The Collected Works of
William Howard Taft

The Collected Works of
William Howard Taft

David H. Burton, General Editor

VOLUME III

PRESIDENTIAL ADDRESSES AND

STATE PAPERS

Edited with Commentary by

David H. Burton

OHIO UNIVERSITY PRESS

ATHENS

Ohio University Press, Athens, Ohio 45701
© 2002 by Ohio University Press
Printed in the United States of America
All rights reserved

Ohio University Press books are printed on acid-free paper ™

09 08 07 06 05 04 03 02   5 4 3 2 1

Presidential Addresses and State Papers of William Howard Taft published New York: Doubleday,
Page & Company, 1910.

Publication of *The Collected Works of William Howard Taft* has been made possible in part through the
generous support of the Earhart Foundation of Ann Arbor, Michigan, and the Louisa Taft Semple
Foundation of Cincinnati, Ohio.

Frontispiece: Photograph of William Howard Taft courtesy of William Howard Taft National
Historic Site.

Library of Congress Cataloging-in-Publication Data
(Revised for volume 3)
Taft, William H. (William Howard), 1857–1930.
Presidential addresses and state papers / edited with commentary by David H. Burton.
     p.   cm. – (The collected works of William Howard Taft ; v. 3)
Includes bibliographical references.
ISBN 0-8214-1404-6 (acid-free paper)
    1. Citizenship–United States.   2. United States–Politics and government–1901–1913.   3. United
States–Foreign relations–1901–1913.   I. Burton, David Henry, 1925–   .   II. Taft, William H.
(William Howard), 1857–1930. Presidential addresses and state papers.   IV. Title.   V. Series:
Taft, William H. (William Howard), 1857–1930. Selections. 2002 ; v. 3.

JK1759.T27 2002
323.6'5'0973–dc21   00-055807

Dedicated to
the Taft family,
for five generations serving
Ohio and the nation

The Collected Works of William Howard Taft

David H. Burton, General Editor

VOLUME ONE

Four Aspects of Civic Duty and *Present Day Problems*

Edited with commentary by David H. Burton and A. E. Campbell

VOLUME TWO

Political Issues and Outlooks

Edited with commentary by David H. Burton

VOLUME THREE

Presidential Addresses and State Papers

Edited with commentary by David H. Burton

VOLUME FOUR

Presidential Messages to Congress

Edited with commentary by David H. Burton

VOLUME FIVE

Popular Government and *The Anti-Trust Act and the Supreme Court*

Edited with commentary by David Potash and Donald F. Anderson

VOLUME SIX

The President and His Powers and *The United States and Peace*

Edited with commentary by W. Carey McWilliams and Frank X. Gerrity

VOLUME SEVEN

Taft Papers on League of Nations

Edited with commentary by Frank X. Gerrity

VOLUME EIGHT

"Liberty under Law" and *Selected Supreme Court Opinions*

Edited with commentary by Francis Graham Lee

Cumulative Index

Contents

Presidential Addresses and State Papers

Commentary

David H. Burton

*P**residential Addresses and State Papers* imparts an appreciation of the range of Taft's interests and his thinking. Beginning with his Inaugural Address and concluding with a detailed exposition of governmental expenses and needed economies, he showed himself willing to tackle the routine as well as the rarefied responsibilities of executive rule. Despite judgments which tend to dismiss the Inaugural Address as far from impressive, it was an honest and forthright effort at laying out his administration's objectives and plans. The president reiterated the key note of his Chicago acceptance speech when he said, "I should be untrue to myself . . . if I did not work for the maintenance and enforcement of [Roosevelt's] reforms as the most important feature of my administration." To accomplish this, "further legislation and executive actions" were needed. This he termed "creative work of the highest order." In words and actions Taft was prepared to be a modern president. Progressive in philosophy—"The scope of a modern government in what it can do and ought to accomplish for its own people had been widened far beyond the principles laid down by the old 'laissez-faire' school of political writers and this widening has met popular approval"—Taft was sober in its proposed application. But then Taft was not an incautious man. The people knew he was not Theodore Roosevelt and therefore did not expect of him Rooseveltian ardor.

The bulk of the addresses in this book reflect "the president as a father figure." His state papers, however, take up many familiar issues, which are dealt with in high seriousness. "Judicial Decisions as an Issue in Politics" is a case in point. In it Taft discusses the standing charge that he favored government by injunction. The tone of his remarks is less judicial than that of a sitting judge, but he clearly believed that the law must be obeyed, whatever the results of a court ruling. Referring to his rulings when he was a federal appeals judge in Ohio, he does not budge from his contention that boycotts growing out of strike action were unacceptable tactics when employed by organized labor. As this was the heart of an article that appeared originally in *McClure's,* a widely read magazine, Taft appears to be verifying the charge of government by judges consistently ruling against workers, organized or not. The president returned to this theme in a Chicago address, "Labor and the Writ of Injunction." In speaking on the issue as opposed to writing about it, Taft displayed a more yielding attitude. His audience was in part a labor audience. The address includes such phrases as "our friends of the great unions" and goes on to expand on the need for drastic reforms in civil and criminal law, as they were then practiced. "Of all the questions that are before the American people I regard no one as more important than this, to wit, the improvement of the administration of justice."

On a number of occasions Taft took up subjects of current controversy: the tariff, income and corporation taxation, the conservation of waterways and other natural resources. But he also showed himself generous in using his time to reach out to the people and to various religious and racial groups. He extended his hand and a good bit of his heart to the three main underclasses: blacks, Catholics, and Jews. Perhaps Taft was not a good politician after all, but a kind man who saw himself as president of all the people.

What further impresses the reader is Taft's willingness to address virtually every part of the nation, thereby showing himself as no mere figurehead but a chief executive truly concerned about problems across the country. His messages to Congress speak to his desire to work with the legislature for a common end. Often thought of as lukewarm on the conservation of natural resources, a judgment that grew out of the Ballinger Pinchot controversy of 1910, Taft delivered a number of important addresses in which he supported conservation legislation. Again, it was a matter of working with Congress. All in all, the collection of these addresses underscores the presidential stature of William Howard Taft.

1

Speech of Acceptance

Delivered at Cincinnati, Ohio, on Tuesday, July 28, 1908

Senator Warner and Gentlemen of the Committee:

I am deeply sensible of the honor which the Republican National Convention has conferred on me in the nomination which you formally tender. I accept it with full appreciation of the responsibility it imposes.

Republican Strength in Maintenance of Roosevelt Policies

Gentlemen, the strength of the Republican cause in the campaign at hand is in the fact that we represent the policies essential to the reform of known abuses, to the continuance of liberty and true prosperity, and that we are determined, as our platform unequivocally declares, to maintain them and carry them on. For more than ten years this country passed through an epoch of material development far beyond any that ever occurred in the world before. In its course, certain evils crept in. Some prominent and influential members of the community, spurred by financial success and in their hurry for greater wealth, became unmindful of the common rules of business honesty and fidelity and of the limitations imposed by law upon their action. This became known. The revelations of the breaches of trust, the disclosures as to rebates and discriminations by railways, the accumulating evidence of the violation of the anti-trust law by a number of corporations, the overissue of stocks and bonds on interstate railways for the unlawful enriching of directors and for the purpose of concentrating control of railways in one management, all quickened the conscience of the people, and brought on a moral awakening among them that boded well for the future of the country.

The man who formulated the expression of the popular conscience and who led the movement for practical reform was Theodore Roosevelt. He laid down the doctrine that the rich violator of the law should be as amenable to restraint and punishment as the offender without wealth and without influence, and he proceeded by recommending legislation and directing executive action to make that principle good in actual performance. He secured the passage of the so-called rate bill, designed more effectively to restrain excessive and fix reasonable rates, and to punish secret rebates and discriminations which had been general in the practice of the railroads, and which had done much to enable unlawful trusts to drive out of the business their competitors. It secured much closer supervision of railway transactions and brought within the operation of the same statute express companies, sleeping car companies, fast freight and refrigerator lines, terminal railroads and pipe lines, and in order to avoid undue discrimination, forbade in future the combination of the transportation and shipping business under one control.

President Roosevelt directed suits to be brought and prosecutions to be instituted under the anti-trust law, to enforce its provisions against the most powerful of the industrial corporations. He pressed to passage the pure food law and the meat inspection law in the interest of the health of the public, clean business methods and great ultimate benefit to the trades themselves. He recommended the passage of a law, which the Republican Convention has since specifically approved, restricting the future issue of stocks and bonds by interstate railways to such as may be authorized by Federal authority. He demonstrated to the people by what he said, by what he recommended to Congress, and by what he did, the sincerity of his efforts to command respect for the law, to secure equality of all before the law, and to save the country from dangers of a plutocratic government, toward which we were fast tending. In this work Mr. Roosevelt has had the support and sympathy of the Republican party, and its chief hope of success in the present controversy must rest on the confidence which the people of the country have in the sincerity of the party's declaration in its platform, that it intends to continue his policies.

Necessary to Devise Some Means of Permanently Securing Progress Made

Mr. Roosevelt has set high the standard of business morality and obedience to law. The railroad rate bill was more useful possibly in the immediate moral effect of its passage than even in the legal effect of its very useful provisions. From its enactment dates the voluntary abandonment of the practice of rebates and discriminations by the railroads and the return by their managers to obedience to law in the fixing of tariffs. The pure food and meat inspection laws and the prosecutions directed by the President under the anti-trust law have had a similar moral effect in the general business community and have made it now the common practice for the great industrial corporations to consult the law with a view to keeping within its provisions. It has also had the effect of protecting and encouraging smaller competitive companies so that they have been enabled to do a profitable business.

But we should be blind to the ordinary working of human nature if we did not recognize that the moral standards set by President Roosevelt will not continue to be observed by those whom cupidity and a desire for financial power may tempt, unless the requisite machinery is introduced into the law which shall in its practical operation maintain these standards and secure the country against a departure from them.

Chief Function of Next Administration to Clinch What Has Been Done

The chief function of the next Administration, in my judgment, is distinct from, and a progressive development of, that which has been performed by President Roosevelt. The chief function of the next Administration is to complete and perfect the machinery by which these standards may be maintained, by which the lawbreakers may be promptly restrained and punished, but which shall operate with sufficient accuracy and dispatch to interfere with legitimate business as little as possible. Such machinery is not now adequate. Under the present rate bill, and under all its amendments, the burden of the Interstate Commerce Commission in supervising and regulating the operation of the railroads of this country has grown so heavy that it is utterly impossible for that tribunal to hear and dispose of, in any reasonable time, the many complaints, queries and issues that are brought before it for decision. It ought to be relieved of its jurisdiction as an executive, directing body, and its functions should be limited to the quasi-judicial investigation of complaints made by individuals and made by a department of the Government charged with the executive business of supervising the operation of railways.

There should be a classification of that very small percentage of industrial corporations having power and opportunity to effect illegal restraints of trade and monopolies, and legislation either inducing or compelling them to subject themselves to registry and to proper publicity regulations and supervision of the Department of Commerce and Labor.

Constructive Work of Next Administration to Organize Subordinate and Ancillary Machinery to Maintain Standards on One Hand, and Not to Interfere with Business on the Other

The field covered by the industrial combinations and by the railroads is so very extensive that the interests of the public and the interests of the businesses concerned cannot be properly subserved except by reorganization of bureaus in the Departments of Commerce and Labor, Agriculture, and Justice, and a change in the jurisdiction of the Interstate Commerce Commission. It does not assist matters to prescribe new duties for the Interstate Commerce Commission which it is practically impossible for it to perform, or to denounce new offenses with drastic punishment, unless subordinate and ancillary legislation shall be passed making possible the quick enforcement in the great variety of cases which are constantly arising, of the principles laid down by Mr. Roosevelt, and with respect to which only typical instances of prosecution with the present machinery are possible. Such legislation should and would greatly promote legitimate business by enabling those anxious to obey the Federal statutes to know just what are the bounds of their lawful action. The practical constructive and difficult work, therefore, of those who follow Mr. Roosevelt is to devise the ways and means by which the high level of business integrity and obedience to law which he has established may be maintained and departures from it restrained without undue interference with legitimate business.

Railway Traffic Agreements Approved by Commission Should Be Valid

It is agreeable to note in this regard that the Republican platform expressly, and the Democratic platform impliedly, approve an amendment to the Interstate Commerce Law, by which interstate railroads may make useful traffic agreements if approved by the Commission. This has been strongly recommended by President Roosevelt and will make for the benefit of the business.

Physical Valuation of Railways

Some of the suggestions of the Democratic platform relate really to this subordinate and ancillary machinery to which I have referred. Take for instance the so-called "physical valuation of railways." It is clear that the sum of all rates or receipts of a railway, less proper expenses, should be limited to a fair profit upon the reasonable value of its property, and that if the sum exceeds this measure, it ought to be reduced. The difficulty in enforcing the principle is in ascertaining what is the reasonable value of the company's property, and in fixing what is a fair profit. It is clear that the physical value of a railroad and its plant is an element to be given weight in determining its full value; but as President Roosevelt in his Indianapolis speech and the Supreme Court have in effect pointed out, the value of a railroad as a going concern, including its good will, due to efficiency of service and many other circumstances, may be much greater than the value of its tangible property, and it is the former that measures the investment on which a fair profit must be allowed. Then, too, the question, "What is a fair profit," is one involving not only the rate of interest usually earned on normally safe investments, but also a sufficient allowance to make up for the risk of loss both of capital and interest in the original outlay. These considerations will have justified the company in imposing charges high enough to secure a fair income on the enterprise as a whole. The securities at market prices will have passed into the hands of subsequent purchasers from the original investors. Such circumstances should properly affect the decision of the tribunal engaged in determining whether the totality of rates charged is reasonable or excessive. To ignore them might so seriously and unjustly impair settled values as to destroy all hope of restoring confidence and forever to end the inducement for investment in new railroad construction which, in returning prosperous times, is sure to be essential to our material progress. As Mr. Roosevelt has said in speaking of this very subject:

"The effect of such valuation and supervision of securities can not be retroactive. Existing securities should be tested by laws in existence at the time of their issue. This Nation would no more injure securities which have become an important part of the National wealth than it would consider a proposition to repudiate the National debt."

The question of rates and the treatment of railways is one that has two sides. The shippers are certainly entitled to reasonable rates; but less is an injustice to the carriers. Good business for the railroads is essential to general prosperity. Injustice to them is not alone injustice to stockholders and capitalists, whose further investments may be necessary for the good of the whole country, but it directly affects and reduces the wages of railway employees, and indeed may deprive them of their places entirely.

From what has been said, the proper conclusion would seem to be that in attempting to determine whether the entire schedule of rates of a railway is excessive, the physical valuation of the road is a relevant and important but not necessarily a controlling factor.

Physical Valuation Properly Used Will Not Generally Impair Securities

I am confident that the fixing of rates on the principles suggested above would not materially impair the present market values of railroad securities in most cases, for I believe that the normal increase in the value of railroad properties, especially in their terminals, will more than make up for the possible overcapitalization in earlier years. In some cases, doubtless, it will be found that overcapitalization is made an excuse for excessive rates, and then they should be reduced; but the consensus of opinion seems to be that the railroad rates generally in this country are reasonably low. This is why, doubtless, the complaints filed with the Interstate Commerce Commission against excessive rates are so few as compared with those against unlawful discrimination in rates between shippers and between places. Of course, in the determination of the question whether discrimination is unlawful or not, the physical valuation of the whole road is of little weight.

Conclusion That There Should Be Physical Valuation

I have discussed this with some degree of detail, merely to point out that the valuation by the Interstate Commerce Commission of the tangible property of a railroad is proper and may from time to time be necessary in settling certain issues which may come before them, and that no evil or injustice can come from valuation in such cases, if it be understood that the result is to be used for a just purpose, and the right to a fair profit under all the circumstances of the investment is recognized. The Interstate Commerce Commission has now the power to ascertain the value of the physical railroad property, if necessary, in determining the reasonableness of rates. If the machinery for doing so is not adequate, as is probable, it should be made so.

The Republican platform recommends legislation forbidding the issue in the future of interstate railway stocks and bonds without Federal authority. It may occur in such cases that the full value of the railway, and, as an element thereof, the value of the tangible property of the railway, would be a relevant and important factor in assisting the proper authority to determine whether the stocks and bonds to be issued were to have proper security behind them, and in such case, therefore, there should be the right and machinery to make a valuation of the physical property.

National Control of Interstate Commerce Corporation

Another suggestion in respect to subordinate and ancillary machinery necessary to carry out Republican policies is that of the incorporation under National law or the licensing by National license or enforced registry of companies engaged in interstate trade. The fact is that nearly all corporations doing a commercial business are engaged in interstate commerce, and if they all were required to take out a Federal license or a Federal charter, the burden upon the interstate business of the country would become intolerable.

Should Be Limited to Small Percentage by Classification

It is necessary, therefore, to devise some means for classifying and insuring Federal supervision of such corporations as have the power and temptation to effect restraints of interstate trades and monopolies. Such corporations constitute a very small percentage of all engaged in interstate business.

Mr. Roosevelt's Proposed Classification

With such classification in view, Mr. Roosevelt recommended an amendment to the anti-trust law, known as the Hepburn Bill, which provided for voluntary classification, and created a strong motive therefor by granting immunity from prosecution for reasonable restraints of interstate trade to all corporations which would register and submit themselves to the publicity regulations of the Department of Commerce and Labor.

The Democratic Proposed Classification

The Democratic platform suggests a requirement that corporations in interstate trade having control of 25 percent of the products in which they deal shall take out a Federal license. This classification would probably include a great many small corporations engaged in the manufacture of special articles, or commodities whose total value is so inconsiderable that they are not really within the purview or real evil of the anti-trust law.

It is not now necessary, however, to discuss the relative merit of such propositions, but it is enough merely to affirm the necessity for some method by which greater executive supervision can be given to the Federal Government over those businesses in which there is a temptation to violations of the anti-trust law.

Construction of Anti-Trust Law—Possible Necessity for Amendment

The possible operation of the anti-trust law under existing rulings of the Supreme Court has given rise to suggestions for its necessary amendment to prevent its application to cases which it is believed were never in the contemplation of the framers of the statute. Take two instances: A merchant or manufacturer engaged in a legitimate business that covers certain states, wishes to sell his business and his good will, and so in the terms of the sale obligates himself to the purchaser not to go into the same business in those states. Such a restraint of trade has always been enforced at common law. Again, the employees of an interstate railway combine and enter upon a peaceable and lawful strike to secure better wages. At common law this was not a restraint of trade or commerce or a violation of the rights of the company or of the public. Neither case ought to be made a violation of the anti-trust law. My own impression is that the Supreme Court would hold that neither of these instances is within its inhibition, but, if they are to be so regarded, general legislation amending the law is necessary.

Democratic Plank to Limit Corporations to Ownership of 50 Percent of Plant and Product Faulty

The suggestion of the Democratic platform that trusts be ended by forbidding corporations to hold more than 50 percent of the plant in any line of manufacture is made without regard to the possibility of enforcement or the real evil in trusts. A corporation controlling 45 or 50 percent of the products may by well-known methods frequently effect monopoly and stamp out competition in a part of the country as completely as if it controlled 60 or 70 percent thereof.

Compulsory Sale of Products at Fixed Price Impractical

The proposal to compel every corporation to sell its commodities at the same price the country over, allowing for transportation, is utterly impracticable.

If it can be shown that in order to drive out competition, a corporation owning a large part of the plant producing an article is selling in one part of the country, where it has competitors, at a low and unprofitable price, and in another part of the country, where it has none, at an exorbitant price, this is evidence that it is attempting an unlawful monopoly, and justifies conviction under the anti-trust law; but the proposal to supervise the business of corporations in such a way as to fix the price of commodities and compel the sale at such price is as absurd and socialistic a plank as was ever inserted in a Democratic political platform.

Difference between Republican and Democratic Policies and Platforms: Former Progressive and Regulative; Latter Radical and Destructive

The chief difference between the Republican and the Democratic platforms is the difference which has heretofore been seen between the policies of Mr. Roosevelt and those which have been advocated by the Democratic candidate, Mr. Bryan. Mr. Roosevelt's policies have been progressive and regulative; Mr. Bryan's destructive. Mr. Roosevelt has favored regulation of the business in which evils have grown up so as to stamp out the evils and permit the business to continue. The tendency of Mr. Bryan's proposals has generally been destructive of the business with respect to which he is demanding reform. Mr. Roosevelt would compel the trusts to conduct their business in a lawful manner and secure the benefits of their operation and the maintenance of the prosperity of the country of which they are an important part; while Mr. Bryan would extirpate and destroy the entire business in order to stamp out the evils which they have practised.

Advantage of Combination of Capital

The combination of capital in large plants to manufacture goods with the greatest economy is just as necessary as the assembling of the parts of a machine to the economical and more rapid manufacture of what in old times was made by hand. The Government should not interfere with one any more than the other, when such aggregations of capital are legitimate and are properly controlled, for they are then the natural results of modern enterprise and are beneficial to the public. In the proper operation of competition the public will soon share with the manufacturer the advantage in economy of operation and lower prices.

What Is an Unlawful Trust?

When, however, such combinations are not based on any economic principle, but are made merely for the purpose of controlling the market, to maintain or raise prices, restrict output and drive out competitors, the public derives no benefit and we have a monopoly. There must be some use by the company of the comparatively great size of its capital and plant and extent of its output, either to coerce persons to buy of it rather than of some competitor or to coerce those who would compete with it to give up their business. There must usually, in other words, be shown an element of duress in the conduct of its business toward the customers in the trade and its competitors before mere aggregation of capital or plant becomes an unlawful monopoly. It is perfectly conceivable that in the interest of economy of production a great number of plants may be legitimately assembled under the ownership of one corporation. It is important, therefore, that such large aggregations of capital and combinations should be controlled so that the public may have the advantage of reasonable prices and that the avenues of enterprise may be kept open to the individual and the smaller corporation wishing to engage in business.

Mere Aggregation of Capital Not a Violation of Anti-Trust Law

In a country like this, where, in good times, there is an enormous floating capital awaiting investment, the period before which effective competition, by construction of new plants, can be introduced into any business, is comparatively short, rarely exceeding a year, and is usually even less than that. Existence of actual plant is not, therefore, necessary to potential competition. Many enterprises have been organized on the theory that mere aggregation of all, or nearly all, existing plants in a line of manufacture, without regard to economy of production, destroys competition. They have, most of them, gone into bankruptcy. Competition in a profitable business will not be affected by the mere aggregation of many existing plants under one company, unless the company thereby effects great economy, the benefit of which it shares with the public, or takes some illegal method to avoid competition and to perpetuate a hold on the business.

Proper Treatment of Trusts

Unlawful trusts should be restrained with all the efficiency of injunctive process, and the persons engaged in maintaining them should be punished with all the severity of criminal prosecution, in order that the methods pursued in the operation of their business shall be brought within the law. To destroy them and to eliminate the wealth they represent from the producing capital of the country would entail enormous loss, and would throw out of employment myriads of workingmen and workingwomen. Such a result is wholly unnecessary to the accomplishment of the needed reform, and will inflict upon the innocent far greater punishment than upon the guilty.

Destructive Policy of Democratic Platform

The Democratic platform does not propose to destroy the plants of the trusts physically, but it proposes to do the same thing in a different way. The business of this country is largely dependent on a protective system of tariffs. The business done by many of the so-called "trusts" is protected with the other business of the country. The Democratic platform proposes to take off the tariff on all articles coming into competition with those produced by the so-called "trusts," and to put them on the free list. If such a course would be utterly destructive of their business, as is intended, it would not only destroy the trusts, but all of their smaller competitors. The ruthless and impracticable character of the proposition grows plainer as its effects upon the whole community are realized.

Effect of Democratic Plans on Business

To take the course suggested by the Democratic platform in these matters is to involve the entire community, innocent as it is, in the punishment of the guilty, while our policy is to stamp out the specific evil. This difference between the policies of the two great parties is of especial importance in view of the present condition of business. After ten years of the most remarkable material development and prosperity, there came a financial stringency, a panic and an industrial depression. This was brought about not only by the enormous expansion of business plants and business investments which could not be readily converted, but also by the waste of capital, in extravagance of living, in wars and other catastrophes. The free convertible capital was exhausted. In addition to this, the confidence of the lending public in Europe and in this country had been affected by the revelations of irregularity, breaches of trust, overissues of stock, violations of law, and lack of rigid State or National supervision in the management of our largest corporations. Investors withheld what loanable capital remained available. It became impossible for the soundest railroads and other enterprises to borrow money enough for new construction or reconstruction.

Will Delay Restoration of Prosperity

Gradually business is acquiring a healthier tone. Gradually all wealth which was hoarded is coming out to be used. Confidence in security of business investments is a plant of slow growth and is absolutely necessary in order that our factories may all open again, in order that our unemployed may become employed, and in order that we may again have the prosperity which blessed us for ten years. The identity of the interests of the capitalist, the farmer, the business man and the wage-earner in the security and profit of investments cannot be too greatly emphasized. I submit to those most interested, to wage-earners, to farmers, and to business men, whether the introduction into power of the Democratic party, with Mr. Bryan at its head, and with the business destruction that it openly advocates as a remedy for present evils, will bring about the needed confidence for the restoration of prosperity.

Republican Doctrine of Protection

The Republican doctrine of protection, as definitely announced by the Republican Convention of this year and by previous conventions, is that a tariff shall be imposed on all imported products, whether of the factory, farm or mine, sufficiently great to equal the difference between the cost of production abroad and at home, and that this difference should, of course, include the difference between the higher wages paid in this country and the wages paid abroad, and embrace a reasonable profit to the American producer. A system of protection thus adopted and put in force has led to the establishment of a rate of wages here that has greatly enhanced the standard of living of the laboring man. It is the policy of the Republican party permanently to continue that standard of living. In 1897 the Dingley Tariff Bill was passed, under which we have had, as already said, a period of enormous prosperity.

Necessity for Revision of Tariff

The consequent material development has greatly changed the conditions under which many articles described by the schedules of the tariff are now produced. The tariff in a number of schedules exceeds the difference between the cost of production of such articles abroad and at home, including a reasonable profit to the American producer. The excess over that difference serves no useful purpose, but offers a temptation to those who would monopolize the production and the sale of such articles in this country, to profit by the excessive rate. On the other hand, there are some few other schedules

Notice and Hearing before Issue of Injunction

I come now to the question of notice before issuing an injunction. It is a fundamental rule of general jurisprudence that no man shall be affected by a judicial proceeding without notice and hearing. This rule, however, has sometimes had an exception in the issuing of temporary restraining orders commanding a defendant in effect to maintain the *status quo* until a hearing. Such a process should issue only in rare cases where the threatened change of the *status quo* would inflict irreparable injury if time were taken to give notice and a summary hearing. The unlawful injury usual in industrial disputes, such as I have described, does not become formidable except after sufficient time in which to give the defendants notice and a hearing. I do not mean to say that there may not be cases even in industrial disputes where a restraining order might properly be issued without notice, but, generally, I think it is otherwise. In some State courts, and in fewer Federal courts, the practice of issuing a temporary restraining order without notice, merely to preserve the *status quo* on the theory that it will not hurt anybody, has been too common. Many of us recall that the practice has been pursued in other than industrial disputes, as, for instance, in corporate and stock controversies like those over the Erie Railroad, in which a stay order without notice was regarded as a step of great advantage to the one who secured it, and a corresponding disadvantage to the one against whom it was secured. Indeed, the chances of doing injustice on an *ex parte* application are much increased over those when a hearing is granted, and there may be circumstances under which it may affect the defendant to his detriment. In the case of a lawful strike, the sending of a formidable document restraining a number of defendants from doing a great many different things which the plaintiff avers they are threatening to do, often so discourages men always reluctant to go into a strike from continuing what is their lawful right. This has made the laboring man feel that an injustice is done in the issuing of a writ without notice. I conceive that in the treatment of this question it is the duty of the citizen and the legislator to view the subject from the standpoint of the man who believes himself to be unjustly treated, as well as from that of the community at large. I have suggested the remedy of returning in such cases to the original practice under the old statute of the United States and the rules in equity adopted by the Supreme Court, which did not permit the issuing of an injunction without notice. In this respect, the Republican Convention has adopted another remedy, that, without going so far, promises to be efficacious in securing proper consideration in such cases by courts, by formulating into a legislative act the best present practice.

Under this recommendation, a statute may be framed which shall define with considerable particularity, and emphasize the exceptional character of the cases in which restraining orders may issue without notice, and which shall also provide that when they are issued, they shall cease to be operative beyond a short period, during which time notice shall be served and a hearing had unless the defendant desires a postponement of the hearing. By this provision the injustice which has sometimes occurred by which a preliminary restraining order of widest application has been issued without notice, and the hearing of the motion for the injunction has been fixed weeks and months after its date, could not recur.

Small Number of Cases Furnish Grounds for Complaint

The number of instances in which restraining orders without notice in industrial disputes have issued by Federal courts is small, and it is urged that they do not therefore constitute an evil to be remedied by statutory amendment. The small number of cases complained of above shows the careful manner in which most Federal judges have exercised the jurisdiction, but the belief that such cases are numerous has been so widespread and has aroused such feeling of injustice that more definite specification in procedure to prevent recurrence of them is justified if it can be effected without injury to the administration of the law.

No Provision in Democratic Platform As to Notice

With respect to notice, the Democratic platform contains no recommendation. Its only intelligible declaration in regard to injunction suits is a reiteration of the plank in the platforms of 1896 and 1904 providing that in prosecutions for contempt in Federal courts, where the violation of the order constituting the contempt charged is indirect, *i.e.*, outside of the presence of the court, there shall be a jury trial.

Dangerous Attack on Power of Courts

This provision in the platform of 1896 was regarded then as a most dangerous attack upon the power of the courts to enforce their orders and decrees, and it was one of the chief reasons for the defeat of the Democratic party in that contest, as it ought to have been. The extended operation of such provision to weaken the power of the courts in the enforcement of its lawful orders can hardly be overstated.

Effect of Jury Trial

Under such a provision a recalcitrant witness who refuses to obey a subpoena may insist on a jury trial before the court can determine that he received the subpoena. A citizen summoned as a juror and refusing to obey the writ when brought into court must be tried by another jury to determine whether he got the summons. Such a provision applies not alone to injunctions, but to every order which the court issues against persons. A suit may be tried in the court of first instance and carried to the Court of Appeals, and thence to the Supreme Court, and a judgment and decree entered and an order issued, and then if the decree involves the defendant's doing anything or not doing anything, and he disobeys it, the plaintiff who has pursued his remedies in lawful course for years must, to secure his rights, undergo the uncertainties and the delays of a jury trial before he can enjoy that which is his right by the decision of the highest court of the land. I say without hesitation that such a change will greatly impair the indispensable power and authority of the courts. In securing to the public the benefits of the new statutes enacted in the present Administration, the ultimate instrumentality to be resorted to is the courts of the United States. If now their authority is to be weakened in a manner never known in the history of the jurisprudence of England or America, except in the constitution of Oklahoma, how can we expect that such statutes will have efficient enforcement? Those who advocate this intervention of a jury in such cases seem to suppose that this change in some way will inure only to the benefit of the poor workingman. As a matter of fact, the person who will secure chief advantage from it is the wealthy and unscrupulous defendant, able to employ astute and cunning counsel and anxious to avoid justice.

I have been willing, in order to avoid a popular but unfounded impression that a judge, in punishing for contempt of his own order, may be affected by personal feeling, to approve a law which should enable the contemnor upon his application to have another judge sit to hear the charge of contempt, but this, with so many judges as there are available in the Federal court, would not constitute a delay in the enforcement of the process. The character and efficiency of the trial would be the same. It is the nature and the delay of a jury trial in such cases that those who would wish to defy the order of the court would rely upon as a reason for doing so.

Maintenance of Full Power of Courts Necessary to Avoid Anarchy

The administration of justice lies at the foundation of government. The maintenance of authority of the courts is essential unless we are prepared to embrace anarchy. Never in the history of the country has there been such an insidious attack upon the judicial system as the proposal to interject a jury trial between all orders of the court made after full hearing and the enforcement of such orders.

The Currency System

The late panic disclosed a lack of elasticity in our financial system. This has been provisionally met by an act of the present Congress permitting the issue of additional emergency bank notes, and insuring their withdrawal when the emergency has passed, by a high rate of taxation. It is drawn in conformity with the present system of banknote currency but varies from it in certain respects by authorizing the use of commercial paper and bonds of good credit, as well as United States bonds, as security for its redemption. It is expressly but a temporary measure and contains a provision for the appointment of a currency commission to devise and recommend a new and reformed system of currency. This inadequacy of our present currency system, due to changed conditions and enormous expansion, is generally recognized. The Republican platform well states that we must have a "more elastic and adaptable system to meet the requirements of agriculturists, manufacturers, merchants and business men generally, which must be automatic in operation, recognizing the fluctuations in interest rates," in which every dollar shall be as good as gold, and which shall prevent rather than aid financial stringency in bringing on a panic.

Postal Savings Bank and Its Advantages

In addition to this, the Republican platform recommends the adoption of a postal-savings-bank system in which, of course, the Government would become responsible to the depositors for the payment of principal and interest. It is thought that the government guaranty will bring out of hoarding-places much money which may be turned into wealth-producing capital, and that it will be a great incentive for thrift in the many small places in the country having now no savings-bank facilities, which are reached by the Post Office Department. It will bring to everyone, however remote from financial centers, a place of perfect safety for deposits, with interest return. The bill now pending in Congress, which of course the Republican Convention had in mind, provides for the investment of the money deposited in National banks in the very places in which it is gathered, or as near thereto as may be practicable. This is an answer to the criticism contained in the Democratic platform that under the system the money gathered in the country will be deposited in Wall Street banks. The system of postal savings banks has been tried in so many countries successfully that it cannot be regarded longer as a new and untried experiment.

Objections to Democratic Proposal to Enforce Insurance of Bank Deposits

The Democratic platform recommends a tax upon National banks and upon such State banks as may come in, in the nature of enforced insurance, to raise a guaranty fund to pay the depositors of any bank which fails. How State banks can be included in such a scheme under the Constitution is left in the twilight zone of State's rights and Federalism so frequently dimming the meaning and purpose of the promises of the platform. If they come in under such a system, they must necessarily be brought within the closest National control, and so they must really cease to be State banks and become National banks.

The proposition is to tax the honest and prudent banker to make up for the dishonesty and imprudence of others. No one can foresee the burden which under this system would be imposed upon the sound and conservative bankers of the country by this obligation to make good the losses caused by the reckless, speculative and dishonest men who would be enabled to secure deposits under such a system on the faith of the proposed insurance; as in its present shape the proposal would remove all safeguards against recklessness in banking, and the chief, and in the end probably the only benefit, would accrue to the speculator, who would be delighted to enter the banking business when it was certain that he could enjoy any profit that would accrue, while the risk would have to be assumed by his honest and hard-working fellow. In short, the proposal is wholly impracticable unless it is to be accompanied by a complete revolution in our banking system, with a supervision so close as practically to create a government bank. If the proposal were adopted exactly as the Democratic platform suggests, it would bring the whole banking system of the country down in ruin, and this proposal is itself an excellent illustration of the fitness for National control of a party which will commit itself to a scheme of this nature without the slightest sense of responsibility for the practical operation of the law proposed.

Postal Savings Banks Much to Be Preferred

The Democratic party announces its adhesion to this plan, and only recommends the tried system of postal savings banks as an alternative if the new experimental panacea is not available. The Republican party prefers the postal savings bank as one tried, safe, and known to be effective, and as reaching many more people now without banking facilities than the new system proposed.

Voluntary Plan for Guaranty

A plan for guaranty of deposits by the voluntary act of the banks involved has been favorably reported to the House of Representatives. This is, of course, entirely different from the scheme in the Democratic platform, omitting, as it does, the feature of compulsory participation. This proposition will unquestionably receive the thoughtful consideration of the National Monetary Commission.

Republican Policies As to Dependencies

The Republican party has pursued consistently the policy originally adopted with respect to the dependencies which came to us as the result of the Spanish war.

Puerto Rico

The material prosperity of Puerto Rico and the progress of its inhabitants toward better conditions in respect to comfort of living and education, should make every American proud that this nation has been an efficient instrument in bringing happiness to a million people.

Cuba

In Cuba, the provisional government established in order to prevent a bloody revolution has so administered affairs and initiated the necessary laws as to make it possible to turn back the island to the lawfully elected officers of the Republic in February next.

Philippines

In the Philippines the experiment of a national assembly has justified itself, both as an assistance in the government of the islands and as an education in the practice of self-government to the people of the islands. We have established a government with effective and honest executive departments, and a clean and fearless administration of justice; we have created and are maintaining a comprehensive school system which is educating the youth of the islands in English and in industrial branches; we have constructed great government public works, roads and harbors; we have induced the private construction of eight hundred miles of railroad; we have policed the islands so that their condition as to law and order is better now than it ever has been in their history. It is quite unlikely that the people, because of the dense ignorance of 90 percent, will be ready for complete self-government and independence before two generations have passed, but the policy of increasing partial self-government step by step as the people shall show themselves fit for it should be continued.

Proposition of Democratic Platform Means Chaos

The proposition of the Democratic platform is to turn over the islands as soon as a stable government is established. This has been established. The proposal then is in effect to turn them over at once. Such action will lead to ultimate chaos in the islands and the progress among the ignorant masses in education and better living will stop. We are engaged in the Philippines in a great missionary work that does our nation honor, and is certain to promote in a most effective way the influence of Christian civilization. It is cowardly to lay down the burden until our purpose is achieved.

Hope of Prosperity in Change in Tariff Recommended by Republican Platform

Many unfortunate circumstances beyond human control have delayed the coming of business prosperity to the islands. Much may be done in this regard by increasing the trade between the islands and the United States, under tariff laws permitting reciprocal free trade in the respective products of the two countries, with such limitations as to sugar and tobacco imported into the United States as will protect domestic interests. The admission of 350,000 tons of sugar from the Philippine Islands in a foreign importation of 1,600,000 tons, will have no effect whatever upon the domestic sugar interests of the United States, and yet such an importation from the Philippine Islands, not likely to be reached in ten years, will bring about the normal state of prosperity in these islands in reference to sugar culture.

The same thing is true of a similar limitation on the importation of tobacco. It is not well for the Philippines to develop the sugar industry to such a point that the business of the islands shall be absorbed in it, because it makes a society in which there are wealthy landowners, holding very large estates, with valuable and expensive plants, and a large population of unskilled labor. In such a community there is no farming or middle class tending to build up a conservative, self-respecting community, capable of self-government. There are many other products, notably that of Manila hemp, to which the energy of the islands can be, and is being, directed, the cultivation of which develops the class of small and intelligent farmers.

Misconception As to Annual Cost of Philippines

One misconception of fact with respect to our Philippine policy is that it is costing the people of the United States a vast annual sum. The expenses of the war in the Philippines from 1898 to 1902 involved the Government in an expenditure of less than $175,000,000. This was incident to war. The fact is that since the close of the war in 1902 and the restoration of order in the islands, the extra cost of the American troops of the regular army in the islands, together with that of maintaining about 4,000 Philippine scouts as a part of the regular army, does not exceed $6,000,000 annually. This is all the expense to which the United States has been put for five or six years last past. The expenses of the Civil Government in the islands since its establishment have been met entirely from the proceeds of taxes collected in the islands, with but one notably generous and commendable exception when the Congress of the United States appropriated $3,000,000 in 1902 to relieve the inhabitants of the islands from the dangers of famine and distress caused by the death from rinderpest of three-fourths of the cattle of the islands.

Veterans of Country's Wars

Both platforms declare, as they should, in favor of generous pensions for the veterans of the Civil and Spanish wars. I stop to note the presence here of a body of veterans of Ohio, and to express my thanks for the honor they do me in coming. I am lacking in one qualification of all Republican Presidents since Lincoln, that of having been exposed to danger and death on the field of battle in defense of our country. I hope that this lack will not make the veterans think I am any less deeply thrilled by the memory of their great comrades gone before—Grant, Hayes, Garfield, Harrison and McKinley— all sons of Ohio, who left records reflecting glory upon their State and Nation, or that my sympathies with the valor and courage and patriotism of those who faced death in the country's crises are any less earnest and sincere than they would be had I the right to wear a button of the Grand Army or of the veteran association of any of our country's wars.

The Rights and Progress of the Negro

The Republican platform refers to the amendments to the Constitution that were passed by the Republican party for the protection of the Negro. The Negro, in the forty years since he was freed from slavery, has made remarkable progress. He is becoming a more and more valuable member of the communities in which he lives. The education of the Negro is being expanded and improved in every way. The best men of both races, at the North as well as at the South, ought to rejoice to see growing up among the Southern people an influential element disposed to encourage the Negro in his hard struggle for industrial independence and assured political status. The Republican platform, adopted at Chicago, explicitly demands justice for all men without regard to race or color, and just as explicitly declares for the enforcement, and without reservation, in letter and spirit, of the Thirteenth, Fourteenth and Fifteenth Amendments to the Constitution. It is needless to state that I stand with my party squarely on that plank in the platform, and believe that equal justice to all men, and the fair and impartial enforcement of these amendments is in keeping with the real American spirit of fair play.

Army and Navy

Mr. McKinley and Mr. Roosevelt, and the Republican party, have constantly advocated a policy with respect to the Army and Navy that will keep this Republic ready at all times to defend her territory and her doctrines, and to assure her appropriate part in promoting permanent tranquillity among the nations. I welcome from whatever motive the change in the Democratic attitude toward the maintenance and support of an adequate Navy, and hope that in the next platform the silence of the present platform, in respect to the Army, will be changed to an acquiescence in its maintenance to the point of efficiency in connection with the efficiently reorganized militia and the National volunteers, for the proper defense of the country in time of war, and the discharge of those duties in time of peace for which the Army, as at present constituted, has shown itself so admirably adapted in the Philippines, in San Francisco, in Cuba, and elsewhere. We are a world power and cannot help it, and, although at peace with all the world and secure in the consciousness that the American people do not desire and will not provoke a war with any other country, we must be prudent and not be lulled into a sense of security which would possibly expose us to national humiliation. Our best course, therefore, is to insist on a constant improvement in our navy and its maintenance at the highest point of efficiency.

Protection of Citizens Abroad

The position which our country has won under Republican administrations before the world should inure to the benefit of everyone, even the humblest of those entitled to look to the American flag for protection, without regard to race, creed or color, and whether he is a citizen of the United States or of any of our dependencies. In some countries with which we are on friendly terms, distinctions are made in respect to the treatment of our citizens travelling abroad and having passports of our Executive, based on considerations that are repugnant to the principles of our Government and civilization. The Republican party and administration will continue to make every proper endeavor to secure the abolition of such distinctions, which in our eyes are both needless and opprobrious.

Asiatic Immigration

In the matter of the limitation upon Asiatic immigration, referred to in the Democratic platform, it is sufficient to say that the present Republican Administration has shown itself able, by diplomatic negotiation, and without unnecessary friction with self-respecting governments to minimize the evils suggested, and a subsequent Republican Administration may be counted on to continue the same policy.

Conservation of National Resources

The conservation of National resources is a subject to which the present Administration has given especial attention. The necessity for a comprehensive and systematic improvement of our waterways, the preservation of our soil, and of our forests, the securing from private appropriation the power in the navigable streams, the retention of the undisposed-of coal lands of the Government from alienation, all will properly claim from the next Administration earnest attention and appropriate legislation.

National Health Bureau

I have long been of the opinion that the various agencies of the National Government established for the preservation of the National health, scattered through several departments, should be rendered more efficient by uniting them in a bureau of the Government under a competent head, and that I understand to be, in effect, the recommendation of both parties.

Publicity of Campaign Contributions and Expenditures

Another plank of the Democratic platform refers to the failure of the Republican Convention to express an opinion in favor of the publicity of contributions received and expenditures made in elections. Here again we contrast our opponents' promises with our own acts. Great improvement has taken place under Republican auspices in respect to the collection and expenditure of money for this purpose. The old and pernicious system of levying a tax on the salaries of Government employees in order to pay the expenses of the party in control of the Administration has been abolished by statute. By a law passed by the Republican Congress in 1907, contributions from corporations to influence or pay the expenses connected with the election of presidential electors or of members of Congress, is forbidden under penalty.

A resident of New York has been selected as treasurer of the Republican National Committee, who was treasurer of the Republican State Committee when Governor Hughes was elected in New York, and who made a complete statement within twenty days after the election, as required by the New York law, of the contributions received by him and the expenditures made by him or under his authority in connection with that election. His residence and the discharge of his duties in the State of New York subject him to the law of that State as to all receipts of the treasury of the National Committee from whatever source, and as to all its disbursements. His returns will be under the obligations and penalties of the law, and a misstatement by him or the filing of a false account will subject him to prosecution for perjury and violation of the statute. Of course, under the Federal law, he is not permitted to receive any contributions from corporations.

If I am elected President, I shall urge upon Congress, with every hope of success, that a law be passed requiring the filing in a Federal office of a statement of the contributions received by committees and candidates in elections for members of Congress, and in such other elections as are constitutionally within the control of Congress. Meantime the Republican party by the selection of a New York treasurer has subjected all its receipts and expenditures to the compulsory obligation of such a law.

Income Tax

The Democratic platform demands two constitutional amendments, one providing for an income tax, and the other for the election of Senators by the people. In my judgment, an amendment to the Constitution for an income tax is not necessary. I believe that an income tax, when the protective system of customs and the internal revenue tax shall not furnish income enough for governmental needs, can and should be devised which under the decisions of the Supreme Court will conform to the Constitution.

Election of Senators

With respect to the election of Senators by the people, personally I am inclined to favor it, but it is hardly a party question. A resolution in its favor has passed a Republican House of Representatives several times and has been rejected in a Republican Senate by the votes of Senators from both parties. It has been approved by the Legislatures of many Republican States. In a number of States, both Democratic and Republican, substantially such a system now prevails.

Inaccuracy and Insincerity of Democratic Charges of Extravagance in Increase of Offices and Expenditures

Our opponents denounce the Republican party for increasing the number of offices 23,000, at a cost of sixteen millions of dollars, during the last year. Such denunciation is characteristic of the Democratic platform. It fails to specify in any way what the offices are, and leaves the inference that the increase was resisted by the representatives of Democracy in Congress. As a matter of fact, the net number of offices increased was just about half the number stated; the increase was due chiefly to the enlargement of the Navy, the construction of the Panama Canal, the extension of the Rural Free Delivery, and to the new offices necessary in the enforcement of the pure food, meat inspection, railroad rate regulation, arid land reclamation, forest preservation and other measures which Congress passed with almost unanimous popular approval. The Democratic platform so far from attacking any of this legislation specifically approves much, and condemns none of it, and it is of course disingenuous to claim credit for approving legislation and yet to denounce the expenditures necessary to give it effect.

Charge of Deficit

Again, it charges that a deficit of sixty millions of dollars between the receipts and expenditures during the fiscal year ending June 30, 1908, occurred. As explained by the Secretary of the Treasury, at least half of this deficit is only an apparent one. The falling off in receipts was, of course, occasioned by the unusual panic, but there is ample free money in the Treasury to meet the difference, and the difference itself is not half of it properly a deficit, because involved in it was the retirement of some thirty-three millions of the bonds of the Government.

During the past seven years the income and expenditures of the Government have been nearly equal, some years showing a surplus, and others, fewer in number, a deficit. Taking one year with another, including this year, there has been an average surplus. The surplus last year, for instance, was greater than the deficit this year, so that, in fact, under the present administration there has been no deficit, but a surplus, which is actually in the Treasury.

The Democratic platform nowhere points out the expenditures which might be reduced or avoided. It would be found generally that to the increases which have occurred, Democratic representatives in Congress made no opposition, but rather supported the measures providing them, and now the party has not the courage to indicate what part of Government cost it would end. It joins the Republican party specifically in approving the outlay of $150,000,000 as pensions. It expressly favors also the cost of greatly increased River and Harbor improvements, the cost of doubling the Navy, and of many other enterprises to which it urges the Government. Its attack, therefore, has nothing in it either of fairness or sincerity.

The truth is that it is known of all fair-minded men that there never has been an administration in the Government more efficiently conducted, more free from scandal, and in which the standard of official duty has been set higher than in the present Republican Administration, which the Democratic platform has thus denounced. It has had to meet the problems arising from the enormous expansion of Government functions under the new legislative measures as well as in the new dependencies, and in the greatest constructive work of modern times, the Panama Canal, and its members may well feel a just pride in the exceptional record for efficiency, economy, honesty and fidelity which it has made. We may rely upon our record in this regard in an appeal to the American people for their approval.

The foreign policy of this country under the present Administration has greatly contributed to the peace of the world. The important part the Administration took in bringing about an end of the Russian-Japanese War by a treaty honorable to both parties, and the prevention of wars in Central America and Cuba are striking instances of this. The arbitration treaties signed with all the important nations of the world mark a great step forward in the development of the usefulness of The Hague tribunal. The visit of Secretary Root to South America emphasized our friendship for our sister republics which are making such strides in the southern hemisphere, and met with a most cordial and gratifying response from our Latin-American colleagues. The assistance which we are rendering in Santo Domingo to enable that Government to meet its obligations and avoid anarchy is another instance of successful work of this Administration in helping our neighbors.

This Administration has by the promptness, skill and energy of its negotiations secured dominion in the Canal Zone of the Isthmus of Panama, without which the construction of the canal would have been impossible. It has subdued the heretofore insurmountable obstacle of disease and made the place of work healthy. It has created such an organization that in six years certainly, and probably in less, the Atlantic and Pacific will be united, to the everlasting benefit of the world's commerce, and the effectiveness of our Navy will be doubled.

The mere statement of the things actually done by this Administration at home, in our dependencies, and in foreign affairs shows a marvel of successful accomplishment, and if ever a party has entitled itself to the approval of its works by a renewed mandate of power from the people whom it served, it is the Republican party in the present campaign.

The only respect in which nothing has been done is in the development of our foreign marine. As long as we uphold the system of protection for our home industries we must recognize that it is ineffectual to assist those of our citizens engaged in the foreign shipping business, because there is no feasible means of excluding foreign competition, and that the only other method of building up such a business is by direct aid in the form of a mail subsidy. I am in favor of the bill considered in the last Congress as a tentative step. The establishment of direct steamship lines between our Atlantic ports and South America would certainly do much to develop a trade that might be made far greater. On the Pacific, the whole shipping trade threatens to pass into the control of Japan. Something ought to be done, and the bill which failed was a step in the right direction.

Independent Democrats

The Democratic party under its present leadership in previous campaigns has manifested a willingness to embrace any doctrine which would win votes, with little sense of responsibility for its practical operation. In its striving for success it has ignored the business prosperity of the country, has departed from sound economic and governmental principles, and has reversed its own traditional views of constitutional construction. Patriotic members of the party have refused to be controlled by party ties, and have either refrained from voting or have supported the Republican candidate. May we not appeal to these courageous and independent citizens again to give us their support in this campaign, because the reasons for their breaking the bonds of party are stronger today than ever before?

Length of Speech Made Necessary by Numerous Issues

I have now reviewed at great length the principles at issue between the two parties. When I began the preparation of this speech of acceptance I had hoped to make it much briefer than it is, but I found on an examination of the platform and on a consideration of the many measures passed during the present Administration and the issues arising out of them, that it was impossible to deal with the subjects comprehensively with proper explanation and qualification in a short discussion. This is my excuse.

Difference Between Parties: Prosperity with Republican Success; Business Disaster with Democratic Victory

I have pointed out that the attitude of the Republican party with reference to evils which have crept in, due to the enormous material expansion of this country, is to continue the Roosevelt policies of progress and regulation, while the attitude of the Democratic party under its present leadership is that of change for the sake of change to the point of irresponsible destruction, and that there is no hope whatever of a restoration of prosperity in returning it to power. As said in our platform, we Republicans go before the country asking the support, not only of those who have acted with us heretofore, but of all our fellow citizens who, regardless of past political differences, unite in the desire to maintain the policies, perpetuate the blessings and make secure the achievements of a greater America.

2

The Republican Party's Appeal

Published in The Independent, *October 15, 1908*

The *Independent* asks me to write on the issues of the campaign. My time is so occupied that I must do it in great haste. To my mind, the issues of the campaign are not different from those which arise in every Presidential election, to wit, whether the work of the existing Administration shall be approved by continuing in power the same party, or shall be condemned by turning the administration of the country's affairs over to the Democratic party.

It can hardly be denied that the administration of the Republican party under Mr. McKinley and under Mr. Roosevelt has been a wonderful series of successes in meeting the new and unprecedented problems which have presented themselves in that period. The successful carrying on of the Spanish War, the establishment of the Cuban Government, and its reestablishment just now promising entire success, the carrying on of the Philippine War, the suppression of the rebellion and the establishment of tranquillity and of a government which is working great good in the Islands, the successful elaboration of the reclamation of arid lands in the West, the enactment of the pure food and meat inspection laws, the enlargement of the navy, the reorganization and great improvement of the army, the continuation of the coast defenses, the successful organization and rapid work toward completion of the Panama Canal, the establishment of the position of this nation as one of the most influential in the world, and the use of the influence thus gained to promote the peace of the world, as shown in the close of the Russian-Japanese War, the settlement of Central American wars, and the making closer the bonds between this country and the South American republics, are all definite things done under the administration of the Republican party which entitle it to the confidence of the people and their belief in its courage and efficiency as an agency in government to effect results.

After the disastrous operation of the Gorman-Wilson Tariff Bill, the Republican party became responsible for the passage of the Dingley Bill, and under that bill, whether it was the sole cause or not, the country was enabled to enjoy a prosperity and an expansion of wealth and material progress never before seen in the world.

It is said now, and truly said, that the tariff rates are generally in excess of what is required by the principle of protection, to wit, they exceed the difference in the cost of production of the same class of articles in this country and abroad. The Republican party is pledged, at a special session of Congress, to take up the tariff schedules and to modify them, so that they shall no longer be excessive; but it also pledges itself to maintain the protective system, upon which a great part of the manufacturing industries of this country and the whole business system rests.

In the course of the unprecedented prosperity and expansion, evils crept into our community, consisting of the violation of the anti-trust law and the illegal creation of unlawful monopolies which were fostered by combining a large part of the plants engaged in the production of the article in question, and by the use of secret rebates and unlawful discriminations in the matter of transportation by the railroads, so as to render helpless the less powerful competitors of the illegal monopoly. More than this, in railroad circles it became clear that the power of issuing stocks and bonds of a par value far in excess of the real value of the property represented by such securities had been used by unscrupulous railroad managers to combine railroad properties and concentrate the control of them in the hands of one man or a few men. These evils, which forced themselves upon public notice most emphatically because of revelations the result of official investigation by State and National authority, were at once taken up by the Republican Administration under Mr. Roosevelt. A railroad rate law was passed, giving greatly increased power to the Interstate Commerce Commission, and prosecutions under the anti-trust law were begun and pressed with a vigor never before shown. The time was ripe, because the construction of the anti-trust law by the slow course of judicial decision had finally become sufficiently clear to make successful prosecutions possible. At the same time with the railroad rate bill were enacted the measures already referred to, the pure food law and the meat inspection law. All these encountered the strongest kind of opposition from the leading corporations, from the railroads and the corporations peculiarly affected by the other two laws. Two of the measures failed of passage in one Congress, though recommended by the President, but in the next Congress they were passed after a hard fight, by the full support of the Republican majorities.

Mr. Roosevelt recommended the Federal restriction of the issue of stocks and bonds on interstate railways for the purpose of preventing future overissue; but this was not taken up at the last session of Congress, to which the recommendation was made. It is, however, a part of the pledge of the Republican platform that such a measure will be passed, and there is no reason to doubt that the Republican majorities, with this direction from the party in convention assembled, will comply with its behest.

The Republican platform also recommends legislation for the purpose of controlling corporations engaged in carrying on interstate commerce which are so large and powerful as to make it a temptation for them, unless restrained by law, to attempt illegal monopolies. The proposed plan is to subject the business of such corporations to the close supervision of the Federal authorities, so as to make their regulation and a keeping of them within the law possible. All these provisions of the Republican platform are in accord with the recommendations of Mr. Roosevelt and Congress, and are a proper and emphatic compliance with his policies.

The action of Mr. Roosevelt and the Republican party in this last Administration has called a halt in the evils and abuses which crept in during the enormous expansion of business during the last twelve years. The rate bill marked a moral revulsion and a purification of business methods in the matter of railway rebates and in the matter of complying with the anti-trust law which are notable in the economic and moral history of the country, and the most important steps now to be taken are those which shall make secure the progress made and clinch it, so that when prosperity is resumed the community shall not again be subjected to such evils and to the growth of enormous fortunes due to the perpetuation of such abuses.

The real issue of the campaign, therefore, is whether the Republican party, because of the record of the administrations of Mr. McKinley and of Mr. Roosevelt in the last twelve years, with this most remarkable array of arduous tasks performed, shall be given a vote of confidence and be entrusted with the further work needed, or whether the country shall be turned over to a party which, under its present leadership, has been doing everything by turns and nothing long. It was a party which proposed to relieve the disaster from which the country suffered during the four years of the operation of the Gorman-Wilson Tariff Bill, not by a new tariff bill, but by adopting a monetary standard of value which would in effect have scaled the debts of all debtors and of the nation as well by 50 percent, and which would have sullied the honor of the nation as one which repudiated its obligations and enabled its citizens to do the same.

Again, in 1900, instead of recommending a change of tariff or suggesting any other of the remedies as paramount which it now proposes, it continued to insist on the adoption of free silver coinage, and attacked the policy of the Government in dealing with its problems which came from the Spanish War, as imperialistic.

Again, in 1904, under a somewhat different leadership, but still claiming to be the same party, it made the paramount issue the executive usurpation of Mr. Roosevelt and attempted to avoid the fear that it might change the tariff by inviting attention, through the letter of its candidate, to the fact that the Republican Senate would prevent any change in the tariff at all. Now that the Republican party has pledged itself to revise the tariff and reduce the excessive rates which have arisen by a change of conditions since 1896, the Democratic party seeks to make the tariff one of the issues of the campaign, after twelve years of what may be described as a substantial ignoring of the issue.

The Democratic party, through its present leader, Mr. Bryan, now claims to be the real successor of Mr. Roosevelt in the purpose and policy to eliminate from our economic system illegal monopolies and railroad rebates, and unlawful discriminations and excessive rates. In other words, having introduced into the last three campaigns issues as of paramount importance of an entirely different character from the trust issue and the railroad issue, and after Mr. Roosevelt and the Republican party have taken long strides toward the remedy of the evils which gave rise to these issues, Mr. Bryan and the Democratic party step forward, and claim, with a courage which in a different cause might well command admiration, that they are the true exponents of the Roosevelt policies, and that they only can be trusted to carry them out, and this in the face of the fact that their remedies as proposed in their platform are exactly the remedies which Mr. Roosevelt, in his message in 1904 and ever since, has consistently pointed out are not the remedies which ought to be pursued. The two remedies which they make prominent are the remedy of putting every article of merchandise made and controlled by a trust upon the free list, a remedy which would totally destroy the industries depending upon the manufacture of such an article, render the capital invested therein and the plant in which it is expended utterly worthless, destroy all the smaller competitors of the trust, greatly injure the prosperity of the country, and throw out of work millions of workingmen and workingwomen.

The second remedy is the revision of the tariff—not on protection lines, but on the lines of a revenue tariff, or on free trade principles. This was attempted in a partial way in the Gorman-Wilson Bill, and resulted most disastrously to the business interests of the country. It means the introducing of such a transition and change in the manufacturing business of this country as to close a very large part of the factories and productive enterprises, and even if theoretically, after the transition and change had been made, the rate of wages would be restored—an assumption I cannot admit—certainly, the transition and change would so halt the business of the country and involve such a paralysis while the change was being effected, that the losses and stagnation in business and the number of men thrown out of employment can hardly be exaggerated. More than this, the Democratic party has so long been engaged in devising sophistical theories upon which to attract votes, rather than in the preparation of practical statutes by which to effect results, that the public may well pause and hesitate to entrust to it any serious, sober work that requires for its accomplishment a strong sense of responsibility to the business interests of the country, in the prosperity of which the comfort and well-being of all classes, farmers, wage-earners and business men alike, are inseparably involved.

The issue in which laboring men are supposed to be particularly interested in this campaign is with respect to injunctions in industrial disputes. The Republican party proposes to meet the objection to the issuing of temporary restraining orders without notice in industrial disputes, which, though only in rare instances, have put at an improper disadvantage men engaged in a lawful strike, by defining the best practice in the issuing of such injunctions in all cases by statute, and limiting the operation of the injunction without notice to a very short period, within which a hearing must be had or the injunction cease to have effect. The Democratic platform recommends no action with respect to notice at all, adopts an enigmatical plank on injunctions in industrial disputes that has practically no meaning, but does recommend the introduction of a jury in all indirect contempt proceedings. This would seriously weaken the power of the court, not alone in industrial disputes, but in all cases both of temporary orders and final judgments, and the Republican party is determined that the power of the courts shall be maintained.

The other issue most closely affecting labor is that of the protective tariff and the proposition to change the system from a protective tariff to a revenue tariff, and drive out business industries that are now really dependent upon protection for their maintenance. This, as already said, would so affect the business of the country, so reduce the number of enterprises that could be carried on in the transition proposed as to throw out of employment millions of workingmen. The question which the laboring man has to answer is, whether the advantage to him and his fellows of a change in the judicial procedure as to injunctions and contempt is so great as to outweigh the public injury arising from a weakening of the power of the courts and the disaster to the wage-earner and the business community which would follow the adoption of the other Democratic economic proposals.

I have omitted from this review the proposition of the Democratic party to give to the Philippines immediate independence, and to initiate a system of enforced guaranty of bank deposits. I have no space to elaborate either proposition, except to say that the first is intended to, and if carried out will, defeat a plan of the Republican Administration to uplift an unfortunate people, to teach them the power of self-government, and to make greatly for the spread of Christian civilization in the Orient. The second is one of those sophistical financial propositions so dear to Mr. Bryan, plausible on its face, but utterly at variance with sound principle. It is supposed to prevent entirely any loss of deposits in all banks to the depositors, and thus to prevent panics. As a matter of fact, it will stimulate reckless and dishonest use of deposits in bank investments, it much reduces the motive for conservative and honest banking in a community, and it would not in the slightest degree prevent runs on banks during panics, for which it is supposed to be a panacea. It imposes upon the honest and conservative banker an obligation to answer for the default of his unscrupulous or inexperienced fellow, without any means on his part of supervising the work of the person whose honest and careful conduct he insures.

The country is just now slowly recovering from a financial depression and a panic which came to us in October and November of last year. It is different from all the other panics in our history, and there are many indications that all that is needed to bring back good conditions is the restoration of confidence on the part of the investing public. It is submitted that for twelve years Mr. Bryan has been upholding financial and economic theories which were calculated to frighten all sound, conservative business men. His free silver and free trade doctrines, with a touch of "greenbackism" in some of his proposals, his quickness to seize upon any remedy, however drastic and impossible, which would please the crowd, and the utter instability of his views on any subject of a financial or economic character, would make his election to the Presidency a menace to prosperity. The necessary capital would be withheld and we should probably have a continuation of the present depression for the coming four years. It is Mr. Bryan's record in the last twelve years that makes this a necessary result of his election. Mr. Bryan says that the argument of the full dinner pail has been worked overtime. The argument of the full dinner pail is just as apt and just as relevant to the present situation as it has been in previous campaigns. As it is, two things can be affirmed of the Democratic party under the leadership of Mr. Bryan: First, that all who have anything to invest distrust him because of his unstable and unsound economic and financial views; and second, that they are justified in their lack of confidence. For that reason, those who wish a restoration of prosperity in the country should vote against the Democratic ticket.

These are the issues of the campaign as I understand them. Mr. Bryan charges that the Republican party is controlled by the corporations through campaign contributions. The record of the present Administration is a complete refutation of that charge. The adoption of statutes which met bitter corporate opposition is utterly inconsistent with it, and his assumption that the use of money in a campaign election can control elections is a charge of venality against the American electorate that has no foundation in fact.

Mr. Bryan says that there is no hope of a genuine revision of the tariff, because he says the Republican party is dependent for its campaign contributions upon the beneficiaries of the excessive rates under the tariff, and therefore that the only possible hope of a reduction in tariff schedules is from the Democratic party. I wish to deny this with the utmost emphasis. It is doubtless true that business men interested in a restoration of prosperity will some of them contribute to Republican campaign funds. Campaign funds are necessary in order to pay the legitimate expenses of a campaign. Certainly the extent of the contributions from any source in this campaign is not enough to indicate such a pecuniary interest in the success of the Republican party as would exist if Mr. Bryan's charges were true. Speaking for myself, as the temporary leader of the party, and as the next President if the party is successful in November, I wish to affirm that no effort of mine will be spared to make the revision of the tariff under Republican auspices and within the conservative protective lines as thorough and as impartial between the consumer and the manufacturing interests as possible. I believe that there are many schedules that ought to be reduced. I believe that there are a few, and only a few, that ought to be raised, but on the whole the revision should be a revision downward and not a revision upward. I am convinced that the people of the country desire such a revision. I am convinced that their representatives coming back to Congress will be imbued with that sentiment, and that no successful obstruction can be placed in the way of such Congressional action.

To restate the issue of the campaign, it is whether the administrations of William McKinley and Theodore Roosevelt, in their wonderful record of meeting new problems and solving them by things done and statutes passed, shall be endorsed by the people, and the progress made assured by proper legislation, or whether there shall be put in power a party the chief characteristic of which in the last twelve years has been that of hunting an issue and seeking a sophistical theory which would attract votes with but little regard for its practical operation, and with but a small sense of responsibility to the business and labor interests of the country.

3

Inaugural Address

March 4, 1909

My Fellow Citizens:

Any one who has taken the oath I have just taken must feel a heavy weight of responsibility. If not, he has no conception of the powers and duties of the office upon which he is about to enter, or he is lacking in a proper sense of the obligation which the oath imposes.

The office of an inaugural address is to give a summary outline of the main policies of the new administration, so far as they can be anticipated. I have had the honor to be one of the advisers of my distinguished predecessor, and, as such, to hold up his hands in the reforms he has initiated. I should be untrue to myself, to my promises, and to the declarations of the party platform upon which I was elected to office, if I did not make the maintenance and enforcement of those reforms a most important feature of my administration. They were directed to the suppression of the lawlessness and abuses of power of the great combinations of capital invested in railroads and in industrial enterprises carrying on interstate commerce. The steps which my predecessor took and the legislation passed on his recommendation have accomplished much, have caused a general halt in the vicious policies which created popular alarm, and have brought about in the business affected a much higher regard for existing law.

To render the reforms lasting, however, and to secure at the same time freedom from alarm on the part of those pursuing proper and progressive business methods, further legislative and executive action is needed. Relief of the railroads from certain restrictions of the anti-trust law have been urged by my predecessor and will be urged by me. On the other hand, the administration is pledged to legislation looking to a proper federal supervision and restriction to prevent excessive issues of bonds and stocks by companies owning and operating interstate-commerce railroads.

Then, too, a reorganization of the Department of Justice, of the Bureau of Corporations in the Department of Commerce and Labor, and of the Interstate Commerce Commission, looking to effective cooperation of these agencies is needed to secure a more rapid and certain enforcement of the laws affecting interstate railroads and industrial combinations.

I hope to be able to submit at the first regular session of the incoming Congress, in December next, definite suggestions in respect to the needed amendments to the anti-trust and the interstate-commerce law and the changes required in the executive departments concerned in their enforcement.

It is believed that with the changes to be recommended, American business can be assured of that measure of stability and certainty in respect to those things that may be done and those that are prohibited which is essential to the life and growth of all business. Such a plan must include the right of the people to avail themselves of those methods of combining capital and effort deemed necessary to reach the highest degree of economic efficiency, at the same time differentiating between combinations based upon legitimate economic reasons and those formed with the intent of creating monopolies and artificially controlling prices.

The work of formulating into practical shape such changes is creative work of the highest order, and requires all the deliberation possible in the interval. I believe that the amendments to be proposed are just as necessary in the protection of legitimate business as in the clinching of the reforms which properly bear the name of my predecessor.

A matter of most pressing importance is the revision of the tariff. In accordance with the promises of the platform upon which I was elected, I shall call Congress into extra session to meet on the 15th day of March, in order that consideration may be at once given to a bill revising the Dingley Act. This should secure an adequate revenue and adjust the duties in such a manner as to afford to labor and to all industries in this country, whether of the farm, mine, or factory, protection by tariff equal to the difference between the cost of production abroad and the cost of production here, and have a provision which shall put into force, upon executive determination of certain facts, a higher or maximum tariff against those countries whose trade policy toward us equitably requires such discrimination. It is thought that there has been such a change in conditions since the enactment of the Dingley Act, drafted on a similarly protective principle, that the measure of the tariff above stated will permit the reduction of rates in certain schedules and will require the advancement of few, if any.

The proposal to revise the tariff made in such an authoritative way as to lead the business community to count upon it necessarily halts all those branches of business directly affected; and as these are most important, it disturbs the whole business of the country. It is imperatively necessary, therefore, that a tariff bill be drawn in good faith in accordance with promises made before the election by the party in power, and as promptly passed as due consideration will permit. It is not that the tariff is more important in the long run than the perfecting of the reforms in respect to anti-trust legislation and interstate-commerce regulation, but the need for action when the revision of the tariff has been determined upon is more immediate to avoid embarrassment of business. To secure the needed speed in the passage of the tariff bill, it would seem wise to attempt no other legislation at the extra session. I venture this as a suggestion only, for the course to be taken by Congress, upon the call of the Executive, is wholly within its discretion.

In the making of a tariff bill the prime motive is taxation and the securing thereby of a revenue. Due largely to the business depression which followed the financial panic of 1907, the revenue from customs and other sources has decreased to such an extent that the expenditures for the current fiscal year will exceed the receipts by $100,000,000. It is imperative that such a deficit shall not continue, and the framers of the tariff bill must, of course, have in mind the total revenues likely to be produced by it and so arrange the duties as to secure an adequate income. Should it be impossible to do so by import duties, new kinds of taxation must be adopted, and among these I recommend a graduated inheritance tax as correct in principle and as certain and easy of collection.

The obligation on the part of those responsible for the expenditures made to carry on the Government, to be as economical as possible, and to make the burden of taxation as light as possible, is plain, and should be affirmed in every declaration of government policy. This is especially true when we are face to face with a heavy deficit. But when the desire to win the popular approval leads to the cutting off of expenditures really needed to make the Government effective and to enable it to accomplish its proper objects, the result is as much to be condemned as the waste of government funds in unnecessary expenditure. The scope of a modern government in what it can and ought to accomplish for its people has been widened far beyond the principles laid down by the old "laisser-faire" school of political writers, and this widening has met popular approval.

In the Department of Agriculture the use of scientific experiments on a large scale and the spread of information derived from them for the improvement of general agriculture must go on.

The importance of supervising business of great railways and industrial combinations and the necessary investigation and prosecution of unlawful business methods are another necessary tax upon Government which did not exist half a century ago.

The putting into force of laws which shall secure the conservation of our resources, so far as they may be within the jurisdiction of the Federal Government, including the most important work of saving and restoring our forests and the great improvement of waterways, are all proper government functions which must involve large expenditure if properly performed. While some of them, like the reclamation of arid lands, are made to pay for themselves, others are of such an indirect benefit that this can not be expected of them. A permanent improvement, like the Panama Canal, should be treated as a distinct enterprise, and should be paid for by the proceeds of bonds, the issue of which will distribute its cost between the present and future generations in accordance with the benefits derived. It may well be submitted to the serious consideration of Congress whether the deepening and control of the channel of a great river system, like that of the Ohio or of the Mississippi, when definite and practical plans for the enterprise have been approved and determined upon, should not be provided for in the same way.

Then, too, there are expenditures of Government absolutely necessary if our country is to maintain its proper place among the nations of the world, and is to exercise its proper influence in defense of its own trade interests in the maintenance of traditional American policy against the colonization of European monarchies in this hemisphere, and in the promotion of peace and international morality. I refer to the cost of maintaining a proper army, a proper navy, and suitable fortifications upon the mainland of the United States and in its dependencies.

We should have an army so organized and so officered as to be capable in time of emergency, in cooperation with the national militia and under the provisions of a proper national volunteer law, rapidly to expand into a force sufficient to resist all probable invasion from abroad and to furnish a respectable expeditionary force if necessary in the maintenance of our traditional American policy which bears the name of President Monroe.

Our fortifications are yet in a state of only partial completeness, and the number of men to man them is insufficient. In a few years, however, the usual annual appropriations for our coast defenses, both on the mainland and in the dependencies, will make them sufficient to resist all direct attack, and by that time we may hope that the men to man them will be provided as a necessary adjunct. The distance of our shores from Europe and Asia of course reduces the necessity for maintaining under arms a great army, but it does not take away the requirement of mere prudence—that we should have an army sufficiently large and so constituted as to form a nucleus out of which a suitable force can quickly grow.

What has been said of the army may be affirmed in even a more emphatic way of the navy. A modern navy can not be improvised. It must be built and in existence when the emergency arises which calls for its use and operation. My distinguished predecessor has in many speeches and messages set out with great force and striking language the necessity for maintaining a strong navy commensurate with the coast line, the governmental resources, and the foreign trade of our Nation; and I wish to reiterate all the reasons which he has presented in favor of the policy of maintaining a strong navy as the best conservator of our peace with other nations and the best means of securing respect for the assertion of our rights, the defense of our interests, and the exercise of our influence in international matters.

Our international policy is always to promote peace. We shall enter into any war with a full consciousness of the awful consequences that it always entails, whether successful or not, and we, of course, shall make every effort consistent with national honor and the highest national interest to avoid a resort to arms. We favor every instrumentality, like that of The Hague Tribunal and arbitration treaties made with a view to its use in all international controversies, in order to maintain peace and to avoid war. But we should be blind to existing conditions and should allow ourselves to become foolish idealists if we did not realize that with all the nations of the world armed and prepared for war, we must be ourselves in a similar condition, in order to prevent other nations from taking advantage of us and of our inability to defend our interests and assert our rights with a strong hand.

In the international controversies that are likely to arise in the Orient growing out of the question of the open door and other issues the United States can maintain her interests intact, and can secure respect for her just demands. She will not be able to do so, however, if it is understood that she never intends to back up her assertion of right and her defense of her interest by anything but mere verbal protest and diplomatic note. For these reasons the expenses of the army and navy and of coast defenses should always be considered as something which the Government must pay for, and they should not be cut off through mere consideration of economy. Our Government is able to afford a suitable army and a suitable navy. It may maintain them without the slightest danger to the Republic or the cause of free institutions, and fear of additional taxation ought not to change a proper policy in this regard.

The policy of the United States in the Spanish war and since has given it a position of influence among the nations that it never had before, and should be constantly exerted to securing to its bona fide citizens, whether native or naturalized, respect for them as such in foreign countries. We should make every effort to prevent humiliating and degrading prohibition against any of our citizens wishing temporarily to sojourn in foreign countries because of race or religion.

The admission of Asiatic immigrants who cannot be amalgamated with our population has been made the subject either of prohibitory clauses in our treaties and statutes or of strict administrative regulation secured by diplomatic negotiation. I sincerely hope that we may continue to minimize the evils likely to arise from such immigration without unnecessary friction and by mutual concessions between self-respecting governments. Meantime we must take every precaution to prevent, or failing that, to punish, outbursts of race feeling among our people against foreigners of whatever nationality who have by our grant a treaty right to pursue lawful business here, and to be protected against lawless assault or injury.

This leads me to point out a serious defect in the present federal jurisdiction, which ought to be remedied at once. Having assured to other countries by treaty the protection of our laws for such of their subjects or citizens as we permit to come within our jurisdiction, we now leave to a State or a city, not under the control of the Federal Government, the duty of performing our international obligations in this respect. By proper legislation we may, and ought to, place in the hands of the Federal Executive the means of enforcing the treaty rights of such aliens in the courts of the Federal Government. It puts our Government in a pusillanimous position to make definite engagements to protect aliens and then to excuse the failure to perform those engagements by an explanation that the duty to keep them is in States or cities not within our control. If we would promise we must put ourselves in a position to perform our promise. We can not permit the possible failure of justice, due to local prejudice, in any State or municipal government to expose us to the risk of a war which might be avoided if federal jurisdiction was asserted by suitable legislation by Congress and carried out by proper proceedings instituted by the Executive in the courts of the National Government.

One of the reforms to be carried out during the incoming administration is a change of our monetary and banking laws, so as to secure greater elasticity in the forms of currency available for trade and to prevent the limitations of law from operating to increase the embarrassments of a financial panic. The monetary commission, lately appointed, is giving full consideration to existing conditions and to all proposed remedies, and will doubtless suggest one that will meet the requirements of business and of public interest.

We may hope that the report will embody neither the narrow view of those who believe that the sole purpose of the new system should be to secure a large return on banking capital or of those who would have greater expansion of currency with little regard to provisions for its immediate redemption or ultimate security. There is no subject of economic discussion so intricate and so likely to evoke differing views and dogmatic statements as this one. The commission, in studying the general influence of currency on business and of business on currency, have wisely extended their investigations in European banking and monetary methods. The information that they have derived from such experts as they have found abroad will undoubtedly be found helpful in the solution of the difficult problem they have in hand.

The incoming Congress should promptly fulfill the promise of the Republican platform and pass a proper postal-savings bank bill. It will not be unwise or excessive paternalism. The promise to repay by the Government will furnish an inducement to savings deposits which private enterprise can not supply and at such a low rate of interest as not to withdraw custom from existing banks. It will substantially increase the funds available for investment as capital in useful enterprises. It will furnish the absolute security which makes the proposed scheme of government guaranty of deposits so alluring, without its pernicious results.

I sincerely hope that the incoming Congress will be alive, as it should be, to the importance of our foreign trade and of encouraging it in every way feasible. The possibility of increasing this trade in the Orient, in the Philippines, and in South America is known to everyone who has given the matter attention. The direct effect of free trade between this country and the Philippines will be marked upon our sale of cottons, agricultural machinery, and other manufactures. The necessity for the establishment of direct lines of steamers between North and South America has been brought to the attention of Congress by my predecessor and by Mr. Root before and after his noteworthy visit to that continent, and I sincerely hope that Congress may be induced to see the wisdom of a tentative effort to establish such lines by the use of mail subsidies.

The importance which the Departments of Agriculture and of Commerce and Labor may play in ridding the markets of Europe of prohibitions and discriminations against the importation of our products is fully understood, and it is hoped that the use of the maximum and minimum feature of our tariff law to be soon passed will be effective to remove many of those restrictions.

The Panama Canal will have a most important bearing upon the trade between the eastern and the far western sections of our country, and will greatly increase the facilities for transportation between the eastern and the western seaboard, and may possibly revolutionize the transcontinental rates with respect to bulky merchandise. It will also have a most beneficial effect to increase the trade between the eastern seaboard of the United States and the western coast of South America, and, indeed, with some of the important ports on the east coast of South America reached by rail from the west coast.

The work on the canal is making most satisfactory progress. The type of the canal as a lock canal was fixed by Congress after a full consideration of the conflicting reports of the majority and minority of the consulting board, and after the recommendation of the War Department and the Executive upon those reports. Recent suggestion that something had occurred on the Isthmus to make the lock type of the canal less feasible than it was supposed to be when the reports were made and the policy determined on, led to a visit to the Isthmus of a board of competent engineers to examine the Gatun dam and locks, which are the key of the lock type. The report of the board shows that nothing has occurred in the nature of newly revealed evidence which should change the views once formed in the original discussion. The construction will go on under a most effective organization controlled by Colonel Goethals and his fellow army engineers associated with him, and will certainly be completed early in the next administration, if not before.

Some type of canal must be constructed. The lock type has been selected. We are all in favor of having it built as promptly as possible. We must not now, therefore, keep up a fire in the rear of the agents whom we have authorized to do our work on the Isthmus. We must hold up their hands, and speaking for the incoming administration I wish to say that I propose to devote all the energy possible and under my control to pushing this work on the plans which have been adopted, and to stand behind the men who are doing faithful, hard work to bring about the early completion of this, the greatest constructive enterprise of modern times.

The governments of our dependencies in Puerto Rico and the Philippines are progressing as favorably as could be desired. The prosperity of Puerto Rico continues unabated. The business conditions in the Philippines are not all that we could wish them to be, but with the passage of the new tariff bill permitting free trade between the United States and the archipelago, with such limitations in sugar and tobacco as shall prevent injury to domestic interests on those products, we can count on an improvement in business conditions in the Philippines and the development of a mutually profitable trade between this country and the islands. Meantime our Government in each dependency is upholding the traditions of civil liberty and increasing popular control which might be expected under American auspices. The work which we are doing there redounds to our credit as a Nation.

I look forward with hope to increasing the already good feeling between the South and the other sections of the country. My chief purpose is not to effect a change in the electoral vote of the Southern States. That is a secondary consideration. What I look forward to is an increase in the tolerance of political views of all kinds and their advocacy throughout the South, and the existence of a respectable political opposition in every State; even more than this, to an increased feeling on the part of all the people in the South that this Government is their Government, and that its officers in their States are their officers.

The consideration of this question can not, however, be complete and full without reference to the Negro race, its progress and its present condition. The thirteenth amendment secured them freedom; the fourteenth amendment, due process of law, protection of property, and the pursuit of happiness; and the fifteenth amendment attempted to secure the Negro against any deprivation of the privilege to vote because he was a Negro. The thirteenth and fourteenth amendments have been generally enforced and have secured the objects for which they were intended. While the fifteenth amendment has not been generally observed in the past, it ought to be observed, and the tendency of southern legislation to-day is toward the enactment of electoral qualifications which shall square with that amendment. Of course, the mere adoption of a constitutional law is only one step in the right direction. It must be fairly and justly enforced as well. In time both will come. Hence it is clear to all that the domination of an ignorant, irresponsible element can be prevented by constitutional laws which shall exclude from voting both Negroes and whites not having education or other qualifications thought to be necessary for a proper electorate. The danger of the control of an ignorant electorate has therefore passed. With this change, the interest which many of the southern white citizens take in the welfare of the

Negroes has increased. The colored men must base their hope on the results of their own industry, self-restraint, thrift, and business success, as well as upon the aid and comfort and sympathy which they may receive from their white neighbors of the South.

There was a time when Northerners who sympathized with the Negro in his necessary struggle for better conditions sought to give to him the suffrage as a protection and to enforce its exercise against the prevailing sentiment of the South. The movement proved to be a failure. What remains is the fifteenth amendment to the Constitution and the right to have statutes of States specifying qualifications for electors subjected to the test of compliance with that amendment. This is a great protection to the Negro. It never will be repealed, and it never ought to be repealed. If it had not passed, it might be difficult now to adopt it; but with it in our fundamental law, the policy of Southern legislation must and will tend to obey it, and so long as the statutes of the States meet the test of this amendment and are not otherwise in conflict with the Constitution and laws of the United States it is not the disposition or within the province of the Federal Government to interfere with the regulation by Southern States of their domestic affairs. There is in the South a stronger feeling than ever among the intelligent, well-to-do, and influential element in favor of the industrial education of the Negro and the encouragement of the race to make themselves useful members of the community. The progress which the Negro has made in the last fifty years, from slavery, when its statistics are revealed, is marvellous, and it furnishes every reason to hope that in the next twenty-five years a still greater improvement in his condition as a productive member of society, on the farm, and in the shop, and in other occupations may come.

The Negroes are now Americans. Their ancestors came here years ago against their will, and this is their only country and their only flag. They have shown themselves anxious to live for it and to die for it. Encountering the race feeling against them, subjected at times to cruel injustice growing out of it, they may well have our profound sympathy and aid in the struggle they are making. We are charged with the sacred duty of making their path as smooth and easy as we can. Any recognition of their distinguished men, any appointment to office from among their number, is properly taken as an encouragement and an appreciation of their progress, and this just policy should be pursued when suitable occasion offers.

But it may well admit of doubt whether, in the case of any race, an appointment of one of their number to a local office in a community in which the race feeling is so widespread and acute as to interfere with the ease and facility with which the local government business can be done by the appointee is of sufficient benefit by way of encouragement to the race to outweigh the recurrence and increase of race feeling which such an appointment is likely to engender. Therefore, the Executive, in recognizing the Negro race by appointments, must exercise a careful discretion not thereby to do it more harm than good. On the other hand, we must be careful not to encourage the mere pretense of race feeling manufactured in the interest of individual political ambition.

Personally, I have not the slightest race prejudice or feeling, and recognition of its existence only awakens in my heart a deeper sympathy for those who have to bear it or suffer from it, and I question the wisdom of a policy which is likely to increase it. Meantime, if nothing is done to prevent it, a better feeling between the Negroes and the whites in the South will continue to grow, and more and more of the white people will come to realize that the future of the South is to be much benefited by the industrial and intellectual progress of the Negro. The exercise of political franchises by those of his race who are intelligent and well-to-do will be acquiesced in, and the right to vote will be withheld only from the ignorant and irresponsible of both races.

There is one other matter to which I shall refer. It was made the subject of great controversy during the election and calls for at least a passing reference now. My distinguished predecessor has given much attention to the cause of labor, with whose struggle for better things he has shown the sincerest sympathy. At his instance Congress has passed the bill fixing the liability of interstate carriers to their employees for injury sustained in the course of employment, abolishing the rule of fellow servant and the common-law rule as to contributory negligence, and substituting therefor the so-called rule of "comparative negligence." It has also passed a law fixing the compensation of government employees for injuries sustained in the employ of the Government. It has also passed a model child-labor law for the District of Columbia. In previous administrations an arbitration law for interstate-commerce railroads and their employees, and laws for the application of safety devices to save the lives and limbs of employees of interstate railroads had been passed. Additional legislation of this kind was passed by the outgoing Congress.

I wish to say that, in so far as I can, I hope to promote the enactment of further legislation of this character. I am strongly convinced that the Government should make itself as responsible to employees injured in its employ as an interstate-railway corporation is made responsible by federal law to its employees; and I shall be glad, whenever any additional reasonable safety device can be invented to reduce the loss of life and limb among railway employees, to urge Congress to require its adoption by interstate railways.

Another labor question has arisen which has awakened the most excited discussion. That is in respect to the power of the federal courts to issue injunctions in industrial disputes. As to that, my convictions are fixed. Take away from the courts, if it could be taken away, the power to issue injunctions in labor disputes, and it would create a privileged class among the laborers and save the lawless among their number from a most needful remedy available to all men for the protection of their business against unlawful invasion. The proposition that business is not a property or pecuniary right which can be protected by equitable injunction is utterly without foundation in precedent or reason. The proposition is usually linked with one to make the secondary boycott lawful. Such a proposition is at variance with the American instinct, and will find no support, in my judgment, when submitted to the American people. The secondary boycott is an instrument of tyranny, and ought not to be made legitimate.

The issue of a temporary restraining order without notice has in several instances been abused by its inconsiderate exercise, and to remedy this, the platform upon which I was elected recommends the formulation in a statute of the conditions under which such a temporary restraining order ought to issue. A statute can and ought to be framed to embody the best modern practice, and can bring the subject so closely to the attention of the court as to make abuses of the process unlikely in the future. The American people, if I understand them, insist that the authority of the courts shall be sustained, and are opposed to any change in the procedure by which the powers of a court may be weakened and the fearless and effective administration of justice be interfered with.

Having thus reviewed the questions likely to recur during my administration, and having expressed in a summary way the position which I expect to take in recommendations to Congress and in my conduct as an Executive, I invoke the considerate sympathy and support of my fellow citizens and the aid of Almighty God in the discharge of my responsible duties.

4

Message Convening Congress in Extra Session

March 16, 1909

To the Senate and House of Representatives:

I have convened the Congress in this extra session in order to enable it to give immediate consideration to the revision of the Dingley Tariff Act. Conditions affecting production, manufacture, and business generally, have so changed in the last twelve years as to require a readjustment and revision of the import duties imposed by that Act. More than this, the present tariff act, with the other sources of Government revenue, does not furnish income enough to pay the authorized expenditures. By July 1st next the excess of expenses over receipts for the current fiscal year will equal $100,000,000.

The successful party in the late election is pledged to a revision of the tariff. The country, and the business community especially, expect it. The prospect of a change in the rates of import duties always causes a suspension or halt in business because of the uncertainty as to the changes to be made, and their effect. It is, therefore, of the highest importance that the new bill should be agreed upon and passed with as much speed as possible consistent with its due and thorough consideration. For these reasons, I have deemed the present to be an extraordinary occasion, within the meaning of the Constitution, justifying and requiring the calling of an extra session.

In my inaugural address I stated in a summary way the principles upon which, in my judgment, the revision of the tariff should proceed, and indicated at least one new source of revenue that might be properly resorted to in order to avoid a future deficit. It is not necessary for me to repeat what I then said.

I venture to suggest that the vital business interests of the country require that the attention of the Congress in this session be chiefly devoted to the consideration of the new tariff bill, and that the less time given to other subjects of legislation in this session, the better for the country.

5

Grover Cleveland

*Address Delivered by the President at the Cleveland Memorial Exercises,
Held in Carnegie Hall, New York City, March 18, 1909*

Grover Cleveland was as completely American in his character as Lincoln. Without a college education, he prepared himself for the Bar. His life was confined to western New York. His vision of government and of society was not widened by foreign travel. He was a pure product of the village and town life of the Middle States, affected by New England ancestry and the atmosphere of a clergyman's home. His chief characteristics were simplicity and directness of thought, sturdy honesty, courage of his convictions and plainness of speech, with a sense of public duty that has been exceeded by no statesman within my knowledge. It was so strong in him that he rarely wrote anything, whether in the form of a private or public communication, that the obligation of all men to observe the public interest was not his chief theme.

His career was a most remarkable one. By his administration of the affairs of his city as its Mayor, he showed his power of resistance to, and of overcoming, the influences that made for corruption and negligence in city government, both in his own party and in the party of his opponents. His reputation in this regard spread over his native state of New York at a time when such an attitude as his seemed exceptional, and his standing before the community became a political asset for the Democratic party, that even those who had but little sympathy with his principles were glad to seize upon as a means of getting into power. Accordingly, he was nominated for the Governorship, and was elected by the votes not only of his own party but of hundreds of thousands of the Republican party. The discharge of his duties as Governor confirmed and strengthened the reputation that he had acquired as a Mayor. Before he had ceased his office as Mayor, he had been elected Governor. Before he had ceased his office as Governor, he had been elected President of the United States.

The presidential campaign of 1884 degenerated into one of slander, scandal and abuse, but Mr. Cleveland came through it, retaining the confidence of the American people in his courage and honesty and his single purpose to better the public service.

Mr. Cleveland was a Democrat. He was a partisan. He believed in parties, as all men must who understand the machinery essential to the success and efficiency of popular government. His impulses were all toward the merit system of appointments in the public service, and against the spoils system; but he had a practical, common-sense view of the problems before him. He dealt with the instruments which he had, and he not infrequently was obliged, in order to accomplish greater objects, to yield to the demands of those who had no ideals, and who were impatient of anything but the use of government offices as a purely political reward. Every time that opportunity offered, however, and there was not some greater object in immediate view, he strengthened and assisted the movement toward the merit system.

Mr. Cleveland's political career was so short that he had a great advantage over the prominent men of his party whose records reached back into, and were governed by, the bitter quarrels of the Civil War. As a political quantity, his history began during the corruption and demoralization in the Republican party which were a necessary result of continued power during the war and the decade succeeding it. He represented in a sense a new Democracy, about which all the older elements rallied, both those strongly in sympathy with his reform views, as well as those elements without such sympathy, who were anxious to secure party power.

At the end of his first term, he was renominated, but was beaten by General Harrison in a close vote. By that time, the politicians of the old school in the Democratic party had drawn away from him, and had no desire to continue his leadership. But so strong a hold had he upon the affections and confidence of the rank and file of his party, and so sure were they that he was stronger than the party in an electoral contest, that he was nominated in the National Convention against the desires of most of the state organization leaders; and in the election which followed, he led his party to the greatest victory in its history.

In this campaign Mr. Cleveland stood for an affirmative idea, that of a reduction of the tariff, so as to make it a tariff for revenue. He attacked the protective theory and system. He stood for something aggressive and affirmative. It was in accordance with the ancient traditions of the party.

I do not need to enter into a discussion of the merits of the issue, but comment on it only as illustrating Mr. Cleveland's character. He was positive. He was affirmative. He was courageous. He believed in parties. He believed in party policies, and he believed in consistency in regard to them, and he did not believe in trimming down a policy to catch the votes of those who really did not agree with it.

The first time Mr. Cleveland was in power he was opposed by a Republican Senate. This gave little opportunity for any radical change by legislation in the previous policies of Republican administrations, but it did offer an opportunity for Mr. Cleveland to point out to the country the fact that our government is a government of three distinct branches, the Executive, the Legislative, and the Judicial, and that the Executive has a sphere which the Legislative branch has no right to invade.

We hear much in these days of the usurpation of the Legislative jurisdiction by the Executive branch. As long as the Legislative branch has the power of the purse, the danger of Executive usurpation is imaginative. The real danger arises from the disposition of the Legislative branch to assume that it has the omnipotence of Parliament and may completely control the discretion conferred upon the Executive by the Constitution. The country is under obligation to Mr. Cleveland for having pointed out in his controversy with the Republican Senate, some of the limitations that there are in the Constitution upon attempted Legislative action to restrict Executive discretion. In the end Mr. Cleveland won in his controversy with the Senate. Whether he might have done so, had both the House and the Senate been against him, is a matter of doubt. The history of Andrew Johnson's controversy with Congress shows how far a partisan legislature may be induced to go in an unconstitutional attempt to cut down Executive power. The limit of Legislative restriction upon Executive action is a difficult line to define. Any one who attempts to do more than to pass on single instances as they arise may find himself in great difficulty, but as such instances are considered and decided, the limits are gradually being defined. We owe to Mr. Cleveland and his courage in dealing with the Senate of the United States, the establishment of some useful precedents.

In Mr. Cleveland's second term, there was a large majority of his party in the House and a working majority in the Senate, so that the whole responsibility of Government fell upon the Democracy, with Mr. Cleveland at its head. The significance of his second administration centers about three issues. The first was the tariff; the second, free silver; and the third, the suppression of lawlessness directed against Federal authority by use of the process of Federal courts and by Federal troops. The same influences in his own party which had sought to defeat Mr. Cleveland for nomination in his third canvass, he found intrencheds in the Senate so strongly as to be able to defeat the declared policy of his party in favor of a revenue tariff, and he refused to sign the Gorman-Wilson Bill but allowed it to become a law after denouncing it as the result of perfidy and dishonor. This was doubtless the greatest disappointment of his political life, for it destroyed the opportunity to test the wisdom of the party policy advocated by him and declared in the party platform, while the business depression which existed before and after its passage furnished ammunition to his political opponents who did not hesitate to argue that the prospect of a revenue tariff on the one hand and the passage of the actual Gorman-Wilson Bill on the other had paralyzed the industries of the country. Whatever one's views upon the tariff, whether he be a protectionist or a free-trader, he cannot but have the deepest sympathy with Mr. Cleveland in his deep indignation at the party disloyalty which defeated the Wilson Bill as it passed the House, and gave us the non-descript bill which became the law.

But there was rising in the Democratic party at the time, especially in the western and southern parts of the country, a desire for economic remedy which should cure everything in our business and body politic. This was the movement in favor of the free coinage of silver. The Republican party and some of its leaders in the west and south had not been free from weakness in this respect, and the law for the monthly purchases of $2,000,000 of silver hung like a stone around the neck of the country. Mr. Cleveland used all the authority that he could command as the Executive to bring about a repeal of this law, and he finally succeeded. The deep gratitude of the country is due to him for this result. Without it disaster would have come. Without it the credit of the country could not have been sustained and there would have been a blot on our financial escutcheon. But when Mr. Cleveland succeeded in securing the repeal of the Sherman Act, it seemed as if his control over the party with respect to the monetary issue had been exhausted. His party became hopelessly divided, and the majority of it declared in favor of the free coinage of silver, a policy which we know today, and which we ought to have known then, was nothing but a policy of repudiation. It was a policy completely contrary to the ancient and traditional views of the old Democratic party. It was a departure from the plainest principles of honesty to those who foresaw its effect in the repudiation and scaling down of public and private debts by legislative fiat. It was a policy which has taken away from the Democratic party the confidence of the business community, whether previously Democratic or Republican. It presented a moral issue so sharp, so clear, as completely to destroy party fealty and party attachments. It took away from the Democratic party that strong, conservative element of which Mr. Cleveland was the leader, and it made it for the time a party which seemed to threaten the foundation of honest business and of honest government. It seemed to make its campaign in 1896 and 1900, an assault upon that which was best in our civilization. In my judgment, the safety of the Republic was threatened by the breaking up of the Democratic party into its radical and conservative elements.

In the campaigns of Mr. Blaine and Mr. Cleveland and of Mr. Cleveland and Mr. Harrison, everyone felt, however deep his partisan desires, that the institutions of the country, as established by the fathers, would be preserved under the leadership of either party, but in the campaign of 1896, and the one which followed it, there was certainly no such confidence on the part of the men who voted for Mr. McKinley. It seemed to be an issue in which the permanence of our institutions was involved.

In this light, it was an unfortunate day for the Republic when the leadership of the Democracy passed from Mr. Cleveland.

The patriotic spirit which moved those under Mr. Cleveland's leadership to break from party ties and save the country from repudiation, entitled them and him to our everlasting gratitude.

Another great debt which the country owes to Mr. Cleveland is the assertion, made through him as its Chief Executive, of the power of the Federal Government directly to defend the Federal jurisdiction through the process of Federal courts and by Federal troops, against the lawless invasion of a mob. Mr. Cleveland was a Democrat and of course respected the traditional construction of the Constitution by that party; but no fear of apparent inconsistency prevented him from asserting the full Federal power to maintain its authority to suppress lawlessness when directed against Federal right and Federal jurisdiction; and so he instituted proceedings in the Federal courts to restrain the Debs' boycott of the country, the tying up of interstate commerce, and the interference with the mails, and he sent the troops under General Miles to Chicago to make his assertion of the power effective. It cost him the support of the thoughtless whose sympathy against the unjust aggressions of corporate power and wealth make them wink at the lawless invasion of vested rights. But he succeeded in stopping what had really grown to the proportions of an insurrection. The highest tribunal created by the Constitution to fix the limits of State and National authority completely sustained his course. There were other issues in his administration; there were other controversies in which he took part in his political life, but time permits me only to discuss those which I have referred to.

Grover Cleveland earned the sincere gratitude of his countrymen and justified recurring memorial occasions like the one in which we are taking part. He was a great President, not because he was a great lawyer, not because he was a brilliant orator, not because he was a statesman of profound learning, but because he was a patriot with the highest sense of public duty, because he was a statesman of clear perceptions, of the utmost courage of his convictions, and of great plainness of speech; because he was a man of the highest character, a father and husband of the best type, and because throughout his political life he showed those rugged virtues of the public servant and citizen, the emulation of which by those who follow him will render progress of our political life toward better things a certainty.

6

Proposed Tariff-Revision Law of 1909
for the Philippine Islands

The White House, April 14, 1909

To the Senate and House of Representatives:

I transmit herewith a communication from the Secretary of War, inclosing one from the Chief of the Bureau of Insular Affairs, in which is transmitted a proposed tariff-revision law for the Philippine Islands.

This measure revises the present Philippine tariff, simplifies it, and makes it conform as nearly as possible to the regulations of the customs laws of the United States, especially with respect to packing and packages. The present Philippine regulations have been cumbersome and difficult for American merchants and exporters to comply with. Its purpose is to meet the new conditions that will arise under the section of the pending United States tariff bill which provides, with certain limitations, for free trade between the United States and the islands. It is drawn with a view to preserving to the islands as much customs revenue as possible, and to protect in a reasonable measure those industries which now exist in the islands.

The bill now transmitted has been drawn by a board of tariff experts, of which the insular collector of customs, Colonel George R. Colton, was the president. The board held a great many open meetings in Manila, and conferred fully with representatives of all business interests in the Philippine Islands. It is of great importance to the welfare of the islands that the bill should be passed at the same time with the pending Payne Bill, with special reference to the provisions of which it was prepared.

I respectfully recommend that this bill be enacted at the present session of Congress as one incidental to and required by the passage of the Payne Bill.

7

Government of the District of Columbia

Address of President Taft at the Banquet Given in His Honor by the
Board of Trade and Chamber of Commerce of Washington, D.C.,
at the New Willard, May 8, 1909

Mr. Chairman and the Solid Men of Washington:

I wish to thank you from the bottom of my heart for the courtesy that
you have extended to me this evening in this magnificent banquet, and in
your coming here to take part in this occasion. I am proud of it, if it be the
case, and I must believe it from the assurances given tonight, that this is the
first time that a President of the United States has ever had the pleasure of
meeting on such an occasion and under such circumstances, the business
men of Washington. I hope for close intimacy; I hope that we may come
together and we may discuss these things, because certainly we need it. I take
the utmost personal pride in the City of Washington. It thrills my heart every
day to look out of the back windows of the White House—for the short time
I have been there—and whenever I get the opportunity, to see this beautiful
city in which we are permitted to live—these avenues and streets constructed
on a magnificent plan, looking forward for centuries; these trees planted with
great foresight to make every part of Washington a park; these vistas into
which always creeps unbidden that beautiful shaft that marks the memory
of the founder of the city.

I have not been here very long in the city of Washington, as some men
count it long. I was here two years between 1890 and 1892; four years from

1904 to 1908—but that is a little bit longer than Justice Stafford. I have been a tax-payer; I have invested some money in land in Washington and have not seen a dollar come out of it; I have sent my children to the public schools; I have hung to straps in street cars, going both ways to the Capitol; I have bathed in the Potomac mud—in a bathtub; I have lunched at Harvey's on those steamed oysters. and I have been a fan with my friend "Sunny Jim" at the baseball park and have had a love, and cultivated it with him, for tail-enders. And therefore, I claim that I have been through experiences that ought to give me some of the local atmosphere and some of the local feeling of Washington. And yet, with all that, gentlemen, as I look about here into these smiling faces, these somewhat rotund forms that give evidence of prosperity, it is a little difficult for me to realize that it was about those "caitiffs" and those "slaves" that Mr. Justice Stafford spoke.

In spite of my experience in Washington, I am a nationalist. This city is a home of the government of a nation, and when men who were just as much imbued with the principles of civil liberty as any who have come after, Washington at the head, put into the Constitution the provisions with reference to the government of the District of Columbia, they knew what they were doing, and spoke for a coming possible eighty millions of people, who should insist that the home of their government should be governed by their representatives; and that if there were in that eighty millions of people men who desired to come and share in the grandeur of that capital and live in a city of magnificent beauty as this was and enjoy all the privileges, then they come with their eyes open as to the character of the government that they are to have, and they must know that they must depend not upon the principles ordinarily governing in popular government, but that they must trust, in order to secure their liberty—to get their guaranties—they must trust to the representatives of eighty millions of people selected under that Constitution.

I want to say, with deference to this discussion, that if this meeting (or subsequent meetings) is to be devoted to securing an amendment to the Constitution, by which you are going to disturb the principle of two Senators from every State, and you are going to abolish the provision that was put in there ex industria by George Washington, you will not get ahead in the matter of better government in Washington by such meetings. I do not want to seem to be abrupt, but I believe it is possible by such meetings as this to arouse the interest of Congress and the Executive to the necessity of consulting the people of Washington, to let them act as Americans act when they don't have the right of suffrage—let them act by the right of petition; and are they not exercising that right all the time? Isn't it possible to determine on the part of the committees of the House and the Senate what the attitude of the Washington citizens is? Why, the government that we have today in Washington everybody admits is a good government. Has it not been brought about through the aid of those very committees in the House and Senate who you say know nothing about Washington, and who make their knowledge, or lack of knowledge, ridiculous by showing it? We are all imperfect. We can not expect perfect government, but what we ought to do is to pursue practical methods, and not, I submit with deference to Justice Stafford, make it seem as if the people of Washington were suffering some great and tremendous load and sorrow, when as a matter of fact they are the envy of the citizens of other cities.

Washington intended this to be a Federal city, and it is a Federal city, and it tingles down to the feet of every man, whether he comes from Washington State, or Los Angeles, or Texas, when he comes and walks these city streets and begins to feel that "this is my city; I own a part of this Capital, and I envy for the time being those who are able to spend their time here." I quite admit that there are defects in the system of government by which Congress is bound to look after the government of the District of Columbia. It could not be otherwise under such a system, but I submit to the judgment of history that the result vindicates the foresight of the fathers.

Now, I am opposed to the franchise in the District; I am opposed, and not because I yield to any one in my support and belief in the principles of self-government; but principles are applicable generally, and then, unless you make exceptions to the application of those principles, you will find that they will carry you to very illogical and absurd results. This was taken out of the application of the principle of self-government in the very Constitution that was intended to put that in force in every other part of the country, and it was done because it was intended to have the representatives of all the people in the country control this one city, and to prevent its being controlled by the parochial spirit that would necessarily govern men who did not look beyond the city to the grandeur of the nation, and this as the representative of that nation.

I have gotten over being frightened by being told that I am forgetting the principles of the fathers. The principles of the fathers are maintained by those who maintain them with reason, and according to the fitness of the thing, and not by those who are constantly shaking them before the mass of the voters when they have no application.

Now, the question arises: What shall we do with the government of Washington? Shall we have the present board of three; shall we have one or shall we have some other form? I confess I do not know. My predecessor has recommended a change of the present form so as to give the responsibility to one, with the view to visiting that one with the responsibility. On the other hand, it is said that three have worked well; that it gives more opportunity, possibly, for counsel, and that it takes away the bureaucratic character of the government. As I have said, I have reached no conclusion as to what recommendation I shall make to Congress on the subject. I fully concur with Justice Stafford in thinking that it would be most unwise to introduce into the District what I understand to be a bureaucratic form of government. That is right. A bureaucratic form of government is one which, as he very well described it, would make the War Department look after the streets; Dr. Wiley, possibly, look after the health—the Agricultural Department through him—and the Treasury Department look after the finances. And so as to each branch of the government you should go to the head of that particular department in the general government. I think that would be a very burdensome, a very awkward, a very clumsy system of government. I am strongly in favor of retaining the municipal form, so that everything which shall affect the city of Washington shall be done under the chief executive of that city, and by that chief executive. In other words, I would give an entity to the city of Washington, or the District of Columbia, and take all of that entity out of the operation of the bureaus of the general government. That is what I understand to be the government today, and the only question that has been mooted is really whether one man should be put at the head of that government as a mayor, or whether you should have three. I agree that probably three men are better, where you have real legislative functions to perform. I am inclined to think that, where the legislative functions are reduced to a minimum and consist in little more than mere executive regulation, possibly the one-headed form is the better, for executive purposes and to fix the responsibility; but I am only thinking out loud, and only because we are here talking right out in meeting I am telling you the reasons as they have been brought to me.

Now I want to talk about the future. And the future of Washington! What an enormous development is before us! Why, I am not an imaginative man, but I would like to come back here a hundred years hence and see the beauties of which this city is capable! Right here, under our noses for a time, under our very eyes, are those beautiful Potomac flats that are going to make as fine parks and parkways as there are in the world! Those parks ought to be connected with the Rock Creek Park by means of the mouth of Rock Creek, or otherwise; and then through them all there ought to be carried a park clear around, including the Soldiers' Home, and completing the circuit with Rock Creek at the other end. Then, too, there is the development in

Anacostia and along the Eastern Branch. Then, the opportunities for playgrounds that there are in Washington! It just makes my mouth water for my poor city of Cincinnati, when I look out and can see clear down to the Potomac and see six and seven baseball matches going on with all the fervor of Young America, and nobody to say them nay! And to think—to think that we had a genius a hundred years ago, almost, in his way, as matchless as Washington, to make the plan for a great Capital, whose remains were buried here the other day, and whose plans were hardly changed in the new plan made by Burnham and his associates. I know there has been discussion as to that plan. There has been a feeling that perhaps it was slipped on to us at one time, and at another; but we all know, even my dear friend, good old Uncle Joe, knows, that we are going to build up to that plan some day. It is not coming at once, but we ought to thank God that we have got a plan like that to build to so that when we go on with the improvement every dollar that we put in goes to make Washington beautiful a hundred years hence.

Then, Justice Stafford, in his very eloquent remarks, called attention to the fact that in 1846—I am sorry to say it ought to be characterized, at least as far as that is concerned, as a day of small things—when the Congress could have recited this: "Whereas, no more territory ought to be held under the exclusive legislation given to Congress over the District, which is the seat of the general government, than may be necessary and proper for the purposes of such a seat. Therefore"—we give back all that we got from Virginia. It is true the early statute said that no buildings should be put on anything but the Maryland side of the river, and perhaps they felt that as we were not going to use that side for buildings, they did not need it at all. I have never been able to satisfy myself that that retrocession was within the power of Congress to make. They did attempt to settle it once in the Supreme Court, but the Supreme Court has a facility in avoiding the main question, born of long practice. And when a gentleman who is paying taxes on this side asks that they be extended to the other side, on the ground that that retrocession did not carry Virginia, so that he might have his taxes reduced, the Supreme Court says that he can not do it in a collateral way; says that, as both parties to the transaction seem to be satisfied up to this time, they do not intend to investigate or seek any burdens that their salaries do not require them to meet. We have never had that question tested. I believe we ought to look forward to a great city of Washington, and while the Anglo Saxon—and especially the Anglo Saxon in Virginia—holds on to territory as long as he can, it might be possible by agitating the question in a legal way to induce another settlement by which we should get the only part of that that we really would like to have, the part that we own now in fee, the eleven hundred acres of the Arlington estate, and a great deal that is unoccupied, leaving Alexandria out, and Falls Church, and taking in only that that is uninhabited, so that we may have in this District, under our fostering control, where we can build roads and make the District still more beautiful, that bank of the Potomac on the other side, as you go up toward Cabin John Bridge. We will need it; the city will continue to grow. It may be, as Justice Stafford has said, that there will be inaugurated a protest by the people living here that they have not political power; but I think that the Justice will find, when he comes to looking into the hearts of the American people, that they will not be convinced when they come to Washington that the Washingtonians are suffering to that degree that requires a reversal of the policy adopted, with entire clearness of mind by the framers of the Constitution. Washington, who doubtless inserted that particular provision in the Constitution, through his influence, also had L'Enfant draw the plans of Washington, and the plans of Washington were not adapted to a village like Alexandria and the village that was in the District at the time we came here—that was adapted to a city of magnificent distances, and to a city of millions of inhabitants; and therefore the clause was adopted, knowing that just such a city we would have here, and just such a city would have to get along, relying upon the training in self-government of the representatives of eighty millions of people to do justice by it and its residents.

Now, my dear friends, I want to say to you that I have got into a constitutional discussion here that I did not anticipate, but I hope it has not clouded my meaning, which I intended to make as clear as possible, that I am deeply interested in the welfare of the District, I am deeply interested in securing good government to every man, woman and child in this District, and to secure so far as is possible, with the original plan under the Constitution, such voice as the people of the District may require in their local matters. But, when it comes to defining how that is to be given, I can not be more explicit than to say it must rest ultimately on the right of petition. I do not see how you can do anything else. I am sure that if you will constantly agitate, and if you will have as eloquent an orator as Justice Stafford talk to the committees of the House and Senate every year, he will rouse them to such a desire to save you from the "slavery" that he has pictured, that you will get the attention you deserve.

8

Concerning Affairs in Puerto Rico

May 10, 1909

To the Senate and House of Representatives:

An emergency has arisen in Puerto Rico which makes it necessary for me to invite the attention of the Congress to the affairs of that island, and to recommend legislation at the present extra session amending the act under which the island is governed.

The regular session of the legislative assembly of Puerto Rico adjourned March 11th last without passing the usual appropriation bills. A special session of the assembly was at once convened by the governor, but after three days, on March 16th, it again adjourned without making the appropriations. This leaves the island government without provision for its support after June 30th next. The situation presented is, therefore, of unusual gravity.

The present government of Puerto Rico was established by what is known as the Foraker Act, passed April 12, 1900, and taking effect May 1, 1900. Under that act the chief executive is a governor appointed by the President and confirmed by the Senate. A secretary, attorney-general, treasurer, auditor, commissioner of the interior, and commissioner of education, together with five other appointees of the President, constitute the executive council. The executive council must have in its membership not less than five native Puerto Ricans. The legislative power is vested in the legislative assembly, which has two coordinate branches. The first of these is the executive council just described, and the second is the house of delegates, a popular and representative body, with members elected by the qualified electors of the seven districts into which the island is divided.

The statute directing how the expenses of government are to be provided leaves some doubt whether this function is not committed solely to the executive council, but in practice the legislative assembly has made appropriations for all the expenses other than for salaries fixed by Congress, and it is too late to reverse that construction.

Ever since the institution of the present assembly, the house of delegates has uniformly held up the appropriation bills until the last minute of the regular session, and has sought to use the power to do so as a means of compelling the concurrence of the executive council in legislation which the house desired.

In the last regular legislative assembly, the house of delegates passed a bill dividing the island into several counties and providing county governments: a bill to establish manual-training schools; a bill for the establishment of an agricultural bank; a bill providing that vacancies in the offices of mayors and councilmen be filled by a vote of the municipal councils instead of by the governor, and a bill putting in the control of the largest taxpayers in each municipal district the selection in great part of the assessors of property.

The executive council declined to concur in these bills. It objected to the agricultural bank bill on the ground that the revenues of the island were not sufficient to carry out the plan proposed, and to the manual-training-school bill because it was in plain violation of the Foraker Act. It objected to the change in the law concerning the appraisement of property on the ground that the law was intended to put too much power, in respect of the appraisement of property for taxation, in the hands of those having the most property to tax. The chief issue was a bill making all the judges in municipalities elective. Under previous legislation there are twenty-six municipal judges who are elected to office. By this bill it was proposed to increase the elective judges from twenty-six to sixty-six in number, and at the same time to abolish the justices of the peace. The change was objected to on the ground that the election of municipal judges had already interfered with the efficient and impartial administration of justice, had made the judges all of one political faith and mere political instruments in the hands of the central committee of the Unionist or dominant party. The attitude of the executive council in refusing to pass these bills led the house of delegates to refuse to pass the necessary appropriation bills.

The facts recited demonstrate the willingness of the representatives of the people in the house of delegates to subvert the government in order to secure the passage of certain legislation. The question whether the proposed legislation should be enacted into law was left by the fundamental act to the joint action of the executive council and the house of delegates as the legislative assembly. The house of delegates proposes itself to secure this legislation without respect to the opposition of the executive council, or else to pull down the whole government. This spirit, which has been growing from year to year in Puerto Rico, shows that too great power has been vested in the house of delegates and that its members are not sufficiently alive to their oath-taken responsibility, for the maintenance of the government, to justify Congress in further reposing in them absolute power to withhold appropriations necessary for the government's life.

For these reasons I recommend an amendment to the Foraker Act providing that whenever the legislative assembly shall adjourn without making the appropriations necessary to carry on the government, sums equal to the appropriations made in the previous year for the respective purposes shall be available from the current revenues and shall be drawn by the warrant of the auditor on the treasurer and countersigned by the governor. Such a provision applies to the legislatures of the Philippines and Hawaii, and it has prevented in those two countries any misuse of the power of appropriation.

The house of delegates sent a committee of three to Washington, while the executive council was represented by the secretary and a committee consisting of the attorney-general and the auditor. I referred both committees to the Secretary of the Interior, whose report, with a letter from Governor Post, and the written statements of both committees, accompany this message.

I have had one personal interview with the committee representing the house of delegates, and suggested to them that if the house of delegates would pass the appropriation bills without insisting upon the passage of the other bills by the executive council, I would send a representative of the Government to Puerto Rico to make an investigation and report in respect to the proposed legislation. Their answer, which shows them not to be in a compromising mood, was as follows:

> "If the legislative assembly of Puerto Rico would be called to an extraordinary session exclusively to pass an appropriation bill, taking into consideration the state of affairs down the island and the high dissatisfaction produced by the intolerant attitude of the executive council, and also taking into consideration the absolute resistance of the house to do any act against its own dignity and the dignity of the country, it is the opinion of these commissioners that no agreement would be attained

unless the council feel disposed to accept the amendments of the house of delegates.

"However, if in the proclamation calling for an extraordinary session the judicial and municipal reforms would be mentioned, and if the executive council would accept that the present justices of the peace be abolished and municipal judges created in every municipality, and that vacancies occurring in mayorships and judgeships be filled by the municipal councils, as provided in the so-called 'municipal bills' passed by the house in its last session, then the commissioners believe that the appropriation bills will be passed in the house as introduced in the council without delay."

Puerto Rico has been the favored daughter of the United States. The sovereignty of the island in 1899 passed to the United States with the full consent of the people of the island.

Under the law all the customs and internal-revenue taxes are turned into the treasury of Puerto Rico for the maintenance of the island government, while the United States pays out of its own Treasury the cost of the local army—i.e., a full Puerto Rican regiment—the revenue vessels, the lighthouse service, the coast surveys, the harbor improvements, the marine-hospital support, the post-office deficit, the weather bureau, and the upkeep of the agricultural experiment stations.

Very soon after the change of sovereignty a cyclone destroyed a large part of Puerto Rican coffee culture; $200,000 was expended from the United States Treasury to buy rations for those left in distress. The island is policed by 700 men, and complete tranquillity reigns.

Before American control 87 percent of the Puerto Ricans were unable to read or write, and there was not in this island, containing a million people, a single building constructed for public instruction, while the enrolment of pupils in such schools as there were, 551 in number, was but 21,000. Today in the island there are 160 such buildings, and the enrolment of pupils in 2,400 schools has reached the number of 87,000. The year before American sovereignty there was expended $35,000 in gold for public education. Under the present government there is expended for this purpose a total of a million dollars a year.

When the Americans took control there were 172 miles of macadamized road. Since then there have been constructed 452 miles more, mostly in the mountains, making in all now a total of 624 miles of finely planned and admirably constructed macadamized roads—as good roads as there are in the world.

In the course of the administration of this island, the United States medical authorities discovered a disease of tropical anaemia which was epidemic and was produced by a microbe called the "hook worm." It so much impaired the energy of those who suffered from it, and so often led to complete prostration and death, that it became necessary to undertake its cure by widespread governmental effort. I am glad to say that 225,000 natives, or one-fourth of the entire population, have been treated at government expense, and the effect has been much to reduce the extent and severity of the disease and to bring it under control. Substantially every person in the island has been vaccinated and small–pox has practically disappeared.

There is complete free trade between Puerto Rico and the United States, and all customs duties collected in the United States on Puerto Rican products subsequent to the date of Spanish evacuation, amounting to nearly $3,000,000, have been refunded to the island treasury. The loss to the revenues of the United States from the free admission of Puerto Rican products is $15,000,000 annually. The wealth of the island is directly dependent upon the cultivation of the soil, to cane, tobacco, coffee, and fruit, for which we in America provide the market. Without our fostering benevolence the business of Puerto Rico would be as prostrate as are some of the neighboring West Indian Islands. Before American control the trade balance against the island was over $12,500,000, while the present balance of trade in favor of the island is $2,500,000. The total of exports and imports has increased from about $22,000,000 before American sovereignty to $56,000,000 at the present day. At the date of the American occupation the estimated value of all agricultural land was about $30,000,000. Now the appraised value of the real property in the island reaches $100,000,000. The expenses of government before American control were $2,969,000, while the receipts were $3,644,000. For the year 1906 the receipts were $4,250,000, and the expenditures were $4,084,000. Of the civil servants in the central government, 343 are Americans and 2,548 are native Puerto Ricans. There never was a time in the history of the island when the average prosperity of the Puerto Rican has been higher, when his opportunity has been greater, when his liberty of thought and action was more secure.

Representatives of the house of delegates insist in their appeals to Congress and to the public that from the standpoint of a free people the Puerto Ricans are now subjected under American control to political oppression and to a much less liberal government than under that of Spain. To prove this they refer to the provisions of a royal decree of 1897, promulgated in November of that year. The decree related to the government of Puerto Rico and Cuba and was undoubtedly a great step forward in granting a certain sort of autonomy to the people of the two islands. The war followed within a few months after its promulgation, and it is impossible to say what its practical operation would have been. It was a tentative arrangement, revocable at the pleasure of the Crown, and had, in its provisions, authority for the governor-general to suspend all of the laws of the legislature of the islands until approved or disapproved at home, and to suspend at will all constitutional guaranties of life, liberty, and property, supposed to be the basis of civil liberty and free institutions. The insular legislature had no power to enact new laws or to amend existing laws governing property rights or the life and liberty of the people. The jurisdiction to pass these remained in the hands of the legislature and included the mass of code laws governing the descent and distribution and transfer of property and contracts, and torts, land laws, notarial laws, laws of waters and mines, penal statutes, civil, criminal, and administrative procedure, organic laws of the municipalities, election laws, the code of commerce, etc.

In contrast with this, under its present form of government the island legislature possesses practically all the powers of an American commonwealth, and the constitutional guaranties of its inhabitants, instead of being subject to suspension by executive discretion, are absolutely guaranteed by act of Congress. The great body of substantive law now in force in the island—political, civil, and criminal code, codes of political, civil, and criminal procedure, the revenue, municipal, electoral, franchise, educational, police, and public-works laws, and the like—has been enacted by the people of the island themselves, as no law can be put upon the statute books unless it has received the approval of the representative lower house of the legislature. In no single case has the Congress of the United States intervened to annul or control acts of the legislative assembly. For the first time in the history of Puerto Rico the island is living under laws enacted by its own legislature.

It is idle, however, to compare the political power of the Puerto Ricans under the royal decree of 1897, when their capacity to exercise it with benefit to themselves was never in fact tested, with that which they have under the Foraker Act. The question we have before us is whether their course since the adoption of the Foraker Act does not show the necessity for withholding from them the absolute power given by that act to the legislative assembly over appropriations, when the house of delegates, as a coordinate branch of that assembly, shows itself willing and anxious to use such absolute power, not to support and maintain the government, but to render it helpless. If the Puerto Ricans desire a change in the form of the Foraker Act, this is a matter for congressional consideration dependent on the effect of such a change on the real political progress on the island.

Such a change should be sought in an orderly way, and not brought to the attention of Congress by paralyzing the arm of the existing government. I do not doubt that the terms of the existing fundamental act might be improved, certainly in qualifying some of its provisions as to the respective jurisdictions of the executive council and the legislative assembly; and I suggest to Congress the wisdom of submitting to the appropriate committees this question of revision. But no action of this kind should be begun until after, by special amendment of the Foraker Act, the absolute power of appropriation is taken away from those who have shown themselves too irresponsible to enjoy it.

In the desire of certain of their leaders for political power Puerto Ricans have forgotten the generosity of the United States in its dealings with them. This should not be an occasion for surprise, nor in dealing with a whole people can it be made the basis of a charge of ingratitude. When we, with the consent of the people of Puerto Rico, assumed guardianship over them and the guidance of their destinies, we must have been conscious that a people that had enjoyed so little opportunity for education could not be expected safely for themselves to exercise the full power of self-government; and the present development is only an indication that we have gone somewhat too fast in the extension of political power to them for their own good.

The change recommended may not immediately convince those controlling the house of delegates of the mistake they have made in the extremity to which they have been willing to resort for political purposes, but in the long run it will secure more careful and responsible exercise of the power they have.

There is not the slightest evidence that there has been on the part of the governor or of any member of the executive council a disposition to usurp authority, or to withhold approval of such legislation as was for the best interests of the island, or a lack of sympathy with the best aspirations of the Puerto Rican people.

9

Address at the Unveiling of the Pennsylvania Memorial

Petersburg, Virginia, May 19, 1909

My Fellow Citizens:

We are met today on the soil of Virginia to dedicate a memorial to the bravery of the sons of Pennsylvania exhibited in a contest to the death with the sons of Virginia and the South. We stand here in the center of the bloodiest and most critical operations of the last year of the civil war, only a few miles distant from that dramatic scene at Appomattox between Grant and Lee, which marked the great qualities of the heart and soul of each, and which was the real end of the terrific struggle between the two sections. Here, in and about Petersburg, the outworks of Richmond, the home of the Confederacy, were carried on those besieging operations begun late in the spring of 1864 and continued with the courage and the tenacity of purpose characteristic of the Federal commander for nearly a year, and resisted with the bravery and strategy and wealth of experience of the Confederate leader until the forces of the South, worn out by the constant assaults and the incessant hammering, were compelled to yield to the greater numbers and the greater resources of the North. To Pennsylvania, as one of the great States of the Union, engaged in the determination to save it, fell the burden of furnishing tens of thousands of men for the struggle in every part of the line of attack; but especially in the Army of the Potomac was the force of her people and their devotion to the cause felt. Besides her serried columns, she contributed to the Union army, Major-General George C. Meade, the commander of the Army of the Potomac; four corps commanders, Hancock, Humphreys, Birney, and Parke, together with Gregg, the commander of the cavalry division—a roster of which she may well be proud.

The mine under the Petersburg works which was successfully exploded in the early summer of '64 was the work of the miners of Pennsylvania enlisted in the 48th Regiment of that State, and the work which was done by them called for special mention in the dispatches of General Meade. In the operations in and about Petersburg, from the early summer of '64 until the surrender at Appomattox in '65, there were engaged from Pennsylvania upward of eighty thousand men, a larger number than now constitutes the army of the United States. Upon the 25th of March, 1865, General Lee determined to make an assault upon the Federal besieging lines east of the town, and successfully carried them by attack of a division under General Gordon, only to be ultimately defeated by the attack offered by Hartranft's two Pennsylvania brigades. These brigades had just been recruited and might have been expected to yield to the terrific onslaught of the Confederate veterans; but, taking on the stubbornness and courage of their great brigade commander, they withstood the battle and turned the enemy and added to the martial renown of the Keystone State.

It is forty-four years since the battle of Fort Stedman and the subsequent victory of the Hartranft brigade. In the time which has passed, the bitterness of the internecine struggle has passed away, and we now treasure as a common heritage of the country the bravery and the valor of both sides in that controversy. A memorial which marks the steadfastness, the courage, and the soldierly qualities of the forces engaged in defense of the Union, finds its true significance and meaning in the corresponding bravery and courage of those with whom the battle was fought.

The Army of the Potomac under Grant and Meade was seconded and supported by a generous government. Constant reinforcements, generous supplies of food and clothing, needful fuel and shelter, the tender ministrations of physicians and nurses, and frequent communication with home and friends—all these abounded in the Union lines. It was hardly so with the Confederate forces. Scantily clothed, rarely on more than half-rations and for considerable periods reduced to an allowance of bacon and meal hardly sufficient to sustain life, the long winter through, their shivering infantry manned the ever-extending siege works, and made head against the vigorous assaults of the Union army until their depleted ranks were no longer equal to the defense of their attenuated lines and they gave up the contest which by any other soldiers but the tried and seasoned veterans of the Army of Northern Virginia would long before have been abandoned. We could not dedicate this beautiful and enduring memorial to the volunteer soldiers of Pennsylvania with such a sense of its justice and appropriateness, had they not been confronted by an enemy capable of resisting their assaults with equal valor and fortitude. Pennsylvania's pride must be in the victory achieved by her men against so brave, resolute and resourceful an enemy.

That we can come here today and in the presence of thousands and tens of thousands of the survivors of the gallant army of Northern Virginia and of their descendants, establish such an enduring monument by their hospitable welcome and acclaim, is conclusive proof of the uniting of the sections and a universal confession that all that was done was well done, that the battle had to be fought, that the sections had to be tried, but that in the end, the result has inured to the common benefit of all.

The men of the Army of Northern Virginia fought for a principle which they believed to be right and for which they were willing to sacrifice their lives, their homes—all, indeed, which men hold most dear. As we recognize their heroic services, so they and their descendants welcome the great commonwealth of Pennsylvania to the soil of Virginia and join that commonwealth in honoring the services rendered by its gallant sons in the struggle for the preservation of the Union. The contending forces of now half a century ago have given place to a new North and a new South, and to a more enduring union in whose responsibilities and whose glorious destiny we equally and gratefully share.

10

Mecklenburg Declaration

Address at the Auditorium, Charlotte, North Carolina, May 20, 1909

Governor Kitchin and Ladies and Gentlemen of the Carolinas:

One of the embarrassments that attends the intense pleasure I have in coming into the Southland is the consciousness that I will have to do some speaking, and that you are so used to eloquence of the highest order that I have to submit myself to a comparison that is always invidious. I am here this afternoon merely to talk to you. What I have to say will not rise to the dignity of a speech.

In the first place, I should like to express my sincere gratitude to the Governor of your State, to the Senators of your State, and to the Representatives of your State, who have done me the honor to be present on this occasion, and to give me welcome. I should like to include, too, those members of the Confederate veterans, those members of the Grand Army of the Republic, those members of the Daughters of the Revolution, that distinguished lady, the widow of Stonewall Jackson, and all the other charming and delightful people who exposed themselves to the elements this morning to celebrate this day, and in part, I hope, to give me welcome.

I wish also to express to the committee of arrangements my deep regret that Mrs. Taft was not able to be present to share the welcome which your committee was good enough to tender her. I assure you I do not make nearly so good a show when the better half of my firm is not with me.

We are here to celebrate a declaration of independence. There are some unregenerate persons who live in South Carolina and elsewhere who for various motives have cast a doubt upon the claim. Now anybody that comes to Charlotte who is not willing to admit in the full the declaration of independence made in Mecklenburg, is in the position of a man of whom a Lord Justice of the Court of Appeals of Ireland told me. I met him in Canada. He had a good deal of experience in courts, and he was redolent with Irish stories. He said that he was holding court in the County of Tipperary, and that a man came before him and a jury charged in the indictment with manslaughter, and that the evidence showed that the deceased had come to his death by a blow from a blackthorn stick in the hands of the defendant; but the evidence also showed that the man who died had a "paper skull," as it is called in medical parlance—unduly thin. The verdict brought in was that of "guilty of manslaughter," and his lordship called the man before him and asked him whether he had anything to say why the sentence of the court should not be pronounced upon him. The defendant, turning to his lordship, said: "No, your Lordship, I have nothing to say, but I would like to ask one question." "What, my man, is that?" said he. "I would like to ask: What the divil a man with a head like that was doing in Tipperary." I would like to ask in explanation of my position, what the "divil" a man who does not believe in the declaration at Mecklenburg is doing in this presence.

The claim is that more than twelve months before the members of the Continental Congress declared that it was necessary to have a separate and independent government in this country, free from British control, that declaration was made in the court-house in this town of Charlotte, by a committee of the County, of whom there are now descendants living among you entitled to your respect and to your congratulation on such ancestry. There is a controversy as to what the exact words were that were used in that declaration. I am not going to enter upon any such discussion, but I am going to point out what seems to me to be, whether you take one version or the other, the very important part of that declaration viewed from the standpoint of practical patriotism and practical statesmanship. The general declaration as to the rights of man I do not count nearly so important, looked at from the standpoint of the responsibility of the people who made it, as the practical provision contained in that declaration for a government which was to succeed the British Government, and to accept all the responsibilities, to maintain a government of law and order, and a government which should have a military force to defend itself. My friends, these general declarations unaccompanied by some sense of the responsibility of self-government are worth little or nothing. It is the men who go forward knowing what they are doing when they are cutting off their relation to one government, and understand that the only justification for so doing is the preparation and the practical preparation of a new government. That is what makes Anglo-Saxon liberty; that is what has distinguished our race for a thousand years, that we dealt with what was practical and not with what was poetical and oratorical and rhetorical.

I want to call your attention in enforcing what I am talking about to the guaranties of life—the guaranties as we know them in the Constitution, of life, liberty and property. They consist not solely in general resolutions, that we believe in liberty, and we believe every man ought to be free, and we believe that he ought to be treated justly, and we believe he ought not to be imprisoned except lawfully. Is that all? No. That is not all we have in our Constitution. If that is all we had, it would not be worth the paper it is written on; it would not be worth more than the hundred constitutions that have been made in various countries, whose names it would be invidious to mention, which constitutions have gone down and haven't made a ripple on the ocean of civilization. What is it in the Constitution of the United States inherited from our British ancestry that makes that instrument and all the instruments of the State constitutions so valuable? It is that each guaranty is a practical method of procedure by which the liberty and the rights of the individual are secured. What are they? The writ of habeas corpus. What is that? That is a method of procedure. It is a method by which a man when he is imprisoned has the right to go to any judge and say to that judge: "I wish you to call my captors here and have them tell you whether I am lawfully imprisoned or not," and if that judge does not do it, he creates a right to action against himself which usually involves imprisonment. That is a practical method. It is a procedure. It is not a general declaration. It is something that everybody can tell about. I am a little more emphatic about this because I have come up against the other kind of declarations in some of my experiences in the Philippines. A gentleman came to see me one morning, the leading counsel in Manila, who had drafted the constitution of the Philippines, and at the same time an old man came in with a petition to me. I was then Chairman of the Philippine Commission, and the petition showed that this old man's son had been six years in Bilibid, imprisoned without a trial, and without knowing what he was there for. I said to the lawyer, "Why don't you get out a writ of habeas corpus?" He said: "What is that writ?" I said: "It is a petition inquiring into the lawfulness of his imprisonment, and

General Otis has issued the order granting that writ or the allowance of that writ, and you can have it here." He asked me to draw up a petition, which I did, and he took it into one of the local courts, which happened to be presided over by an American. He went out to Bilibid prison and before he got through that day he had filed ninety petitions for the writ of habeas corpus to release people at Bilibid prison who had been there from four to ten years. When they heard at whose instance he had gotten them out, they wanted to attend in a mass and come and thank me at my house. I expressed my appreciation of their gratitude, but as I was not quite sure but that half of them ought to have been where they were anyhow, I excused them from coming and received an acknowledgment in the form of a table ornament, such as they give in the Philippines, which consists of a bundle of toothpicks.

To go on, the writ of habeas corpus is one thing; an indictment by grand jury is another. That is mere procedure. That is not a general right. It is a mere form of procedure. The right of trial by jury is another form of procedure. Then there is the 14th amendment and the other, the 15th amendment to the Constitution, which accords to everyone the right not to be deprived of his property without due process of law. That does not say that you are not to be deprived of your property unjustly. You may be. All that says is that you shall have a hearing before a tribunal, and that if a man is going to rob you he has got to rob you in a regular way. Now, that is practical. The Anglo-Saxon ancestor knew that if he could once get it before court he would have "a show for his white alley," that he would have a day in that court, and that that was the true basis of civil liberty. So it is with the declarations that were made at Mecklenburg. You go over them and see that they create selectmen, they create military guards, they create courts with jurisdiction, they create courts to make collection of debts, and they made every provision which a single community like this could make, together with commitments for felony, to await the decision of courts to be created by the highest authority under the authority of the General Congress. Now, there are things in that declaration that make me thrill with pride that there was a community in this country—and I venture to say this was not the only community, but it seems to have been the one most charged with its sense of responsibility—which knew that self-government was not a mere gift, but it was something which when it is to be enjoyed must be enjoyed with a full sense of the responsibility of those enjoying it, and with the idea that there is a duty imposed on everyone who enjoys it of seeing to it that it is carried on for the benefit of all.

The Scotch-Irishmen who lived in this community were hard-headed. They were willing to take upon themselves the risk of being strung up as traitors to Great Britain; they were willing to fight it out, as they did so often thereafter in the Hornet's Nest; but they recognized their responsibility as citizens and as individuals, that if they went into the business of self-government, they must make that government worthy of the name. Now, it is a fact that by reason of the lax government which Great Britain was able to give our colonies—I say lax—it was lax, though it was unjust by fits and starts—our ancestors were the best-prepared people for self-government that ever assumed an independent government. They had had two hundred years of independence in the sense of distance from the home government. When brought to mind they were attacked occasionally by such tyranny as Governor Tyrol manifested in North Carolina and as was manifested by other governors at different times throughout the other colonies, but all that time we were gathering experience, we were gathering a sense of responsibility as to our own communities so that when in '75 you declared your independence here, and in '76 we all declared our independence at Philadelphia, we were in a condition with men as great, as able, as full of the knowledge of statecraft as any nation in Europe or any nation that ever lived, to step into the ranks of nations and carry on a government worthy the consideration of the entire world. Now, we have had a great deal of experience since that time. We have been through a number of wars. We watched the institution of slavery grow by unfortunate circumstances until it seemed to be an issue that had to be fought out, and that we could not cure the body politic except by an excision that threatened the whole physical structure of the nation. But we have lived that through. You in the Southland had the troubles, the suffering, the sad losses burned into your hearts with much more emphasis than we in the Northland, because here was the center of the war. And it is entirely natural that in that forty years which have succeeded the war, with the continuance here of the race whose fate was the cause of the war, that their condition, even after the magnanimous spirit shown on both sides at Appomattox was manifested to the world, there should continue a bitterness of feeling that time and long time could only erase; but when we look back I think we must congratulate ourselves that even in that time the feeling has largely disappeared, and that we are now a more united country than ever since—I should say even decades before—the war. One could not stand, as I did, on the platform yesterday, and see 1,200 Union veterans from Pennsylvania who had taken part in the battles about Petersburg, meet and fraternize with five hundred veterans of the Confederacy in their gray, and hear the expressions of mutual esteem and mutual appreciation of the bravery on both sides and the desire to further unite, without being convinced that that is a sincere and a deep-rooted feeling on both sides. It is true that political divisions have continued in such a way as at some times to seem to perpetuate the lines which were made at the time of the war, but even those lines are rapidly disappearing; and it is the duty of all of us with respect to political partisanship to wipe out those lines as far as we can, and to see, so far as we may, that in each State the tolerance of opinion shall continue until there shall be respectable parties on both sides of the line, because it is essential to have a good opposition to have a good government. Now, if there is anything that I can do in my administration to make that feeling of union more close, I shall do it. When I was running for the presidency, I prided myself on having been the first Republican candidate that ever came into North Carolina seeking suffrages for the Republican Party. I did not carry the State, but I had a mighty good time. I am anxious, of course, speaking from a partisan standpoint and leaving my official position for a moment, that the Republican party of North Carolina should be strengthened merely to have a good fight every election, and, of course, in so far as I may legitimately, I should be glad to build up the Republican Party. Now, I understand that some of my Republican friends think that I have lost sight of the Republican Party in putting on the Federal Bench in North Carolina, a gentleman recently upon the Supreme Bench of the State, a lawyer of the highest eminence and learning and integrity, and a Democrat. I promised, after I was President-elect— not before the election—to the South that I would do the best I could to wipe out the feeling that the central Government at Washington was a government alien to the Southland, and I pointed out that the only way by which the Executive could cure that feeling was, in so far as in him lay, to put into office men in whom the community at large, without regard to party, would have the highest confidence.

Now, I am trying to do that, and I am going to appoint Republicans and I am going to appoint Democrats, striving in each case to get a man who will commend himself to the community in which he lives. It is suggested that it is an insult to the Republicans of a district to appoint a Democrat a Judge because from that is to be inferred that there is no Republican worthy of the appointment, and I understand that there are some gentlemen in the Democratic party who are willing to make that inference as strong as possible, in order to stir up Republican dissatisfaction. But I venture to say that when the whole account is added up, that spirit will have disappeared and the Democrats who seek to utter it will find that it is not such a popular method of attacking the Republican Administration after all.

I plead to my Republican friends as a vindication and justification for my course, the course of as orthodox a Republican as ever filled the executive chair, and a man than whom there never was a President who did so much to maintain the standard of the Federal Judiciary, Benjamin Harrison, for he deemed it his duty to put one Democrat on the Supreme Bench and two on the Circuit Court of Appeals. The Federal Judiciary, my dear friends, to my mind is the strongest bulwark that we have in all this country to protect ultimately our institutions of civil liberty. It is the guaranties of civil liberty in the Federal Constitution that we must love and must hug to our bosom if we continue this civilization. Therefore there is no more sacred duty that the Executive has than in the selection of men whose appointment and service on the Bench will strengthen it with all the people at large; and therefore ordinary considerations of political partisanship have much less application to the appointment of judges than they do to other and temporary offices. The Federal Judiciary should be as much appreciated in the South as it is in the North, and if I have an opportunity to make any appointments in the South, it will continue to be the chief duty I have to make such appointments as shall appeal to all the people whether they be Republican or Democrat, and I urge all citizens whether they be Republicans or Democrats, to accept the appointments made as men, if they are men, who will carry on their high duties with a single eye to the administration of justice, to accept them, and congratulate the people on their appointment, and not to make use of them for any partisan argument or partisan appeal.

But now, my dear friends, I have got to the end of my speech, I believe. I think not that we are at a point where there is to be political revolution in the South. I never had such a dream, but I believe we are on the eve of such a condition in the South that there shall be complete tolerance of opinion, and that there shall grow into respectable power an opposition in each State which shall tend to the betterment of the Government as it exists in the State, which shall give us occasionally, as you have already given us in North Carolina, a Republican in a crowd of Democrats, in order that we may have represented in the Congress at Washington your views without regard to some past issue, without regard to the ghost of an issue that really ought not to influence you in enforcing those particular economic views that you really entertain. Let me again say to you how my heart has been aroused by the cordiality of your reception, by the nonpartisan welcome of your distinguished Governor and your Congressmen and your Senators, whether Republicans or Democrats, and to say to you that I haven't spoken here consciously a word to influence you in a partisan way, but it is impossible to discuss the conditions without mentioning the parties. I hope you will, therefore, forgive me for an apparent reference to political conditions when I am really only extending to you the right hand of fellowship as Americans, explaining possibly by inference some of the difficulties of conducting this Government as its Chief Executive. I thank you!

11

The Negro and the South

Address at Howard University, Washington, D. C. May 26, 1909

Mr. President, and Young Ladies and Gentlemen of the Graduating Class:

I have a good many engagements and I am tempted into them sometimes—before the engagements are to be met and the work is to be done—by
such a mellifluous and forceful gentleman as your President; and then I am
not reminded of the obligation thus assumed until I pick up the morning
paper and find myself advanced as one of the chief attractions at some meeting where I don't feel myself at all as entitled to figure in that capacity.

When your President came to me and asked me to come to Howard
University he said that he expected to celebrate the laying of the cornerstone
of a new building here, given by Mr. Carnegie, and that incidentally there
would be commencement exercises. I am a fairly good hand at a trowel and
I thought possibly I might engage in the exercises of laying the cornerstone
without being involved in a speech. But I find it to be otherwise. Nevertheless, I am glad to seize the opportunity of looking into your faces, you young
men and women who are about to go out into the world and meet the
obstacles which are before you and to overcome them successfully, as I sincerely hope you may. I am glad to be able to be here to testify to you my
profound sympathy in your careers and my hope that they all may be successful.

This institution here is the partial repayment of a debt—only partial—to a race to which a government and the people of the United States are eternally indebted. They brought that race into this country against its will. They planted it here irretrievably. They first put it in bondage and then they kept it in the ignorance that that bondage seemed to make necessary, under the system then in vogue. Then they freed it and put upon it the responsibilities of citizenship. Now, some sort of obligation follows that chain of facts with reference to the people who are responsible for what that government did. The obligation would be clearer, or rather, the method of its discharge would be easier, were it not for our constitutional system which throws generally upon the States the burden of education and leaves to the general government only certain limited jurisdiction with respect to the people. However, in so far as the District of Columbia is concerned, and the establishment of institutions of learning in this District, we are free from any embarrassment with respect to the carrying out of the obligation, and it is fitting that the Government of the United States should assume the obligation of the establishment and maintenance of a first-class University for the education of colored men. I am far from saying—and I wish to put in this caveat in advance, in order not to be met by an argument which has weight but has not weight when improperly used—that the colored race today, all of them, would be better off if they all had university education. I think they would be in a very bad way if they had, because they would not know how to use it and they would not find means of using it. No race would be better off if they were all educated as university men. The great body of the colored race, as the great body of the white race, must depend for their livelihood upon their manual labor, skilled or unskilled, or upon some occupation which requires less education than that which is conferred by a university, and if it is too widely extended, the effect of it is to put a lot of men into life who do not find occupations which are suited to their tastes, and to make them unhappy and really not fit for the life which is before them. On the other hand, that admission is far from a concession that it is not necessary for the success of the colored race that there be among them leaders of that race fitted by university education for that leadership. There is not any likelihood, with deference to persons who occupy a different position, that either in the generosity of the general government or in the generosity of individuals who found colored colleges and universities, there is to be such an opportunity given as is likely to lead too many colored men to acquire university education as compared with the number of colored men that there are in the community and especially south of Mason and Dixon's line. The opportunity that there is for educated colored men to aid their race in the struggle before them for economic success and the maintenance of themselves as worthy and valuable members of the community—the opportunity that there is for university men among colored men to assist in that movement, I say is very great indeed.

Through the South one of the things that is essential is the cultivation of greater sanitation and greater attention to the laws of hygiene among the colored race. What they need in the South is a great many more physicians of their own color and race to tell them how to live and to enable them to recover when they are subject to the many sicknesses to which they are subject by reason of the kind of life they lead in the South. I have had occasion to look into it and I am glad to offer to the young doctors to whom I am addressing myself an opportunity for a successful livelihood as physicians in the growing Southern communities where there are so many colored people coming to the front and where physicians well educated are able to make a good livelihood on the one hand, and on the other to do a substantial good to their race.

The benefit that teachers educated here can do to their race goes without saying. Of course, the basis of the education of the colored people is in the primary schools and in the industrial schools—in schools framed after Hampton and Tuskegee and even those less ambitious, but still furnishing an industrial department. In those schools must be introduced teachers from such university institutions as this, and it is in furnishing the material for the faculties of those smaller—not smaller, but less ambitious schools—that such an institution as this shall have its chief function.

Then, too, among the colored race, the ministers have a great influence. Now, if they are to wield that influence they can not be too highly educated; they can not know too much in order that they may carry on their sacred function and discharge it to the highest benefit of the race.

I say these things with a good deal of emphasis because I know there are many who dispute the wisdom of large contributions to universities of the colored race like this, and at one time I was very much perplexed with the argument to know whether or not it was proper. But what is the fact? There are several universities in this country, besides Howard University, devoted to the colored race; those are Lincoln, Fisk, Atlanta, Talladega and Wilberforce, and they have not, taken together, an endowment that exceeds $250,000. Now, when you consider that there are ten millions of Negroes in this country, you see how utterly inadequate, even for the education of the leaders, those universities, together with this, are; and there is opportunity for the founding of more, or certainly for the enlargement of this, as Congress and the people of the United States shall understand the useful part that this institution and institutions like it play in the real uplifting and on-ward progress of the race.

I am delighted to think, because I have been in the South a good deal of late and have studied some of the conditions there, that they are getting bet-ter and better for the Negro race in certain respects that are not published to the world, but that really affect very much the conditions of those who live there. In all the growing communities of the South—I mean where there is a touch of the modern and a touch of progress and a touch of civilization—the white men of progress are beginning to appreciate the advantage of hav-ing a class like the colored men that they have there. They are anxious that they have an industrial education. They are anxious that they should make their way in the world and show their usefulness in the community. The truth is that the greatest hope that the Negro has, because he lives chiefly in the South, is the friendship and the sympathy of the white men with whom he lives in that neighborhood. I know it is not the habit to think so, but it is growing, and one of the things that misleads us most is the desperate, the extreme statements of white men from the South on the subject, but really they don't mean what they say. They are the last people that want to be taken literally. They have a theory that it may give them sometimes a little boost politically to talk in extremes and superlatives, but I have heard expressions from leading Negroes in various cities that confirm my judgment that the situation is growing better and better. I remember hearing the Reverend Dr. Walker, that Negro who went abroad and preached in Spurgeon's pulpit and was worthy to preach in that pulpit, express his friendship for the white people of Augusta where I spent five or six weeks, and express his view of the proposition that the Negro race should be moved to some other country than this. He said they were mighty well satisfied to live in Augusta until they went to glory, and that they did not want to go anywhere else until they did go to glory. That is the same sentiment I found in Charlotte and in Peters-burg. I don't mean to say that there are not exceptions. I mean to say that those communities that are moving forward are moving forward with a keen eye to progress and that they realize the advantage they have in the presence of the Negro race who are almost their only laborers.

We have a gentleman at the head of the Jeanes trust fund who tells a good story. He said he was in one of the towns—I think it was in North Carolina—where they were bringing in some Italian immigrants and that an old colored man there inquired as to what they were doing. He said they were white men who had come into the country from abroad. "Why," he said, "we's got white men enough already to work for—we can't do no more." Now, the fact is that the progress of the race is outlining itself with great clearness, to me at least, in making itself a useful part of the community where it is, so that it shall not only awaken an altruistic spirit, or spirit of humanity, but, what is a good deal better to tie to, shall awaken the economic spirit of those with whom you live and who value your services as members of the community and know how much you add to its success by being there and being valuable members of that community in accumulation, in your providence and in making the homes that are made in a successful community of Negroes in the South.

It seems to me that the future is in the hands of the race itself. I do not mean to say that cruelties are not to exist in the future, and injustices, and a great many reasons why complaints should be made against the inhumanity of man, but I do mean to say that there never has been a time in the history of the Negro race when the future offered such a basis for belief in your success as a race and for the belief that you have it in your hands to make that success as it is today. Everything that I can do as the Executive in the way of helping along this University I expect to do. I expect to do it because I believe it is a debt of the people of the United States, it is an obligation of the Government of the United States, and it is money constitutionally applied to that which shall work out in the end the solution of one of the great problems that God has put upon the people of the United States.

12

Rodelph Shalom Temple

Pittsburgh, Pennsylvania, May 29, 1909

My dear Friends:

I do not claim to conform very strictly to religious observances, but it has remained for the city of Pittsburgh to bring me to church, both on Saturday and on Sunday.

I esteem it a great privilege to appear before this intelligent and patriotic audience—at the instance of your leader, your Rabbi, who was a warm friend of my predecessor, and who, I am glad to think, has transferred his friendship for the time to me.

I am not altogether out of place in a Jewish tabernacle, for the church that I attended in Cincinnati, in my boyhood and young manhood, was immediately next to the Jewish tabernacle of the Reverend Dr. Wise; and there were times in the history of both churches when there was an exchange between the pulpits. I am glad to be here this morning—this beautiful morning and in this beautiful church—to show if possible by my presence how this is a Government of all the people, and how the Constitutional provision that there shall be no religious requirement or qualification for office or citizenship in this country is evidenced by the presence of the President of the United States in a Jewish tabernacle, where he feels himself as much at home and with as much support as he does in any other church in the country.

The prayer to which we just listened, full of that liberality and love of humankind, makes one feel ashamed of all narrowness and bigotry in religion, and it gives me the greatest pleasure to say, as I do from the bottom of my heart, that never in the history of the country, in any crisis and under any conditions, have our Jewish fellow citizens failed to live up to the highest standard of citizenship and patriotism.

I thank your Rabbi, and I thank you, for the opportunity to appear before you and say this much. I am not a preacher. I am not in the habit of appearing in pulpits. It was not until I returned from the Philippines that I appeared once in a Presbyterian pulpit, once in an Episcopalian pulpit, once in a Unitarian pulpit, and now before a Jewish audience in the pulpit of a Jewish tabernacle. That makes a round, I think, that justifies my saying that I hope to be the President of all the people, and to have your support, as you have given it to my predecessors, without stint and with every desire to make this a great country and a great Government.

13

The Regular Army of the United States

Gettysburg, Pennsylvania, May 31, 1909

We are gathered at this historic spot today to dedicate a monument to the memory of the officers and the enlisted men of the Regular Army who gave up their lives for their country in the three days' battle. It is but a tardy recognition of the Nation's debt to its brave defenders whose allegiance was purely to the Nation, without local color or strengthening of State or municipal pride.

The danger of a standing army, entertained by our ancestors, is seen in the constitutional restrictions and the complaints registered in the Declaration of Independence. It has always been easy to awaken prejudice against the possible aggressions of a regular army and a professional soldiery, and correspondingly difficult to create among the people, that love and pride in the army which we find today and frequently in the history of the country aroused on behalf of the navy. This has led to a varied and changeable policy in respect to the regular army. At times it has been reduced to almost nothing. In 1784, there were but eighty men who constituted the regular army of the United States, and in Battery F of the 4th Artillery were fifty-five of them; but generally the absolute necessities in the defense of the country against the small wars, which embrace so large a part of our history, have induced the maintenance of a regular force, small to be sure, but one so well trained and effective as always to reflect credit upon the Nation.

In the War of 1812, had we had a regular army of 10,000 men, trained as such an army would have been, we should have been spared the humiliation of the numerous levies of untrained troops and the enormous expense of raising an army on paper of 400,000 or 500,000 men, because with an effective force of 10,000 men, we might have promptly captured Canada and ended the war.

The service rendered by the regular army in the Mexican War was far greater in proportion than that which it rendered in the Civil War, and the success which attended the campaigns of Taylor and of Scott were largely due to that body of men.

To the little army of 25,000 men that survived the Civil War, we owe the opening up of the entire western country. The hardships and the trials of frontier Indian campaigns, which made possible the construction of the Pacific railroads, have never been fully recognized by our people, and the bravery and courage and economy of force compared with the task performed shown by our regular troops have never been adequately commemorated by Congress or the Nation.

Today, as a result of the Spanish War, the added responsibilities of our new dependencies in the Philippines, Puerto Rico, and for some time in Cuba, together with a sense of the importance of our position as a world power, have led to the increase of our regular army to a larger force than ever before in the history of the country, but not larger in proportion to the increase in population and wealth than in the early years of the Republic. It should not be reduced.

The profession of arms has always been an honorable one, and under conditions of modern warfare, it has become highly technical and requires years of experience and study to adapt the officers and men to its requirements. The general purpose of Congress and the American people, if one can say there is a plan or purpose, is to have such a nucleus as a regular army that it may furnish a skeleton for rapid enlargement in time of war to a force ten or twenty times its size, and at the same time be an appropriate instrument for accomplishing the purposes of the government in crises likely to arise, other than a war.

At West Point, we have been able to prepare a body of professional soldiers, well trained, to officer an army, and numerous enough at the opening of the Civil War to give able commanders to both sides of that internecine strife.

Upon the side of the North many of the officers were drafted to command the volunteer troops from the States, while the regular army, aggregating about 10,000 at the opening of the war, was increased to about 25,000 during its first year. More than half this army was engaged in the Battle of Gettysburg. Eleven regiments of infantry, five regiments of cavalry, twenty-six batteries of artillery, and three battalions of engineers. The infantry of the regular army were embraced in two brigades of the Third Division of the Fifth Corps under Major-General Sykes, himself a most able regular army officer. The cavalry was included in a Reserve Division under General Merritt, and the batteries were distributed among various army corps of the entire Federal force.

Two of the most important and determining crises of the three days' battle were, first, the seizure of the Round Tops and the maintenance of the Federal control over that great point of vantage, the possession of which by the Confederate forces would have taken the whole Federal line in the reverse; and the second was the resistance to Pickett's charge on the third day of the battle when the high point in the Confederate advance into Pennsylvania was turned, and Lee was defeated and hurried back into Southern territory, never again to plant his Confederate battle-flags on Northern soil. The taking of the Round Tops and the driving back of the Confederate forces was the work of Sykes' Fifth Army Corps, and especially of the two brigades of the Regular Infantry regiments, in which in killed and wounded alone the regulars lost 20 percent. of their full number, and some of their brigades, notably Burbank's, lost 60 percent. in killed and wounded of the men engaged. With a desperate bravery worthy of the cause, they drove back the Confederate forces and enabled General Meade to unite the left of Sickles' 3rd Corps with the right of the 5th Army Corps, and thus presented a shorter but a firmer front with which to withstand the onslaught of Lee's army upon the third day.

Without invidious comparison and in no way detracting from the courage and glory of the other branches of the service who united to resist Pickett's charge, it is well known that much of the effective resistance was by the artillery. The batteries of the regulars and volunteers under General Hunt made the resistance to that awful charge that gave the victory to the Union forces. The soul of Cushing, in charge of Battery F, 4th Artillery, went up with the smoke of the last shots which sent Pickett's men reeling back from the point now marked as the high tide of the Confederacy.

Time does not permit me to mention the names of the heroes of the regular army whose blood stained this historic field, and whose sacrifices made the Union victory possible. With my intimate knowledge of the regular army, their high standard of duty, their efficiency as soldiers, their high character as men, I have seized this opportunity to come here to testify to the pride which the Nation should have in its regular army, and to dedicate this monument to the predecessors of the present regular army, on a field in which they won undying glory and perpetual gratitude from the Nation which they served. They had not the local associations, they had not the friends and neighbors of the volunteer forces to see to it that their deeds of valor were properly recorded and the value of their services suitably noted in the official records by legislation and congressional action, and they have now to depend upon the truth of history and in the cold, calm retrospect of the war as it was, to secure from Congress this suitable memorial of the work in the saving of the country which they wrought here.

All honor to the Regular Army of the United States! Never in its history has it had a stain upon its escutcheon. With no one to blow its trumpets, with no local feeling or pride to bring forth its merits, quietly and as befits a force organized to maintain civil institutions and subject always to the civil control, it has gone on doing the duty which was its to do, accepting without a murmur the dangers of war, whether upon the trackless stretches of our western frontier, exposed to the arrows and the bullets of the Indian, or in the jungles and the rice paddies of the Philippines, on the hills and in the valleys about Santiago in Cuba, or in the tremendous campaigns of the Civil War itself, and it has never failed to make a record of duty done that should satisfy the most exacting lover of his country.

It now becomes my pleasant duty to dedicate this monument to the memory of the regular soldiers of the Republic who gave up their lives at Gettysburg and who contributed in a large degree to the victory of those three fateful days in the country's history.

14

An Answer to the Panama Canal Critics

McClure's, *May, 1909*

The Panama Canal continues to furnish copy for the newspapers and the magazines of the country. It is being constructed by the United States Government for the benefit of world commerce, and every citizen of the United States, and indeed any citizen of the world, properly feels himself authorized to criticize the work as it is being done and to express his opinion as to the type of canal that is selected. In such an enormous work as the construction of the canal is likely to be, it would seem wise to have fixed definitely, at the beginning, the type and plan to be followed.

When De Lesseps, having completed in triumph the Suez Canal, came to Panama, he began the construction of what his board of management and he intended to be a sea-level canal. Between that time and 1902, when the canal was offered for sale to the United States for $40,000,000 several boards were appointed for the purpose of recommending the best course to be taken in the construction of the canal. Two of these boards were French, and all of them recommended the lock type of canal, with a dam at Bohio. We all remember that the Nicaragua route had a great many adherents in and out of Congress, and that for a time it seemed likely that that route would be selected. The natural conditions made it necessary that the canal across Nicaragua should be of a lock type. When the change of plan from Nicaragua to

Panama was made, it is quite evident, from the discussion, from the law, and from direct evidence, that it was expected that the canal to be built would be of the lock type and would not be on the sea level.

One of the most careful of the French boards that recommended the lock type pointed out that a lock canal was necessary because the floods of the Chagres River would be uncontrollable in case of a sea-level canal, and made such a canal impossible. In 1906 thirteen engineers were invited to consider the question of the proper type of the canal. Of these, eight were Americans and five foreigners. A majority, consisting of the five foreigners and three Americans, decided in favor of a canal that should be 150 feet across the bottom for more than nineteen miles and 200 feet across the bottom for a little more than twenty miles. Five American engineers—including Mr. Alfred Noble, chief engineer of the Pennsylvania Company, constructor of the "Soo" canal and locks, and dean of American engineers; Mr. Frederic P. Stearns, the chief engineer of the Metropolitan Water Board Company of Boston; and Mr. Randolph, the constructor of the Chicago Drainage Canal—recommended the construction of a lock canal, the main feature of which was to be a lake with the level of the water at eighty-five feet above the sea. These reports were considered by the Isthmian Canal Commission, itself composed of engineers and men familiar with works of construction, and that commission, by a vote of five to one, recommended to the War Department and to the President the adoption of the minority report. This action of the commission was concurred in by Mr. John F. Stevens, then chief engineer of the commission in charge of the work at the Isthmus. The Secretary of War and the President also approved the report of the minority of the consulting board and decided in favor of a lock canal.

The question was submitted by President Roosevelt to Congress. It was unnecessary to do this, because, under the Spooner Act, the President had authority to build the canal, and so had authority to determine what the type should be. The fact is that in reading the Spooner Act of 1902, directing the construction of the canal, it is impossible to escape the construction that Congress at that time contemplated, not a sea-level, but a lock canal. However, the question was again fairly submitted to Congress upon all the reports made and all the evidence.

After the reports had been made, the Senate Committee on Interoceanic Canals conducted an examination of all the engineers and others with knowledge, in order to arrive at a conclusion in respect to the question thus submitted to Congress. The Senate Committee by a majority reported in favor of a sea-level canal, but when the matter was considered in open Senate, where it was very fully discussed, the Senate accepted the minority report of that

Committee and decided in favor of the lock canal. In the House of Representatives the resolution in favor of the lock canal was carried by a very decided majority. And so the law of Congress today fixes the type of the canal as a lock canal, at a level of eighty-five feet. Meantime, the organization of the instrumentalities for construction on the Isthmus has gone on with great rapidity and effectiveness, until the excavation has reached the very large amount of three millions of cubic yards of material a month. More than half of this has been made by steam shovels in the dry, while the rest has been made by steam dredges. The steam dredges have been working in the softer material in the harbors and channels near the ocean on each side of the Isthmus.

All the plans have been made and all the work done with a view to the construction of the lock canal. It is true that a large part of the work, until recently, would have had to be done for a sea-level canal, except for the expensive change or relocation of the Panama Railroad, and the excavations for the locks and for the spillway of the great Gatun Dam, which is the key of the lock type. I presume it would be difficult to say how many millions of dollars have now been spent that would be thrown away, were the canal to be changed from a lock to a sea-level type, but certainly fifteen million dollars is not an overestimate of the amount.

With a plan settled and the organization becoming more and more perfect, and the work of excavation going on at an unexpected rate of progress, suddenly those responsible for the work are confronted with a newspaper war upon the type of the canal, and a discussion in the Senate of the United States, seriously suggesting a change from the lock type solemnly adopted by law two years ago, to a sea-level canal. What has given rise to this renewed discussion of the type of the canal and this assumption that the question of the type is still really open for consideration and settlement? Three circumstances, and only three, that I can trace.

The first is that a newspaper correspondent on the Isthmus, while detained by a washout on the railroad in one of the heavy rains that are frequent on the Isthmus, heard that the rock and earth which is now being deposited in great quantities to form the Gatun Dam, had, under the effect of the flood, sunk out of sight into a subterranean lake, and cabled to the United States that the whole structure of the Gatun Dam had given way.

The second circumstance was that the estimates of the engineers in the actual construction of the work and the expenditure of the money from time to time showed quite clearly that the cost of the construction of the lock type of canal would be at least twice that which had been estimated as its cost by the minority of the board of consulting engineers.

The third circumstance was that under the present efficient organization, with the use of steam shovels and dredges, the amount of excavation has considerably exceeded that which had been anticipated.

In this wise, the argument in favor of a change from the lock canal to the sea-level canal apparently is given great additional force because it is said that by the sinking and giving way of the Gatun Dam, the indispensable feature of the lock type, it has been demonstrated that the lock type is unsafe, dangerous, and impossible.

Second, it is said that the argument which has been made in favor of the lock type of canal on the ground of economy is shown to be unfounded because the real cost of the lock type of canal is demonstrated by actual construction to be equal to, or in excess of, the estimated cost of the sea-level canal.

Third, it is said that the argument that the sea-level canal would be a great many years in process of construction, which was vigorously advanced, is now shown to be erroneous by the great increase in the daily, monthly, and yearly excavation as compared with the total amount of excavation needed in the sea-level type.

I propose in a general way to examine these three reasons to see how much real weight they have.

First, as to the sinking of the Gatun Dam. The report of the newspaper correspondent, like so many other statements made with respect to a matter two thousand miles away, under the influence of a desire to be sensational and startling, was founded purely on imagination. The only foundation for the statement was that in a comparatively small stretch on the site of the dam, perhaps two hundred feet across, some rough material had been piled up on the upward side of the dam, and there had been excavated immediately back of this pile or dump a lot of material from an old French diversion channel; that the water accumulated above this dump in the very heavy rains; that the water behind the dump and the material there had been taken out; and that there was a slide down into the cavity that had been made just back of the dump. The slide could not have been more than one hundred feet. The whole mass was not more than two hundred feet across, and on a personal examination, for I was there, it was evidently nothing more than an ordinary slide, such as frequently occurs in the construction of railroad banks and other fills when they are not properly balanced, and are without the proper slope. The material on the inside of the dam, that which is to be impermeable and puddled, has not yet been deposited at all. This was a mere deposit on the edge of the bottom of the dam upstream. The dam at that point, when constructed, will be nearly half a mile wide. The insignificance of the circumstance, when one takes into consideration the whole size of the dam, and the relation of this particular material to the entire dam, is apparent. It appears that there is clay in the material taken out of the excavation at Culebra which is slippery and upon which other material will slide if the pressure is unequal and the usual precautions against sliding are not taken. But this has always been known, and is true of most clays. It is not a danger that can not be provided against, and, indeed, the shape and form and exact method of building the dam are for the very purpose of producing the stability needed, and of avoiding any danger of a slide due to a lack of proper balance and weight in the material put into the dam.

President Roosevelt, in view of the widespread report as to the failure of the dam, concluded to send a competent board of engineers to find out whether anything had occurred on the Isthmus that should lead to a change from that type of canal which had the Gatun Dam as its chief feature. The board was made up of Mr. Stearns of Boston, and Mr. Randolph, the chief engineer of the Chicago Drainage Canal, both of whom had been on the original minority board; Mr. Freeman, who had visited the canal two years before with a view to ascertaining whether there was a proper foundation for the locks at the Gatun Dam; and four other engineers, who had not given their opinion before as to the proper type of canal. These were the chief engineer of the Reclamation Service, Mr. Davis, who has had wide experience in the construction of dams and locks; Mr. Schuyler, one of the two or three great engineers of the West Coast, who has written a text-book on the subject of earthen dams and their proper construction; Mr. Hazen, perhaps, the greatest authority on filtration in the country; and Captain Allen, a hydraulic engineer of high standing in Chicago. Their report was unanimous. They decided that the dam as projected was heavier and more expensive than it need be. They reduced the cost and the amount of material in it. They reported that the lock type of canal was entirely feasible, and safe as projected; and they pointed out and emphasized the difficulties of the proposed sea-level canal.

The report of this board has been attacked on the ground that it was a packed jury, and that two of its members had already expressed their opinion in recommending the lock type of canal as part of the minority board. This is utterly unjust. It is quite true that the two gentlemen named had expressed their opinion in favor of a lock type of canal and had recommended the plan that was adopted, but it is also true that five of the board had not so committed themselves, and there was not the slightest reason why, if they differed from the other two, they should not express their opinion. Two of the old board were taken for the reason that they were as competent engineers as the country afforded and knew well the grounds on which the lock type had been originally adopted. It is entirely proper, when it is claimed that a judgment should be set aside on the ground of newly discovered evidence, that at least part of the same court should sit to hear what that new evidence is and pass upon its weight with reference to the previous judgment. The truth is that the judgment of this new board of engineers ought to remove all doubt as to the safety of the Gatun Dam from the minds of the interested public. But engineers are like members of other professions, and I presume we may expect from time to time, as the construction of the canal goes on, further attacks upon the feasibility, safety, and usefulness of the type adopted after so much care.

Not only has this board determined on the entire safety and practicability of the Gatun Dam, but the army engineers, Colonel Goethals and his assistants, who are in charge of the actual work, are perfectly certain that the Gatun Dam can be and will be made as safe as the adjoining hills in resisting the pressure of the water of the lake against it and in maintaining it there for purposes of navigation. These army engineers are not responsible for the type of the canal. They did not take hold of the work until after the type had been settled by act of Congress, and they had no preconceived notions in respect to the matter when they took charge and assumed that intimate relation to the whole project which makes their judgment of great value.

Mr. Frederic P. Stearns is one of the greatest authorities in the world on the construction of dams. He has built a dam at the Wachusetts Reservoir of the Metropolitan Board of Public Works in Massachusetts, upon foundations much less favorable for stability than those of the Gatun Dam, and the water is now standing at 65 feet in the reservoir. The dam has been tested, and his judgment has the benefit, therefore, of actual test and verification.

The judgment of the engineers in 1906 as to the sufficiency of the foundation upon which to construct the Gatun Dam was based on borings made with wash drills into the material underneath the proposed dam site, and material was washed from depths varying from 20 to 250 feet below the surface. The wash of the water affected the material to such an extent as to give a wrong impression regarding some of it. The borings seemed to show that at considerable depth, that is, from 200 to 250 feet down, there was loose sand and gravel such as to permit the free flow of an underground stream. Since these borings were taken, pits have been sunk that make possible the removal of the material in place so that it can be seen just exactly what the foundation consists of, and it turns out that, instead of there being loose sand and gravel at the bottom, there appears to be a conglomerate of sand, clay, and gravel so united as to require a pick to separate it, and entirely impervious to water. In other words, a full examination of the foundations of the Gatun Dam strengthens greatly the opinion of those who held that there was a foundation of a blanket 200 feet in depth entirely impervious to water, below the surface, and substantially incompressible.

A most interesting exhibit can be seen at the headquarters of the commission at Culebra, of the various layers of material which form the foundations under the Gatun Dam, and when they are examined, the truth of the assertion that this makes an excellent foundation can be readily understood.

The second circumstance is with reference to the cost of the work. The estimate of the cost of the canal, exclusive of the interest during construction, sanitation, and expense of Zone government, and the $50,000,000 paid Panama and the French company, was $139,705,200. The present estimate of the cost of the canal as now projected, exclusive of the same items, is $297,766,000, or a grand total of $375,000,000. The increase arises, first, from the fact that the yardage or excavation to be made was 50 percent underestimated. This was due, first, to insufficient surveys, and second, to changes of plan. These changes of plan involved a widening of the canal, for a distance of four thousand feet, from 500 feet to 1,000 feet in width, just below the Gatun locks on the north side, in order to furnish a wider and more commodious place for vessels anchoring before entering the locks. The canal has also been widened for five miles from 200 feet to 300 feet across the bottom; this in the Culebra cut. Again, the material supposed to be easy of dredging turns out to be in many places more of rock than was supposed, and the average cost of excavation has been increased generally about 20 percent. In addition to that, the locks as originally projected were 900 feet usable length and 95 feet in width. They have been increased now, in response to a request from our Navy Department, from 900 feet to 1,000 feet usable length and from 95 feet to 110 feet in width. This greatly increases the amount of concrete, greatly widens the gates, and greatly increases the whole cost of the locks at both ends of the canal. Then, too, it was thought wise not to follow the minority report which contemplated dams immediately on the shore of the Pacific at La Boca, in Sosa Hill, but to move them back to Miraflores and San Pedro Miguel, some four miles or more from the shore. This was chiefly done for military reasons, in order to take the lock construction out of sight of an enemy approaching the canal on the Bay of Panama.

All these changes were substantial increases in the amount of work to be done, which, taken with the increased unit price, explains the discrepancy between the estimate and the actual expenditure. Much money was expended in the construction and repair of buildings in which the employees of the canal lived. Much money, not included in the estimate, was expended for the purpose of making their lives more enjoyable while on the Isthmus. The wages per day are higher than those which were estimated. Colonel Goethals has submitted a detailed statement showing exactly where the difference is between the original estimate and the actual cost. This has been examined by the present board of engineers, who report that in their judgment the estimate presented by Colonel Goethals is an outside figure, and that the cost will probably be less for the present type of canal than $297,000,000, as estimated.

The advocates of the sea-level canal point to the fact that the estimate by the Consulting Board in 1906 of the cost of the sea-level canal was $247,000,000, plus cost of sanitation, government, and the $50,000,000 paid Panama and the French company, or fifty millions less than the admitted cost of the lock type. They assume, therefore, that the difference in cost originally advanced as an argument against a sea-level canal has now been refuted. The defect of this argument is that the same circumstances that have increased the cost of the lock type of canal would increase the actual cost of a sea-level canal. Much of the work that has been done—indeed, a very large part of it—is work that would have had to be done for a sea-level canal, and we are furnished now by Colonel Goethals with an estimate of what the sea-level canal would cost, in the light of the actual cost of the work and unit prices on the Isthmus. This would be $477,601,000 without cost of sanitation or government and exclusive of the original $50,000,000 payment. When the loss of interest and loss of revenue by delay is taken into consideration, the cost is easily increased $200,000,000 beyond the cost of the lock type of canal, so that the difference between the cost of the lock type and the sea-level canal is shown by actual construction on the Isthmus to be greater than was estimated when the lock type of canal was selected as the proper one.

Third, the date of completion for the lock type of canal has been fixed as the 1st of January, 1915. I hope that it may be considerably before that. At the rate of excavation now going on in the Culebra cut, it could probably be completed in less than three years, but the difficulty is that as the cut grows deeper, the number of shovels that can be worked must necessarily be decreased. Therefore, the excavation per day, per month, and per year must grow less. Hence it is not safe to base the estimate of time on a division of the total amount to be excavated by the yearly excavation at present. Then, too, the Gatun Dam and locks and the manufacture and adjustment of the gates may take a longer time than the excavation itself, so that it is wiser to count on the date set. The enthusiastic supporters of the sea-level canal, basing their calculation on the amount of material now being excavated, and upon the total amount to be excavated, for a sea-level canal, reach the conclusion that the sea-level canal could be constructed in a comparatively short time as compared with the estimate of twelve or fifteen years made at the time of the decision in favor of the lock type. They have fallen into the error, already pointed out, of assuming that the present rate of excavation could continue as the work of building the sea-level canal went on, which in the case of the sea-level canal is even more erroneous and misleading than in the case of the lock canal, for the reason that the construction, below the forty-foot level above the sea down to the level of forty feet below the sea, is work of the most difficult character, more than half of it always under water, and necessitating either pumping or dredging in rock and working in a narrow space, which greatly reduces the possible rate of excavation.

It is said that new methods of removing rock under water are available so as greatly to reduce the price and the time. I shall take up this statement a little later, but it is sufficient now to say that these methods are in use on the Isthmus, and that the actual employment of them in the character of material that exists on the line of the canal completely refutes the claim that they can accomplish anything more than, or as much as, the excavation in the dry.

Then, too, in this calculation of time, a third great error of the sea-level enthusiasts is the failure to take into consideration the time actually needed to construct the Gamboa Dam to retain the waters of the Chagres River and the other dams and the great diversion channels that would absolutely have to be built before the sea-level excavation could be carried on. The Gamboa Dam as projected is a masonry dam, 180 feet above sea level, with a level of the water 170 feet against the dam and above the bed rock of the stream, and of a length 4,500 feet along the top. It would be the highest dam known in the world and its construction would have to be of the most careful character, and would take an indeterminate time. It has never been definitely settled that there is at the only available site a foundation suitable for such a dam.

I have thus examined the circumstances relied upon by the present advocates of the sea-level canal to show that the known conditions are different today from those that influenced the selection of the lock type. I have not gone into the matter in detail, but the records will bear out my general statements and show that not in the slightest respect has the argument been changed by newly discovered facts in favor of the sea-level canal.

The memory of the reading public, however, is not very long, and, relying on this fact, the opponents of the lock canal do not hesitate to bring out again, as if newly discovered, the same old arguments that failed to convince when the issue was fresh and the supposedly final decision was given. We are again met with the statements of gentlemen who claim to be and really are familiar with the steamship business, that mariners would prefer a sea-level canal and would use a lock canal with reluctance. With a great show of enthusiasm and a chain of reasoning as if newly thought out, the ease with which vessels can be navigated on the level is held up in contrast with the difficulties involved in lifting them eighty-five feet at one side of the Isthmus and lowering them the same distance on the other. Such an argument always proceeds on the hidden premise that the question whether we should have a lock or a sea-level canal is a mere matter of preference freely open to our choice, and wholly without regard to the real difficulties involved in the construction of a sea-level canal such as the discussions of the present day seem to assume a sea-level canal will be.

We hear much of the Straits of Panama described as a broad passage of from 400 to 600 feet in width across the bottom, 40 to 45 feet in depth, and piercing the Isthmus with a volume of water sufficient to do away with all difficulty from rapid currents produced by the water of swollen tropical streams, or cross currents resulting from the discharge of such streams into the canal from heights ranging all the way from ten feet to fifty feet above the level of the water. Such a comparison is utterly misleading. The only sea-level canal that has been projected with respect to which estimates of any substantial and reliable kind have been made is a canal, one-half the length of which is 150 feet across the bottom and the other half of which is 200 feet across the bottom. It is a canal that for twenty miles, from the point where the Chagres River and the canal converge, to Gatun, has four times the curvature of the Suez Canal, and in which at flood stages, under any plan that has been devised for preventing the destruction of the canal by the flood waters of the Chagres River and the other streams emptying into that river, there will be a current of nearly three miles an hour. Such a current in the Suez Canal, with one-fourth of the curvatures, makes the steering of large vessels dangerous, and in this canal, with its great curvature, would make the passage of large vessels impossible.

The lock canal as projected has a width at the bottom of 300 feet for about 25 percent of its length, of from 500 to 800 feet for 50 percent, and of 1,000 feet, or the entire lake width, for the remainder. With such widths the curvature, of course, is immaterial.

In the projected sea-level canal, it would be impossible for vessels safely to pass one another at any speed at all. Therefore one vessel would have to tie up while the other went by. This fact would greatly reduce the speed with which a vessel could pass through the sea-level canal, and the greater the business, the slower would be the passage. As the tonnage increased, therefore, the lock canal of the projected type, in spite of the time taken going through the locks to the 85-foot level and descending from that level, in case of large steamers, would furnish a quicker passage. As business increased, the time taken in going through the sea-level canal and the danger to the vessel would be very considerably greater than in the lock canal. The danger of accidents and of the destruction of the locks, if certain machinery is used and certain precautions are taken in the warping of the vessels into and out of the locks, will be practically nothing. We are able to gage this by the infrequency of dangerous accidents at the "Soo" locks, in which the business is enormous and the size of the locks through which the vessels go is but a small percentage less than that of the locks projected at Panama. The devices for preventing the outflow of the water in case of a destruction of the upper gates are complete, and in the opinion of many engineers unnecessarily elaborate.

Mr. Bunau-Varilla and Mr. Granger and Mr. Lindon Bates have all lent the weight of their voices in denunciation of the present lock type of the canal. In denouncing the type that is under construction, they always compare it with a sea-level canal of a width from 300 to 600 feet; when the actual canal projected for the sea-level is only 150 feet across the bottom in one-half the length, and 200 feet the other half. They always point with severest criticism to the instability and experimental character of the Gatun Dam, but never refer to the Gamboa Dam, which is an essential part of the sea-level plan, and which in its measurements and in the height of the water behind it exceeds the proportions of any dam in the world. In addition to this the sea-level canal involves the construction of three or four other dams in order to turn back the water of streams entering the Chagres Valley over the height of land into other valleys away from the canal. One of these dams is 75 feet high by 4,000 feet in length; another 2,800 feet long; another 1,200 feet; and another 800 feet. No one knows what the character of the foundation is for these dams thus projected in the sea-level plan. No one is able to estimate the cost involved in their construction, because they are now far away from the railroad and considerable expense would be involved in delivering material for their construction. None of these difficulties connected with the making of the sea-level canal are ever mentioned in the discussion of the comparative merits of the present lock-type canal and the sea-level canal as projected. We can only approximately arrive at the cost of a sea-level canal such as that suggested in the articles of Mr. Granger and Mr. Bunau-Varilla in this wise: Colonel Goethals's estimate of the cost of the sea-level canal exactly as projected is $500,000,000; that is, $477,000,000 with the addition of interest and other items that might bring it up to $500,000,000. This does not include the cost of sanitation, of the Zone government, or the $50,000,000 originally paid.

An estimate was made of the additional cost by the Board of Consulting Engineers of widening the sea-level canal 100 feet. That would make a canal, half of it 250 feet wide, and half of it 300 feet wide. It was said it would cost from $86,000,000 to $100,000,000. Considering now the discrepancy between the estimate and the actual cost of the sea-level canal, that is, between $247,000,000 and $477,000,000, it is certainly not exaggerating to say that the cost of a sea-level canal 300 feet wide from end to end would involve an expenditure of not less than $650,000,000 and probably $700,000,000, and this without including the cost of sanitation, of government, or the $50,000,000 originally paid. As already said, an outside estimate for the present cost of the lock type of canal is $297,000,000, exclusive of the cost of sanitation and of government and of the $50,000,000 originally paid, or $375,000,000 including everything, as against $750,000,000 for such a canal as that advocated by Mr. Bunau-Varilla or Mr. Granger.

I have already commented on the utter impossibility of calculating the time that it would take to construct the sea-level canal. No estimate has been made of the time it would take to construct the Gamboa Dam or other dams and the great diversion channels needed to keep the Chagres River out of a sea-level canal, and no estimate has been made as to the additional time that would be required for the excavations below the sea level and the pumping needed to keep the canal prism in a condition for such excavation. Another difficulty about the sea-level canal, but one rarely referred to, is the obstacle to its construction in the Black Swamp between Gatun and Bohio. This would probably necessitate retaining walls or the draining of the swamp with such an extended area as to make the task a huge one.

Of the critics of the present type of the canal, Mr. Bunau-Varilla and Mr. Lindon Bates were advisers of the consulting board of thirteen engineers appointed to recommend types of a canal. That board divided as between the 85-foot canal, which was adopted, and the sea-level canal 150 feet wide for half of the distance and 200 feet wide for the other half; but they all, whether sea-level or lock-type advocates, united in rejecting the plans of Mr. Bunau-Varilla and Mr. Bates. Those gentlemen are now engaged in criticizing the Gatun Dam and the locks that form part of the approved and adopted type; but if their plans as they recommend them are examined, it will be found that they contemplated dams and locks more in number, with a great deal more uncertainty as to the foundation, than the Gatun Dam and the dams at Miraflores and at Pedro Miguel in the present lock-type. It will be found that in the original plan of Mr. Bunau-Varilla he projected a canal that should have a high level of at least 130 feet to be reached by a series of locks, and that Mr. Bates had a series of lakes to be reached by locks quite like that of the Gatun Dam, although the lakes were not so extended and the locks not so high. Under these circumstances, the criticism of these gentlemen in asserting great danger from earthquakes and other causes to the Gatun Dam and the locks of the adopted type may be received with a measure of caution.

Mr. Bunau-Varilla's chief argument in reference to the speed and ease and economy with which his type of canal could be constructed, ultimately resulting in a sea-level canal, is based on the facility with which a certain Lobnitz process and machine for dredging rock under water can be successfully carried on. This is also one of the bases for the proposition of Mr. Granger that a sea-level canal can be easily constructed. In addition to that, Mr. Granger has invented a machine for the elevation of material in water, to be carried by gravity through a flume a long distance. It has never been tested on any great work of construction, and rests wholly on theory.

The Lobnitz method of excavating rock under water is on trial today on the Pacific side of the Isthmus at Panama, and the result of the work there confirms the judgment of practical engineers elsewhere that the machine will work in comparatively soft rock with thin laminations, but that it will not work in hard rock or in rock in which the strata are widely separated, of which there is much to be excavated in constructing the Panama Canal. In other words, the arguments of both these gentlemen advocating the Straits of Panama are either based on theory without practical test of the usefulness of the processes they recommend, or, when practical test has been given, the process has failed to come up to what is claimed for it by these advocates.

Mr. Bunau-Varilla early proclaimed that the heavy machinery of the Americans in the steam shovels at the Isthmus was not accomplishing nearly as much as the lighter machinery of the French. Now we have gone far beyond any record of the French in the excavation in the dry per day, per month, and per year. The lack of soundness in Mr. Bunau-Varilla's conclusions is thus made apparent.

The facts today are the same as they were when the lock type was adopted, namely, that it would take at least $200,000,000 more of money and at least five years more of time to construct the sea-level type of canal 150 to 200 feet in width; that the canal when constructed would be dangerous for the passage of the larger vessels; and that the lock type of canal constructed at $200,000,000 less in cost and five years less in time will be a better canal, a safer canal, and one in which the time of passage for large vessels will be even less than in the sea-level type.

For these reasons the administration is proceeding to construct the canal on the type authorized and directed by Congress, and the criticisms of gentlemen who predicate all their arguments on theory and not upon practical tests, who institute comparisons between the present type of canal and the sea-level type of 300 to 600 feet in width that never has been or "will be on sea or land," cannot disturb the even tenor of those charged with the responsibility of constructing the canal, and will only continue to afford to persons who do not understand the situation and are not familiar with the history of the canal and of the various plans proposed for the canal, an unfounded sensation of regret and alarm that the Government is pursuing a foolish and senseless course. Meantime the canal will be built and completed on or before the 1st of January, 1915, and those who are now its severest critics will be glad to have their authorship of recent articles forgotten.

15

Judicial Decisions as an Issue in Politics

McClure's, *June, 1909*

Last summer at Hot Springs, after the Convention and before the electoral campaign had been actively begun, Mr. McClure asked me to furnish him two articles for his magazine, to be printed after the election. I suggested to him that if I were defeated he might not desire the articles, but he said he would run the risk. One subject which he proposed was my labor decisions, and the article that follows is a compliance with the promise I then made.

I believe it is true that I am the only successful candidate for the Presidency who ever had extended judicial experience. Mr. Van Buren had been a surrogate or probate judge early in his career, and Andrew Jackson, I believe, did serve as a judge of the Supreme Court of North Carolina, but it was a very unimportant part of his life, and his service did not bring into the issues of his campaigns any discussion of his work as a judge.

Judge Parker, so far as I know, is the only other candidate who had been for any number of years on the Bench; and while there was some reference in the campaign to his judicial opinions, they did not involve any issues made in the platform, and were not given special prominence on the stump or in political editorials.

In 1896 the judgment of the Supreme Court in the income-tax case was made a subject of heated discussion, and suggestions that the court might be increased if one party was successful, so as to bring about a reversal of the decision, were not wanting. Still, I think it may be truly said that in no campaign since the beginning of the government has there been directly involved as an issue a question considered and decided by one of the Presidential candidates as a judge.

It is not the first time in my family that a judicial decision has played an important part in the political fortunes of the judge deciding it. While my father was a judge of the Superior Court of Cincinnati, the question arose whether the school board of the city had the power by resolution to change the rule under which schools were opened in the morning by the reading of the King James version of the Bible. Two of the judges of the Superior Court held that this was beyond the power of the school board, while my father, the third judge, dissented. The case proceeded to the Supreme Court, and that court, in a unanimous judgment, approved the views of my father as a dissenting judge in the court below. Notwithstanding this result, in three gubernatorial campaigns my father was defeated in Republican conventions on the ground of his decision in the Bible case; but it never fell to his lot to be nominated as a party candidate and to find it necessary to go upon the stump to explain or defend his decisions. I think I may say that my experience in this respect has been truly exceptional.

To make the controversy clear, it is necessary to refer to the efforts made by the American Federation of Labor and the railroad labor organizations to secure legislation against what they claimed to be the abuses of the power of injunction by courts of equity in labor disputes. Mr. Gompers and the American Federation of Labor were much more radical and drastic in their demands than were the railroad organizations. Mr. Gompers demanded the passage of a bill containing two sections: The first section provided that no injunction should issue from a court of equity except to protect property rights from irreparable injury where there was not adequate remedy at law, and contained the proviso, which embodied the whole intent of the section, that injury to business of a complainant in such labor disputes should not be considered an injury to property rights; and the second section contained a provision which in effect legalized the secondary boycott and rendered immune from criminal or civil prosecution or injunctive process those taking part in such a boycott. This was known as the Pearre Bill. President Roosevelt and the members of his Cabinet whom he called into consultation, of whom I was one, were quite willing to concede that the power of the issuing of injunctions in the form of temporary restraining orders, without notice to the party affected, had been abused in some cases by Federal judges, and that it might be wise to take away the power of issuing such orders without notice and restore the law to the condition in which it had been when the Federal Judiciary Act of 1789 was put in force. At that time no temporary injunction could issue without a notice to the party affected and an opportunity to be heard. A bill to effect such a change was introduced and probably would have passed if Mr. Gompers and the American Federation of Labor had been willing to accept it as a compromise.

At the head of a delegation of labor-union men, Mr. Gompers visited the President. The President told him very plainly that he would not and did not favor the bill known as the Pearre Bill, for he thought that the power of injunction ought to be exercised quite as much against lawless working-men as against lawless capitalists.

Thus the issue was made in the Congressional campaign of 1906, and Mr. Gompers summoned assistance from his fellows of the American Federation of Labor to defeat Mr. Littlefield in Maine, Mr. Cannon in Illinois, and a great many other Congressmen who were put upon the so-called "black list" because they declined to consent to the passage of the Pearre Bill, and refused to withdraw the protecting influence of injunctive process from a man's business rights and to legalize boycotts. The electoral campaign carried on by Mr. Gompers was not successful in defeating any Congressman whom he had blacklisted, and into whose district he went for the purpose of defeating him. Of course in each district many other issues played a part, and it is difficult to tell how much influence Mr. Gompers exerted in taking away votes from the successful candidate. He renewed his efforts in the next Congress, but without avail.

Then came the presidential conventions of the two parties. Mr. Gompers appeared before the Committee on Resolutions of the Republican Convention, and demanded the approval of the Pearre Bill or its equivalent. The President and I favored the following resolution:

Injunctions

"We declare for such an amendment of the statutes of procedure in the Federal courts with respect to the use of the writ of injunction as will, on the one hand, prevent the summary issue of such orders without proper consideration, and, on the other, will preserve undiminished the power of the courts to enforce their process, to the end that justice may be done at all times and to all parties."

A great many of the delegates were opposed to any resolution on the subject, regarding it as an attack upon the courts; but finally, as a compromise, the following resolution was adopted in the platform:

Court Procedure

"The Republican party will uphold at all times the authority and integrity of the courts, State and Federal, and will ever insist that their powers to enforce their process and to protect life, liberty, and property shall be preserved inviolate. We believe, however, that the rules of procedure in the Federal courts with respect to the issuance of the writ of injunction should be more accurately defined by statute, and that no injunction or temporary restraining order should be issued without notice, except where irreparable injury would result from delay, in which case a speedy hearing thereafter should be granted."

It will be observed that the Republican Convention declined to take away the power to issue temporary restraining orders without notice, but preferred to hedge the power about with a statutory declaration of the instances in which they might issue, and offered an opportunity for limiting their life or duration by statute to such a short time as would necessitate a hearing within a few days. In this respect the convention did not go as far as Mr. Roosevelt and I were willing to go. Mr. Gompers and his associates expressed dissatisfaction with the action of the Republican Convention, and then went to Denver, where, after the fullest discussion, the resolution which was adopted read as follows:

Labor and Injunctions

"The courts of justice are the bulwark of our liberties, and we yield to none in our purpose to maintain their dignity. Our party has given to the Bench a long line of distinguished judges, who have added to the respect and confidence in which this department must be jealously maintained. We resent the attempt of the Republican party to raise a false issue respecting the judiciary. It is an unjust reflection upon a great body of our citizens to assume that they lack respect for the courts.

"It is the function of the courts to interpret the laws which the people create, and if the laws appear to work economic, social, or political injustice, it is our duty to change them. The only basis upon which the integrity of our courts can stand is that of unswerving justice and protection of life, personal liberty, and property. If judicial processes may be abused, we should guard them against abuse.

"Experience has proved the necessity of a modification of the present law relating to injunctions, and we reiterate the pledge of our National platforms of 1896 and 1904 in favor of the measure which passed the United

States Senate in 1896, but which a Republican Congress has ever since refused to enact, relating to contempts in Federal courts and providing for trial by jury in cases of indirect contempt.

"Questions of judicial practice have arisen especially in connection with industrial disputes. We deem that the parties to all judicial proceedings should be treated with rigid impartiality, and that injunctions should not be issued in any cases in which injunctions would not issue if no industrial dispute were involved."

I have been informed that the resolution was drafted by Mr. Gompers and was passed exactly as drafted.

In one of Mr. Roosevelt's letters written during the campaign, he invited attention to an article published by Mr. Gompers in the *American Federationist* in defense of what he had done in supporting the Democratic candidate, and pointed out that in that article Mr. Gompers said, or plainly intimated, that Mr. Bryan was in complete accord with the attitude taken by the American Federation of Labor before the last two Congresses, and that this necessarily involved not only the abolition of the use of the injunction in labor disputes where only the business of the plaintiff was to be injured, but also the legalizing of the secondary boycott.

Neither Mr. Gompers nor Mr. Bryan ever attempted to answer the query put by Mr. Roosevelt as to whether this statement was true. Read in the light of this explanation, we can see what the resolution of the Denver Convention was intended to mean. The key necessary to understand the resolution was the principle of equity procedure advanced by Mr. Gompers and his legal counsel, that the right of a man to pursue a lawful business is not a property or pecuniary right which a court of equity would ever, according to proper rules of its procedure, issue an injunction to protect. The question has been distinctly passed upon by dozens of courts, and Mr. Gompers's proposition has not received the slightest support except in one dissenting opinion.

The instances in which courts of equity, both in England and in this country, have issued injunctions to protect business rights are so many as to be overwhelming. But assuming Mr. Gompers's proposition of law to be correct, namely, that no injunction could ever issue merely to protect the rights of business, as distinguished from property rights, then the meaning of the resolution of the Democratic platform becomes clear. It resolves that injunctions ought not to issue in labor disputes under any circumstances except those in which they would issue in other disputes, and as, according to Mr. Gompers, they would never issue in other disputes to protect business rights, they ought to be prohibited from being issued to protect a man's business in labor disputes.

A boycott is ordinarily not directed toward anything but a man's business. It is intended to injure his business and is well adapted to do so. If, therefore, by the resolution as interpreted above, all injuries to business and confined to business alone, and not reaching to rights in material property, were excluded, it would have the effect of limiting the recourse of one injured by a boycott to the inadequate remedy of a suit for damages, and thus in an indirect way the object of the American Federation of Labor in the Pearre Bill would be accomplished.

There was another and a very important issue in respect to which the Democratic platform by its expressed declaration and the Republican platform by its silence left no doubt, and that was the question whether in punishments for contempt in all classes of cases, except those committed in the presence of the court, punishment should not be inflicted by the court until after a conviction in a trial by jury.

I have thus defined certain so-called labour issues of the campaign, in order that the relevancy of my decisions may become apparent. At the risk of being tedious, I shall attempt to state shortly what those decisions were.

The first one was rendered by me when I was a judge of the Superior Court of Cincinnati, a State court of general jurisdiction, where I sat under appointment and subsequent election for three years. The case was a suit for damages by Moores & Company, lime-dealers, against the Bricklayers' Union of Cincinnati.

The undisputed facts shown were these: Parker Brothers were a firm of boss bricklayers. They had quarreled with Bricklayers' Union. The Bricklayers' Union had withdrawn its members from the employ of Parker Brothers and had declared a strike against the firm, and had threatened all material-men that it would boycott any one of them who furnished material to Parker Brothers. Moores & Company were lime-dealers and sold Parker Brothers lime for cash. This was discovered by a walking delegate of the Union, and a boycott was declared against Moores & Company, who were thereby prevented from enjoying the profit of a number of valuable contracts, and whose business suffered severely in other ways.

I sat as the trial judge, and charged the jury that upon this state of fact Moores & Company were entitled to recover as damages the loss that had been inflicted by the boycott of the Bricklayers' Union. The jury immediately returned a verdict for $2,500. A motion for a new trial was made, and I reserved the motion, as I had the power to do, to the general term of the Superior Court for the consideration of three judges, including myself, and there I delivered the opinion of the court, and in this opinion, which was an elaborate one. I attempted to explain what was the illegality of a boycott. If I were writing the opinion again, I should hope to make it shorter. As between two persons, when one refuses to deal with the other and thus injures the other, no unlawful injury is committed if he is not under special contract to do the thing that he refuses to do. It is what in law is called *damnum absque injuria.*

A body of workmen are dissatisfied with the terms of their employment. They seek to compel their employer to come to their terms by striking. They may legally do so. The loss and inconvenience he suffers he can not complain of. But when they seek to compel third persons, who have no quarrel with their employer, to withdraw from all association with him by threats that unless such third persons do so the workmen will inflict similar injury on such third persons, the combination is oppressive, involves duress, and if injury results, it is actionable. It is true that the result of the rule is that an act is actionable or not as the intent with which it is done varies. This is not frequent in civil injuries, but it is not unknown.

This I understand to be the view of the Anthracite Coal Commission, of which Judge Gray of the Third Circuit was certainly the most conspicuous lawyer member, and I think that it is a safe rule of distinction in all labor controversies. Such a view does not render illegal the union of all members of a trades union, whether employees of the particular employer or not, to withdraw from association with him. It permits them thus to express their sympathy with their fellows. But it does forbid them, by threatening men who otherwise would be entirely willing to associate with their former employer, to compel that third person to join them in the fight.

The decision in Moores & Company against the Bricklayers' Union sustained the verdict and gave judgment against the Union. The Union took the case to the Supreme Court of Ohio, where it was affirmed without opinion. The decision was won in a local court and did not attract any immediate attention. Subsequently the fact that the reasoning was quite elaborate and the citation and consideration of authorities extended, elicited considerable reference to it in other decisions, and in the discussions of a naturally interesting subject in legal periodicals, and at bar association meetings; but it did not arouse labor-unions to resolutions of protest, so far as I can recollect.

The next case was one that attracted far greater attention because of the prominence of one of the parties, and the very large body of men more or less indirectly interested in the issues. I had then become United States Circuit Judge for the Sixth Judicial Circuit. The Toledo & Ann Arbor Railroad

was a railroad running from Michigan to Toledo, Ohio, where it made connections with six different railroads. It had had a controversy with its locomotive engineers as to their wages, and through Mr. Arthur, who was the
Grand Chief of the Brotherhood of Locomotive Engineers, a strike had been
declared against that railroad.

The Brotherhood had a secret rule (No. 12) which provided that it was
a violation of obligation for any member of the Brotherhood engaged with
a connecting line to haul the cars of a railroad company against which a strike
had been approved by the Grand Chief. The six railroads who were made
parties defendant to this action had been notified by their engineers that they
probably must refuse to haul the cars of the Toledo & Ann Arbor road. This
had come to the knowledge of the Toledo & Ann Arbor Railroad Company,
and it accordingly filed a bill in equity in the United States Court at Toledo,
asking that the six railroads be compelled to haul the cars of the Toledo &
Ann Arbor Railroad, on the ground that this was their specific duty under
the Interstate Commerce Law, which imposed a fine and penalty upon all
officers, employees, and servants of any road engaged in interstate commerce
who should refuse to perform it.

Judge Ricks accordingly issued a temporary restraining order against all
the defendant railroad companies, their officers and employees, and had the
injunctive process served on all the locomotive engineers. After this injunction was issued, Mr. Arthur, the Grand Chief, sent a telegram to the engineers of the Lake Shore, advising them that he had approved the strike
against the Toledo & Ann Arbor Railroad, and inviting their attention to the
laws of the order, including secret Rule No. 12, and directing them to act
accordingly. A supplemental petition was then filed in the same cause, and I
was applied to, as circuit judge, to enjoin Mr. Arthur by mandatory injunction to withdraw his order to the engineers of the Lake Shore road. I issued
without notice a temporary mandatory restraining order, requiring Mr. Arthur to withdraw his telegram until the case could be heard. Mr. Arthur
obeyed the order. The case was promptly heard in the course of a day or two
at Toledo.

Meantime one of the engineers who had received notice of the injunction on the Lake Shore road, an engineer named Lennon, had refused to haul
the cars of the Toledo & Ann Arbor road. He was brought before Judge
Ricks on an attachment for contempt of the order. The two causes were
heard the same day in Toledo. My recollection is that I did not sit in the
Lennon case, and that Judge Ricks did not sit in the Arthur case.

The result of the Lennon case was that Judge Ricks sentenced Lennon
to confinement for thirty days for contempt. After a release by writ of *habeas*

corpus to test the legality of Lennon's confinement was denied by Judge Ricks, an appeal was taken to the Court of Appeals at Cincinnati, and thence to the Supreme Court of the United States, and the confinement of Lennon was held to be legal.

In the Arthur case I made the temporary order of injunction permanent and wrote an opinion giving my reasons. No appeal was taken from this ruling in the Arthur case, although a direct appeal on the merits lay to the Court of Appeals and thence by certiorari to the Supreme Court of the United States. What I decided in the Arthur case was this: That the Toledo & Ann Arbor road had a right under the Interstate Commerce Law to have its cars hauled by the Lake Shore road, and that a conspiracy by the servants of the Lake Shore company to compel it to decline to perform that duty in order that they might injure the Toledo & Ann Arbor road, thus involving the Lake Shore company in a controversy in which it had no interest and in which it was an unwilling participant, was a secondary boycott at common law. I also held that this was unlawful under the statutes of the United States, and injuries arising therefrom were of such a recurrent character and the loss was so difficult to estimate, that a suit at law offered no adequate remedy, and therefore a court of equity would prevent the injury by injunction.

It will be observed that Judge Ricks in his decision had held that Lennon as an engineer of the Lake Shore road had violated the injunction requiring him to haul the cars of the Toledo & Ann Arbor road, and that I had by mandatory injunction directed Arthur to withdraw his telegram directing all engineers of the Lake Shore road to do that which Lennon had done; the point being, not that Lennon and the engineers of the Lake Shore road could not leave the employ of the Lake Shore road freely and without restraint by injunction, but only that as long as they remained in the employ of the Lake Shore company they were *pro tanto* the company itself and burdened with the duties of the company and must obey the injunctions that would lie against the company itself. In no decision was it affirmed that an injunction could compel a man to remain in the service against his will, or that in any labor dispute could a man in the employ of another be enjoined from striking.

Though this distinction was made clear in both decisions, it was generally reported, and believed by many who did not look into it, that we had enjoined men from striking and had punished them in contempt proceedings for exercising the right to strike. It is easy to see, therefore, how it was possible for members of the Brotherhood of Engineers and of labor organizations generally to believe that a blow had been struck at organized labor from which it could never recover, and that the instrumentality of the strike, which in the last resort is the chief weapon that the laboring man has to secure better wages and better terms of employment, had been taken away. Judge Ricks and I were denounced from one end of this country to the other, in resolutions of labor organizations and kindred associations, as enemies of labor who had sought by judicial process to subject the workingman as a slave to the complete control of his employer. As a matter of fact, I had laid down, not only in the Moores case but in the Arthur case, the principles upon which the success of labor organizations must always depend, and upon which in the last ten years they have grown to their very great proportions and increased in their very great usefulness.

These principles were stated in a somewhat more specific way in the Phelan case, to which I shall presently refer, and from which I shall quote.

I was attacked further, and this attack was heard in the late campaign, on the ground that I had denounced the Brotherhood of Locomotive Engineers as a criminal conspiracy against the laws of the United States. What I did in the opinion was to point out the fact that secret Rule No. 12, if enforced, would involve all those engaged in its enforcement, both those who actually took part in it and those who ordered it, in a criminal conspiracy against the laws of the United States. I did so in these words:

"We have thus considered with some care the criminal character of Rule 12 and its enforcement, not only because, as will presently be seen, it assists in determining the civil liabilities that grow out of them, but also because we wish to make plain, if we can, to the intelligent and generally law-abiding men who compose the Brotherhood of Locomotive Engineers, as well as to their usually conservative chief officer, what we can not believe they appreciate, that, notwithstanding their perfect organization, and their charitable, temperance, and other elevating and most useful purposes, the existence and enforcement of Rule 12, under their organic law, make the whole Brotherhood a criminal conspiracy against the laws of their country."

The effect of that admonition, which was intended to be kindly, and it seems to me was couched in a perfectly friendly tone, was to lead the Brotherhood to repeal Rule No. 12; and I understand now that all the railroad labor organizations, which are among the best conducted of trades unions in the country, deprecate the use of the boycott as a weapon in labor controversies.

The third reported decision for which I was attacked in the late campaign was what was known as the Phelan case. It was presented as a phase of the Debs insurrection.

Debs was the president of the American Railway Union, a labor association organized as a rival of the older railway brotherhoods. Soon after the organization was complete, Debs, as president of the directors of the association, became interested in the question whether the Pullman Company, manufacturing Pullman cars near Chicago, paid their employees sufficient wages. It was decided that the wages were not sufficient. The employees were induced to strike, and then it was sought by the American Railway Union to compel the Pullman Company to pay higher wages by threatening a universal boycott against all the railroads of the country that had contracts with the Pullman Company for the use of the Pullman cars, and to compel them to withdraw from or break these contracts and to discontinue the use of the Pullman cars.

Although this was the original purpose, it degenerated into an attempt to tie up every railroad in the country by withdrawing all the railway employees from railroad work without regard to whether the railroads had business for the Pullman Company or not. In other words, it became a boycott against the public in an attempt to make the public compel the Pullman Company to raise the wages it paid its employees, although the public had no relation to the Pullman Company, which was a private corporation doing a private business, so far as its manufacturing of cars was concerned, and had no power over the question of the amount of wages to be paid by it to those whom it employed.

In pursuance of this plan, Debs sent Phelan to Cincinnati to tie up all the railroads in that city, and among others was the Cincinnati, New Orleans & Texas Pacific Railway Company, which operated as a lessee the Cincinnati Southern Railroad, and which for the time being was in the hands of the court in charge of Mr. Felton, receiver. I was the circuit judge, resident in Cincinnati, who had appointed the receiver, and was conducting the affairs so far as the court had to interfere in that receivership.

The receiver filed a petition in the proceeding, asking an attachment of Phelan for contempt of court. The petition charged that Phelan was attempting to prevent the receiver from carrying out the order of the court directing him to run the road, and was advising all those who had left the employ of the receiver, and others, to use violence in compelling the receiver's employees to leave his employment; that in consequence the receiver was obliged to hire constables to protect his men.

Phelan was brought in on a warrant, and was served with an injunction to prevent his continuing in that which he was already charged to have done, and the cause was set for a trial at his convenience. It was promptly heard, and a week was consumed in the trial. At the end of that time I found Phelan guilty of contempt of court, and sentenced him to six months in the Lebanon jail. His actions after the injunction was served on him were exactly what they had been before, and he conducted himself avowedly and flagrantly in violation of the court's orders. In this case, as in the others, I pointed out, with all the clearness of which I was capable, the distinction between the strike and the boycott, and perhaps more fully than in previous cases explained what were the rights and responsibilities of the trades unions engaged in a controversy with an employer. In this case I said:

"Now, it may be conceded in the outset that the employees of the receiver had the right to organize into or join a labor union which should take joint action as to their terms of employment. It is of benefit to them and to the public that laborers should unite in their common interest and for lawful purposes. They have labor to sell. If they stand together, they are often able, all of them, to command better prices for their labor than when dealing singly with rich employers, because the necessities of the single employee may compel him to accept any terms offered him. The accumulation of a fund for the support of those who feel that the wages offered are below market prices is one of the legitimate objects of such an organization. They have the right to appoint officers who shall advise them as to the course to be taken by them in their relations with their employer. They may unite with other unions. The officers they appoint, or any other person to whom they choose to listen, may advise them as to the proper course to be taken by them in regard to their employment, or, if they choose to repose such authority in any one, may order them, on pain of expulsion from their union, peaceably to leave the employ of their employer because any of the terms of their employment are unsatisfactory."

In the Arthur case it was brought out quite distinctly that while employees who struck for an unlawful purpose could not be enjoined from doing so, because to enjoin them would be to compel the specific performance of a contract of service, in violation of the Thirteenth Amendment against involuntary servitude, it was left open as an undecided question whether men who were inciting employees to quit their employer in violation of some legal duty might not be restrained from doing so; and in the Phelan case, the effect of the decision was to hold that where one was inciting employees to quit in pursuance of an unlawful boycott, he could be enjoined, although the employees could not be.

There was one other case—indeed, there may have been more, though I do not recollect them—in which I issued an injunction growing out of a labor dispute and in which I punished men for a violation of the order of the injunction. A number of miners on the Ohio side of the Ohio River combined together in a conspiracy to prevent the importation into Ohio of West Virginia coal, and every time that a train of one of the West Virginia railroads was delivered to the Ohio railroad, the miners jumped upon the train and by physical force prevented the further transportation of the coal.

The Baltimore & Ohio road, which was the West Virginia road, brought suit against the Cleveland, Lorain & Wheeling to compel the Cleveland, Lorain & Wheeling to take its cars and transport them, and then it was made to appear by the Baltimore & Ohio that certain defendants, who were named, had conspired to prevent the Baltimore & Ohio from securing transportation over the Cleveland, Lorain & Wheeling.

I issued a mandatory injunction against the Cleveland, Lorain & Wheeling compelling it to receive and transport the cars, and named as defendants to the action a number of the Ohio miners engaged in the conspiracy. They were duly served, and, after a full notice, were brought into court. They did not deny their guilt, and I sentenced them to six months in jail. It was a case of blockade of interstate commerce by force, and it was only by the decree of an equity court that the passage of coal from one State to another was made free and uninterrupted. There was no report of the opinion in this case, which presented questions similar to those in the Arthur case. When I reached Wheeling in the campaign, I was confronted by the exploitation of this case in the local paper, and explained it as I have explained it here.

With this record of decisions in labor cases, in which I have had each time to decide against the labor organizations, or the cause with which they sympathized, I had always been of opinion that it would be utterly impossible for me to run for office before the people even if I desired to do so. My ambition was not political. I desired if possible to resume my work on the Bench, and the disqualification which these decisions seemed to me to make clear and certain did not really involve in my judgment any sacrifice on my part. I think it fell to my lot to take part in more cases of this kind than most judges, and had I had political ambition, it might have been regarded as a misfortune.

The attacks made upon me in labor circles and by labor journals did not particularly trouble me, because I thought that in the course of time it would appear that what I had decided was clearly the law, and that the principles that I had laid down were those upon which trades unions properly conducted would thrive and attain their greatest usefulness.

The decision of the Supreme Court in the Debs case, in an opinion by Mr. Justice Brewer, removed all doubt, if any had before existed, as to the right of a court of equity to issue an injunction in such cases, and I don't think that in any respectable court it is now disputed. But the effect of Mr. Gompers's action and that of the Democratic party in its platform was to appeal, so to speak, from the decision of the court to the decision of the electorate. They had done this once before in appealing against the decision of the Supreme Court in the Debs case, which was characterized in the platforms of 1896 and of 1900 as government by injunction, but the appeals apparently had not met with great success.

They were now able, however, to appeal in a more concrete way to the people, by asking them to vote against the candidate who was as much responsible for the enunciation of the principles that they contended against as any judge on the Bench. I was characterized as the "father of injunctions." This attributed to me something that I did not deserve, for injunctions had already been issued in labor disputes by Vice-Chancellor Malins in England; by the Supreme Judicial Court of Massachusetts in the case of Sherry vs. Perkins; by Judge Sage in the case of Casey vs. Typographical Union; by Judge Beatty in the Coeur d'Alene strike troubles, and by other judges.

It had fallen to my lot, because of the number of cases that I had subsequently to consider, to write rather more elaborate opinions on the subject and perhaps state the principles more at length than other judges, but I was not entitled to either the credit or discredit of having introduced a new equity jurisdiction in labor troubles. There was no new jurisdiction. It was merely an application of plain equity principles to novel situations. The character of the injury in cases of boycott when business is injured is such that it is impossible to estimate what the injury is. This is palpable. Moreover, the injury is a result of a series of acts combined together, each one of which would not justify a suit for damages, but all of which taken together with their recurrent effect bring about the injury which can only be remedied adequately by an injunction to prevent the carrying out of the combination. This has always justified the issuing of an injunction in equity, and its use is not an enlargement of equity jurisdiction but a mere application of the oldest and most well-known principles.

Viewing as I did the effect on my political attitude of these decisions, it may well be supposed that I was surprised when I discovered the strength that I had developed in the Republican Convention, and found that the opposition to me on the ground of my labor decisions, although sufficiently elaborated, did not lose for me a great many votes among the delegates; but while this was the result in the Convention, there was very great reason to believe that the objection to me as a candidate was much more formidable. Mr. Gompers, through the American Federation of Labor, used all the machinery that that association afforded to secure votes for Mr. Bryan against me, and I constantly received most discouraging reports of the defection in the ranks of labor because of my injunction decisions. This was particularly noticeable among the railway employees who remembered the fact that I had enjoined Arthur, and carried in their memories, though indistinctly, the attacks that had been made upon me at the time of that decision as a judge determined to strike down labor organizations. As the injunction had been directed toward the chief of the most conservative, useful, and powerful brotherhood, that of the locomotive engineers, it was not unnatural that it should have been remembered and cherished.

I was very reluctant to go on the stump and discuss my own decisions. I knew no precedent for it, and I felt that if the decisions themselves did not support the conclusions reached, there was little use in my attempting to supply additional explanation or defense. I found, however, that Mr. Bryan was constantly referring to me as the father of injunctions, and that the Democratic managers were making as much of this part of the issues of the campaign as possible, and I concluded, therefore, that the only thing for me to do was to seek an opportunity to tell what I had decided to audiences composed as largely of labor men as possible, and then leave it to their sense of justice whether the attacks upon me as an enemy of labor were justified.

The first speech I made upon it was rather unpremeditated; it was given at Athens, Ohio, before a lot of miners who were trades unionists. I don't know how the speech impressed the audience other than by the way in which it was received. My friends who heard it commended its presentation and urged that I seek other opportunities to deal with the same subject. A large meeting of railway employees was organized in Chicago by a friendly club, at Orchestra Hall. There for the first time I went over in full my labor decisions. I shook hands afterward with every one of the audience, and I am quite certain that my treatment of the subject met with the approval of those who were present and induced them to believe what I contended was the fact, and believe now to be the fact, that of all judges who had had occasion to consider the question, I had laid down the law as favorably as possible for the lawful and useful organization of trades unions. I was careful to state that I did not apologize in any way for the decisions that I had rendered, and I only sought the opportunity to state what the decisions were and their effect, in order to enable my hearers to judge whether I was the man against whom they should cast their ballots.

I had similar meetings in Minneapolis, South Omaha, Lorain, East St. Louis, Kansas City, East Cleveland, and at Cooper Union in New York. I was able to point out that although the brotherhoods had attacked my decision against Arthur, later on, in a labor controversy which got into court in St. Louis between the brotherhoods and the Missouri Pacific road, my decisions in the Arthur case and in the Phelan case had been successfully cited as authorities upon which Judge Adams modified the injunction already issued in such a way as to enable the brotherhoods to win the strike and secure a betterment of the conditions of employment with that company. I was also able to point out to the brotherhoods that in the Phelan case in sentencing Phelan, I was merely sentencing a man who had done everything that he possibly could to incite his followers to violence against the members of the old brotherhoods who had declined to follow Debs and who stuck to the cabs of their engines in faithful service of the receiver.

It is impossible, of course, to tell which of the many reasons that enter into the decision of an electorate is most influential. It is very certain that Mr. Gompers was not able to carry with him his followers in the American Federation of Labor; the two million votes that he claimed were controlled by that organization. It is very clear that in the large cities the labor vote did not go in unusual numbers to Mr. Bryan as against me. In Greater New York, in Boston, in Philadelphia, in Baltimore, in Cleveland, in Cincinnati, in Chicago, in St. Louis, and in San Francisco I received certainly a full party vote and in many of them a very much larger vote than the party vote, and in those States the Federation of Labor is stronger than in any other parts of the country.

I am, of course, not blind to the fact that one of the chief arguments in my favor with the wage-earner in this campaign was the fear that the election of Mr. Bryan would make the hard times permanent, and the hope that the continuance of the Republican party in power would insure a return of good times. This argument doubtless neutralized the one directed against me as a man unfair to labor; and there were probably a number of men who voted for me without approving me, because while they liked Mr. Bryan's attitude in the injunction matter, they preferred to give victory to that side which was likely to insure steadier work and better wages. Still, I think, in spite of all this, it must be conceded that the showing made by Mr. Gompers upon the issue against me as an enemy of labor was considerably less than he expected it to be, and that this was due in part at least to the fact that no one can control the vote of the intelligent laboring man; that he does not yield to mere sentiment or the calling of names, but that he himself investigates the reasons and makes up an independent mind.

I did not hesitate to meet the issue on the question of a trial by jury in contempt cases. I attempted to point out the dreadful weakening of the power of the court that would ensue if every order to be performed outside of the presence of the court might be violated and no punishment ensue except after a trial by jury. I think I showed that the result of such a change in the law would be to put the means of evading decrees of the court of equity into the hands of the wealthy and unscrupulous, and that it would work but little benefit to the poor and needy wage-earner. The appeal made to the farmer, merchant, business man, and the public at large, including the intelligent wage-earner, against the weakening of the power of the court, in the interest of a particular class, was, if one can judge from the attitude of the audiences addressed, as strong a vote-getting argument as the Republican party had in the late campaign. Certainly it was next in force and persuasiveness to that based on a prospective restoration of good times in a Republican victory.

16

Concerning the Government of Cuba

June 5, 1909

To the Senate and House of Representatives:

I have the honor to transmit herewith a communication from the Acting Secretary of War, under date of May 8th, submitting the report, with accompanying exhibits, of the Honorable Charles E. Magoon, provisional governor of Cuba, for the period from December 1, 1908, to January 28, 1909, when the provisional government was terminated and the island again turned over to the Cubans. I recommend, in accordance with the suggestion of the Acting Secretary of War, that this report and the exhibits be printed.

I think it only proper to take this opportunity to say that the administration by Governor Magoon of the government of Cuba from 1906 to 1909 involved the disposition and settlement of many very difficult questions and required on his part the exercise of ability and tact of the highest order. It gives me much pleasure to note in this public record the credit due to Governor Magoon for his distinguished service.

The army of Cuban pacification under Major-General Barry was of the utmost assistance in the preservation of the peace of the island and the maintenance of law and order, without the slightest friction with the inhabitants of the island, although the army was widely distributed through the six provinces and came into close contact with the people.

The administration of Governor Magoon and the laws recommended by the advisory commission, with Colonel Crowder, of the Judge-Advocate-General's Corps at its head, and put into force by the Governor, have greatly facilitated the progress of good government in Cuba. At a fair election held under the advisory commission's new election law General Gomez was chosen President and he has begun his administration under good auspices. I am glad to express the hope that the new government will grow in strength and self-sustaining capacity under the provisions of the Cuban constitution.

17

Concerning Tax on Net Income of Corporations

June 16, 1909

To the Senate and House of Representatives:

It is the constitutional duty of the President from time to time to recommend to the consideration of Congress such measures as he shall judge necessary and expedient. In my inaugural address, immediately preceding this present extraordinary session of Congress, I invited attention to the necessity for a revision of the tariff at this session, and stated the principles upon which I thought the revision should be effected. I referred to the then rapidly increasing deficit, and pointed out the obligation on the part of the framers of the tariff bill to arrange the duty so as to secure an adequate income, and suggested that if it was not possible to do so by import duties, new kinds of taxation must be adopted, and among them I recommended a graduated inheritance tax as correct in principle and as certain and easy of collection. The House of Representatives has adopted the suggestion and has provided in the bill it passed for the collection of such a tax. In the Senate the action of its Finance Committee and the course of the debate indicate that it may not agree to this provision, and it is now proposed to make up the deficit by the imposition of a general income tax, in form and substance of almost exactly the same character as that which in the case of Pollock vs. Farmers' Loan and Trust Company (157 U.S., 429) was held by the Supreme Court to be a direct tax, and therefore not within the power of the Federal Government to impose unless apportioned among the several States according to population. This new proposal, which I did not discuss in my inaugural address or in my message at the opening of the present session, makes it appropriate for me to submit to the Congress certain additional recommendations.

The decision of the Supreme Court in the income-tax cases deprived the National Government of a power which, by reason of previous decisions of the court, it was generally supposed that Government had. It is undoubtedly a power the National Government ought to have. It might be indispensable to the nation's life in great crises. Although I have not considered a constitutional amendment as necessary to the exercise of certain phases of this power, a mature consideration has satisfied me that an amendment is the only proper course for its establishment to its full extent. I therefore recommend to the Congress that both Houses, by a two-thirds vote, shall propose an amendment to the Constitution conferring the power to levy an income tax upon the National Government without apportionment among the States in proportion to population.

This course is much to be preferred to the one proposed of re-enacting a law once judicially declared to be unconstitutional. For the Congress to assume that the court will reverse itself, and to enact legislation on such an assumption, will not strengthen popular confidence in the stability of judicial construction of the Constitution. It is much wiser policy to accept the decision and remedy the defect by amendment in due and regular course.

Again, it is clear that, by the enactment of the proposed law, the Congress will not be bringing money into the Treasury to meet the present deficiency, but by putting on the statute book a law already there and never repealed, will simply be suggesting to the executive officers of the Government their possible duty to invoke litigation. If the court should maintain its former view, no tax would be collected at all. If it should ultimately reverse itself, still no taxes would have been collected until after protracted delay.

It is said the difficulty and delay in securing the approval of three-fourths of the States will destroy all chance of adopting the amendment. Of course, no one can speak with certainty upon this point, but I have become convinced that a great majority of the people of this country are in favor of vesting the National Government with power to levy an income tax, and that they will secure the adoption of the amendment in the States, if proposed to them.

Second, the decision in the Pollock case left power in the National Government to levy an excise tax which accomplishes the same purpose as a corporation income tax, and is free from certain objections urged to the proposed income-tax measure.

I therefore recommend an amendment to the tariff bill imposing upon all corporations and joint stock companies for profit, except national banks (otherwise taxed), savings banks, and building and loan associations, an excise tax measured by 2 percent on the net income of such corporations. This is an excise tax upon the privilege of doing business as an artificial entity and of freedom from a general partnership liability enjoyed by those who own the stock.

I am informed that a 2 percent tax of this character would bring into the Treasury of the United States not less than $25,000,000.

The decision of the Supreme Court in the case of Spreckels Sugar Refining Company against McClain (192 U.S., 397) seems clearly to establish the principle that such a tax as this is an excise tax upon privilege and not a direct tax on property, and is within the federal power without apportionment according to population. The tax on net income is preferable to one proportionate to a percentage of the gross receipts, because it is a tax upon success and not failure. It imposes a burden at the source of the income at a time when the corporation is well able to pay and when collection is easy.

Another merit of this tax is the federal supervision which must be exercised in order to make the law effective over the annual accounts and business transactions of all corporations. While the faculty of assuming a corporate form has been of the utmost utility in the business world, it is also true that substantially all of the abuses and all of the evils which have aroused the public to the necessity of reform were made possible by the use of this very faculty. If now, by a perfectly legitimate and effective system of taxation, we are incidentally able to possess the Government and the stockholders and the public of the knowledge of the real business transactions and the gains and profits of every corporation in the country, we have made a long step toward that supervisory control of corporations which may prevent a further abuse of power.

I recommend, then, first, the adoption of a joint resolution by two-thirds of both Houses proposing to the States an amendment to the Constitution granting to the Federal Government the right to levy and collect an income tax without apportionment among the States according to population, and, second, the enactment, as part of the pending revenue measure, either as a substitute for, or in addition to, the inheritance tax, of an excise tax upon all corporations, measured by 2 percent of their net income.

18

Address at the Unveiling of the Memorial to Dr. Benjamin F. Stephenson, Founder of the Grand Army of the Republic

Washington, D.C., July 3, 1909

Mr. Chairman; My Fellow Citizens:

We are met to dedicate a memorial to a Union soldier who served four years as a surgeon in the Civil War, and who also builded an institution by which there should be united in the bonds of fellowship all the sweet association, all the deep lesson of loyalty, and all the pride of patriotism that such a civil war as that could arouse in millions of hearts. When men at the formative period in life—from 18 to 22—are associated in any work, whether it be in college, in society, in church, or otherwise, they carry with them afterward the fondest memories and associations for each other because they have passed through a common mold. But how much greater must be the sweet association and the bond of union between men who for four years passed through the dangers of the Civil War; those who survived thinking of the tender memories of those who gave up their lives for their country; those surviving carrying with them the sweet association, the stories of courage, and tales full of humor and of pathos. I can conceive no bond of union stronger than that which unites the men who fought from '61 to '65 in the Grand Army; and it was to the credit of the founder of the Grand Army of the Republic that he saw the solid basis upon which such a structure as that great society could be erected.

You will recollect that there were prophets of evil with respect to the fate of the United States after the war should cease, after the end should be accomplished for which the North was fighting, and it was said that the aggregation of a million men in arms threatened our free institutions. They recalled that the Pretorian Guard of Rome was an instrument in furthering the ambition of those who would suppress free institutions and who were to assume despotic power. But all those prophecies faded into nothingness. The men who composed that million were men in favor of free institutions, who had fought for them, and did not intend to sacrifice them to anything else. There was no man with the ambition to improve that army as an instrument of despotism even if it had been willing to furnish itself as such; and so it was the marvel of other countries that this great body of organized force, than which there never was a stronger or better-disciplined army, faded out and disappeared into the paths of peace, preserving nothing but the sweet memory and association they had formed during the war and the consciousness that they had in their own hearts of having rendered that greatest service, to wit: the preservation of their country.

Stephenson organized this Grand Army of the Republic to preserve the essence of that army in its finest characteristic, in its democracy and in its patriotism. Far be it from me to criticize in the slightest such organizations as the Cincinnati and the Loyal Legion. They are great organizations, and those who belong to them may well have pride in them. But the Grand Army of the Republic knows no limitation but service to the Government in the Civil War; and therefore it is that Congress, recognizing the usefulness of such an organization in preserving patriotism, in maintaining it in its intensity during those years when commercial greed seemed to make many people forget it, properly contributed $10,000 to this memorial and recognized the Grand Army of the Republic as an institution which may well have national gratitude and national recognition. More than that, the Grand Army of the Republic is most useful in this: it represents the concentrated opinion of the men who fought in the war to preserve the Union, and it therefore may give authoritative expression, which no other body and no other part of the people can give, to that forgetfulness of the bitterness of the strife which existed during the four years of the war. I am glad to say that, while that bitterness may in a few instances obtain, you will never find it to exist between the men who actually exposed their lives on one side and the men who exposed their lives on the other. The union of the two sections has been molded strongly and more strongly by those meetings which ought to be encouraged between the blue and the gray to occur as often as possible. Even within my recollection on occasions like this and on Memorial Day and on

Fourths of July I have seen the ranks of the Grand Army thinned. I know there are many who by jaunty step and by keeping their hats on are able to deceive the people as to their age; but the fact is, that those ranks are thinning from day to day; perhaps a hundred a day are going to their long home. It is fitting that such an association, which in the course of the next generation will pass away, should have such an enduring monument as this to testify not only to the patriotic service that they rendered during the war, but also to the service to the country that they have rendered by their holding high loyalty and patriotism since the war to the present day.

Mr. Commander-in-chief of the Grand Army of the Republic, inasmuch as Congress contributed to this monument and provided for its erection, I am here officially to accept at your hands, on behalf of the Government of the United States, this fitting memorial of fraternity, charity, and loyalty.

19

Address at the Two Hundred and Fiftieth Anniversary of the Founding of Norwich, Connecticut

July 5, 1909

My Friends:

I think it was last year that I had the pleasure of addressing a Norwich audience. Then I talked to you on the subject of the Panama Canal and I promised to come back here at the 250th anniversary of your city's foundation, whether I was nominated and elected for the Presidency or not. I said that probably you would not want me if I was not elected, and I haven't had an opportunity to test you on that. But it is a great pleasure to come back to this beautiful town. I like to call it a town because while you make a distinction between the city and the town, the term town suggests its wonderful history. Well may it be called the Rose of New England. Its beauties today and its sweet memories of the past justify the use of that term, and if I were a Norwich man I should hug it to my bosom. There is something about the town differing from most towns whose history I know, in the individuality of the town itself. There are other towns that have had noted individuals who have made history. Norwich has had noted individuals whose characters, continued through three great crises, have given a character and an individuality to the town itself.

Major John Mason was a great man and he had a son-in-law, James Fitch, a minister of the gospel in this town for forty years, who was a good man; and there were in those thirty-five men in whose name the nine square miles were given by Uncas, men of bone and sinew fit to meet the tremendous trials of those early days.

Then you came to the revolutionary time and you were not wanting, for out of the descendants of your first settlers you furnished great force to that which was needed to separate this country from England. And then again in the Civil War you furnished much more than your quota, and the names of the men who marched out from Norwich would have done credit to many a larger city with a much greater population to draw from.

One of the things that the history of this town suggests is the character of the government that you had here in the early days. Like that of the government of other New England towns, but perfect in its way, it was almost a theocracy. The minister, James Fitch, was not alone a minister of the gospel as we know him today, exercising a beneficent influence in the community, but he spoke by authority, the State was behind him, and the men and women of the community were obliged to conform to the rules of morality and life which he laid down.

We speak with great satisfaction of the fact that our ancestors—and I claim New England ancestry—came to this country in order to establish freedom of religion. Well, if you are going to be exact, they came to this country to establish freedom of their religion and not the freedom of anybody else's religion. The truth is, in those days such a thing as freedom of religion was not understood. Erasmus, the great Dutch professor, one of the most elegant scholars of his day, did understand it and did advocate it, but among the denominations it certainly was not fully understood. We look with considerable horror and with a great deal of condemnation on those particular denominations that punished our ancestors because our ancestors wished to have a different kind of religion, but when our ancestors got here in this country and ruled they intended to have their own religion and no other. But we have passed beyond that and out of the friction. Out of the denominational prejudices in the past we have developed a freedom of religion that came naturally and logically as we went on to free institutions. It came from those very men who built up your community and made its character. The Rev. James Fitch could not look upon any other religion in this community with any degree of patience, but his descendants, firm in the faith as he was, now see that the best way to promote Christianity and the worship of God and religion is to let every man worship God as he chooses. This community was well supervised by the clergy, and did well by the clergy. The Rev. James Fitch, after fourteen years at Saybrook, came here and presided in the First Church for forty more years. I have heard clergymen say that after a clergyman passes his fiftieth year he ought to be made emeritus and step out of the profession. They did not say so in those days. There was an authority about a minister of the gospel that meant a good deal more than mere persuasiveness, and the clergyman's authority is one that seems to cultivate a long life.

The Rev. James Fitch was succeeded by Dr. Benjamin Lord and he was succeeded by Dr. Strong, all of the same church, and the Doctors Lord and Strong presided together, including six years when they were both ministers of this town, one hundred and seventeen years. Now, think of the influence in a community of God-fearing men with force of character, with power to condemn wrong and uphold right, and then you can understand how Norwich has survived and preserved an individuality.

Major Mason was a statesman. He was deputy governor. His chief was Governor Winthrop and Governor Winthrop, while Major Mason presided over the colony of Connecticut, went to London and found King Charles the Second in such good humor that he got that far-famed charter to Connecticut. They said that Charles II, was a monarch who never said a foolish thing and never did a wise one. Whether it was wise for him or not, the charter of Connecticut that he gave, with its principles of free institutions and its latitude to the people of Connecticut in carrying on their government, was certainly from our standpoint a wise act, and I don't wonder that when they tried to get it away they put it in that oak where it was not found.

The truth is, my dear friends, we hear a great deal of discussion of free government and references made to the declaration of independence which this day celebrates. And some people so construe that instrument that they would make it mean that any body of men or women or children are born with the instinct of self-government so that they can frame a government as soon as they begin to talk. Now, that is not true. Self-government has been fought out in the history of this world and by certain races has been hammered out by a thousand years of struggle and men have taught themselves how to govern themselves. Men are not fit to govern themselves until they have sense and self-restraint enough to know what is their interest and to give every other man all that is coming to him according to right and justice.

Now, what is true with respect, therefore, to our ancestors is true with respect to many races in this world. They have to be led on and taught the principle and lesson of self-government. But our ancestors, by a wise negligence in the home government for nearly two hundred years, came to be the best-prepared people there were in the world for self-government. Take the town of Norwich and see how those thirty-five men and the people who followed them made up a government; how they were conscious of the responsibility that they took upon themselves when they attempted a government themselves, and how they carried on an orderly government, a government of liberty, regulated by law. So it was in every town in the thirteen colonies. They were all men of strength, of individuality, of self-restraint, and they knew what it cost to build up a government and maintain it; and when on the fourth of July, 1776, they declared their independence of Great Britain, they did it with reluctance and with hesitation because they knew the tremendous burden on their backs, and they knew the responsibilities that they owed to the world and that they owed to the people for whom they were making the declaration.

No better example of the character of those men who made that declaration of independence and who subsequently framed the Constitution of the United States could be found than right here among your representatives of the town of Norwich. Your selectmen, your leaders, had the education and the experience that fitted them, as all the Americans of that day were fitted, to organize and maintain a civil government and preserve the free institutions and liberty regulated by law.

Now you have stood and looked at the procession so long that your eyes are strained and I do not mean to strain your ears. I wish again to testify to the profound pleasure I have had in studying the history of the town of Norwich, of going over the characters of your great men and of realizing that the strength of your community—the character of your community—is in the character of the men that made it up; and I doubt not that right here under these beautiful elms, and in these houses, so many of which preserve the memories of the past, there is the same respect for virtue, for individual character, for honesty, for freedom and for law that was left to you as a legitimate legacy from the ancestors whose memory you honor today.

20

Address at the Catholic Summer School of America

Cliff Haven, New York, July 7, 1909

Your Eminence, Governor Hughes, Dr. McMahon and my Fellow Citizens of the Catholic Summer School of America:

Governor Hughes and I are going through these three or four days delivering speeches at each other, and expressing our opinions of each other in a way that will enable us, when we get through, to do it with greater facility. The truth is that the gift of eloquence and speech which Governor Hughes has needs no practice, but I have to have a little.

I would be without that which makes a man if I did not appreciate to the full the kindly words of your distinguished Governor, and if I did not congratulate the State of New York on having a Governor who represents the highest ideals. One is almost carried off his feet before such an audience. There is something in the atmosphere that suggests a flying machine, as if you were all so full of joy that that element in you could raise you up, and that is the way you ought to be, and I congratulate you that such is the feeling.

The combination of work and pleasure, the cultivation of health on the one hand and of intellect on the other, and of religious faith above all under such beautiful surroundings is calculated to make everyone enthusiastic, and I share that enthusiasm to the full.

I am not a Catholic, but I have had in the last ten years a great deal to do with the Catholic Church. My lot did not carry me into a part of the world that made me as familiar with the French Explorers, the French leaders of civilization, like Champlain, as it did into the regions of those leaders that came from Spain—into the Philippines where the same influence that carried Champlain here and the same ideal that controlled him, controlled men equally brave, and in certain respects more successful. There was Magellan and later Legaspi who came out to the Philippines and with four or five Augustinian monks converted to Christianity that entire Archipelago now having some seven or eight million souls, and then perhaps 500,000—the only community, the only people in the entire Orient that today as a people are Christians. There is on the Luneta, the great public square facing the ocean in Manila, a statue carved by a great Spanish sculptor, Querol, in which there are two figures, Legaspi, holding the standard of Spain and with his sword drawn, and behind him Urdeneta, a Recolleto monk, holding aloft behind all the cross, and there is in that statue such movement, such force, such courage that I used to like, even in the hot days of Manila, to stand in front of it and enjoy, as I thought I got, the spirit that the sculptor had tried to put in there, of loyalty to country and faith in God.

I think we are reaching a point in this country where we are very much more tolerant of everything and everybody than in the past, and where we are giving justice where justice ought to be given. We are no longer cherishing those narrow prejudices that came from denominational bigotry, and we are able to recognize in the past those great heroes of any religious Christian faith and appreciate the virtues they exhibited as examples for us.

Religious tolerance is rather a modern invention. Those of us of Puritan ancestry have been apt to think that we were the inventors of religious tolerance. Well, as a matter of fact, what we were in favor of, if I can speak for Puritan ancestry, was having a right to worship God as we pleased, and having everybody else worship God in the same way. But we have worked that out now; and there has been a great change, I am sure His Eminence the Cardinal will agree with me, even in the last twenty-five years. I have had personal evidence of it in some of the work that we had to do in the Philippines. Fifty years ago if it had been proposed to send a representative of the Government to the Vatican to negotiate and settle matters arising in a country like the Philippines between the Government and the Roman Catholic Church, it would have given rise to the severest condemnation and criticism on the part of those who would have feared some diplomatic relation between the Government and the Vatican contrary to our traditions; but within the last ten years that has been done, with the full concurrence of all religious denominations, believing that the way to do things is to do them directly, and when a matter is to be settled that it should be settled with the head of the church who has authority to act. And so it fell to my lot, my dear friends, and in that respect just by good luck, I came to be an exception, which will perhaps stand for many years as the sole exception, of being the representative of the United States at the Vatican. There I had the great pleasure of meeting that distinguished statesman and pontiff, Leo XIII, a man of ninety-two, whom I expected to find rather a lay figure directed by the council of the Cardinals than one active in control of the church. But I was most pleasantly disappointed, for even at ninety-two he was able to withstand an address of mine of twenty minutes, to catch the points of that address, and to respond in a speech of some fifteen minutes, showing how fully he appreciated the issue that there was and its importance.

We did not succeed in bringing about exactly the agreement which we asked, and he realized that, but he was full of friendly enthusiasm for the settlement of the issue and after two audiences which I had the honor of holding with him, at the close of the second one, he said, "You haven't, got exactly what you want in exactly the way you want it, but," said he, "I am going to send a representative of mine to the Philippines with instructions to see that the matter is settled justly in accordance with the wishes of the Government of the United States." And it was so settled. I am gratified to say that now every question between the Church and the State in the Philippine Islands, which were so closely united that it seemed almost impossible to make a separation of the two as it ought to be made under our Constitution, has been settled fairly and justly to both sides, and that no bad taste or feeling of injustice exists on either side with respect to those questions.

And now, my dear friends, I ought to talk about Champlain, and I would talk something about him because I appreciate as highly as any one can those motives that governed him and his high character as a man and the obstacles that he had to overcome; but when I get up to talk on any subject, I am a little bit in the attitude of the doctor who could cure fits and that is all he could cure and so he wanted to throw his patients into that condition. I can only talk about the Philippines, and that is what I have done, but I hope they have some application to the thoughts of the morning.

I thank you, my dear friends, I thank the reverend fathers and His Eminence the Cardinal, for the cordial reception that you have given to the civil head of New York and to the civil head of the Nation.

21

Speech at the Banquet, Boston Chamber of Commerce

September 14, 1909

Mr. President, Gentlemen of the Boston Chamber of Commerce, My Fellow Citizens:

I have been under a promise to come to Boston and speak to its Chamber of Commerce for more than a year. It is a great pleasure to redeem that promise. To be the guest at a magnificent feast like this, to be thus received in Boston, one of the greatest centers of the wealth, of the culture and art, of the educational influences, and of the moral forces of our country, and to be welcomed by so distinguished a company, the Governor of the State, a Justice of the Federal Supreme Court, Foreign Ministers, members of the State Judiciary, United States Senators and Representatives, powerful and broad-minded prelates and ministers of religion, together with the men who are the bone and sinew of the commerce of this great section—make this occasion most memorable in my life, and properly call for an expression on my part of deep gratitude and high appreciation.

I congratulate Boston on a union in one organization of all of her business men, for it insures a concentration of influence that must make for good. The opportunities for usefulness are great in civic improvement and progress and in State and National affairs. While you doubtless include in your ranks persons of all political views, many questions must arise upon which you can all unite, and thus exert a most effective influence.

As Boston is the commercial center of New England, your association really speaks for New England, a part of the country whose importance can be measured by the emphasis with which sectional writers and speakers sometimes attack it. It is no mere exaggeration of speech or flattery, therefore, for me to point out that this Chamber of Commerce, by the ideals which it may maintain in the matter of business integrity and scrupulous business methods and in maintenance of law in the conduct of corporations, has great power and corresponding responsibility.

I am very grateful for the hospitable reception which I have had on the North shore of Massachusetts. A vacation which I had planned of more than two months has been whittled down to a little more than one month; but every minute of it I have enjoyed.

The bracing and pure air, the beautiful roads, the fine golf links, the prosperous towns and villages, the intelligent and considerate people, all have contributed to make my stay a delightful one. The beauties of that region are nothing but an expansion and enlargement of the wonderful park system and suburbs of Boston.

I have attempted to keep within the speed limit and before a broad-minded judge I could establish this by satisfactory evidence. But it has not prevented me from motoring into every village and town and countryside of Essex County. I am delighted at the prospect of returning here again next summer, when I hope and pray that no tariff or other bill will shorten my days of leisure.

I am on the eve of beginning a journey 13,000 miles in length, which will enable me to see tens and hundreds of thousands of my fellow citizens, and enable them, I hope, to see me. Occasionally I hear a query, why should I start off on such a trip and what particular good does it do to anybody?

Well, it certainly is not going to be a pleasure trip, although I shall enjoy it. It will involve much hard work and a great deal of mental effort to think of things to say, and to say them simply and clearly so that they can be understood.

It will strain the digestion not only of myself and those who accompany me, but also of the many who extend hospitality along the way; and it will very considerably reduce the appropriation of $25,000 made by Congress for the traveling expenses of the President.

On the other hand, it will certainly give me a very much more accurate impression as to the views of the people in the sections which I visit. It will bring closely to me the needs of particular sections, so far as national legislation and executive action are concerned, and I believe it will make me a wiser man and a better public officer.

Moreover, it will give the people an opportunity to see the man whom they have chosen, for the time being, to act as their chief executive, and who, because of this office, in a sense temporarily typifies nationality. I ought to be able to explain to the people some of the difficulties of government and some of the problems of solution from the standpoint of the executive and the legislator, as distinguished from that of the honest but irresponsible critic.

The personal touch between the people and the man to whom they temporarily delegate power of course conduces to a better understanding between them. Moreover, I ought not to omit to mention as a useful result of my journeying that I am to visit a great many expositions and fairs, and that the curiosity to see the President will certainly increase the box receipts and tend to rescue many commendable enterprises from financial disaster.

This is an innocent, but it has come to be a very useful, function of the presidential office.

The thing that I most object to and look forward to with most fear is the necessity for speaking every day on some subject or other to a listening multitude. It becomes a brain-racking performance before one gets through with a trip of two months.

At first everything the President says is reported in the newspapers. If after a time he repeats himself, as he must do, and the correspondents and reporters exercise the discretion which they ought, and cut the report, a suffering public will thank them.

One of the reasons why I hesitated to fix the time for meeting the Boston Chamber of Commerce on the eve of my departure for the West was because I would have to make a speech here and I needed all the material that I could think of for speeches in the West.

When I explained this to the committee who were good enough to wait upon me to tender your hospitable invitation I was relieved greatly to hear from Mr. Frederick P. Fish, who was one of the committee, the statement that I need give myself no concern in that regard, because commonplace remarks would be entirely appropriate from me here.

Now, whether Mr. Fish meant by this to characterize the intellectual capacity of the speaker, or the intellectual demands of the audience, I am at a loss to say. But if what I say tonight is commonplace, you may know that I am only filling the order which Mr. Fish gave me, and complying with the invitation as I have understood it.

This is the second week of September. We are all ending our vacations and going home. This is the time of the year, rather than the first of the calendar year, when good resolutions ought to be made—and kept, as far as possible. This is the time when, looking forward to the coming again of Congress in December, one must consider the needs of the country so far as they may be relieved by congressional legislation, and attempt to state what that legislation should be.

Your chairman has made some reference to a number of subjects to which the attention of Congress may well be directed. In the first place, there is the monetary situation. While it is probable that the Vreeland Bill passed by the last Congress would aid us in case of another financial crash, it is certain that our banking and monetary system is a patched-up affair which satisfies nobody, and least of all those who are clear-headed and have a knowledge of what a financial system should be.

The matter has been referred by Congress to a monetary commission, which has been studying with much interest and enthusiasm the financial and banking systems of the great Governments of Europe and has embodied and will soon publish in interesting and attractive form the best accounts of the financial systems of the world.

It is quite apparent from the statements of Mr. Vreeland, who is now the head of the committee on banking and currency in the House of Representatives, and from the conversations of Mr. Aldrich, who is the chairman of the monetary commission and of the finance committee of the Senate, that the trend of the minds of the monetary commission is toward some sort of arrangement for a central bank of issue which shall control the reserve and exercise a power to meet and control the casual stringency which from time to time will come in the circulating medium of the country and the world.

Mr. Aldrich states that there are two indispensable requirements in any plan to be adopted involving a central bank of issue. The one is that the control of the monetary system shall be kept free from Wall Street influences, and the other, that it shall not be manipulated for political purposes. These are two principles to which we can all subscribe.

It is quite possible that the report of the commission of a definite conclusion may be delayed beyond the next session of Congress.

Meanwhile, the members of the commission intend to substitute a campaign of education in order to arouse public opinion to the necessity of a change in our monetary and banking systems, and to the advantages that will arise from placing some form of control over the money market and the reserve in the hands of an intelligent body of financiers responsible to the Government.

I am told that Mr. Aldrich will "swing around the circle" in the present fall, and will lecture in many of the cities of the Middle West on the defects and needs of our monetary system. I can not too strongly approve of this proposal. Mr. Aldrich, who is the leader of the Senate, and certainly one of the ablest statesmen in financial matters in either house, has been regarded with deep suspicion by many people, especially in the West.

If, with his clear-cut ideas and simple but effective style of speaking, he makes apparent to the Western people what I believe to be his earnest desire to aid the people and to crown his political career by the preparation and passage of a bill which shall give us a sound and safe monetary and banking system, it would be a long step toward removing the political obstacles to a proper solution of the question.

I do not need to argue with this audience that a change in our monetary and banking systems is necessary. You are too good business men not to know it, and I sincerely hope that the whole force of your association will be exerted to insist upon the adoption of a satisfactory system before the end of this Administration.

It is a subject that the general public has very little conception of, and when they suffer from the radical defects of the system they are utterly unable to tell how and why. We all need education on the subject. We must all unite to mend our roof before the storm and rain shall show us again its leaky and utterly inadequate character.

I am not going to discuss the merits and demerits of the new tariff bill with you. I shall have often to refer to that before my journey is ended and I must save something for other audiences. Suffice it to say that the passage of the bill has removed a disturbing element in business.

Nor shall I dwell at length on the necessity for amendments to the interstate-commerce law, to the anti-trust law, and the organization of the Departments in Washington with a view to promoting greater efficiency and expedition in the settlement of controversies arising under them.

During Mr. Roosevelt's Administration we were all struck with the necessity for reform in business methods, for more scrupulous attention to the conduct of business in accordance with the law, and with the necessity for simplifying the law in such a way as to make it clear to corporate managers what they can do and what they can not do.

We are, I believe, unless all signs fail, on the eve of another great business expansion, and an era of prosperity. Indeed it is already here in many branches of business.

The hum of prosperity and the ecstasy of great profits are likely to dull our interest in these reforms and to lead us back again to the old abuses, unless we insist upon legislation which shall clinch and enforce those standards by positive law.

Nothing revolutionary, nothing disturbing to legitimate business is needed; but we must set the marks clear in the statute by which the lines can be drawn and the proper legitimate paths be laid down upon which all business shall proceed, and must have it understood by means of prompt prosecution and punishment that the law is for all and is to be enforced even against the most powerful.

Then, too, the needs in respect to the conservation of our national resources; the amendment to the public land system; the execution of the pure-food law; and all the rest of the important matters that should demand attention, make the legislative and executive labor of the next three years heavy enough, if our purposes are carried out, to exhaust the energy of the most enthusiastic and hopeful.

Still the world is making progress—our country is making progress. Occasionally one hears a note like that of Governor Johnson, denouncing the East and calling upon the West to organize in a sectional way against the East, because the East is deriving more benefit from the governmental policy than the West, and at the expense of the West.

It is difficult for one to treat such an appeal seriously. Throughout the country there is free trade of the freest character; and due to this the prosperity of the West, especially of the agricultural West, is even more pronounced than that of the East.

Moreover, the East is too close to the Pacific Coast, too close to the Middle West, too close to the Rocky Mountains, because all the people of these western stretches have eastern ancestry and eastern associations and eastern connections, and because they have eastern capital with which their sections have been largely built up, and because they are too much assisted by eastern markets in enhancing the prices which their products bring, to make such an attempt at sectionalism successful.

It is true that at times public questions will be given a local color by what is thought to be a local benefit, as distinguished from the general and the national benefit.

But such attitude is generally temporary, and it takes but a few years of business experience, it takes but a panic or two, to present the most convincing evidence that in this country we are all in the same business boat, and that the prosperity of one section adds to the prosperity another, and the business disaster in one section is only the forerunner of business depression and disaster in another.

I was born and brought up in the Middle West. I have had a New England ancestry and New England associations. Fortune threw me out into the Pacific so that I know something of the feelings of the West coast. Jurisdiction as a judge gave me a somewhat intimate knowledge of Southern feelings and Southern aspirations.

I feel, therefore, as if I could speak with confidence in respect to the whole nation, and as President of the United States may well lift up my voice to protest against any effort, by whomsoever made, to arouse section against section, and Americans against Americans.

Not in the history of the country since the war has the feeling between the North and the South been more cordial and friendly than it is today, and a political attempt to make a cleavage between New England and the East on the one side and the West on the other, will be found to be so utterly hopeless as to confound those who propose it.

And now, my friends and fellow citizens, as I take my departure for the West I feel that I carry from you to every citizen and inhabitant of the United States whom I shall meet, the cordial greetings of New England and the East, your congratulations on the prospective prosperity in the whole country, and an earnest wish that the national Government shall be conducted in such a way as to ensure peace with all the nations of the world and tranquillity and prosperity at home, growing out of the conduct of business on lines of commercial integrity and within the law which forbids the organization and maintenance of monopolies and the systematic suppression of competition.

Things are not perfect; but we have made progress. We have a right to be optimistic and believe that further progress is likely; that conditions are improving and that we may continue to maintain for all citizens of the country that equality of opportunity which it is the highest object of a well-conducted Government to preserve.

22

Labor and the Writ of Injunction

Orchestra Hall, Chicago, Illinois, September 16, 1909

My Fellow Citizens of Chicago:

It is just about a year ago tonight that I made a speech in this hall to some 1,800 members of the railroad labor organizations, in which I attempted to convince them that there was nothing in my decisions as a Circuit Judge in labor injunction cases which ought to make them vote against me for the Presidency. It was a critical time in the campaign. It was a critical question in the campaign, and as I review that whole controversy, there was hardly another speech in my campaign of greater importance to me than that one; and in view of the result of the election I look back upon it now with especial interest. This hall, therefore, suggests one of the subjects upon which I shall speak to you.

You will remember perhaps that the head of the Federation of Labor, who had declared for my opponent, was anxious to carry the whole union labor vote against me, and as the ground for his action was my decisions as a Judge, I was put under the burden which I think no other candidate for the Presidency ever had to bear of explaining and defending in a political contest the decisions which I had made as a Judge upon the Bench. It was assumed by many, who thought themselves familiar with the situation, that I would lose a part of the labor vote which had theretofore been evenly divided between the Republicans and the Democrats. The result showed that this assumption was incorrect and that labor men—union labor as well as non-union labor men—thought for themselves, voted according to their own judgment, and declined to be delivered as a body to one party or the other; and on the whole, I do not think that in that election I suffered materially from the loss of labor votes. In the discussions I asserted that I was as much interested as any one in maintaining the cause of labor, when labor, organized or unorganized, by proper methods sought to better its condition by legislation or otherwise. I said that I expected to recommend to Congress, if I were elected, that interstate railroads be required to adopt any additional devices found useful for the purpose of saving from loss of life or limb employees engaged in the dangerous business of railroading. I also said that I favored the adoption of legislation looking to a proper definition of the cases in which preliminary injunctions might issue without notice and defining the proper procedure in such matters. Now that the election has come and gone, I want to take this opportunity of saying that I have not forgotten my own promises or those of the platform, and I propose in the next session of Congress to recommend the legislation on the subject of injunction which was promised in the Republican platform, and to see whether by such legislation it is not possible to avoid even a few cases of abuses that can be cited against the Federal courts in the exercise of their jurisdiction.

I do not think trades-unionism was greatly aided by the attempt to drag all organized labor into politics, and to induce it to vote one way; but that does not prevent my placing a proper estimate upon the immense good for labor in general which its organization and its efforts to secure higher wages have accomplished.

I know there is an element among employers of labor, and investors of capital which is utterly opposed to the organization of labor. I can not sympathize with this element in the slightest degree. I think it is a wise course for laborers to unite to defend their interests. It is a wise course for them to provide a fund by which, should occasion arise and strikes or lock-outs follow, those who lose their places may be supported pending an adjustment of the difficulties. I think the employer who declines to deal with organized labor and to recognize it as a proper element in the settlement of wage controversies is behind the times. There is not the slightest doubt that if labor had remained unorganized, wages would be very much lower. It is true that in the end they would probably be fixed by the law of supply and demand, but generally before this law manifests itself, there is a period in which labor, if organized and acting together, can compel the employer promptly to recognize the change of conditions, and advance wages to meet the rising market and increase in profits; and on the other hand can delay the too quick impulse of the employer facing a less prosperous future to economize by reducing wages.

There is a higher standard of living among American laborers than in any country in the world, and while there have doubtless been a good many other reasons for this, certainly the effect of the organization of labor has been to maintain a steady and high rate of wages making such a standard of living possible.

Nothing I have said, or shall say, should be construed into an attitude of criticism against, or unfriendliness to those workingmen who for any reason do not join unions. Their right to labor for such wages as they choose to accept is sacred, and any lawless invasion of that right can not be too severely condemned. All advantages of trades-unionism, great as they are, cannot weigh a feather in the scale against the right of any man lawfully seeking employment to work for whom and at what price he will. And I say this with all the emphasis possible even though the fact is that, if I were a workingman, I should probably deem it wise to join a union for the reasons given.

The effect of organized labor upon such abuses as the employment of child labor, as the exposure of laborers to undue risk in dangerous employments, to the continuance of unjust rules of law exempting employers from liability for accidents to laborers, has been direct, immediate and useful, and such reforms in those matters as have taken place would probably be long delayed but for the energetic agitation of the questions by the representatives of organized labor. Of course, when organized labor permits itself to sympathize with violent methods, with breaches of the law, with boycotts and other methods of undue duress, it is not entitled to our sympathy. But it is not to be expected that such organizations shall be perfect, and that they may not at times and in particular cases show defective tendencies that ought to be corrected.

One notable defect which has been pointed out has been in the disposition of the majority of members in labor unions to reduce the compensation of all men engaged in a particular trade to a dead level, and to fail to recognize the difference between the highly skilled and very industrious workman and the one only less skilled and less industrious. I think that there is a movement among trades-unions themselves to correct this levelling tendency, and nothing could strengthen the movement more than the adoption of some plan by which there should remain among union workmen the impetus and motive to be found in the greater reward for greater skill and greater industry.

There is one thing to be said in respect to American trades-unionism that its critics are not generally alive to. In France the trades-unions are intensely socialistic. Indeed, in some of the late difficulties it was plain that there was a strong anarchistic feeling among them and that they opposed all authority of any kind. It is also plain that the tendency toward socialism in England and England's trades-unionism is growing stronger and stronger. I need not point out the deplorable results in this country if trades-unionism became a synonym for socialism. Those who are now in active control, the Federation of Labor and all the great railroad organizations, have set their faces like flint against the propagandism of socialistic principles. They are in favor of the rights of property and of our present institutions modified by such remedial legislation as to put workingmen on equality with their opponents in trade controversies and trade contracts and to stamp out the monopoly and the corporate abuses which are an outgrowth of our present system unaccompanied by proper limitation; and I think all of us who are in favor of the maintenance of our present institutions should recognize this battle which has been carried on by the conservative and influential members of trades-unionism, and willingly give credit to these men as the champions of a cause which should command our sympathy, respect and support.

Our friends of the great unions at times complain of our courts, more perhaps because of the decisions in injunction cases than for anything else. I have already referred to this particular phase of litigation in which they have an interest, but when the subject of courts is mentioned it suggests to me a larger field for complaint and reform in which all citizens are interested and have a right to be heard.

There is no subject upon which I feel so deeply as upon the necessity for reform in the administration of both civil and criminal law. To sum it all up in one phrase, the difficulty in both is undue delay. It is not too much to say that the administration of criminal law in this country is a disgrace to our civilization, and that the prevalence of crime and fraud, which here is greatly in excess of that in the European countries, is due largely to the failure of the law and its administrators to bring criminals to justice. I am sure that this failure is not due to corruption of officials. It is not due to their negligence or laziness, though of course there may be both in some cases; but it is chiefly due to the system against which it is impossible for an earnest prosecutor and an efficient judge to struggle. We inherited our system of criminal prosecutions and the constitutional provisions for the protection of the accused in his trial from England and her laws. We inherited from her the jury trials. All these limitations and the jury system are still maintained in England, but they have not interfered with an effective prosecution of criminals and their punishment. There has not been undue delay in English criminal courts. In this country we have generally altered the relation of the judge to the jury. In England the judge controls the trial, controls the lawyers, keeps them to relevant and proper argument, aids the jury in its consideration of the facts, not by direction but by suggestion, and the lawyers in the conduct of the cases are made to feel that they have an obligation not only to their clients but also to the court and to the public at large not to abuse their offices in such a way as unduly to lengthen the trial and unduly to direct the attention of the court and the jury away from the real facts at issue. In this country there seems to have been on the part of all State legislatures a fear of the judge and not of the jury, and the power which he exercises in an English court has by legislation been reduced from time to time until now, and this is especially true in Western States, he has hardly more power than the moderator in a religious assembly. The tendency of legislation is to throw the reins on the back of the jury and to let them follow their own sweet will, influenced by all the arts of counsel for the defendant in leading them away from the real points at issue, and in awakening their emotions of pity for the defendant in forgetfulness of the wrongs of the prosecuting witness, or it may be of the deceased, and of the rights of society to be protected against crime, and all these defects are emphasized in the delays which occur in the trials—delays made necessary because the trials take so great a time. A murder case in England will be disposed of in a day or two days that here will take three weeks or a month, and no one can say, after an examination of the record in England, that the rights of the defendant have not been preserved and that justice has not been done. It is true that in England they have enlarged the procedure to the point of allowing an appeal from a judgment in a criminal case to a court of appeals, but this appeal is usually taken and allowed only on a few questions easily considered by the court above and promptly decided. Counsel are not permitted to mouse through the record to find errors that in the trial seemed of little account, but that are developed into great injustices in the court of appeal. This is another defect of our procedure. No criminal is content with a judgment of the court below, and well may he not be because the record of reversals is so great as to encourage it in every case and to hang important judgments in appellate proceedings sometimes for years. I don't know when the reforms are to be brought about in this country. Until our people shall become fully aware and in some concrete way be made to suffer from the escape of criminals from just judgment in this country, the system may continue. One of the methods by which it could be remedied in some degree is to give judges more power in the trial of criminal causes and enable them to aid the jury in its consideration of facts and to exercise more control over the arguments that counsel see fit to advance. Judges, and especially judges who are elected, ought not to be mistrusted by the people. A judgeship is a great office and the man who holds it should exercise great power and he ought to be allowed to exercise that in a trial by jury. Then it is undoubtedly true that in England, lawyers in the conduct of their cases feel much more and respect much more their obligations to assist the court in administering justice and restrain themselves from adopting the desperate and extreme methods for which American lawyers are even applauded. The trial here is a game in which the advantage is with the criminal, and if he wins he seems to have the sympathy of a sporting public. Trial by jury, as it has come to us through the Constitution, is the trial by jury under the English law, and under the law the vagaries, the weaknesses, the timidities and the ignorance of juries were to be neutralized by the presence in court of a judge to whom they should look for instruction upon the law and sound advice in respect to the facts, although of course with regard to the facts their ultimate conclusion must be their own, and they were fully at liberty to disregard the judicial suggestion.

But reform in our criminal procedure is not the only reform that we ought to have in our courts. On the civil side of the courts there is undue delay, and this always works for the benefit of the man with the longest purse. The employment of lawyers and the payment of costs all become more expensive as the litigation is extended. It used to be thought that a system by which cases involving small amounts could be carried to the Supreme Court through two or three courts of intermediate appeal was a perfect system, because it gave the poor man the same right to go to the Supreme Court as the rich man. Nothing is further from the truth. What the poor man needs is a prompt decision of his case and by limiting the appeals in cases involving small amounts of money so that there shall be a final decision in the lower court, an opportunity is given to the poor litigant to secure a judgment in time to enjoy it and not after he has exhausted all his resources in litigating to the Supreme Court.

I am a lawyer and admire my profession, but I must admit that we have had too many lawyers in legislating on legal procedure, and they have been prone to think that litigants were made for the purpose of furnishing business to courts and lawyers, and not courts and lawyers for the benefit of the people and litigants. More than this, I am bound to say that in the matter of reducing the cost of litigation, and, indeed, the time of it, Congress and the Federal courts have not set a good example. Probably under the Constitution it is impossible in the Federal courts to unite suits at law and cases in equity in one form of action, as has been done in the codes of the States, but it certainly is possible to introduce a simpler form of procedure both in suits in law and suits in equity. This last form of procedure—that is, equity—has been entirely in the control of the courts and especially the Supreme Court, and yet in years no real reform has taken place in that regard, and the procedure is just about as clumsy, just about as expensive, just about as likely to produce delay as it was thirty or forty years ago. The fact that no reform has been instituted may perhaps be due to the circumstance that our judges have been overloaded with work in the Supreme Court, and thus opportunity has not been seized for this reform. But I conceive that the situation is now ripe for the appointment of a commission by Congress to take up the question of the law's delays in the Federal courts and to report a system which shall not only secure quick and cheap justice to the litigants in the Federal courts but shall offer a model to the legislatures and courts of the States by the use of which they can themselves institute reforms.

I would abolish altogether the system of payment of court officers by fee. The fee system may be properly continued for the reimbursement of the public treasury by litigants specially interested, but the fees ought to be reduced to the lowest point and the motive for increasing the expense of litigation that arises from the payment of the compensation of court officers out of fees should be removed. I do not think that the delays in justice are due to any niggardliness on the part of the public in appropriating money to meet the expenses of administration. The evil lies deeper in the system which I have referred to only in a most summary way.

Of all the questions that are before the American people I regard no one as more important than this, to wit, the improvement of the administration of justice. We must make it so that the poor man will have as nearly as possible an opportunity in litigating as the rich man, and under present conditions, ashamed as we may be of it, this is not the fact.

And now, my friends, I have subjected you to a rather solemn discussion of a rather solemn subject.

I always like to visit Chicago because it is in a sense the center of the country. Much more than Boston is it the hub about which many people and many interests revolve. In making up the personnel of my Cabinet and my administration I have been surprised to find how many admirable men you have in your community, and I must apologize for the drain which I have made upon your resources by calling to Washington and foreign courts at least half a dozen of your most prominent and able citizens. In doing so I had to ask them all to make personal sacrifices in the matter of compensation and to gather their reward from disinterested desire to serve the public and a patriotic willingness to put their abilities at the disposition of the country.

We are entering now upon an era of prosperity which I hope will be long continued. We have just passed a tariff bill which has ended for the time the disturbance of business that always arises from the consideration and agitation over such a bill, and there is nothing now to prevent the application of all the capital and all the forces which have been suspended for the last year and a half or two years by a lack of confidence and a waiting for such settlement, to the expansion of business and the further development of the resources of this country. But this prospect of prosperity must not blind us to the necessity for carrying out certain great reforms advocated by Mr. Roosevelt, recommended in the Republican party platform, which I believe are needed to prevent a return to the abuses of which all men recognize the evil in our previous business methods and the management of our great corporations. I expect to consider these questions more at length at another stage in my journey, as I do also the character of the tariff bill which has been adopted and which has been subjected to much criticism, but tonight I feel that I have wearied you far beyond any claim I have had to your attention.

23

Postal Savings Banks

State Fair Grounds, Milwaukee, Wisconsin, September 17, 1909

Mr. President, Governor, Senators, Ladies and Gentlemen, and Citizens of Wisconsin:

I am only too conscious of my lack of experience and knowledge in the presence of farmers. You have a Governor who is a farmer. You have Senators who are farmers. I think all your business men must be farmers if I can judge by the crowd that greets me here. I must admit that I am a city-bred man, and while the spirit would be willing I am afraid I could not milk a cow. Nevertheless, he must be blind indeed to the interests of his country, he must be lacking indeed in acquaintance with the progress of the world who does not realize what, in the fifty years since that noble patriot, Abraham Lincoln, stood here, has been accomplished in the way of improvement of agriculture and scientific investigation into the methods of breeding and into the methods of treating the soil. But I do not intend to occupy your time in discussing something that you know a great deal better than I do. I want to get on to something that perhaps we are both equally ignorant of, but which it will help us to discuss.

Something was said about a man's being a ruler and a servant of the people. I have had occasion to say a number of times that it is perhaps true that the President of the United States has a great deal of power, but while he is in office the thing that strikes him is the limitations and the difficulties of exercising that power. The real power is in the House of Representatives and in the Senate. But the man who gets the blame for everything is the fellow at the top. Now, parties make platforms. They are said to be, in the language of the cynical, something to get in on but not to stand on. Our party, if I may make a partisan reference when I am here only in a non-partisan capacity—the Republican party agreed that we ought to have an institution, the benefit and virtue of which I wish to discuss this morning, in the shape of postal-savings banks. We heard discussed in the Senate last winter the question of how planks were introduced into a party platform, and when they grew a little burdensome to carry out, it was said that they were put in at three o'clock in the morning when more than half the convention were asleep, and when the minority was awake enough to push them in. I don't mean to say that the question of postal-savings banks binds every one who calls himself a Republican—I don't mean that a plank binds every one who calls himself a Republican—because that is not the kind of people the Americans are. If they do not like a plank in a platform, or if they do not like the platform, they cease to be Republicans, or they are Republicans with an exception, and that indicates a free, enlightened and discriminating people. But I am here to uphold the doctrine of postal-savings banks, because I believe that they will fill in this country a long-felt want.

In the first place I want to describe a little bit what it was proposed to put into the savings-bank law, in order that you may understand something about which we are speaking. It was proposed to make every money-order office in the United States, of which there are 40,000, and such other post offices as the Postmaster General might think fit, postal-savings banks. It was proposed to allow anybody to deposit there a dollar or anything more than a dollar, in multiples of ten cents. It was proposed to limit the amount of the deposit in any one month to $200, and to limit the amount of total deposits to $1,000, and to agree to pay interest at the rate of 2 percent on not more than $500. The money thus accumulated was to be invested by a committee consisting of the Postmaster-General, the Attorney-General and the Secretary of the Treasury, either in the neighboring national bank in the county, or if there was no such bank, in the nearest national bank, or if that was impracticable, in State, county or Federal bonds. They were required to secure in everything but Federal bonds $2^1/_4$ percent annually. Now, our friends the bankers—and they are friends; I am not attacking them. It is not wise to attack bankers either, for really we have a right to be proud of our banking fraternity.—But there are a good many who object to the postal-savings banks on a number of grounds, and I wish to take up those objections.

In the first place it is said that the postal-savings bank is a very paternal institution; that it has a leaning toward State socialism, and that it proposes to take the banking business out of the hands of private persons and put it in those of the Government. Now I am not a paternalist, and I am not a socialist, and I am not in favor of having the Government do anything that private citizens can do as well, or better. We have passed beyond the time of what they call the laisser-faire school which believes that the Government ought to do nothing but run a police force. We do recognize the interference of the government because it has great capital and great resources behind it, and because sometimes it can stand the lack of an immediate return on capital and help out. We did it in our Pacific roads. We have done it in a great many different ways, and this particular postal-savings bank's business is a business which the government is especially fitted to do, and which no system of private banks can do. In the first place they have this great organization of the post office, with skilled employees sprinkled all over this country in every nook and cranny of it. Whether there are many people or few, the post offices have to be maintained. Therefore it will be a most economic means of establishing a system of savings banks merely to add one function to the duty of the postmasters all through this country. It can be done most cheaply. The Government can afford it and nobody else could do it. It is said that we have enough banking in this country and therefore we ought not to put the Government into it. It is said, moreover, that if we did put the Government into it, it would not be very long before the Government would do all the banking, discounting and everything else, and the bankers would be driven out of business. I don't think that that argument amounts to much. It is to say, that the American people have not sense enough to discriminate between what is a right use of the post office and what is a right thing to do with reference to savings banks and the going into the general business of discounting and banking which the government has no business to do. I believe in the discriminating sense of the American people to know the degree to which they ought to go in a good thing and then to know that when they get beyond it, it becomes a bad thing. To say that if the people go into one good thing, they are necessarily going to get into something which is not good, is to question the intelligence and the discrimination of our people, and I don't propose to do it.

Let us see about banking and the amount that the people of the United States have in the way of opportunities to deposit money. In 14 States the deposits of savings banks amount to $3,600,000,000. I won't say that in those States there was a crushing demand for postal-savings banks, although even there they would discharge a certain function, but when you come to consider the other 32 States and territories, the deposits are only $70,000,000. In other words, 98 percent of all the deposits in the savings banks in the country are in 14 States, which tends to show conclusively that in the 32 States the banking facilities—at least the savings-bank facilities—for the deposit of funds to encourage thrift on the part of the people are very inadequate, and it is in those States that we expect, if the postal-savings bank system is put in, that the people will be induced to save more money instead of spending it, or instead of putting it into the sock where it does not do much good until it is withdrawn. Now, in New England in the savings banks there are two citizens to one savings-bank account. In every other part of the United States the savings-bank accounts are one to every 157 people, which tends to show the concentration of savings-bank deposits in the East. Another fact showing the need for such a system is that today in the distant States to which I have referred there are $8,000,000 deposited by men who take out money orders and just leave the money in the money-order office of the post office without drawing any interest at all. They just put it there because they don't know where else to put it, which is an indication that they ought to have some place where they can put it and draw some interest. Our new citizens send abroad every year over $90,000,000, and a very large proportion of that goes into the savings banks abroad. Our new immigrants when they come here are distrustful of the local banks, they are distrustful of the private savings-deposit banks, and what they want is a government guaranty in order to secure to them the certainty that when they want their money, they can get it. They are not so insistent on the rate of interest as they are on the certainty of getting their money back, and if they have the government guaranty that they will get it, they can be counted upon rather to deposit their money than to waste it. The great usefulness of the postal-savings bank is an encouragement of thrift on the part of those who are just wavering in the balance whether they shall save the money or spend it, because they do not know where they can put it safely. It is said that this will interfere with the system of savings banks and other banks. I most urgently deny that, because we only propose to pay 2 percent and every savings bank that you know pays at least three and sometimes three and one-half or four. Therefore, those who put their money in a postal-savings bank at 2 percent are not those who would be likely to put the money in a savings bank at three. Instead of that it will furnish more money to the savings banks, and I will tell you how, and I will tell you this in confidence, because this is the way it is worked in other countries. You stir up a lot of people to begin to save money and put it in at 2 percent and they put it in there because they know they can get the money back. That is the whole idea they have at first, but after they begin to calculate what a low rate 2 percent is they begin to look around; they learn for themselves; they acquire some discrimination, and they understand that in the neighboring bank they can get 3 or 3¹/₂ percent. They acquire more intelligence and more knowledge in respect to the matter and then they begin to estimate the security of the private or State savings bank. Under these conditions this fund, which never would have come at all, will be available for the savings banks as the intelligence of the depositor grows greater and as his willingness to risk a little more in order to get a little more interest becomes more acute. We are not usually backward in adopting new and proper assistance to our people and to the government, but we may look abroad frequently to learn lessons in the matter of finance, and even in the matter of some departments of the Government. I want to read you a list of the countries that have postal-savings banks. Let me first say, in Italy there are $273,000,000 deposited in the postal-savings banks of the country. In Russia $130,000,000; in Great Britain and Ireland $766,000,000; in Canada $47,000,000; in Japan $47,000,000. Now, I want to refer to Canada. Canada has postal-savings banks and what is the result along the border up in the Northwest? You find Americans going over the border and making deposits in those savings banks. Why? Because they have the guarantee of the Canadian Government. Now, it is right that when the Government takes custody of money it should agree to return it. It is upon the agreement to return that the basis of the postal-savings bank may be put. There are postal-savings banks in Austria, Belgium, Japan, France, Hungary, Italy, Holland, Russia, Sweden, Great Britain and Ireland, Bahamas, Canada, India, Ceylon, Straits Settlements, Cape Colony, Tasmania, Western Australia, New Zealand and the Gold Coast, and I may add in the Philippines, because I had something to do with putting them there. In Germany they do not have them, but they have a system of town and provincial banks which fills the measure of the demand.

You know we have issued upward of $700,000,000 of 2 percent bonds of the United States, and we have prided ourselves, and our heads have been a little bit swelled on the theory, that we could float bonds at 2 percent and no other country could. We did float those at par at 2 percent—I don't know but that it was a little more—but we did it by getting the banks into a corner so that they had to have under the law some government security, and so they were obliged to buy those 2 percent bonds. Now they are liable to be on the market. We have to take care of them in some way. We have got to prevent their going down below par because the normal interest rate that a government can get is quite above 2 percent—somewhere between 2 and 3 percent, and if we have the postal-savings banks, if we have a large fund of

$500,000,000 to $600,000,000 or $700,000,000, as we may expect to have in view of what has happened in Great Britain, we can use that fund to put in Government bonds and take care of that issue, which is our child and which after all we ought not to be so proud of, because we fooled the world into thinking that we were getting something at 2 percent and that our credit was worth that, when as a matter of fact we were forcing the banking fraternity into taking them because of certain other advantages which they had to have. It was just a little sharp game which the Government played, and it is necessary that in any legislation which comes along we should take care of that issue of 2 percent before issuing any more bonds at a higher rate.

I observed yesterday in the convention of bankers the proposition was urgently and ably fought. Nevertheless, it seems to me, looking at it from a larger field of view possibly than bankers can have, because we are all subject to the prejudices of our profession—I am a lawyer, and I know I am prejudiced as a lawyer, and I think bankers are likely to be prejudiced as bankers; nevertheless, I believe that the arguments in favor of instituting such a system, backed up by the experience of so many other nations as those I have named to you, justify our going into the business of encouraging our people by something that will be inexpensive to the Government, encouraging our people, those of them who have not the sense of security in private banks, encouraging them to a thrift and furnishing the means by which they shall save on small interest. We are looking forward, I hope, with confidence, to a readjustment of our whole financial and banking system. Certainly it needs it, and it has been suggested that the postal-savings bank might well await that. I am bound to say that I do not see the necessity for uniting them. It seems to me that one system can stand by itself, and if we adopt the postal-savings bank it would be easily worked into a general system of banking because those savings banks will furnish us $500,000,000 or $600,000,000, and that is a very tidy pile to have around for the Government to use legitimately in order to carry on any financial operations.

24

The Tariff

Winona, Minnesota, September 17, 1909

My Fellow Citizens:

As long ago as August 1906, in the Congressional campaign in Maine, I ventured to announce that I was a tariff revisionist and thought that the time had come for readjustment of the schedules. I pointed out that it had been ten years prior to that time that the Dingley Bill had been passed; that great changes had taken place in the conditions surrounding the productions of the farm, the factory, and the mine, and that under the theory of protection in that time the rates imposed in the Dingley Bill in many instances might have become excessive; that is, might have been greater than the difference between the cost of production abroad and the cost of production at home with a sufficient allowance for a reasonable rate of profit to the American producer. I said that the party was divided on the issue, but that in my judgment the opinion of the party was crystallizing and would probably result in the near future in an effort to make such revision. I pointed out the difficulty that there always was in a revision of the tariff, due to the threatened disturbance of industries to be affected and the suspension of business, in a way which made it unwise to have too many revisions. In the summer of 1907 my position on the tariff was challenged, and I then entered into a somewhat fuller discussion of the matter. It was contended by the so-called "standpatters" that rates beyond the necessary measure of protection were not objectionable, because behind the tariff wall competition always reduced the prices, and thus saved the consumer. But I pointed out in that speech what seems to me as true today as it then was, that the danger of excessive rates was in the temptation they created to form monopolies in the protected articles, and thus to take advantage of the excessive rates by increasing the prices, and therefore, and in order to avoid such a danger, it was wise at regular intervals to examine the question of what the effect of the rates had been upon the industries in this country, and whether the conditions with respect to the cost of production here had so changed as to warrant a reduction in the tariff, and to make a lower rate truly protective of the industry.

It will be observed that the object of the revision under such a statement was not to destroy protected industries in this country, but it was to continue to protect them where lower rates offered a sufficient protection to prevent injury by foreign competition. That was the object of the revision as advocated by me, and it was certainly the object of the revision as promised in the Republican platform.

I want to make as clear as I can this proposition, because, in order to determine whether a bill is a compliance with the terms of that platform, it must be understood what the platform means. A free trader is opposed to any protective rate because he thinks that our manufacturers, our farmers, and our miners ought to withstand the competition of foreign manufacturers and miners and farmers, or else go out of business and find something else more profitable to do. Now, certainly the promises of the platform did not contemplate the downward revision of the tariff rates to such a point that any industry theretofore protected should be injured. Hence, those who contend that the promise of the platform was to reduce prices by letting in foreign competition are contending for a free trade, and not for anything that they had the right to infer from the Republican platform.

The Ways and Means Committee of the House, with Mr. Payne at its head, spent a full year in an investigation, assembling evidence in reference to the rates under the tariff, and devoted an immense amount of work to the study of the question where the tariff rates could be reduced and where they ought to be raised with a view to maintaining a reasonably protective rate, under the principles of the platform, for every industry that deserved protection. They found that the determination of the question, what was the actual cost of production and whether an industry in this country could live under a certain rate and withstand threatened competition from abroad, was most difficult. The manufacturers were prone to exaggerate the injury which a reduction in the duty would give and to magnify the amount of duty that was needed; while the importers, on the other hand, who were interested in developing the importation from foreign shores, were quite likely to be equally biased on the other side.

Mr. Payne reported a bill—the Payne tariff bill—which went to the Senate and was amended in the Senate by increasing the duty on some things and decreasing it on others. The difference between the House bill and the Senate bill was very much less than the newspapers represented. It turns out upon examination that the reductions in the Senate were about equal to those in the House, though they differed in character. Now, there is nothing quite so difficult as the discussion of a tariff bill, for the reason that it covers so many different items, and the meaning of the terms and the percentages are very hard to understand. The passage of a new bill, especially where a change in the method of assessing the duties has been followed, presents an opportunity for various modes and calculations of the percentages of increases and decreases that are most misleading and really throw no light at all upon the changes made.

One way of stating what was done is to say what the facts show—that under the Dingley law there were 2,024 items. This included dutiable items only. The Payne law leaves 1,150 of these items unchanged. There are decreases in 654 of the items and increases in 220 of the items. Now, of course, that does not give a full picture, but it does show the proportion of decreases to have been three times those of the increases. Again, the schedules are divided into letters from A to N. The first schedule is that of chemicals, oils, etc. There are 232 items in the Dingley law; of these, 81 were decreased, 22 were increased, leaving 129 unchanged. Under Schedule B—earths, earthenware and glassware—there were 170 items in the Dingley law; 46 were decreased, 12 were increased, and 112 left unchanged. C is the schedule of metals and manufactures. There were 321 items in the Dingley law; 185 were decreased, 30 were increased, and 106 were left unchanged. D is the schedule of wood and manufactures of wood. There were 35 items in the Dingley law; 18 were decreased, 3 were increased, and 14 were left unchanged. There were 38 items in sugar, and of these 2 were decreased and 36 left unchanged. Schedule F covers tobacco and manufactures of tobacco, of which there were 8 items; they were all left unchanged. In the schedule covering agricultural products and provisions there were 187 items in the Dingley law; 14 of them were decreased, 19 were increased, and 154 left unchanged. Schedule H—that of spirits and wines—contained 33 items in the Dingley law; 4 were decreased, 23 increased, and 6 were left unchanged. In cotton manufactures there were 261 items; of these 28 were decreased, 47 increased, and 186 left unchanged. In Schedule J—flax, hemp, and jute—there were 254 items in the Dingley law; 187 were reduced, 4 were increased, and 63 left unchanged. In wool and manufactures thereof, there were 78 items; 3 were decreased, none were increased, and 75 left unchanged. In silk and silk goods there were 78 items; of these, 21 were decreased, 31 were increased, and 26 were left unchanged. In pulp, papers, and books there were 59 items in the Dingley law, and of these 11 were decreased, 9 were increased, and 39 left unchanged. In sundries there were 270 items, and of these 54 were decreased, 20 were increased, and 196 left unchanged. So that the total showed 2,024 items in the Dingley law, of which 654 were decreased, 220 were increased, making 874 changes, and 1,150 left unchanged.

Attempts have been made to show what the real effect of these changes has been by comparing the imports under the various schedules, and assuming that the changes and their importance were in proportion to the importations. Nothing could be more unjust in a protective tariff which also contains

Schedules.	Items in Dingley law.	Changes in Dingley law by Payne law.			Unchanged.
		Decreases.	Increases.	Total changes.	
A. Chemicals, oils, etc.	232	81	22	103	129
B. Earths, earthenware, and glassware	170	46	12	58	112
C. Metals and manufactures of	321	185	30	215	106
D. Wood and manufactures of	35	18	3	21	14
E. Sugar, molasses, and manufactures of	38	2	0	2	36
F. Tobacco and manufactures of	8	0	0	0	8
G. Agricultural products and provisions	187	14	19	33	154
H. Spirits, wines, etc.	33	4	23	27	6
I. Cotton manufactures	261	28	47	75	186
J. Flax, hemp, jute, and manufactures of	254	187	4	191	63
K. Wool and manufactures of	78	3	0	3	75
L. Silk and silk goods	78	21	31	52	26
M. Pulp, papers, and books	59	11	9	20	39
N. Sundries	270	54	20	74	196
Total	2,024	654	220	874	1,150

revenue provisions. Some of the tariff is made for the purpose of increasing the revenue by increasing importations which shall pay duty. Other items in the tariff are made for the purpose of reducing competition, that is, by reducing importations, and, therefore, the question of the importance of a change in rate can not in the slightest degree be determined by the amount of imports that take place. In order to determine the importance of the changes, it is much fairer to take the articles on which the rates of duty have been reduced and those on which the rates of duty have been increased, and then determine from statistics how large a part the articles upon which duties have been reduced play in the consumption of the country, and how large a part those upon which the duties have been increased play in the consumption of the country. Such a table has been prepared by Mr. Payne, than whom there is no one who understands better what the tariff is and who has given more attention to the details of the schedule.

Now, let us take Schedule A—chemicals, oils, and paints. The articles upon which the duty has been decreased are consumed in this country to the extent of $433,000,000. The articles upon which the duty has been increased are consumed in this country to the extent of $11,000,000. Take Schedule B. The articles on which the duty has been decreased enter into the consumption of the country to the amount of $128,000,000, and there has been no increase in duty on such articles. Take Schedule C—metals and their manufactures. The amount to which such articles enter into the consumption of the country is $1,221,000,000, whereas the articles of the same schedule upon which there has been an increase enter into the consumption of the country to the extent of only $37,000,000. Take Schedule D—lumber. The articles in this schedule upon which there has been a decrease enter into the consumption of the country to the extent of $566,000,000, whereas the articles under the same schedule upon which there has been an increase enter into its consumption to the extent of $31,000,000. In tobacco there has been no change. In agricultural products, those in which there has been a reduction of rates enter into the consumption of the country to the extent of $483,000,000; those in which there has been an increase enter into the consumption to the extent of $4,000,000. In the schedule of wines and liquors, the articles upon which there has been an increase, enter into the consumption of the country to the extent of $462,000,000. In cottons there has been a change in the higher-priced cottons and an increase. There has been no increase in the lower-priced cottons, and of the increases the high-priced cottons enter into the consumption of the country to the extent of $41,000,000. Schedule J—flax, hemp, and jute: The articles upon which there has been a decrease enter into the consumption of the country to the extent of $22,000,000, while those upon which there has been an increase enter into the consumption to the extent of $804,000. In Schedule K, as to wool, there has been no change. In Schedule L, as to silk, the duty has been decreased on articles which enter into the consumption of the country to the extent of $8,000,000, and has been increased on articles that enter into the consumption of the country to the extent of $106,000,000. On paper and pulp the duty has been decreased on articles, including print paper, that enter into the consumption of the country to the extent of $67,000,000, and increased on articles that enter into the consumption of the country to the extent of $81,000,000. In sundries, or Schedule N, the duty has been decreased on articles that enter into the consumption of the country to the extent of $1,719,000,000; and increased on articles that enter into the consumption of the country to the extent of $101,000,000.

It will be found that in Schedule A the increases covered only luxuries—perfumeries, pomades, and like articles; Schedule H—wines and liquors—which are certainly luxuries and are made subject to increase in order to increase the revenues, amounting to $462,000,000; and in Schedule L—silks—which are luxuries, certainly, $106,000,000, making a total of the consumption of those articles upon which there was an increase and which were luxuries of $579,000,000, leaving a balance of increase on articles which were not luxuries of value in consumption of only $272,000,000, as against $5,000,000,000, representing the amount of articles entering into the consumption of the country, mostly necessities, upon which there has been a reduction of duties, and to which the 650 decreases applied.

Now, this statement shows as conclusively as possible the fact that there was a substantial downward revision on articles entering into the general consumption of the country which can be termed necessities, for the proportion is $5,000,000,000 representing the consumption of articles to which decreases applied, to less than $300,000,000 of articles of necessity to which the increases applied.

Now, the promise of the Republican platform was not to revise everything downward, and in the speeches which have been taken as interpreting that platform, which I made in the campaign, I did not promise that everything should go downward. What I promised was, that there should be many decreases, and that in some few things increases would be found to be necessary; but that on the whole I conceived that the change of conditions would make the revision necessarily downward—and that, I contend, under the showing which I have made, has been the result of the Payne bill. I did not agree, nor did the Republican party agree, that we would reduce rates to such a point as to reduce prices by the introduction of foreign competition. That

Statement.

Schedule.	Article.	Consumption value.	
		Duties decreased.	Duties increased.
A	Chemicals, oils, and paints	$ 433,099,846	$ 11,105,820
B	Earths, earthenware, and glassware	128,423,732	....
C	Metals and manufactures of	1,221,956,620	37,675,804
D	Wood and manufactures of	566,870,950	31,280,372
E	Sugar, molasses, and manufactures of	300,965,953	....
F	Tobacco and manufactures of (no change of rates)	....	....
G	Agricultural products and provisions	483,430,637	4,380,043
H	Spirits, wines, and other beverages	....	462,001,856
I	Cotton manufactures	....	41,622,024
J	Flax, hemp, jute, and manufactures of	22,127,145	804,445
K	Wool and manufactures of (no production statistics available for articles affected by changes of rates)		
L	Silk and silk goods	7,947,568	106,742,646
M	Pulp, papers, and books	67,628,055	81,486,466
N	Sundries	1,719,428,069	101,656,598
	Total	4,951,878,575	878,756,074

Of the above increases the following are luxuries, being articles strictly of voluntary use:

Schedule A. Chemicals, including perfumeries, pomades, and like articles	$ 11,105,820	
Schedule H. Wines and liquors	462,001,856	
Schedule L. Silks	106,742,646	
Total	579,850,322	

is what the free traders desire. That is what the revenue-tariff reformers desire; but that is not what the Republican platform promised, and it is not what the Republican party wished to bring about. To repeat the statement with which I opened this speech, the proposition of the Republican party was to reduce rates so as to maintain a difference between the cost of production abroad and the cost of production here, insuring a reasonable profit to the manufacturer on all articles produced in this country; and the proposition to reduce rates and prevent their being excessive was to avoid the opportunity for monopoly and the suppression of competition, so that the excessive rates could be taken advantage of to force prices up.

Now, it is said that there was not a reduction in a number of the schedules where there should have been. It is said that there was no reduction in the cotton schedule. There was not. The House and the Senate took evidence and found from cotton manufacturers and from other sources that the rates upon the lower class of cottons were such as to enable them to make a decent profit—but only a decent profit—and they were contented with it; but that the rates on the higher grades of cotton cloth, by reason of court decisions, had been reduced so that they were considerably below those of the cheaper grades of cotton cloth, and that by undervaluations and otherwise the whole cotton schedule had been made unjust and the various items were disproportionate in respect to the varying cloths. Hence, in the Senate a new system was introduced attempting to make the duties more specific rather than *ad valorem,* in order to prevent by judicial decision or otherwise a disproportionate and unequal operation of the schedule. Under this schedule it was contended that there had been a general rise of all the duties on cotton. This was vigorously denied by the experts of the Treasury Department. At last, the Senate in conference consented to a reduction amounting to about 10 percent on all the lower grades of cotton, and this reduced the lower grades of cotton substantially to the same rates as before and increased the higher grades to what they ought to be under the Dingley law and what they were intended to be. Now, I am not going into the question of evidence as to whether the cotton duties were too high and whether the difference between the cost of production abroad and at home, allowing for a reasonable profit to the manufacturer here, is less than the duties which are imposed under the Payne Bill. It was a question of evidence which Congress passed upon, after they heard the statements of cotton manufacturers and such other evidence as they could avail themselves of. I agree that the method of taking evidence and the determination was made in a general way, and that there ought to be other methods of obtaining evidence and reaching a conclusion more satisfactory.

Criticism has also been made of the crockery schedule and the failure to reduce that. The question whether it ought to have been reduced or not was a question of evidence which both committees of Congress took up, and both concluded that the present rates on crockery were such as were needed to maintain the business in this country. I had been informed that the crockery schedule was not high enough, and mentioned that in one of my campaign speeches as a schedule probably where there ought to be some increases. It turned out that the difficulty was rather in undervaluations than in the character of the schedule itself, and so it was not changed. It is entirely possible to collect evidence to attack almost any of the schedules, but one story is good until another is told, and I have heard no reason for sustaining the contention that the crockery schedule is unduly high. So with respect to numerous details—items of no great importance—in which, upon what they regarded as sufficient evidence, the committee advanced rates in order to save a business which was likely to be destroyed.

I have never known a subject that will evoke so much contradictory evidence as the question of tariff rates and the question of cost of production at home and abroad. Take the subject of paper. A committee was appointed by Congress a year before the tariff sittings began, to determine what the difference was between the cost of production in Canada of print paper and the cost of production here, and they reported that they thought that a good bill would be one imposing $2 a ton on paper, rather than $6, the Dingley rate, provided that Canada could be induced to take off the export duties and remove the other obstacles to the importation of spruce wood in this country out of which wood pulp is made. An examination of the evidence satisfied Mr. Payne—I believe it satisfied some of the Republican dissenters—that $2, unless some change was made in the Canadian restrictions upon the exports of wood to this country, was much too low, and that $4 was only a fair measure of the difference between the cost of production here and in Canada. In other words, the $2 found by the special committee in the House was rather an invitation to Canada and the Canadian print-paper people to use their influence with their government to remove the wood restrictions by reducing the duty on print paper against Canadian print-paper mills. It was rather a suggestion of a diplomatic nature than a positive statement of the difference in actual cost of production under existing conditions between Canada and the United States.

There are other subjects which I might take up. The tariff on hides was taken off because it was thought that it was not necessary in view of the high price of cattle thus to protect the man who raised them, and that the duty imposed was likely to throw the control of the sale of hides into the hands of meat packers in Chicago. In order to balance the reduction on hides, however, there was a great reduction in shoes, from 25 to 10 percent; on sole leather, from 20 to 5 percent; on harness, from 45 to 20 percent. So there was a reduction in the duty on coal of 33 1/3 percent. All countervailing duties were removed from oil, naphtha, gasoline, and its refined products. Lumber was reduced from $2 to $1.25; and these all on articles of prime necessity. It is said that there might have been more. But there were many business interests in the South, in Maine, along the border, and especially in the far Northwest, which insisted that it would give great advantage to Canadian lumber if the reduction were made more than 75 cents. Mr. Pinchot, the Chief Forester, thought that it would tend to make better lumber in this country if a duty were retained on it. The lumber interests thought that $2 was none too much, but the reduction was made and the compromise effected. Personally I was in favor of free lumber, because I did not think that if the tariff was taken off there would be much suffering among the lumber interests. But in the controversy the House and the Senate took a middle course, and who can say they were not justified.

With respect to the wool schedule, I agree that it is too high and that it ought to have been reduced, and that it probably represents considerably more than the difference between the cost of production abroad and the cost of production here. The difficulty about the woolen schedule is that there were two contending factions early in the history of Republican tariffs, to wit, woolgrowers and the woolen manufacturers, and that finally, many years ago, they settled on a basis by which wool in the grease should have 11 cents a pound, and by which allowance should be made for the shrinkage of the washed wool in the differential upon woolen manufactures. The percentage of duty was very heavy—quite beyond the difference in the cost of production, which was not then regarded as a necessary or proper limitation upon protective duties.

When it came to the question of reducing the duty at this hearing in this tariff bill on wool, Mr. Payne, in the House, and Mr. Aldrich, in the Senate, although both favored reduction in the schedule, found that in the Republican party the interests of the woolgrowers of the Far West and the interests of the woolen manufacturers in the East and in other States, reflected through their representatives in Congress, were sufficiently strong to defeat any attempt to change the woolen tariff and that, had it been attempted, it would have beaten the bill reported from either committee. I am sorry this is so, and I could wish that it had been otherwise. It is the one important defect in the present Payne tariff bill and in the performance of the promise of the platform to reduce rates to a difference in the cost of production, with reasonable profit to the manufacturer. That it will increase the price of woolen cloth or clothes, I very much doubt. There have been increases by the natural increase in the price of wool the world over as an agricultural product, but this was not due to the tariff, because the tariff was not changed. The increase would therefore have taken place whether the tariff would have been changed or not. The cost of woolen cloths behind the tariff wall, through effect of competition, has been greatly less than the duty, if added to the price, would have made it.

There is a complaint now by the woolen clothiers and by the carded-woolen people of this woolen schedule. They have honored me by asking in circulars sent out by them that certain questions be put to me in respect to it, and asking why I did not veto the bill in view of the fact that the woolen schedule was not made in accord with the platform. I ought to say in respect to this point that all of them in previous tariff bills were strictly in favor of maintaining the woolen schedule as it was. The carded-woolen people are finding that carded wools are losing their sales because they are going out of style. People prefer worsteds. The clothing people who are doing so much circularizing were contented to let the woolen schedule remain as it was until very late in the tariff discussion, long after the bill had passed the House, and, indeed, they did not grow very urgent until the bill had passed the Senate. This was because they found that the price of woolen cloth was going up, and so they desired to secure reduction in the tariff which would enable them to get cheaper material. They themselves are protected by a large duty, and I can not with deference to them ascribe their intense interest only to a deep sympathy with the ultimate consumers, so called. But, as I have already said, I am quite willing to admit that allowing the woolen schedule to remain where it is, is not a compliance with the terms of the platform as I interpret it and as it is generally understood.

On the whole, however, I am bound to say that I think the Payne tariff bill is the best tariff bill that the Republican party ever passed; that in it the party has conceded the necessity for following the changed conditions and reducing tariff rates accordingly. This is a substantial achievement in the direction of lower tariffs and downward revision, and it ought to be accepted as such. Critics of the bill utterly ignore the very tremendous cuts that have been made in the iron schedule, which heretofore has been subject to criticism in all tariff bills. From iron ore, which was cut 75 percent, to all the other items as low as 20 percent, with an average of something like 40 or 50 percent, that schedule has been reduced so that the danger of increasing prices through a monopoly of the business is very much lessened, and that was the chief purpose of revising the tariff downward under Republican protective principles. The severe critics of the bill pass this reduction in the metal schedule with a sneer, and say that the cut did not hurt the iron interests of the country. Well, of course it did not hurt them. It was not expected to hurt them. It was expected only to reduce excessive rates, so that business should still be conducted at a profit, and the very character of the criticism is an indication of the general injustice of the attitude of those who make it, in assuming that it was the promise of the Republican party to hurt the industries of the country by the reductions which they were to make in the tariff, whereas it expressly indicated as plainly as possible in the platform that all of the industries were to be protected against injury by foreign competition, and the promise only went to the reduction of excessive rates beyond what was necessary to protect them.

The high cost of living, of which 50 percent is consumed in food, 25 percent in clothing, and 25 percent in rent and fuel, has not been produced by the tariff, because the tariff has remained the same while the increases have gone on. It is due to the change of conditions the world over. Living has increased everywhere in cost—in countries where there is free trade and in countries where there is protection—and that increase has been chiefly seen in the cost of food products. In other words we have had to pay more for the products of the farm, for meat, for grain, for everything that enters into food. Now, certainly no one will contend that protection has increased the cost of food in this country, when the fact is that we have been the greatest exporters of food products in the world. It is only that the demand has increased beyond the supply, that farm lands have not been opened as rapidly as the population and the demand has increased. I am not saying that the tariff does not increase prices in clothing and in building and in other items that enter into the necessities of life, but what I wish to emphasize is that the recent increases in the cost of living in this country have not been due to the tariff. We have a much higher standard of living in this country than they have abroad and this has been made possible by higher income for the workingman, the farmer, and all classes. Higher wages have been made possible by the encouragement of diversified industries, built up and fostered by the tariff.

Now, the revision downward of the tariff that I have favored will not, I hope, destroy the industries of the country. Certainly it is not intended to. All that it is intended to do, and that is what I wish to repeat, is to put the tariff where it will protect industries here from foreign competition, but will not enable those who will wish to monopolize to raise prices by taking advantage of excessive rates beyond the normal difference in the cost of production.

If the country desires free trade, and the country desires a revenue tariff and wishes the manufacturers all over the country to go out of business, and to have cheaper prices at the expense of the sacrifice of many of our manufacturing interests, then it ought to say so and ought to put the Democratic party in power if it thinks that party can be trusted to carry out any affirmative policy in favor of a revenue tariff. Certainly in the discussions in the Senate there was no great manifestation on the part of our Democratic friends in favor of reducing rates on necessities. They voted to maintain the tariff rates on everything that came from their particular sections. If we are to have free trade, certainly it can not be had through the maintenance of Republican majorities in the Senate and House and a Republican administration.

And now the question arises, what was the duty of a Member of Congress who believed in a downward revision greater than that which has been accomplished, who thought that the wool schedules ought to be reduced, and that perhaps there were other respects in which the bill could be improved? Was it his duty because, in his judgment, it did not fully and completely comply with the promises of the party platform as he interpreted it, and indeed as I had interpreted it, to vote against the bill? I am here to justify those who answer this question in the negative. Mr. Tawney was a downward revisionist like myself. He is a low-tariff man, and has been known to be such in Congress all the time he has been there. He is a prominent Republican, the head of the Appropriations Committee, and when a man votes as I think he ought to vote, and an opportunity such as this presents itself, I am glad to speak in behalf of what he did, not in defense of it, but in support of it.

This is a government by a majority of the people. It is a representative government. People select some 400 members to constitute the lower House and some 92 members to constitute the upper House through their legislatures, and the varying views of a majority of the voters in eighty or ninety millions of people are reduced to one resultant force to take affirmative steps in carrying on a government by a system of parties. Without parties popular government would be absolutely impossible. In a party those who join it, if they would make it effective, must surrender their personal predilections on matters comparatively of less importance in order to accomplish the good which united action on the most important principles at issue secures.

Now, I am not here to criticize those Republican Members and Senators whose views on the subject of the tariff were so strong and intense that they believed it their duty to vote against their party on the tariff bill. It is a question for each man to settle for himself. The question is whether he shall help maintain the party solidarity for accomplishing its chief purposes, or whether the departure from principle in the bill as he regards it is so extreme that he must in conscience abandon the party. All I have to say is, in respect to Mr. Tawney's action, and in respect to my own in signing the bill, that I believed that the interests of the country, the interests of the party, required me to sacrifice the accomplishment of certain things in the revision of the tariff which I had hoped for, in order to maintain party solidarity, which I believe to be much more important than the reduction of rates in one or two schedules of the tariff. Had Mr. Tawney voted against the bill, and had there been others of the House sufficient in number to have defeated the bill, or if I had vetoed the bill because of the absence of a reduction of rates in the wool schedule, when there was a general downward revision, and a substantial one though not a complete one, we should have left the party in a condition of demoralization that would have prevented the accomplishment of purposes and a fulfilment of other promises which we had made just as solemnly as we had entered into that with respect to the tariff. When I could say without hesitation that this is the best tariff bill that the Republican party has ever passed, and therefore the best tariff bill that has been passed at all, I do not feel that I could have reconciled any other course to my conscience than that of signing the bill, and I think Mr. Tawney feels the same way. Of course if I had vetoed the bill I would have received the applause of many Republicans who may be called low-tariff Republicans, and who think deeply on that subject, and of all the Democracy. Our friends the Democrats would have applauded, and then laughed in their sleeve at the condition in which the party would have been left; but, more than this, and waiving considerations of party, where would the country have been had the bill been vetoed, or been lost by a vote? It would have left the question of the revision of the tariff open for further discussion during the next session. It would have suspended the settlement of all our business down to a known basis upon which prosperity could proceed and investments be made, and it would have held up the coming of prosperity to this country certainly for a year and probably longer. These are the reasons why Mr. Tawney voted for the bill. These are the reasons why I signed it.

But there are additional reasons why the bill ought not to have been beaten. It contained provisions of the utmost importance in the interest of this country in dealing with foreign countries and in the supplying of a deficit which under the Dingley bill seemed inevitable. There has been a disposition in some foreign countries to take advantage of greater elasticity in their systems of imposing tariffs and to make regulations to exclude our products and exercise against us undue discrimination. Against these things we have been helpless, because it required an act of Congress to meet the difficulties. It is now proposed, by what is called the maximum and minimum clause, to enable the President to allow to come into operation a maximum or penalizing increase of duties over the normal or minimum duties whenever in his opinion the conduct of the foreign countries has been unduly discriminatory against the United States. It is hoped that very little use may be required of this clause, but its presence in the law and the power conferred upon the Executive, it is thought, will prevent in the future such undue discriminations. Certainly this is most important to our exporters of agricultural products and manufactures.

We have imposed an excise tax upon corporations measured by 1 percent upon the net income of all corporations except fraternal and charitable corporations after exempting $5,000. This, it is thought, will raise an income of

26 to 30 millions of dollars, will supply the deficit which otherwise might arise without it, and will bring under Federal supervision more or less all the corporations of the country. The inquisitorial provisions of the act are mild but effective, and certainly we may look not only for a revenue, but for some most interesting statistics and the means of obtaining supervision over corporate methods that has heretofore not obtained.

Then, we have finally done justice to the Philippines. We have introduced free trade between the Philippines and the United States, and we have limited the amount of sugar and the amount of tobacco and cigars that can be introduced from the Philippines to such a figure as shall greatly profit the Philippines and yet in no way disturb the products of the United States or interfere with those engaged in the tobacco or sugar interests here. These features of the bill were most important, and the question was whether they were to be sacrificed because the bill did not in respect to wool and woolens and in some few other matters meet our expectations. I do not hesitate to repeat that I think it would have been an unwise sacrifice of the business interests of the country, it would have been an unwise sacrifice of the solidarity, efficiency, and promise-performing power of the party, to have projected into the next session another long discussion of the tariff, and to have delayed or probably defeated the legislation needed in the improvement of our interstate commerce regulations, and in making more efficient our anti-trust law and the prosecutions under it. Such legislation is needed to clinch the Roosevelt policies, by which corporations and those in control of them shall be limited to a lawful path and shall be prevented from returning to those abuses which a recurrence of prosperity is too apt to bring about unless definite, positive steps of a legislative character are taken to mark the lines of honest and lawful corporate management.

Now, there is another provision in the new tariff bill that I regard as of the utmost importance. It is a provision which appropriates $75,000 for the President to employ persons to assist him in the execution of the maximum and minimum tariff clause and in the administration of the tariff law. Under that authority I conceive that the President has the right to appoint a board, as I have appointed it, who shall associate with themselves, and have under their control, a number of experts who shall address themselves, first, to the operation of foreign tariffs upon the exports of the United States, and then to the operation of the United States tariff upon imports and exports. There are provisions in the general tariff procedure for the ascertainment of the cost of production of articles abroad and the cost of production of articles here. I intend to direct the board, in the course of these duties and in carrying them out, in order to assist me in the administration of the law, to make what might be called a glossary of the tariff, or a small encyclopedia of the tariff, or something to be compared to the United States Pharmacopoeia with reference to information as to drugs and medicines. I conceive that such a board may very properly, in the course of their duties, take up separately all the items of the tariff, both those on the free list and those which are dutiable, describe what they are, where they are manufactured, what their uses are, the methods of manufacture, the quality of the manufacture, the cost of production abroad and here, and every other fact with respect to each item which would enable the Executive to understand the operation of the tariff, the value of the article, and the amount of duty imposed, and all those details which the student of every tariff law finds it so difficult to discover. I do not intend, unless compelled or directed by Congress, to publish the result of these investigations, but to treat them merely as incidental facts brought out officially from time to time, and as they may be ascertained and put on record in the Department, there to be used when they have all been accumulated and are sufficiently complete to justify executive recommendation based on them. Now I think it is utterly useless, as I think it would be greatly distressing to business, to talk of another revision of the tariff during the present Congress. I should think that it would certainly take the rest of this administration to accumulate the data upon which a new and proper revision of the tariff might be had. By that time the whole Republican party can express itself again in respect to the matter and bring to bear upon its Representatives in Congress that sort of public opinion which shall result in solid party action. I am glad to see that a number of those who thought it their duty to vote against the bill insist that they are still Republicans and intend to carry on their battle in favor of lower duties and a lower revision within the lines of the party. That is their right and, in their view of things, is their duty.

It is vastly better that they should seek action of the party than that they should break off from it and seek to organize another party, which would probably not result in accomplishing anything more than merely defeating our party and inviting in the opposing party, which does not believe, or says that it does not believe, in protection. I think that we ought to give the present bill a chance. After it has been operating for two or three years, we can tell much more accurately than we can today its effect upon the industries of the country and the necessity for any amendment in its provisions.

I have tried to state as strongly as I can, but not more strongly than I think the facts justify, the importance of not disturbing the business interests of this country by an attempt in this Congress or the next to make a new revision; but in the meantime I intend, so far as in me lies, to secure official data upon the operation of the tariff, from which, when a new revision is attempted, exact facts can be secured.

I have appointed a tariff board that has no brief for either side in respect to what the rates shall be. I hope they will make their observations and note their data in their record with exactly the same impartiality and freedom from anxiety as to result with which the Weather Bureau records the action of the elements or any scientific bureau of the Government records the results of its impartial investigations. Certainly the experience in this tariff justifies the statement that no revision should hereafter be attempted in which more satisfactory evidence of an impartial character is not secured.

I am sorry that I am not able to go further into detail with respect to the tariff bill, but I have neither the information nor the time in which to do it. I have simply stated the case as it seemed to Mr. Tawney in his vote and as it seemed to me in my signing the bill.

25

Amendment of Interstate Commerce Law

Des Moines, Iowa, September 20, 1909

Fellow Citizens of Iowa:

I have great pleasure in meeting such a concourse of citizens of one of the most purely agricultural States in the union—one which has enjoyed to the full the prosperity which has come to the man who has invested his money and his labor in the farm for the last decade.

Iowa has come to be a State in which there is great independence of view, and in which the voters exercise intelligent discrimination with reference to candidates and policies that keeps those who are looking for political victories in a constant state of doubt and anxiety.

The last general election was held in November of 1908, and resulted in the success of the Republican party in the national contest. In both chambers of Congress the Republicans have a majority and they have the President. Looking forward to the legislation that ought to be expected from that party, we must refer back to the platform upon which the party was elected. In the extra session recently closed a tariff bill was passed as was promised in the platform. I do not intend to dwell upon the much-disputed question whether that bill complied with the bill promised, for I have considered that at another time and at another place. What I wish to invite your attention to this morning is, with the tariff bill out of the way for the time at least, what there is for the Republican party in Congress under the promises of its platform to do in the coming regular session.

Now, in the first place one of the great issues in the last campaign—one in which I took a deep personal interest because the issue concerned me personally—was the claim that the Republican party was opposed to labor organizations, and had favored the use of the injunction in labor disputes in behalf of the employer, and, therefore, that its candidate should be opposed by all of organized labor and of all other kinds of labor on this account. As you perhaps remember, I had decided a number of the important labor cases in which permanent injunctions were issued, and I was characterized as the "father of labor injunctions." It became necessary for me to go about the country explaining and defending my labor decisions and showing, as I was able to show, that my attitude, while it was in favor of certain punishment of disturbance of the peace and other violations of the law in connection with labor disputes, was that of one favorable to the organization of labor as necessary to enable it to stand upon an equality of resources with capital in the necessary controversies that arise between labor and capital with respect to the fixing of their compensation and arranging the other terms of employment. I discussed this subject at Chicago the other night at length. I do not intend to discuss it here other than to say that I have not forgotten the promise of the platform, and Congress should take up the question of injunctions and labor disputes and should adopt a law embodying the procedure as to issuing of injunctions without notice and framing it in such a way as to prevent such injunctions save in rare and meritorious cases.

More than this, I am prepared to recommend that Congress require the interstate railroads to adopt any other safety device that can be proved as valuable in order to protect the lives and limbs of men engaged in that dangerous employment. While I believe that every man ought to be permitted to work for whom and at what wage he pleases—and I am prepared to go to the extreme limit in defending this right—I am nevertheless one of those who approve the organization of labor and, if I were a workingman, would probably become a member of a trades union if I could gain admission. My attitude on this point is based upon the belief that the organization of labor has secured better terms of employment, higher wages, a safer place to work in, and other advantages which but for the organization and its demands in a form that could not be denied might have been long delayed in coming. The leading men of the labor organizations of this country, many of whom opposed my last election, are greatly to be commended because of the stand that they have taken against the prevalence of socialism in labor unions. They favor the preservation and maintenance of our institutions under the Constitution, which recognizes the right of property as well as the liberty of the individual; and they are entitled to our sympathy in this struggle, which by reason of the socialistic and anarchistic tendencies of European labor organizations, they have much difficulty in maintaining.

But legislation with respect to the laborer is not all the legislation that the Republican party is pledged to. Indeed, when I look forward to the next session and realize how much there is to be considered, I tremble lest the session will not be long enough, and lest it will not be possible to do all that has been promised.

Immediately after Mr. Roosevelt's election in 1904, he wrote a message to Congress in which he recommended to Congress that the interstate commerce law be amended so that the Interstate Commerce Commission, finding a rate to be unreasonable and unduly discriminatory, might change the rate and fix one which should be fair. In other words, his recommendation embodied the fixing of the rates by the Interstate Commerce Commission. The suggestion of the message was followed by the introduction of a bill in the House which in the first regular session of the newly elected Congress was passed by the House as the Hepburn Rate Bill. It went to the Senate and received a good many amendments, and then after a long and acrimonious fight it was passed almost unanimously. The chief feature of the bill was the new authority of the Commission after determining that an existing rate complained of was unreasonable, to say what would be a reasonable rate; in other words, to fix the rate if the rate complained of was unjust. There were many other features to the rate bill, but the one I have given is perhaps the most important. A provision was made for appeal from the action of the Commission to the court, and this was wisely done for, even if no provision was made, the court would still have jurisdiction to consider whether the rate fixed was confiscatory or not. If the act had attempted to prevent such an appeal to the court, it probably would have rendered it invalid under the Constitution. The rate bill has now been in operation some three years and it must be admitted that it has not furnished the relief against unduly discriminatory rates with the expedition and effectiveness which were expected. The Republican platform promised additional legislation in aid of enforcing the interstate commerce law, and I have been engaged in the consideration of what I ought to recommend to Congress in order to comply with that promise. Those who opposed the provision by which appeal from the order of the Commission might be taken to the court did so because they thought such a right to appeal would offer much opportunity to delay the proceedings. An examination of the decisions of the Commission and the resort to the courts by the way of temporary injunctions, fully justifies the conclusion that one of the defects of the present interstate commerce law is the delay entailed by litigation in the court over the correctness of the order of the Commission. The court appeal can not be abolished because it is a constitutional right. Something must be done to reduce its effect by way of delay, so that the decision of the court shall be prompt, final, and effective. It is proposed now by a number of gentlemen of my Cabinet, who have conferred with some members of the Interstate Commerce Commission, to facilitate these appeals from the Commission by the creation of a separate interstate commerce court of five members which shall sit in Washington and which shall be the only court to which petitions to set aside or nullify the orders of the Interstate Commerce Commission can be made; and it is proposed to allow a single judge to make an order staying the proceedings of the Interstate Commerce Commission but sixty days, and thereafter that no injunction shall be allowed against the order of the Commission unless granted by the whole court of five members. I know that objection will be made to the creation of this court. In one of the bills originally introduced such a separate court was provided for, but the provision was defeated. A tariff court has been provided in the new tariff bill to consist of five members whose judgment shall be final on all questions arising under the administration of the tariff. I am strongly inclined to think that a similar court, except that an appeal ought to lie from it to the Supreme Court, will serve the purpose of expedition and the dispatch of business in respect to the orders of the Commission. I know that there is a well-grounded objection to increasing Federal courts and to the provision for the appointment of Federal judges, whose terms and salaries last for life and who become a permanent expenditure of the Government. But there is this to be said, that if the establishment of such a court proves to be a mistake, the demand for judges throughout the country and their increase will furnish an opportunity to use the judges thus appointed for other and general judicial work. The uniformity of decisions, and the promptness of decision, which may be expected from a court whose experience will soon make them experts in the disposition of such cases, would promise to the shipper and railroad litigants quick decision as to their rights.

A second change in the interstate commerce law ought to give to the Commission the power to hear and entertain complaints against unjust classification of merchandise for transportation. The classification of merchandise is just as important in determining the expense of transportation as the fixing of the rates, because rates are fixed according to classes, and if an article is classed in one class this determines the rate at which that article is to be carried. The classification should be as near as possible so that each class includes within it all the various merchandise that can reasonably be carried by the railroad at the same cost and rate. It is perfectly clear that by including articles in the same class which ought to pay different rates, a railroad can commit exactly the same kind of injustice as it would by imposing an exorbitant rate as to any class. Hence, I haven't the slightest hesitation in recommending to Congress that the power of the Commission should be extended to include not only the fixing of rates after complaint, but also the readjustment of classification if it proves on investigating to be unjust.

The Interstate Commerce Commission has found great embarrassment in the proper administration of the law in the fact that it is limited in its action to investigating only those rates which are specifically complained of by a shipper or some other interested person. It has frequently found that in the examination of one rate complained of and the discovery that it is unjust, there are many other rates connected with this rate equally unjust that if it had the power of initiating complaints of itself it could promptly reach and readjust and fix to the benefit of persons who have not seen fit or have not had the courage or money to contest the fairness and correctness of the rates. I am aware that the question was hotly discussed in Congress at the time of the passage of the rate bill, and it was thought wise to limit the power of the Commission to the consideration of rates actually complained of by persons interested. It would now seem from the experience of the Commission that it is the extension of its power so as to institute complaints of its own that is necessary to make its work truly effective. This is the proper method of legislation—to pass the bill and if it does not operate as fully in the direction intended as we had hoped, then amend the bill so as to improve it in that direction. I do not think that until we try this new amendment and see how it works, we ought to put down the bars entirely and give to the Interstate Commerce Commission the absolute power to fix rates in advance and on their own initiative, and without complaint filed and investigation made as is done in some of the States. I think it a great deal better to proceed cautiously in this matter and feel our way to a satisfactory act which shall accomplish the purpose without too drastic or radical action.

Under the interstate commerce law, a new rate or classification is to be filed with the Commission. It is proposed now to authorize the Commission to postpone the date that such new rate or classification is to take effect, provided that within thirty days of the date of the order a complaint be filed that such rate or classification is unreasonable or unjust, or, provided, second, that the commission itself shall institute an inquiry into the reasonableness or justice of such rate or classification. This introduces a somewhat new element into the act by placing the railroad company in the situation when it proposes to make a change in the rate, that it should be prepared to show to the Commission affirmatively that the change to the new rate is justified. I am inclined to think that this is a fair change in the provisions of the law. It gives to the public the same right to have changes which affect them injuriously, investigated before they go into effect as it does changes of rates by the railroad, by appeal to the courts to have the order of the Commission subjected to investigation and hearing. Railroads ought not to be permitted to change rates unless they can give reason for it.

A third amendment to the act should provide that the Commission may by order suspend, modify or annul any changes in the rules or regulations which impose undue burdens on shippers. No doubt ought to be left with respect to the power of the Commission on such a subject, because the rules and regulations of a railway are the means by which injustice may be done to the shipper. There has been a good deal of difficulty encountered by shippers over connecting lines, and the power of the Commission in respect to this has been quite limited. It would seem well to empower the Commission on the application of one carrier, or an individual, or at the instance of the Commission itself, to compel connecting carriers to unite in forming a through route and fix the rate and the apportionment thereof among the carriers. The Commission should also be empowered to prescribe the rules and regulations under which the shippers shall have the privilege to designate the route over which their shipments shall be carried to the destination beyond that of the first carrier.

Another most important amendment of the interstate commerce law— part of which was specifically promised in the platform—is a prohibition against any interstate railroad company acquiring stock in any competing railroad in the future, and a further provision that no railroad engaged in interstate commerce shall after a certain date hold stock in a competing railroad; and the further amendment that after the passage of the amending act, no railroad company engaged in interstate commerce shall issue any additional stock or bonds or other obligations except with the approval of the Commission, based upon a finding by the Commission that the same are issued, first, for purposes authorized by law, and, second, for a price not less than par for stock, and not less than the reasonable market value for bonds, such price being paid either in cash or in property or services, and if in property or services, then at the fair value thereof as determined by the Commission.

By these provisions enforced with reason, and drawn with a view not to be too drastic with railroads in the beginning, we shall gradually abolish that evil which is involved in the union of competing roads by one road's owning the stock of another; and we shall prevent the over-issue of stock and bonds so as to prevent watering, and to keep the railroad efficient for the service for which it was intended. It greatly interferes after a time with the power of the owners to improve a railroad if it is loaded down with securities, the interest upon which it cannot pay because those securities were not represented by actual value put into the railroad; and I think it, therefore, plainly within the power of Congress in dealing with interstate railroad companies that are organized under state corporations to insist that in order to maintain efficient instruments of transportation the watering of stock and bonds on them shall cease.

These suggested amendments to the interstate commerce law will entrust to the Interstate Commerce Commission considerably more power than that tribunal has at present. But we have entered upon a course of regulating railroads, and as the laws which we passed have not been as effective for the purposes as it was hoped, we must continue to introduce amendments to bring about a law which will serve the purpose which we have.

You in Iowa have been perhaps more successful than elsewhere in the country in regulating your railroads. The difficulties of the interstate commerce regulation are, however, very much greater than those in a State, and present much more difficult questions; but as we are now entering upon a period of the greatest prosperity, in which the railroads are sure to share, it seems wise to remedy as promptly as we can the defects in the present regulation in order that we shall not under the influence of prosperity forget to insist that we are not to return to former abuses.

One great trouble with railroad management was the allowance by railroads of illegal and discriminatory rebates. Those have now largely ceased, and that was one of the great accomplishments of Mr. Roosevelt's administration. But the question of rates and their justice still remains. The scope of the authority of the Interstate Commerce Commission has not been wide enough to make the regulation as effective as it ought to be, and to bring under consideration as many of the rates as it should within a reasonable time.

In addition to these amendments to the law which are looking to a rather more drastic regulation of railroad rates than heretofore, another provision should be added by which railroads may be permitted to agree upon traffic rates, and make contracts with respect to rates that shall not be pooling contracts, but shall constitute agreements as to rates—provided always that such agreements shall receive the approval of the Interstate Commerce Commission. In this wise the operation of the anti-trust law against traffic agreements between railroads will be abolished; and against their absolute prohibition would be substituted a requirement that such agreements shall meet the approval of a properly constituted tribunal.

This last section brings me to the question of the anti-trust law. While we have not threshed the whole matter out so as to reach a definite conclusion, I am strongly inclined to the view that the way to make the anti-trust law more effective is to narrow its scope somewhat, so that it shall not include in its prohibition and denunciation as a crime anything but a conspiracy or combination or contract entered into with actual intent to monopolize or suppress competition in interstate trade. At the common law all contracts in restraint of trade, except those which were called reasonable, the courts would decline to enforce and leave the parties in the condition in which they were found. The anti-trust law denounces such contracts when in restraint of interstate trade as criminal—and that whether made with intent to monopolize or to suppress competition or without intent to do either. The theory seemed to be that a contract in restraint of interstate trade tended to a monopoly, and therefore should be denounced because of its tendency, whether there was any actual purpose on the part of the person making it to monopolize or suppress competition or not. This feature of the present anti-trust law has, it seems to me, weakened its force because it has seemed to bring within the condemnation of the law contracts and other arrangements which were actually innocent in their character, and which were not included in those vicious combinations which it was the real intent of the law to suppress. This wider scope of the law, which I would narrow, has been seized upon by those who do not favor the law at all as a ground for ridiculing its provisions and as a means of demonstrating its absurdity. If the crimes denounced in the law were confined to combinations, conspiracies and contracts made with intent to monopolize or partially monopolize interstate trade, or to suppress competition in interstate trade, then the real object of the law would come within its denunciation, and no one could declare its operation to be unreasonable in that it included a lot of innocent contracts or arrangements.

It has been suggested that the law ought to limit its denunciation to those contracts in restraint of trade that are unreasonable. I do not favor any such limitation for the reason that in the common law the reasonable restraint of trade came to have a very different meaning. It was a narrow one, and one which would have but exceptional application. A reasonable restraint of trade was one made ordinarily in the sale of the good will of a business in which the vendor agreed not to go into business within the territory covered by the business, the good will of which he was selling, and this was to enable him to sell what he had acquired and to enable the buyer to maintain in its integrity the good will which he had bought; but if the restraint went beyond the territory covered by the business, it was regarded as an unreasonable restraint of trade and was unenforceable. But the proposal of introducing the word "reasonable" into the act goes much farther than this exceptional case in the common law. It seems to be proposed to leave to the judges to decide what combinations and contracts in restraint of trade ought to be permitted to exist and to be enforced on general grounds of public policy—in other words, to have the court attempt to establish some line between what are called good and bad trusts, as if the suppression of competition in some cases was a good thing and in other cases was bad. I can not agree that any such distinction can properly be made. All combinations to suppress competition, or to maintain a monopoly in whole or in part, of interstate trade, is and should be in violation of the anti-trust law and should be punished as such; and there is no room for the expression "reasonable" or "unreasonable" in this general view of the statute. If the statute were limited to combinations, conspiracies and contracts to restrain trade with the intent to monopolize interstate trade, or with intent to suppress competition therein, it would probably not include within its denunciation a boycott against goods going into interstate trade, because such a boycott is a restraint against interstate trade with the intention to restrain it, but it is not a restraint of interstate trade with intent either to suppress competition or to maintain a monopoly of the goods with respect to which the contract is made. I am entirely opposed to excepting from the operation of any law of general application a class of persons like laborers or workingmen or farmers or ministers or teachers or lawyers. Take the present anti-trust law, therefore, and insert a special exception to the application of that law by providing that it should not apply to the trades unions class and it would be legislation of the most vicious character; but when you make the law apply only to conspiracies seeking to suppress competition or to monopolize the trade, then the labor boycott is probably not included, simply because the statute would not seem wide enough to include it in its scope, and this result is obtained without class legislation at all.

I am in favor of this change because I believe that the ordinary action in equity by injunction in any place where the boycott is operative can accomplish effectively all the purposes that ought to be accomplished in the suppression of such an evil. On the other hand, to employ the anti-trust law for the purpose of suppressing evils growing out of the labor organizations is to take advantage against such unlawful labor organizations of the literal terms of statute which were probably not intended to include that which judicial construction could not avoid including within its words.

It would probably seem wise to establish an accusatory bureau in the Department of Justice to institute prosecutions for violations of the interstate commerce law and of the anti-trust law, while it will be wise to continue the Bureau of Corporations, enlarging its scope somewhat perhaps to maintain the registration of corporations and the investigation into their operation so far as interstate trade is concerned.

It has been found most difficult to separate the administrative from the quasi-judicial functions of the Interstate Commerce Commission, but it is thought that it would be wise to take away from them any responsibility in regard to the investigation of the validity of their orders before the Interstate Commerce Commission court and to leave the maintenance of those orders to the Department of Justice when the appeal comes on to be heard in the court.

The two statutes which must claim the attention of our Congress in its next session are the interstate commerce law and the anti-trust law, and I have outlined in a tentative way what I am inclined to recommend to Congress as proper amendments. I do so for the purpose of promoting public discussion of them in order that when Congress shall meet the subjects shall not be entirely new and arguments pro and con shall not be lacking. I believe it will facilitate consideration of matters in Congress itself.

Another series of questions for Congress is with reference to the conservation of resources. These I shall not discuss now, but shall do so later in my journey. As I look forward to the coming session of Congress, it seems to me that the work to be done will involve close attention and much discussion, which I hope will be temperate, entered into with a view of reaching a clear and satisfactory conclusion.

The monetary commission will probably report so that its final conclusion may be considered at the end of the coming session or at the beginning of the next. In any event, as we look forward to the work which this Congress has to do, we must be conscious that the measures I have proposed will consume all the time there is.

All this is in the line of performing the promises of the Republican platform, and we can certainly be discharging no higher or more sacred duty. If by the legislation we shall have defined with exactness the proper course for railroads to pursue and also the proper course for great industrial corporations to pursue and make clear the path of lawfulness, we shall have vindicated the good sense of the people in placing the Republican party in power.

26

Corporation and Income Taxes

Auditorium, Denver, Colorado, September 21, 1909

Fellow Citizens of Colorado:

It gives me great pleasure again to visit the Centennial State, and to find here, as elsewhere, the signs of a coming period of prosperity which promises to be exceptional in the history of the country.

I have undertaken a trip of 13,000 miles, with a view to getting a somewhat more accurate and reliable impression of the needs of the country, and with the view to coming into personal touch with the people of the country, and especially in those States so far distant from the seat of government that their people are apt to suppose that their interests are forgotten in the conduct of the Government. It certainly serves to bring the Chief Magistrate into closer union with the eighty millions of people of this country, for he can at reasonably short intervals come into contact with those to whom he is responsible for the proper discharge of his duties during the temporary delegation of power with which they have honored him. The great difficulty and burden of such a trip upon the one making it is the indispensable accompaniment of speeches along the way. It may also be hard on the people to have to hear the speeches, but in a country where the people rule, discussion is necessary, and if the Chief Executive in going about among the people does not discuss something, he will seem to be in the position of wishing to avoid consideration of the interests of the public, or to be afraid of bringing to their attention and rendering account to them of what the Government has done or intends to do. For that reason I have attempted on this trip, at various centers of population of importance, to take up some topic of immediate interest, and explain my views upon it, and if it is a matter already acted upon, to show the wisdom of the action if I can, or if it is to be acted upon, outline what I deem to be the proper course to be taken. In the pursuit of this plan I have selected tonight for consideration and discussion the corporation tax which was embodied in the tariff bill recently passed, and the income tax proposition which at the same session of Congress, and really as a part of the tariff bill, though formally included in a joint resolution, was submitted to the States to amend the Constitution of the United States by giving to the Congress power to levy an income tax generally, without regard to the apportionment of the tax among the States according to population.

The necessity for the revision of the tariff arose not only because the rates in a number of the schedules had become excessive and were quite beyond the measure of the tariff set by the Republican platform, to wit, the difference between the cost of production of the article at home and that abroad, together with a reasonable allowance for profit to the American manufacturer, but also because within the last year or two the tariff had ceased to produce enough revenue in connection with the internal revenue law, to pay the expenses of the government.

There are two ways of meeting the difficulty which arises when your expenditures exceed your receipts; one is to reduce your expenditures, and the other is to increase your receipts. It is the proposal of the Administration and the Government to take both courses in this regard, and I have no doubt that the appropriations for that coming year will show a very considerable reduction in expenditures, perhaps reaching $40,000,000 or $50,000,000. But even this is not enough to make up for the probable deficit under the old tariff law, or under the tariff law as it has passed, unless accompanied by some additional method of taxation.

It was first proposed, and I recommended it in my Inaugural Address, that the central government impose a tax upon inheritances—a graduated inheritance tax; that is, a tax, the percentage of which increased as the inheritance was greater, in a certain proportion; but this was seriously objected to by many of the States, some of whose legislatures passed protests against it, on the ground that that was a field of taxation which the States had preempted, and in respect to which it would be rather unfair to impose a double burden. I have no disposition to quarrel with that conclusion, although I think a good deal might have been said in favor of the Federal inheritance tax because the truth is that even although the State and Federal Governments imposed the inheritance tax at the rate proposed, it would not have been particularly heavy. Still with the inheritance tax foreclosed, the question then arose as to what tax should be imposed in order to make up the deficit. This question arose in the Senate, for the inheritance tax had passed the House, and had been stricken out by the Finance Committee of the Senate. A part of the Republicans and all of the Democrats of the Senate united in pressing for consideration a general income tax on individuals throughout the United States. It left an exemption of those whose income did not exceed $5,000, but upon the rest it imposed a general income tax of 2 percent. It also imposed a tax under the former income tax upon inheritances, and it was as inquisitorial as possible in subjecting the business of every individual in the community to investigation, and permitted the examination of his books and all private evidences of what his business consisted of, and what his income was; this investigation to be carried on by the collectors and deputy collectors of internal revenue. The law was as near as it could be made that income tax law which had once been considered by the Supreme Court some ten years ago, and which was held to be unconstitutional by a vote of five to four. It was conceded that the tax would probably raise $150,000,000 to $200,000,000, which was far in excess of the needs of the Government if the tariff bill was to retain its general form, as proposed, and so to produce revenues which should be reasonably expected from it. Our friends the Democrats favored the income tax with a view to substituting it for the tariff as an income-producing measure, thus minimizing the office of the tariff in protecting the industries of this country. In other words, the passage of the income tax bill would have lent support probably to the proposition to have a tariff for revenue only, and would have interfered with the protective policy to which the Republican party is pledged.

One further objection to the income tax amendment was that it had been declared to be unconstitutional by the Supreme Court, and to invoke a second decision upon that issue was to question the uniformity of the decisions of the Supreme Court and to drag the Court into a political discussion which, whatever its decision, could not make for its standing as an impartial tribunal before the people. It indicated a diversity of view between the Congress and the Court—two coordinate branches—with reference to the constitutionality of the law which it seemed unwise to perpetuate in a formal statute. But the income tax amendment seemed quite likely to pass by the vote of all the Democrats and a sufficient number of Republicans. Therefore those who were opposed to the income tax amendment looked about to see if a compromise could not be proposed less objectionable than the income tax amendment, which would satisfy enough Republicans who were advised to favor the income tax amendment to prevent the passage of that amendment, and such a compromise was found in a proposal to pass the present corporation tax, and also the joint resolution already referred to, proposing to the States an amendment authorizing the General Government to impose an income tax without apportioning it as a direct tax according to the population of the States. When Congress assembled, the Ways and Means Committee of the House had adopted a bill in which they made up the proper deficit by an inheritance tax and also by a tax upon tea and coffee. There were serious objections to the tax on tea and coffee on the ground that it increased the expenses of living, especially among those least able to bear such expense, and therefore the Ways and Means Committee was induced to omit the coffee and tea tax. And then the question arose, what should be substituted for that tax in the bill?

In my Letter of Acceptance of the Republican nomination for the Presidency, I said I thought that an income tax could be devised which could conform to the Constitution of the United States, and therefore that the income tax amendment was not necessary, and when this situation arose which I have described, I directed the Attorney-General to prepare a law which should impose what in effect would be an income tax and still conform to the Constitution. The Attorney-General did so, and I recommended the imposition of that tax to the Committee on Ways and Means. After some deliberation, the committee concluded that even without the coffee and tea tax the income produced would be sufficient, by means of the inheritance tax, to make an additional form of taxation unnecessary. So the matter went to the Senate, where the situation became changed, as I have described it, and the question arose whether we could find some substitute for a general income tax that would satisfy the majority of that body and prevent the passage of a general income tax held by the Supreme Court to be unconstitutional. Accordingly a compromise was reached by which the present corporation tax was passed, and the amendment to the Constitution proposed.

For the sake of clearness, I may say that the Constitution does not forbid the levying of an income tax by the Central Government. The section of the Constitution involved in general terms forbids the levy of a direct tax by the Central Government unless such direct tax is apportioned among the States according to their population. The Supreme Court, in the last decision referred to, held that the income tax was a direct tax, and if levied at all by the Central Government must be apportioned according to the population of the States. This made the imposition of such a tax utterly impracticable, and so construed in effect forbade a general income tax at all. But there are decisions of the Supreme Court authorizing an excise tax to be levied on business corporations and to be measured by the gross income or the net income of the business; and therefore it seemed to the Attorney-General, as it has to a great many excellent lawyers, entirely within the decision of the Supreme Court as constitutional to provide that all corporations engaged in a business for profit should pay to the Central Government an excise tax equal to one percent of their net earnings. At first it was thought that two percent would produce about $25,000,000. Subsequent investigation seemed to show that this was a very decided underestimate, and that one percent would produce that amount, and that that amount would be sufficient to meet the probable difference between the net receipts from the internal revenue and tariff bill and the expenditures of the Government. The provisions for the corporation tax in the bill exempt all corporations whose net income does not exceed $5,000. It is, therefore, in effect an income tax; that is it taxes earnings actually made. It is a tax upon success and not failure.

Complaint is made that it is a discriminating tax in that it taxes business conducted under a corporate form, whereas when the business is conducted by a partnership the business escapes taxation altogether. The justification for the distinction arises from the advantages which the business enjoys under a corporate form, first in that the individuals who really own the business by being the share owners of the corporation have only a limited liability and are not bound to meet the debts of the corporation beyond their stock investment, or in some States more than 100 percent beyond their stock investment; and, on the other hand, the advantage of a permanent establishment in the business, because no matter whether the present owners and managers die or not, the business continues in its corporate form without a settlement thereof in the administration of the estate of the deceased owners.

Again, objection is made that the tax is really a tax upon the dividends of the corporation, and that in the stock of the corporation may be interested a great many people having but little property—widows, orphans and others. I am not disposed to deny that theoretically it would be better to impose a higher rate of taxation upon those having large fortunes than upon those having only a competence. As I shall elaborate farther on, I am very much opposed to exempting incomes above the actual living wage, because I think everyone in the Government ought to pay something toward its sustenance, because everyone derives benefit from it, and while an increase in the percentage of the tax, as the fortune of the individual taxed increases, is fair, it is fair because the burden of the taxation at the same rate is heavier upon a man with a small income than upon a man with a large income or fortune.

Still it is not practical with such a tax as the corporation tax, where you tax the sources of the income before it reaches the individual who is to pay the tax, to impose a graduated tax, and the tax upon the net earnings of the corporation of one percent or two percent is so small that small holders of the shares will feel the burden to be very light. In all probability it will hardly affect their dividends at all, because most corporations do not declare all their earnings in dividends, and will simply take the tax out of the surplus.

We have had very little experience with income taxes in this country, but those we have had have shown the inquisitorial feature of the tax to be most harassing; that is, the power given to collectors of internal revenue and deputy collectors to look into a man's private affairs and to compel him to produce his private papers in order that his actual income may be ascertained. Moreover, the most objectionable feature of the tax is the premium upon perjury which it offers to those who were willing to conceal their income—a matter not at all difficult to do—and who thus subject to a much heavier proportionate burden, those who are conscientious in making their returns and who pay the tax as the law intended. So great was this evil in the levy of an income tax in England that when that tax was imposed directly upon individuals, as was proposed here in the so-called income tax amendment bill, it was found that the proceeds of the tax at 10 percent were less than the proceeds of an income tax of 5 percent imposed as our corporation tax is, not upon the individuals directly but upon the income before it came into their hands. This is a practical argument in favor of the corporation income tax as against an individual income tax that is altogether unanswerable.

In England, after a hundred years of experience, the income tax is levied in only exceptional instances on the individual directly. It is first levied on the declared dividends of corporations; secondly, on rents before they leave the hands of the tenants, and, finally, on the individual with respect to matters that are not covered by rents and corporate investments.

Another distinction which is made in the English law, and which commends itself to everyone with a sense of justice, is that the income tax on passive and permanent investments like the stocks and bonds in a corporation, should be higher than on earned incomes, that is, incomes earned by the services of the individual as salary, or as a professional income. Earned incomes thus described are really the proceeds of an application of the capital of the individual which is being consumed and will be entirely used up at the end of his professional life of twenty or thirty years, whereas the income from corporate and business investments will continue permanently without regard to whether the owner lives or dies, and will pass on by succession of law undiminished and without reducing the capital. This distinction justifies making a difference between a tax upon the income of corporations and that of individuals where they earn their income by services, either by making the rate less or by not taxing the earned incomes at all. The latter is the effect of the corporation tax.

Another criticism of the corporation tax in the present bill is that only shares of stock in corporate enterprises are thus taxed, and that those who own bonds secured by mortgage upon the entire property or plant of the corporation, do not pay any tax at all. This is true, and the defect was fully recognized by those who drafted the corporation tax. They would have been glad if possible to impose a tax upon the bondholders who are only less interested in the earnings and success of the corporations than are stockholders; but the difficulty of including them and of collecting from the corporation before the payment of interest on the bonds, an income tax proportioned to a percentage of the interest to be paid on the bonds, was that Congress could not authorize a corporation to recoup itself in the payment of such a tax from the interest to be paid, because thus to impose a tax on the bondholder proportioned to the interest he received would be in violation of the Constitution as interpreted by the Supreme Court, as an income tax not apportioned among the States. Now, if the proposed amendment to the Constitution authorizing the imposition of an income tax without apportioning it among the States according to population passes, it will be possible to add to our corporation tax the feature of imposing a tax on the bonded interest in that corporation by a percentage tax upon the interest to be paid, thus reducing the amount of interest which the corporation would pay to the bondholder to the extent of the tax collected. This would make the corporation tax a more beneficial measure, and one reaching interests that ought to be reached, because under modern systems of financing corporations, the bondholders and the stockholders are all of them in a sense joint investors and a corporation income tax ought to include them all. Under the conditions that existed with reference to the Constitution it seems to me clear that the corporation tax is an equitable burden—one reaching active business not too heavy to retard it, but enough to collect a substantial revenue from those who are successful in business. It is a tax easily collected—one that no corporation can escape—one in which perjury can not play any important part at all in an effort to escape it.

Another feature of it is that incidentally it will give the Federal Government an opportunity to secure most valuable information in respect to the conduct of corporations, and their actual financial condition which they are required to show in general terms in a public return. In addition, the law provides the means under proper limitations of investigating fully and in detail their course of business. This is to be done only after the Commissioner of Internal Revenue shall have ascertained from evidence that their returns required by law are not correct. Then the evidence which he secures by his investigations of books and papers and examination of witnesses is not to be made public but is to be held in the secret archives of the Government until the President shall deem it of public interest and according to justice to make the facts known. Up to this time we have no adequate statistics concerning our corporations. Even the stockholders, whatever their right may be to know the course of business of corporations, are generally in a state of complete ignorance, and any instrumentality by which the corporation shall be compelled to disclose with accuracy a general statement of their condition certainly makes for the public good. Indirectly it would help very much in another revision of the tariff, whenever that shall come, because corporations engaged in business said to be affected by the tariff will have upon record in Washington their exact financial condition from year to year in the matter of their income, their expenditures and their debts.

Having said this much with respect to the corporation tax as it is, I want to say a few words in favor of the passage of the income tax amendment as proposed by Congress to the States. Assuming the constitutional authority to have been given, I am opposed to a general individual income tax law except in times of great national stress. I am opposed to it because of the difficulty already alluded to, that it puts such a premium on perjury as to have led other governments to abandon that method of levying an income tax and of imposing the tax wherever possible on the sources of income in the hands of those who are not ultimately to pay it. The instance I have already given of an increase of 100 percent in the proceeds of the tax when changed from a personal tax to one upon the sources of the income, like our corporation tax, is a most forceful argument in favor of the proposition— that the inquisitorial feature of an income tax levied directly upon the person, together with the inevitable opportunities for escape from the tax by use of perjury, make it desirable if possible to avoid such a direct method of levying an income tax.

But I am most strongly in favor of the adoption by the States of the amendment authorizing Congress to impose an income tax without apportioning it among the States according to population; and I am strongly in favor of this because in times of great stress, if war or some other calamity were to visit this country and we should need to strain our resources, the income tax would be one of the essential instruments by which we could collect a large amount of money to enable us to meet the exigency. It has been so in the past, for during the Civil War it was understood that the levy of an income tax without apportionment was constitutional, and such a tax was levied and was collected. And I consider it in the Constitution, as at present construed, an elemental weakness on the part of the Central Government not to be able in times of emergency to levy such a tax.

Of course, it will be said by those who are opposed to the income tax that there will be a disposition to impose a direct income tax merely as a means of collecting ordinary income taxes in normal times and that no distinction can be made in the Constitution by which the power to levy such a tax can be limited to times of emergency, because it is impossible to describe what the emergency should be. I agree with that, and I agree that there is a probability that at times the desire to tax accumulated wealth will lead to the movement in favor of a direct income tax, but I am also confident that its inquisitorial character, and the fact that in time the opportunity for perjury will show it to be so ineffective in reaching the persons whom it is sought to reach by a proportionate burden, that it will be wise to adopt the course taken in England and other countries having great experience with such a tax, and to follow the course of our corporation tax rather than by direct personal imposition, except in great emergencies.

If the income tax amendment passes, as I hope it may, we can then enlarge the corporation tax so as to include a proper burden on the bondholders in corporations as well as upon the shareholders; and this will make this instrument of taxation even more equitable than it now is.

Those who favor a directly personal income tax to use it for the purpose of permanently restraining great wealth will probably find it ineffective for the reasons given. I have already considered in a speech which I made at Columbus in 1907 how our great fortunes could be divided without drastic confiscatory methods. It seems to me now, as it did then, that the proper authority to reduce the size of fortune is the State rather than the Central Government. Let the State pass laws of inheritance which shall require the division of great fortunes between the children of the decedents, and shall not permit a multi-millionaire to leave his fortune in trust so as to keep it in a mass; make much more drastic the rule against perpetuities which obtains at common law; and then impose a heavy and graduated inheritance tax, which shall enable the State to share largely in the proceeds of such large accumulations of wealth that could hardly have been brought about save through its protection and its aid. In this way, gradually but effectively, the concentration of wealth in one hand or a few hands will be neutralized and the danger to the Republic that has been anticipated by a continuation through generations of such accumulating fortunes, will be obviated. The use of the income tax itself for this purpose will, I think, never be very successful because of the defect already indicated—the difficulty of finding the income upon which to impose the tax and the opportunity that perjury will offer to escape it. An inheritance tax can not be thus escaped because when a man dies his property must come before some court for consideration and adjudication with a view to its legal transmission, and therefore those who are to succeed, however reluctant, must always make a showing of just what the deceased left in order that they may acquire valid title to the succession.

It seems, therefore, that the present Congress has taken the wisest course in adopting as much of the feature of an income tax as conforms to the Constitution, and by recommending an amendment to the Constitution which shall enable us to round out and perfect this corporation tax so as to make it more equitable, and so as to make it an instrument of supervision of corporate wealth by Federal authority. I doubt not that the information thus obtained may be made a basis for further legislation of a regulative character, applicable only to those corporations whose business is so largely of an interstate character as to justify greater restrictions and more direct supervision.

27

A Soft Answer Turneth away Wrath, but Grievous Words Stir up Anger

Mormon Tabernacle, Salt Lake City, Utah, Sunday, September 26, 1909

Mr. Chairman, Ladies and Gentlemen:

I thank you from the bottom of my heart for this expression of welcome and good will. I have been oppressed since I have come into this magnificent structure with the thought that you had gathered here in part to hear me, and that I have nothing to address to you worthy of such a magnificent presence. I am told that my distinguished predecessor, under the inspiration of an audience like this, delivered an address in the nature of a sermon upward of two hours in length. Now, he had the capacity; he had the spirit; and he had the mission to make such a preachment, of moral force and inspiration. He knew how to appeal to the best that is in a man and a woman, and arouse them to uplift themselves to higher standards and higher ideals. But it has not been given to me to exercise that great influence which was his and which shone forth from him as he stood before men upon a platform. Yet I have felt that on this Sunday morning it was necessary for me to make such effort as I could to follow him in something that may sound a bit like a sermon. And as sermons are begun with the quotation of a text, having more or less relation to what follows it, I am going to give you the text from Proverbs: "A soft answer turneth away wrath, but grievous words stir up anger."

It is a text that has enforced itself upon my mind during the last ten years with especial emphasis, because I have come into contact with Oriental peoples and with those descended from the Latin races of Europe, and I have had a chance to compare their views of life and their methods of speech, and their social conventions and amenities with those of the Anglo Saxon race. We Anglo Saxons are, we admit, a great race. We have accomplished wonders in hammering out against odds that seemed insurmountable the principles of civil liberty and popular government and making them practical and showing to the world their benefits. But in so doing, and in the course of our life, it seems to me we have ignored some things that our fellows of Southern climes have studied and made much of; and those are the forms of speech and the method of every-day treatment between themselves and others. An Oriental will tell you in all the various beautiful forms, of his anxiety for your health, his respect for your character, his almost love of you and your family, and he will put you in a good humor with him and with the world, and he will not expect exactly that you take him literally but he will hope that you will understand that he has good will toward you, as you have toward him. Now that, to our Anglo Saxon nature, seems at first hypocritical, when probably you think, and perhaps rightly, that he does not care much about you at any rate, but he understands and hopes that you understand that what he means to do is to make life more agreeable to you and life more agreeable to him, to lubricate, so to speak, the wheels of society, and to make things move more smoothly without jarring and jolting the nerves of either side. At first that seems superficial to us, who prefer "No" and "Yes," and abrupt methods and the communication in the shortest and curtest sentences. But, my friends, we have much to learn from people of that kind, of courtesy and politeness.

The truth is that a man's life in his family, with his wife, with his children, with his mother, with his neighbors, is not made up of grandstand plays and defiance of the elements and all that sort of thing. It is made up of a series of little acts, and those little acts and little self-restraints are what go to make up the man's character. I agree that there are men, and many of them, I hope, who are a great deal better than they seem to be in their families and to their wives and to their children and to their neighbors, and that when exigencies arise they do betray and show forth elements of strength of character that ought to commend them to their fellow citizens and their families. But it does seem as if they were depriving their families and their neighbors of something in their not living up to that standard all the time in little things as well as in big things; and the truth is that if we yield to negligence in the little things, if we yield to the momentary desire to be lazy and not attentive, and not courteous to everyone, so as to make everyone feel as comfortable as possible during the day, we are going to cut down that higher character that we assume to have under greater exigencies when we are showing forth its strength. And so I say that our friends of the Southern climes and our Oriental friends have touched a point in philosophy, the philosophy of life, that we may well learn from them, and introduce into our lives more courtesy and more politeness—more real, genuine desire to make everybody happy by the little things of life, which after all constitute nearly all there is in life.

I don't for a moment decry the necessity at times for speaking out and speaking out with all the emphasis possible, but what I am urging upon you, and what I have seen in other countries with the advantage of having had an opportunity to see both civilizations, is the added happiness that comes to the whole human race when each member of it in a small but effective way tries to make each other member whom he happens to meet happy for the moment, for life is made up of moments and that contributes to the happiness of all.

Now, another corollary from the text which I would like to draw, is that we ought to ascribe to our neighbors and to those with whom we come in contact, or with respect to whose action we have to express an opinion—we ought to ascribe as high motives as we can. We ought to avoid this acrimonious discussion, that consigns everybody who is opposed to our view to perdition, and to having the most corrupt motives, and that ascribes to those who stand with us only the purest. Life is too valuable to waste in anger and hatred, and the charging and denunciation of our fellowmen when they don't deserve it.

Now, there are to me some things as full of humor as possible. Just within the recent three or four months we have had an illustration. You know something about the pure-food law which has been passed for the purpose of saving the public from food that will injure the health, or from deceiving the public by giving to it in a form that does deceive something for consumption as food. Well, there has arisen in this reform a discussion over—what? You don't know what it is, and I don't know what it is, but for lack of more definite information we will call it benzoate of soda. Now that question has been submitted to experts. Some experts have said that it was deleterious when used in connection with food, and other experts have said that it was harmless, but if you read the discussions you will think that benzoate of soda is a moral line and that any who take their place on one side of it are doomed to hopeless corruption and those on the other side are carrying on a cause of the highest morality. I don't mean to say that the pure-food law is not one of the most important laws on the Federal statute books—and it ought to be. But what I do mean to say is that in its enforcement and in viewing its construction, we must assume that where men differ they differ honestly unless a corrupt motive can be shown, and that while it may be necessary or useful for the public press to encourage the idea that somebody is being moved by corrupt motives, in order to make the headlines a little more salacious, and attractive, and increase the circulation of the paper, it is not necessary for the happiness of the people that it be thought that that question presents a great moral issue which is going to divide men between the bad and the good. We will reach a proper solution some time. It will probably be found, when the differences are examined closely, that those who oppose each other do not stand so far apart.

Another subject that is making a great deal of trouble is the question of what is whiskey, and I have that subject on my hands now. I get letter after letter indicating that if I decide that whiskey is one thing, the whole pure-food law might just as well be abolished, and that I will yield to an element in the community that ought to be condemned and that ought to have no right to live here anyhow. It puts a man in rather an embarrassing situation when the question is really one of fact and law, mixed together, largely one of fact, and one in which I say in passing I have no expert knowledge.

The truth is, my friends, this matter of hatred and resentment which accompanies the attributing of a bad motive to those who differ with you is a waste of nervous strength, of time, of worry, without accomplishing one single good thing. I don't know how it has been with you, but it has happened time and time again with me that some man has done something that I did not like which I thought had a personal bearing, and that I have said in my heart, times will change and I will get even with that gentleman. I don't profess to be free from those feelings at all. But it has frequently happened, I may say generally, that the time did come when I could get even with that man, and when that time came, it seemed to me that I would demean myself and that it would show me no man at all if I took advantage of the opportunity.

Now I am going to tell you a story that interested me greatly when it was told to me, and that I can make applicable to this sermon, by the reason for its introduction and its telling. When I was Solicitor-General, it became my duty, in company with the Attorney-General, to call upon each of the Justices of the Supreme Court in Washington; and among those on the Bench at that time was that distinguished statesman, that great orator, and that most excellent judge, Mr. Justice Lamar of Mississippi. As you know, he was on the other side supporting the Confederacy during the Civil War.

It happened that we found him the night of our visit in a most talkative and communicative mood, and when in that mood he was as charming a man as I have ever met. Something arose which led him to say a number of things along the line that I have followed in what I have said to you—that early in life he rather cherished resentments and hatreds, and he thought it was an evidence of great strength of character if only he could remember them a long time; but as he had grown older, as God had seemed to be better to him, as the years had grown mellow, and as he had come to love everyone of his race, with real affection and interest, he had seen the utter lack of wisdom in allowing his time and mind and nerves to be taken up in cherishing those unworthy thoughts. "Well," I said, "Mr. Justice Lamar, you seem to have had some experience. Perhaps you can say what has led you to this." "Well," he said, "there are a good many instances, but I can give you one. I was the agent of the Confederacy in visiting England to secure the recognition of our belligerency during the Civil War. Mr. Mason and Mr. Slidell were Ambassadors really but I was the active agent, and a resolution had been introduced in the lower house of Parliament, the House of Commons, recognizing the belligerency and, I am not sure but the independence of the Confederacy. Our great friend was a member of Parliament named Mr. Roebuck, and walking on the Thames embankment the day before the resolution was to be discussed in the House, he expressed his great confidence in the success of our side and in the passage of the resolution; and I said to him, 'Yes, Mr. Roebuck, I hope that is true, but every once in a while there comes over me the fear that the House will be carried off its feet by the eloquence of John Bright.' 'Oh,' said Mr. Roebuck, 'Mr. Bright is a great orator for a set occasion, but in a debate I have measured swords with him myself, and I may say I didn't come off second best. Or, to change the metaphor, it was a case of the swordfish and the whale.' I was not entirely satisfied," continued the Justice, "but with hopefulness I attended the House of Commons the next morning and had as my company Mr. Charles Dickens, the novelist. Seated just beyond Mr. Dickens was a gentleman of the most distinguished appearance, whose face I had never seen before in the flesh but whom I soon recognized as the Reverend Henry Ward Beecher, who had come over to England to defend the Northern cause. We three sat there and listened to the debate: there was first an address by Sir Roundell Palmer, the Attorney-General, who defended the resolution; then Mr. Gladstone, who did not support the resolution, although he expressed great sympathy with the Southern Confederacy."

And so Mr. Justice Lamar went on describing one speaker and another. He loved oratory; he could repeat what he had heard, and I am sorry I can not repeat it to you. But finally said he, "Mr. Roebuck arose and proceeded to attack the North, its motives in assuming to be interested in the freeing of the slaves, its greed; its character as nothing but a commercial people," and so on and so on. To use Mr. Justice Lamar's expression, "He did give it to you fellows in a way that I very much enjoyed and I could not help, every time that he made a point and sent it home, looking around Mr. Dickens to see how Mr. Beecher took it."

"Well," the Justice said, "the debate went on and the hour for dinner approached, and I was hoping that the debate was over, because it seemed clearly with us and that no other prominent personage would take part, when I heard a voice like an organ note, a voice of volume and sweetness, the like of which I had never heard before and never have heard since, and I followed the note to the lips of the speaker. When I saw the speaker I saw that the whale was in the fight, and that John Bright had risen to meet the occasion. And bitter as I was on the subject, full as I was of the wrongs of the South and the righteousness of our cause, I could not but appreciate the strength of his sentences and the greatness of his oratory, and, to complete my humiliation and disappointment, every time in a glowing period that he drove home what he called the iniquity of slavery and the iniquity of our cause, Mr. Beecher leaned around Mr. Dickens to see how I took it.

"Now," said Justice Lamar, "from that moment, I hated Mr. Beecher, but subsequently in Mr. Beecher's life, when he became subjected to charges and a great strain and a trial that developed the real sweetness of his character and the grandeur and force of what he was as a man, I lost all that feeling. I did not rejoice in the trials that he had, but I came personally to know him and to recognize in that instance, as in many others, the utter fatuity, the utter uselessness of cherishing a personal feeling, a personal hatred beyond the moment when you can suppress it."

And so, my friends, what I am urging is less acrimony in public discussion—more charity with respect to each other as to what moves each man to do what he does do—and that you do not charge dishonesty and corruption until you have a real reason for doing so. I am the last man to pardon or mitigate wrongs against the public or against the individual. I believe, and I regret to say it, that throughout this country the administration of the criminal law and the prosecution of crime is a disgrace to our civilization; but it is one thing to prosecute a criminal when you have evidence and it is another thing to ascribe motives to the acts of men when you haven't any evidence and are just relying on your imagination in respect to what you infer.

My friends, I can not in the presence of so great an audience as this, an audience that inspires one with higher thought of country and patriotism, fail to refer to the depth of feeling that has been awakened in me, of gratitude for your welcome, of an appreciation of the basis of that welcome which is loyalty to your flag and country. I understand that in the great office of the President the personality of the man who fills it for the time sinks, and that the office typifies the nation, so that all people of whatever party ought to feel that toward the man who for the time being holds the office they are manifesting a respect for the nation for which they live and for which they would be willing to die.

The advantage of such a trip as that I am taking is of course that I come into personal touch with the people, and I am thus enabled to learn a great many things which otherwise I should be ignorant of, and on the other hand that they come into personal touch with me and find out the kind of personality in a way—very superficially—that they have selected through good fortune or misfortune temporarily to preside over them. A man of an inquiring mind said to me the other day, "It is quite true that you are speaking a good deal so that the people may learn something about your views, but how do you, if you do all the talking, learn anything about what the people think?" Well, stated simply, that would seem to be unanswerable unless you have a knowledge of the people whom I meet along the way, of the persons with whom I talk and of the opportunities for observation that are presented in so long a trip as that of 13,000 miles. If a man can not absorb a good deal from the newspapers, from talks along the way, of what is going on in a community, he had better not take a trip. But if he has the ordinary pores in his skin and the ordinary brain tentacles for holding on to things that are in the air, he is apt to get a pretty good knowledge of what is in the atmosphere, what is on the earth, in the communities that he visits. I am not here to justify my coming, because you have been kind enough to be so cordial in your welcome that I do not think it is necessary, and yet I do wish to explain some of the advantages that come from information at first hand and by personal touch, that one who is charged with the responsibility for four years of carrying on the executive department of the government may pick up.

And now, my friends, I say to you again how grateful I am for your cordial welcome, and express to you as sincerely as possible my earnest hope for your further progress and development in order to cap that wonderful advancement and seizure of opportunities that this community displays in its history. I thank you!

28

Remarks at the Young Men's Christian Association

Salt Lake City, Utah, September 26, 1909

Young Men:

It is always a great pleasure for me to attend a Young Men's Christian Association in any city and to assist, as I have a number of times, in the dedication of new buildings for the purpose of the Association. I have done that in I don't know how many cities and even as far as Shanghai and Hong-Kong and Manila, and the reason is because I feel that the Young Men's Christian Association supplies a need in every community which no church, no institution, nothing else that I know of can meet. It supplies an opportunity for rational amusement, and at the same time for the study of ideals and for religious worship at appropriate times; and it saves young men of the city who have not the opportunity of home surroundings. As our cities grow, the number of young men who leave their homes in the country and go to the city increases and it offers to them an opportunity for a rational occupation of their leisure hours—hours which if they do not have the opportunity to spend in rational amusement and occupation are only too frequently devoted to vicious pursuits. Now, that is true in every city. It is especially true in the newer and younger cities. It is very true in the Orient where, so far away from home, young men especially forget the restraints and the obligations that neighborhood life puts upon them, and they first take one drink and then another, and as there is nothing else to do, a third, and as those drinks in those far distant countries seem to offer a stimulus that is agreeable, the end is not until they are in the gutter.

I congratulate you sincerely on the evidence of the especial excellence of your Association here. I am told that two or three times you have taken prizes offered to those interested in the Associations the country over for the excellence of your work and the skill and persistence of those who superintend it and engage in it. That is an admirable sign of your usefulness to the community. The Young Men's Christian Association offers a lesson which can not be too deeply impressed upon the people—the lesson of tolerance. It means the brotherhood of man and the Fatherhood of God, and the recognition of the advantages of all religion within the Christian brotherhood bringing one nearer to that ideal that we all aspire to and from which we so often fall away.

Now, my friends, I should be glad to talk with you longer on some of the details of Young Men's Christian Association work, but it is impossible for me to do so. I can only express my pleasure at having this opportunity in the somewhat strenuous program of the last three days to express to you my congratulation on the work that you have done and my hope for your continued usefulness in the community.

29

Conservation of National Resources

Spokane, Washington, September 28, 1909

Ladies and Gentlemen of Spokane; Fellow Citizens of Washington:

I am going to take up today the subject of the conservation of our natural resources. This has been given a very wide scope. I do not propose to cover the whole ground today. I shall confine my attention to those parts of the policy which are certainly within the jurisdiction of the National Government, and which especially concern the country west of the Missouri River.

I refer, first, to the preservation of the national forests; second, to the reclamation of the arid and semi-arid lands by irrigation; third, to the disposition of water-power sites upon public lands with proper restrictions upon the use both in respect to the compensation, its extent in point of time, and the adjustment of rates to be charged to the public by the beneficiary of the grant; fourth, to the disposition of coal, oil and phosphate lands owned by the Government with such restrictions as will permit their development for private profit, and yet will prevent monopoly and extortion in the sale of the product.

The national forests as reserved by Executive Order contain about 167,000,000 acres of land in the United States proper. All of this land is now under the direct control of the Forestry Bureau and is being preserved from fire and from other destruction, and is being treated in accordance with the best modern methods of treating forests under the supervision of Mr. Pinchot, the Chief Forester, and the head of the Bureau of Forestry in the Department of Agriculture.

It appears that the Government timber land is only about one-fourth of the timber land owned by private individuals, and that only three percent of the timber land owned by private individuals is properly looked after according to modern methods of forestry. The destruction by fire of forests is estimated to be $50,000,000 a year. It would seem, therefore, imperative that the States should exercise their jurisdiction over these forests to which I have referred and which are held by private individuals, and require some system of fire protection and the adoption of the best methods of forestry. It would seem that the States have a right to do this because of the general interest which the public has in the preservation of the forests, in their equalizing of the water supply, and in their effect upon the climate. The equalization of the water supply, of course, prevents erosion of the soil and the wasteful destruction of the best part of the soil, which is carried down the river with the floods.

The regulation of forests in private ownership within State boundaries is plainly not within the scope of Federal jurisdiction, and it should be undertaken by the States. I do not think the States have taken up the matter with as much energy as they ought, and they have not improved the opportunity which was given them by way of example by the Forestry Bureau of the United States. The question whether the Federal Government, with the purpose of equalizing the flow of water in navigable streams, and to promote navigation during the entire year, may enter upon a plan of regulating existing forests and reforesting certain denuded territory in the States, I need not now discuss. The subject would involve a wider discussion than I have time to give it.

The plan of the Government to reclaim the arid and semi-arid lands manifested in the reclamation act has been carried out most rapidly by the Bureau charged with its execution. I had the honor the other day in Colorado of opening the most ambitious of these projects, at least the most difficult of them—the Gunnison tunnel—which is to bring water into a valley in Colorado, known as the Uncompahgre Valley, with some 150,000 acres, and to put it in a condition to grow fruit and cereals. There are some thirty projects which have been entered upon by the Reclamation Bureau, and I believe that all of them are to be commended for their excellent adaptation to the purpose for which they were erected, and for the speed with which the work has been done. It is said, however, that in the planning of a number of these improvements, the enthusiasm of the projectors has carried them to a point where they begin to feel embarrassed in the matter of resources with which to complete the projects, and begin to show that prudence was not observed by those engaged in executing the act; that the projects were too many and more than could be completed in a reasonable time after their beginning, because of a lack of funds. The reclamation act provides for the expenditure of funds made up of the proceeds of the sale of public lands and reimbursed from time to time by the instalments to be paid by the settlers who take up the irrigated land, and it also provides that no part of a project is to be contracted for and begun, until the money for the completion of that part of the project contracted for shall be in the reclamation fund. Now, it appears that it will take $10,000,000 or more, which is not available in the reclamation fund at present, fully to complete the projects, and it also appears that a great number of persons by reason of the beginning of the projects have been led into the making of settlements, the expenditure of time and labor, with the hope and upon the reliance that such reclamation enterprises would be carried through in a reasonable time.

I think there is no doubt that it was the intention of Congress that projects should not be multiplied in such a way that they could not be completed within a reasonable time out of the reclamation funds provided by the sale of public lands, and it probably would have been wiser to adhere strictly to the limitation thus construed, even though the language of the act, by dividing up the projects into parts in terms permits the beginning of more projects than there was likely to be money enough to complete within a reasonable time. The pressure was doubtless very great, and the reclamation service yielded to the pressure within the letter of the law, and now find themselves in the situation described. The work has been well done and reflects great credit on the engineers who have had charge of it. But something must be done to relieve the present situation, which is one of disappointed hopes to many settlers upon the arid lands, who counting upon an early completion of the projects undertaken have invested their money and spent their time and seem to be no nearer the goal of satisfactory irrigation than they were when the projects were begun. I think it wise to apply to Congress for relief by urging the passage of an enabling act, which shall permit the Secretary of the Interior to issue bonds in the sum of $10,000,000 or more, to complete all the projects now projected. These bonds should be redeemed from the money paid into the reclamation funds after the completion of the projects.

From conversation with the Senators who have visited much of the reclamation work and given an examination to its progress, I infer that such a proposal as this seems to them to be the best way out of the present difficulty, and I shall take pleasure in recommending the passage of such a remedial measure by the next Congress.

No one can visit this western country without being overwhelmingly convinced of the urgent necessity for the proper treatment of arid and semi-arid lands by the extension of systems of irrigation. The results in the productivity of the soil when irrigated are marvellous. The mere fact that the reclamation service has gone ahead too fast ought not to prevent Congress from lending its aid to overcome the difficulty. We shall know better in the further treatment of the subject and in the further use of the $50,000,000 fund how to avoid putting ourselves in a similar position again. Meantime irrigation works under private auspices are being projected in every direction, and the prospect of reclaiming millions of acres from the deserts is most encouraging. The examples of Government engineering and of ingenuity in planning the structures in these various Government projects for irrigation are of immense utility as models for private enterprise.

One subject that is now being agitated in some quarters calls for notice. Payment for irrigated lands is required in ten annual instalments. Suggestions are now being made that these should be lengthened into a longer term. I sincerely hope that Congress will not listen to such appeals. It may be well to make the first three or four instalments nominal, but after that time the instalments should be large enough to pay the total amount due, upon which no interest is calculated, in ten years. Any other course will encourage a lack of thrift and industry and will greatly embarrass the extension and continuance of the work of irrigation.

When the Government became possessed of its public domain and took measures to secure its settlement by the passage of the homestead act and other acts offering, after certain steps prescribed, to vest title to a specific part of the public lands in individuals, the chief object of Congress seemed to be to secure development by inducing people to settle on public lands and acquire it for themselves. The thought of conserving the resources which were thus opened to private acquisition hardly occurred to Congress. Its generosity to the Pacific railroads in offering the public lands in such extensive grants to them is an instance of the spirit which actuated Congress thirty and forty and fifty years ago. I am not criticizing Congress in the slightest for this policy. It certainly was necessary to make extensive grants to secure the construction of a railroad which should unite the Pacific Coast with the Atlantic Coast, and bring closer to the Eastern seaboard the far distant regions of this country. I merely refer to it in a historical way to explain the character of the statutes now upon the statute books with reference to the sale and disposition of public lands. There has always been a distinction made between agricultural lands and mineral lands, because it was recognized that mineral lands would probably be much more valuable, and a different method was required for the acquisition of the one from that of the other. But never until now has adequate provision been made for a classification of lands so as to show distinctly what are mineral lands and what are agricultural lands. The truth is, that the needs of the country have developed so, and the demand for land has so much increased, that in order to secure a sensible, business-like disposition of the lands remaining in the public domain, there must be an authoritative classification of lands by the proper bureau so as to show whether they are agricultural lands, forest lands or lands available for water-power sites on the banks of rivers and other streams, or mineral lands, coal lands, oil lands, or phosphate lands. Had this classification been made earlier, it would have saved a great amount of litigation and would have saved to the Government millions of acres patented as one kind of land when in fact it was another. The classification so far as authorized is being rapidly executed by the Geological Survey. After classification, legislation should be and doubtless will be directed to the means by which such lands should be disposed of and the restrictions specified in the interest of the public upon the tenure and use to which the owner is to put such lands.

As to lands which are purely agricultural, there would seem to be no reason for departing from the ordinary method of disposition under the homestead and other laws, including the reclamation acts, by which citizens acquire title in them.

With respect to forest lands owned by the public, they should be surveyed and held by the Government under the regulation of the Forestry Bureau permitting a sale of such timber as shall be necessary in the proper forestry preservation.

As to water-power sites, there has been such a change in conditions that a special provision should be made in the interest of the public for their transfer to private control.

The development of electrical appliances and the transfer of power through electric lines for long distances has made the use of water power to produce electricity one of the most important sources of power that we have in this country, and it will so affect the cost of production in all the fields of manufacture and production of the necessities of life as to require the Government to retain control over the use by private capital of such power when it can only be exercised upon sites which belong to the Government. Such sites can be properly parted with under conditions of tenure, use and compensation, consistent on the one hand with reasonable profit to the private capital invested and on the other with the right of the public to secure the furnishing of such power at reasonable rates to everyone. There should be a condition of forfeiture if the owner of the power site does not within a certain time expend capital sufficient to double the power, and after development shall charge rates to the public beyond what is a reasonable profit on the capital invested in the improvement to be regulated by the Government. The amount of compensation that ought to be charged by the Government for the use of the water-power sites might perhaps be left to readjustment every ten or fifteen or twenty years. The compensation to be charged in the outset might well be purely nominal, but after the project has become a complete success and the profit has grown to a considerable percentage of the amount invested, then there would seem to be no reason why the public might not be benefited by sharing in the profits of the transaction to an amount to be fixed upon arbitration or in some other method at the end of a stated period of fifteen or twenty years. This is an arrangement toward which the tenure of all public utilities is tending, and I know of no reason why it should not be introduced into the governmental disposition of such sources of continuous power as the water sites upon public lands are likely to be. I know it has been the course in the past under the bounteous and generous disposition of the Government to give these water sites away under existing inadequate acts; but we have reached a time now when the importance of these water-power sites has greatly increased, and there would seem to be no reason why it would interfere with a speedy development of the country to impose restrictions upon the use of such water sites, equitable as between the public and the investor. This is a matter which Congress must take up. The water-power sites are now generally disposed of under the same kind of a procedure as that by which agricultural lands are taken up, and there is no power on the part of the Secretary of the Interior in the disposition of such sites to impose the conditions suggested. This matter has become so important that under the last administration large tracts of lands amounting to upward of four million acres were temporarily withdrawn from settlement in order to prevent the acquisition of water-power sites under the general land laws. This amount has been reduced under the present administration to 450,000 acres, which include even more ascertained water sites than the original withdrawals. It should be understood that these withdrawals are temporary and can only be justified as made in order to permit Congress to legislate on the subject of water-power sites. Should Congress conclude not to do so, it would be difficult for the executive to find the authority indefinitely to withhold these lands from settlement under the general laws, on the ground that they contain water-power sites. The legislative power is vested in Congress and not in the executive. I shall, therefore, urge upon Congress at its next session, the passage of a law authorizing the disposition of such water-power sites upon terms to be agreed upon by the Secretary of the Interior with the proposed purchaser of the character already indicated. It may turn out that restrictions of this sort are so burdensome as to discourage the investment of capital, and it may be necessary to modify the requirements on this account. But my own impression is that the demand for water power is going to be so great that these restrictions will not prevent the investment of capital but will ultimately bring to the public coffers a revenue from an entirely proper source and will secure the development of a power for manufacturing industries that will probably in time exceed the utility and value of coal, and become a substitute for it.

I now come to what should be the proper disposition of coal lands, oil lands and phosphate lands. The anthracite coal strike evoked a great deal of discussion in respect to the evils of the ownership by private persons of a monopoly of the coal supply of the country, and led Mr. Roosevelt to declare the necessity for preserving from acquisition by monopolizing syndicates the public coal lands still undisposed of. The truth is that in Alaska the deposits of coal are so great that when they are developed they will doubtless furnish coal to the entire Pacific Coast. They have been reserved from filings since 1906. There are some 900 claims but it is probable that under the evidence adduced most of these claims will prove to have been defective. With such an immense tract of coal land at a place near the sea as this is, from which coal easily can be furnished by water to the entire Pacific Coast, it becomes highly important to settle, before this land shall be disposed of under present laws, whether we are to retain any different control over these lands from those which have been already sold by the Government in other parts of the country.

It seems wise in the disposition of coal lands, and indeed of all mineral lands having agricultural value, to separate the surface of the land from its mineral contents; and then either to lease the right to take coal from the land at a specified compensation per ton—that is to provide a system of royalties—or to sell the deposits of the land outright to the coal miner. In every case, restriction by way of forfeiture ought to be included to prevent a monopoly of ownership of the coal land in any one set of men so as to enable them to control the price of coal. This is the great object of a change in the method of their disposition.

Some provision should be made with reference to the disposition of phosphate land. This land, which is found in Wyoming and in Idaho, contains the wonderful fertilizer which it will soon be necessary to use on much of the land in the United States, and as the need for the use of this fertilizer on much land is growing, we should see to it, if possible, that the product be not subject to monopoly or sold outside of the United States.

The oil lands of California, as well as the phosphate lands, and practically all the coal lands have been withdrawn from settlement in order to await the action of Congress; and I expect to recommend to Congress legislation on the lines above indicated, with the general purpose of enabling the Secretary of the Interior in the administration of the land laws to secure more benefit to the public and greater certainty in the security against the monopoly of resources. What, however, I wish to make as plain as possible is that these purposes can not be accomplished unless Congress shall act, and that the burden of carrying out the policy of the conservation of our resources, in respect to the matters I have discussed is upon Congress. The Executive can recommend but the legislature must enact. After the enactment of general authority, it is easy for the Executive to make proper regulations calculated to carry out in detail the general purpose which Congress had, but the first duty in respect to the conservation of resources falls upon Congress.

There has been a good deal of discussion in the newspapers as to the attitude of the present administration toward the general policy of the conservation of resources, and some very unfair and altogether unfounded inferences have been drawn. The truth is, my administration is pledged to follow out the policies of Mr. Roosevelt in this regard, and while that pledge does not involve me in any obligation to carry them out unless I have Congressional authority to do so, it does require that I take every step and exert every legitimate influence upon Congress to enact the legislation which shall best subserve the purposes indicated. I do not think that Congress, if properly approached, will object to adopting legislation of the general character which I have outlined. In the past it has aided the forestry service by what seemed to be ample appropriations. It has in a measure provided for a classification of lands by the head of the Geological Survey. These are both important steps. I hope nothing will prevent our taking the further steps needed when Congress meets. Secretary Ballinger of the Interior Department, upon whom will fall the duty of executing the new provisions of law, is in entire accord with me as to the necessity for promoting in every legitimate way the conservation of the resources which I have named, and he can be counted upon to use the great influence which he must have as Secretary of the Interior to this proper end. Indeed, it will be found that in his reports as Commissioner of the General Land Office he brought these matters to the attention of Congress and urged the adoption of a general policy along the lines I have indicated.

30

Alaska

Alaska-Yukon-Pacific Exposition, Seattle, Washington,
September 29, 1909

Ladies and Gentlemen, Fellow Citizens of Seattle, of Washington, and of the
Pacific Coast:

This great Alaska-Yukon-Pacific Exposition was the objective point on my trip to the West, and I am glad to have arrived here after two weeks' travel from the old Bay State. As I look about me at this wonderful exhibition of the progress of the Northwest, of Alaska, and the Pacific Coast, I feel a great pride in having urged upon the proper Congressional committee, with all the emphasis of which I was capable, the importance and the utility of the enterprise. And it is gratifying to know that under the administration of Seattle men the Exposition has been a great success both in arousing world-wide interest in the growth of the Far Northwest and in showing a profit over the immense outlay needed in its construction and maintenance.

When I first planned my visit to Seattle, I had included with it a trip to Alaska in order that I might by a personal investigation make myself better acquainted with the character of that great territory and with the best method of securing its development. I greatly regret that the time consumed by Congress in the consideration of the tariff bill prevented my carrying out the part of the plan embraced in a visit to this most interesting territory.

One of Mr. Seward's substantial claims to the gratitude of his country-men and to a place among the statesmen of his country was the broad view which he took of the value of Alaska and his wisdom in effecting its purchase. The cession of Virginia and the ordinance of 1787, which gave to the nation the Middle West, the purchase by Jefferson of Louisiana Territory, which carried our domain to the Rocky Mountains, the annexation of Texas, and the treaty of Guadalupe Hidalgo, which extended our territory to the Pacific Coast, were properly supplemented by the acquisition of Alaska, and this Exposition may well be regarded as a celebration of the foresight of Seward in his policy of expansion.

It would seem that the wealth of Alaska in minerals, in fish, in furs, and even in agriculture, was still but inadequately known, and yet its value from a mere money standpoint to the nation, as shown by the wealth which has been extracted from it, exceeds by many fold the cost of it to the Government of the United States. A review of the history of the territory will show that Congress has been very slow to extend to it a proper form of government.

Alaska is a country of immense expanse, and the governmental needs of the southeastern portion near to Washington and the Northwest are quite different from those of Nome and the Seward peninsula and of the valley of the Yukon. Such a territory has need of local legislation and local govern-ment, which can only be understood by those who are on the ground, and it is utterly impossible and impractical for Congress in its legislation to gov-ern the details by legislation required for the best development of the terri-tory. There has been no authority in the territory having an adequate jurisdiction to meet the exigencies of such a young but potentially prosper-ous territory.

It has been proposed that Congress should give to Alaska the regular form of territorial government under which a legislature and a Governor might be elected, and between the two they might be given the powers ordi-narily given to the legislature and executive of regularly organized territories. I think this would be a great mistake, because I don't think that the territory has a population of sufficient number or sufficient stability and permanence of residence to warrant the delegation to a locally elected legislature of such authority. Many of the places in Alaska, where there is a considerable popula-tion, are nothing but mining camps, with all the migratory and temporary features of such settlements. More than that, the population is so small, as compared with the vast expanse of the territory, that it would be unwise to provide that a comparatively small population in southeastern Alaska should elect representatives and legislate for the enormous territory reaching from British Columbia clear to the Bering Sea and the Arctic Ocean.

Local self-government or home rule, in a country so large as Alaska, with a scattered nomadic population, intense local and sectional feeling, should not be given serious consideration until the population and developed resources of the country have increased to such an extent as to warrant the division of the territory into more limited areas, where the inhabitants of each would have an opportunity to become acquainted, and where there would be some degree of similarity of interests. Before such an experiment, an earnest effort should be made to secure a larger percentage of permanent residents and endeavor to attach some of the population to the soil.

My own judgment is that the only way properly to develop Alaska for the benefit of everybody in it, is to bring the Territory under the management of one bureau and department in Washington, so that all the officials in the Government shall have to report to one head, and so also that the interests of the entire Territory shall be centered in one responsible bureau chief in Washington, whose business it shall be through his Department chief to present to Congress the needs of the Territory, to follow legislation, and to attend to everything at the National Capital in which the people of the Territory are interested. It is not necessary that the delegate shall be dispensed with, but an executive office, with records, with information and constantly active, can greatly contribute to the welfare of a territory for which it is responsible when located at the National Capital, and when understood to have the proper authority and responsibility.

Certain general laws, like the mining laws, the forestry laws, the customs laws and the land laws should be passed by Congress and perhaps executed by national officers, but this would leave a wide domain for domestic legislation which it seems to me ought to be intrusted to some local authority on the ground and having a knowledge of local needs. Of course if the Territory were so settled with a permanent population more or less equally distributed through its extent, such legislative power might be entrusted to an elected legislature, but for the reasons I have given, it seems to me that it would be much wiser to entrust this local legislative power to a commission of five or more members, appointed by the President, to act with the Governor in the discharge of such legislative functions. It seems wise not to confer legislative functions on the Governor alone, but to assist him in its exercise by the addition of competent persons who will live in the Territory, familiarize themselves with its local needs and bring to the attention of Congress and the Executive such additional legislation as may from time to time be wise.

It will be observed that this is practically the government which was given to the Philippine Islands, although the Commission there had more legislative authority than it would be wise or necessary to give to the Alaskan

Commission. Objection will be made on the ground that this is treating the people of Alaska, who are generally free-born American citizens, as if the Territory were a dependency of persons unfit to exercise the power of self-government. I can not deny that the conditions in Alaska are such as in my judgment to prevent the extension of local self-government safely to that Territory. It is not because of the character of the people if they were permanent residents and sufficient in number and sufficiently distributed to warrant the establishment of a representative government, but the conditions that exist are such as to put them for the time being in a position justifying a similar treatment to that of the Philippines. Indeed it would be a great deal better government than at present, because it would be vesting power in a local authority familiar with local needs, and today no such power exists. In other words, it would be a great advance over the present conditions. I don't know that Congress will agree with me in this view, but a personal experience in the practical operation of such a system of government for the benefit of the territory governed leads me to feel justified in making such a recommendation. The Territory will develop much more rapidly and the boon of self-government will come much more quickly under such a system than as the government is being carried on at present.

The future of Alaska is big with prosperity and great productiveness, but it needs intelligent legislation to develop it quickly and in the right way; and I know no better method of securing such a result than by a properly constituted Commission. There is an opportunity for Congress to aid in the construction of certain railroads that will largely develop the Territory, and which private enterprise is not able or willing to undertake unless it receives some sort of guaranty from the Government. That I would unhesitatingly recommend, because Alaska is a territory in which private capital can not be expected to build the first railroads.

I am especially interested in Alaska because her development has been delayed by a lack of appropriate legislation and because I know something of the needs of a land so far distant. Of course the law-making power of the Commission should be subject to the approval of the head of the department at Washington responsible for the government of Alaska, just as is provided now by the law governing the Philippines.

Since I last visited the Coast, I am glad to say that the Philippines have had extended to them in the matter of a tariff law a measure of justice, which ought to have been adopted nine years ago. If it had been adopted, the city of Seattle, the city of San Francisco, and the whole Pacific Coast would have profited by its enactment. Free trade with the Philippines as now established between the Islands and this country will develop an exchange of business between the two countries which will be greatly to the advantage of both. Trade in the Philippines has long had one trend, and it will take some time, perhaps two or three years, to effect a change, even now that the law is passed; but a familiarity with the situation in the Islands makes me confident that the Pacific Coast will come to value more and more highly the trade from the Philippines which will fall to it. There are many industries in the Philippines the products of which will sell well in the United States now that the tariff is lifted from them, and with similar relief from burden in entering the Philippines, American manufactures will have a far wider sale in those distant islands on the Pacific.

The Panama Canal will be completed on or before the first of January, 1915, and with its completion the trade between the Eastern and Western coasts of this country will be revolutionized, for the carriage of heavy bulk merchandise between the Pacific and the Atlantic Coast is almost certain to be by water. This will reduce the transcontinental business to the carriage of the more valuable classes of merchandise, which can profitably pay a higher rate of transportation. More than this, it will change the avenues of international trade, will bring the eastern coast of America closely in touch with the western coast of South America, and will greatly facilitate the direct transportation from the west coast of America to European ports.

China is waking up. She is approaching a period of development that can not but increase her trade and augment her importance as customer and as a trader with this country, while Japan and all the other Oriental countries are moving onward with giant steps in the commercial competition of the world. The many prophecies that have been made that in the next half-century the commercial progress of the world is to be seen more decidedly in the Pacific than anywhere else are certainly well founded; and under those conditions it behooves us as Americans interested in pushing her trade into every quarter of the globe to take steps to repair a condition that exists in respect to our merchant marine that is humiliating to our national pride and most burdensome to us in competition with other nations in obtaining international trade.

We maintain a protective tariff to encourage our manufacturing, farming, and mining industries at home and within our jurisdiction, but when we assume to enter into competition upon the high seas in trade between international ports, our jurisdiction to control that trade so far as the vessels of other nations are concerned, of course ceases, and the question which we have to meet is how with the greater wages that we pay, with the more stringent laws we enact for the protection of our sailors, and with the protective system making a difference in the price between the necessaries to be used in the maintenance of a merchant marine, we shall enable that merchant marine to compete with the marine of the rest of the world.

This is not the only question either, for it will be found on an examination of the methods pursued in other countries with respect to their merchant marines, that there is now extended by way of subsidies by the various governments to their respective ships, upward of $35,000,000, and this offers another means by which in the competition the American merchant ship is driven out of business and finds it utterly impossible to bid against its foreign competitors. Not only this, but so inadequate is the American merchant marine today that in seeking auxiliary ships with which to make our navy an instrument of offense or defense, or indeed in sending it around the world as a fleet, we have to call on vessels sailing under a foreign flag to carry the coal and to supply the other needs of such a journey. Were we compelled to go into a war today, our merchant marine lacks altogether a sufficient tonnage of auxiliary unarmed ships absolutely necessary to the proper operation of the navy, and were a war to come on we should have to purchase such vessels from foreign countries, and this might under the laws governing neutrals be most difficult.

The trade between the eastern ports of the United States and South America is a most valuable trade, and now equals something like $250,000,000; but European nations, appreciating the growing character of this trade, have by subsidies and other means of encouragement so increased the sailings of large and well-equipped vessels from Europe to the ports of South America as visibly to affect the proportion of trade which is coming to the United States by the very limited service of a direct character between New York and South American ports.

I need not tell you of the inadequacy of the American shipping marine on the Pacific Coast and the growing power for commercial purposes in this regard of the Empire of Japan. Japan is one of the most active and generous countries in the matter of subsidies to its merchant marine that we have, and the effect is only too visible in an examination of the statistics.

For this reason, it seems to me that there is no subject to which Congress can better devote its attention in the coming session than the passage of a bill which shall encourage our merchant marine in such a way as to establish American lines directly between New York and eastern ports and South American ports, and between our Pacific Coast ports and the Orient and the Philippines. We earn a profit from our foreign mails of from $6,000,000 to $8,000,000 a year. The application of that amount would be quite sufficient to put on a satisfactory basis two or three Oriental lines and several lines from the East to South America. Of course, we are familiar with the argument that this would be contributing to private companies out of the treasury of the United States; but we are contributing in various ways on similar principles in effect, both by our protective tariff law, by our river and harbor bills, and by our reclamation service. We are not putting money in the pockets of ship owners, but we are giving them money with which they can compete for a reasonable profit only with the merchant marine of the world.

From my observation I think the country is ready now to try such a law and to witness its effect in a comparatively small way upon the foreign trade of the United States. If it is successful, experience will show how the policy can best be expanded and enlarged and the American commercial flag be made to wave upon the seas as it did before our Civil War. It is true that our foreign trade is great and increasing, and this without the merchant marine, but it is also true that the ownership of a merchant marine greatly enhances the opportunities for the merchants of the country having such a merchant marine. This is shown by consular reports and a reference to statistics in an indisputable way.

There is no part of the country more interested in the development of this policy than Seattle, Washington and the whole Pacific Coast. With the enormous energy and potential force that you have developed in your community here for trade and business expansion, it cannot have escaped the foresight of your business captains that the development of a merchant marine means the growth of Seattle into a port of such importance that hardly the lively imagination of her ambitious citizens can compass.

31

Alaska, Merchant Marine, and Subsidy

The Armory, Tacoma, Washington, October 1, 1909

Mr. McCormick, Mr. Mayor, Ladies and Gentlemen:

After what your Mayor has said I don't know exactly what I ought to say. It is a good deal of a burden to bear to start off with that kind of an introduction. It invites a hope that I am sorry to say you will hardly be able to realize; but I am very glad to meet a Tacoma audience again. My recollection is that I stole into your town and ran around with a friend on my way to Portland two years ago; that I returned, and then met an audience in the Park; and that I had the honor then of being introduced by your Congressman, Mr. Cushman—"Old Cush," as we called him affectionately in Washington. It saddens my visit to think that he is no more; that he has gone from you and has left to you but a sweet and fragrant memory. It was my good fortune to come into contact with him early in my service as Secretary of War, and to know how he cherished his dear old home of Tacoma. I think I told you when I was here two years ago that he wore out the steps of the War Department trying to get me to recommend that a government reservation should be turned over to the city as a park. He said, "Mr. Secretary, if you will only do this my people of Tacoma will put a monument in that Park that can be seen way down Puget Sound"; and I said to him, "Why, Cush, old man, you would make a good deal better monument than I would, and what I will do is to get that park and then they will put up a monument to you." Of course, those things were said in kindly jest, but I am here to suggest to the people of Tacoma that they could not honor a more loving son— one who had served them better—than by putting up a monument to Francis Cushman in Wright's Park. First, he was an honest man; second, he was a courageous man; third, he was a man of intellect; fourth, he had a genial, kindly heart; and, fifth, he had that delicious flavor of humor that made everybody love to be with him and to come under its influence. There was something about Cushman that always reminded me of Lincoln. He was not a handsome man—neither was Lincoln—but it is impossible to think of either without an admiration for something about his physical make-up that appealed to you as an evidence of his straight-forward simplicity and love of his fellow-men. His humor, flashes of which have outlasted his life in Washington, comes back every time I think of him. He was going into the tariff debate, and he had known that his committee had voted for a dollar on lumber, and he wanted to keep it up to $2, but he was a party man; he believed in party; he believed that the maintenance of the solidarity of the Republican party on the whole was more important than his opinion on a particular issue, and so he was marching up to meet that particular thing he expected to be done, lumber carried from $2 to $1, but when he rose in that House, he said he wasn't hastening the moment because he felt a little bit like that gentleman who in the early days had established a small ranch, and then increased his herd of cattle by a judicious selection from his neighbors' herds until they came to the conclusion that it was necessary for him to swing from a limb; and when they asked him to come, he said he was coming—that he wasn't hurrying because he said that while it was an event in which he had very considerable interest, he could not describe his attitude as one of enthusiasm.

I remember another of his witticisms. There was a gentleman in office in Washington whom "Cush" didn't think to be very popular in the West, and so at a Gridiron dinner, at which the President was present, after it was announced that this gentleman was about to retire, "Cush" expressed proper regret at his going, but said that he was bound to admit that when news of that retirement came to the West there would not be a dry throat west of the Missouri River. And so, my friends, Cushman went on through life— helping everyone by his optimism—helping everyone by his apt story— helping everyone by his good fellowship, by his high standard, and by his wish to stand by his fellows. I am sorry, deeply sorry, that you have lost him as a Representative. I am sorry, deeply sorry, that I have lost him as a friend. And I could not come into this community after having been introduced to you, as I was by him two years ago, and having been associated with him since in a close and intimate way, without paying this tribute to a man who loved his people, to a man who deserved well of his people, to a man who loved his country, and to a man who deserved well of his country.

Now, my friends, I do not know what I am going to talk about exactly. I have delivered six or eight set speeches on subjects that I think ought to command the attention of Congress, and I have gotten rid of those. I felt about them very much as boys do about written examinations, and now I do not have anything to tie me down. I can talk to you about anything, if I can think of anything to say. There are one or two things I would like to argue with you, because perhaps you differ with me. It isn't of much use to talk with a man and to try to convince him of something he is already convinced of, to talk with him about something that he believes even more strongly than you do; but there is a subject in which possibly in this audience I shall find a number who disagree with me. I talked to an audience over in Seattle about it, and that is the question as to what we ought to do about Alaska. You are interested in Alaska here. The State of Washington—Seattle and Tacoma are the nearest ports to that great possession of the United States. Now, in the first place, we have to admit that we haven't any reason to be proud of the governmental arrangements that we have made in Alaska. Unfortunately, there is right next to Alaska a country that has been governed by our neighbors on the north, and that government compares most favorably with our government of Alaska, and we ought to do something about it. It is proposed that we should give to Alaska a territorial form of government, permitting the thirty or forty thousand people who are there, to elect a legislature, a governor and other territorial officers to exercise legislative power in that vast territory. Well, that sort of a proposition, of course, appeals to Americans because we Americans are generally in favor of popular government. We believe that popular government among intelligent people is better, because we believe that each set of men, call it class or otherwise, as you choose, men similarly situated are better able generally to decide through their representatives what is to their interest than if you leave it to somebody else; and hence we favor popular government and representative government, but that assumes certain conditions that make it possible for the people to act intelligently.

Now, what is the condition in Alaska? They have 35,000 or 40,000 people there, but they are a nomadic people. There are very few permanent residents attached to the soil. There are miners, moving from one mining camp to another. There are saloon-keepers, for that seems to be a very important element in that territory, who change from one place to another, and they are not so situated with reference to the permanent attachment to the soil, or with reference to a distribution through the entire territory, which is enormous, reaching from British Columbia to the Arctic Ocean—they are not so situated that they could provide a government of people having similar interests and reaching similar conclusions with reference to the whole territory. They are situated in one corner, or they are so scattered that it seems most unwise to me to attempt to make out of so small a community an organized territory and a territorial government. But you say, "If you don't do that, what are you going to do? They ought to have some authority in the territory that has power to legislate upon domestic matters. They ought to have some authority in the territory exercised by people who are on the ground and who understand the local needs." I agree to that. I think that is one of the things that has been most lacking. We have, of course, a commission of army officers there to build roads. We have some judges up there who exercise judicial jurisdiction and some sort of other jurisdiction. We have collectors of internal revenue, and we have a Governor, who has some authority, chiefly of making recommendations to Congress; and then we have a Delegate who comes to Congress, who does not vote but who suggests methods by which improvements can be made. But there is nobody to do anything in the sense of acting on the ground and making laws and regulations, which shall meet the needs of that territory.

Now, how are you going to bring it about? If they are not in a condition justifying local self-government, as I believe they are not, there is only one other way by which they can do it, and that is the way we pursued in the Philippines. There President McKinley appointed a commission of five persons, who went out to the Philippines and lived there and familiarized themselves with the needs of the Islands. The commission had the power to legislate on all matters of domestic concern except customs, and here in Alaska we might well omit land laws, mining laws and possibly a number of other general statutes with reference to the jurisdiction of courts. But if you give to the President the power to appoint five men who are to go there and settle and live there while they exercise their office, pay them good salaries— men who have no interest in the territory—and make it essential that they shall have no interest there of any sort, so that they will be entirely free from factionalism and sectionalism. Then you will get a body of men who will pass intelligently on measures needed to build up the territory and whose recommendations Congress will be glad to follow. Congress, on the other hand, will give to these men the power of local legislation—power to make certain things crimes, to make other things misdemeanours—power to levy internal taxation, power to make improvements; and then if you get such a commission, I doubt not that it will recommend to Congress to help railroads, because railroads can not be built by private enterprise in a country so far away and where so much risk attends the investment. There is no reason why we should not help Alaska, as we have in the Philippines helped the railroads there, by guaranteeing for a certain time the interest on railroad bonds.

There is not a subject in which I take a deeper interest than I do in the development of Alaska, and I propose, if Congress will follow my recommendation, to do something in that territory that shall make it move on. The ground has hardly been scratched there. Seward was laughed at for paying seven million dollars for that territory, and I think we have drawn from there already $200,000,000 of gold. The agricultural possibilities of the country, the forests and the timber that are there, are not fully understood. We do know that there is a wealth of coal that can be mined and that will make coal cheaper along the whole Pacific Coast. It is worth while, therefore, for us to take it up as a business matter. These things are to be treated from a common sense standpoint, not from a purely sentimental one, and if you believe in your hearts, as I believe in mine, that for ten years at least we will give a better government there by sending up five able, honest, disinterested men to pass laws, to recommend legislation to Congress, and to do the things that are needed to lead that territory on to proper development—if you believe it in your heart, then you ought to say so, and you ought not to be led aside by what seems to be for the moment a popular cry.

I know that the newspapers of Alaska have forwarded a telegram, and I think it got into the papers, in which they recommend that they have a territorial legislature. Now, I am not going to impugn their motives. It is not necessary. I do think that their situation is such that they are much more likely to look upon themselves as able to legislate than perhaps men who look at it from a standpoint of indifference and who understand the nomadic or moving character of the population. You would hardly arrange for a mining camp to be a territory. It is agricultural soil and attachment to the ground itself that makes a permanent population and that is safe to legislate and maintain a popular government.

Now, I have said as much on that subject as I intend to say, except this, that there are a great many people who agree with me and I think there are a majority in Congress who believe that the territory is not in a condition to justify an organized territorial government. Those who are in favor, intensely in favor of developing Alaska, will perceive that my proposition is much more likely to receive support, and that, even if they really believe that they ought to have organized territorial government on a popular basis, it is a great deal better to get half a loaf than none at all, and it is better to take the proposition of a commission with legislative power than it is to have the present unsatisfactory condition of nobody able to legislate there and nobody to develop the country. I am appealing, therefore, to those who differ with me as to what would be wiser—to come over to my side, because on my side we are much more likely to get reform and remedial legislation with respect to Alaska, or to insist upon territorial organization by popular legislation?

I like to come out here, because I believe that here I find a people that sympathize deeply with me about the Philippines. The truth is, my political life began in the Philippines, and I rather feel as if I hailed from the gem of the Pacific than from any state of the Union, in a political sense. Certainly if it would not have been for them, I would not be President of the United States; and when I come to a people who are as interesting as you are, I like to talk with them because my sympathy and my hopes are far out in the Pacific from a personal standpoint.

I am convinced that with the adoption in this last tariff bill of free trade with the Philippines, the people of Tacoma, Seattle and San Francisco are going to live to see the day when they will thank God for the passage of that bill. I came over from Seattle this afternoon with a gentleman who congratulated me on the immediate effect of the bill, and said that if I wanted to I could use his certification that the trade has already begun. He said that he had just sold 100,000 barrels of flour to Manila, and that a great many other things had been sold in the same direction. They are going to have a good many cloths, like piña cloth, that will attract the attention of the ladies, and will lead them to buy it because it will come over at a cheap rate and because it is very pretty. I am not a judge of it myself. There are summer hats of a delightful texture—I know because I have worn them—and there are many other things that the deft fingers of the Filipinos will make and export into this country. On the other hand, your manufactures, your flour and other things that you raise will go out to the Philippines, all because the duties have been taken off at both ends.

I want to congratulate you on the fact that in the next fifty years the growth of this world's business is to be in the Pacific—and you are on the Pacific. You have one of the most magnificent harbors in the world. I do not need to convince you about that I believe, and here at the end of three or four great transcontinental lines you have an opportunity to play an important part in the Oriental trade of this country.

Japan is making giant strides to control the Oriental trade. She is trying to get trade in China, just as we are. China is waking up from her dream of centuries past. She is developing and the more she develops the more we ought to like it. We ought not to proceed on the theory that the proper kind of a country for us to deal with is a country that sells to us things at a cheaper price than they ought to bring, and that will give us a higher price than our things ought to bring. That is the way modern commerce is carried on. The great countries that deal with us profitably are the countries who know what they want and whose business is of such great extent that they are able to deal with us on a level, and that is the kind of development that we ought to hope for China. With China growing, with Japan growing, with the Philippines growing, and you here at the end of two or three transcontinental lines, with a harbor so magnificent as this is, I do not know what your future is going to be. It is full of hope and if I did not know that you are just as full of hope as you ought to be, I would emphasize it.

But, that trade is to be carried in what? It is to be carried in ships. Now, whose ships ought it to be carried in? [Cries of "ours".] Yes, you are right—you ought to go to the head. And yet we haven't a ship—well, you have; there is the *Minnesota*, and I am not going to cross the bridge that carried me over; it is a comfortable ship and it took me across the ocean, but it is the one ship you have here with an American flag. There are some in the Pacific Mail in San Francisco.

If the bill introduced in Congress by one of your Congressmen from Washington, Mr. Humphrey, passes, offering a subsidy, we shall have a number of lines to the Orient and several lines between New York and the southeastern coast of South America, where there is another trade we are likely to lose because Europe is putting on many fast lines running to that part of the world.

This bill is an experiment. We are earning by our foreign mail upward of six or eight million dollars a year profit, that is, the stamps that we sell and our part of the money that is collected for foreign mail exceed our expenditures from six to eight million dollars. And all this bill proposes is that that sum shall be invested in subsidies to be paid to a number of lines to the Orient and to several lines to South America, so that we may try it out and see how it will work. Now, I say that it is wise to do that. There are gentlemen who will oppose it, and oppose it consistently, because they say it is paying money out of the public treasury into the pockets of private individuals. It is, but it is not paying it for them to keep it there. It is paying it for them to run ships out of which they can make no profit at all unless they get it out of what we pay to them; in other words, out of what is paid to them they will have to pay a large proportion in order to be able to compete with the ships of other nations, so that it is not paying the subsidy into their pockets for nothing. It is paying something into their pockets for them to do something which will inure to the benefit of the country.

234

Mr. Thomas B. Reed used to express his opinion of men who opposed what he regarded as beneficial legislation because somebody was likely to profit by it. "Oh, yes," he said, "he is one of those men opposed to the bill because a man might make $1.50." Now, that spirit I deprecate. We have proceeded to invest money in our rivers and harbors so that steamboats could run on them. Well, that money came out of your pocket and mine and through other sources of taxation to put water into the stream so that the steamboats should run on it. The man who runs the steamboat on the water gets profit out of it. Are not we helping him by direct contribution to do his business? So it is with the protective tariff. We put up a tariff for the purpose of increasing prices and making everybody contribute a little bit in order to have our industries diversified. This subsidy is exactly on the same principle. We cannot protect it by the tariff because the competition is by foreign vessels which we can not control, and the only thing we can do is to pay the money directly instead of making a protective tariff.

People run away from the name subsidy. It is a subsidy. I am not afraid to call it so. It is paid for the purpose of giving a merchant marine to the whole country so that the trade of the whole country may be benefited thereby, and the men running the ship will of course make a reasonable profit. It is difficult for anybody with any amount of money to run a vessel if he be an American and subject to American laws and make a profit. He can not do it; and we are trying to help him out with this subsidy so that he may make a reasonable profit. We are not making him a millionaire either. When he gets the subsidy he has to work hard to earn it and to make a reasonably small profit. We are gradually convincing those through the Middle West of the mistake of their opposition and the wisdom of paying such subsidies for the purpose of increasing our merchant marine.

It is said we have a great foreign trade at any rate. It is increasing every year, so what is the need of this. Let the rest of the world do our carrying business. If they will do it at a cheap rate, let's get it and save our money. The difficulty about that is that when you control the merchant marine, you do control trade. It is seen in South America. The facility with which steamer lines can be established between Europe and the ports of South America has led to their getting more and more proportionately of the trade between the eastern ports and South America, and so it is everywhere. When you control the merchant marine you control the avenues of trade, and you are able to divert it in one direction or another; therefore, it is a great instrument to help us increase our international trade.

I ought to say about that trade that one of our troubles is that we are altogether too conceited. We feel, for instance, that we have so much business here that if they do not like the patterns which we make, if they do not like the looms upon which our textile fabrics are made, they need not take them, and the consequence is we lose the trade. We need our foreign trade, and our merchants have to learn that they must make the same effort with the foreign trade as with the domestic trade. This is the course which has been followed by great companies that have made foreign commerce a success. But I merely note in passing that which has been made most apparent to those of us who have lived in the Orient—that the German and Swiss and Japanese manufacturers consult with the utmost attention the desires of the Oriental, and it is just as well that we should. If we want to sell something, we had better make it attractive to the men who wish to buy it.

Now, something which ought to appeal to all of us is that unless we have a merchant marine, our navy if called upon for offensive or defensive work is going to be most defective. We haven't tonnage enough today in our foreign trade to enable us to give to the navy the auxiliary ships that will be necessary to carry ammunition, coal and those other things that are necessary in order to fit the sailors and maintain the ships. Therefore, we ought to exert ourselves to produce that tonnage so when the time comes that the life of the nation is in danger and we need the navy to protect us against invasion or against attack, we should have the auxiliary under our own flag in order to make the operations of the navy effective.

I have talked a good deal longer than I have had a right. I have become interested in these subjects, and have gotten into a perspiration over them, but I believe thoroughly what I have said to you, and I hope when you go home and think it over, you will come over to my side; at any rate, if you do not, that you will believe I have been in earnest in what I have said.

I thank you sincerely for your attention. I hope your community will go on increasing in wealth and in intelligence, if that is possible.

32

The Tariff, Income and Corporation Taxes

The Armory, Portland, Oregon, October 2, 1909

Mr. Mayor; Ladies and Gentlemen; Citizens of Portland:

I wish to extend to your distinguished Mayor and your people of this beautiful city my heartfelt acknowledgment of the cordial reception which I have had at your hands since reaching your city this morning. I wish to thank the veterans of the Grand Army for the honor which they have done me tonight in escorting me to this hall. I appreciate the motive of these men who helped preserve the Union, who recognize in me the Commander-in-Chief, under the Constitution, of that country which they did so much to preserve and save.

I am going tonight, my friends, if my voice holds out, and your patience holds out, to take a little review of the present administration, of what it has done, and of what it has agreed to do. In the first place the party of the administration agreed to revise the tariff, and in my judgment, that agreement involved a revision downward, because, under the theory of the protective tariff after a ten years' trial, the effect of competition ought to have made rates of tariff less necessary generally than they were ten years ago. Now the tariff bill which was passed was, in my judgment, a substantial revision downward, but it was not, in certain important respects, a compliance with the terms in respect to the woolen schedule, and perhaps there might be

237

some other things mentioned of that character, but the truth was, that the States that were interested in the manufacture of woolens and the states that were interested in the preservation of the woolen industry united and prevented a change of that tariff, which had been reached by agreement after very difficult negotiation.

Now, the question was whether, because that bill did not, in all respects, comply with the terms of the party, members of the House and of the Senate should decline to vote for it, and the President should decline to sign it. After thinking the matter over, I became convinced that it was my highest duty to sign it, for the reason that while, in certain respects, it was defective, it was nevertheless the best tariff bill which the Republican party had ever offered to the people, and it was necessary that a tariff bill should be passed, in order that the prosperity which we were awaiting should come. As long as there remained unsettled the important question of the tariff, business would not resume with the prosperity and the energy and the enterprise which it would have when business conditions became settled.

Again, we are engaged in running a government by party, and because some of us are disappointed with respect to some things that the party does not do, if we think that party considerations are of higher importance, if we think that in order to accomplish anything, we must have solidarity of party, then we may well weigh our personal predilections with reference to some issues, in order that we may maintain a strong party front and accomplish affirmatively the steps that we believe we ought to accomplish. It is easy enough to break up a party; it is easy enough to prevent legislation, but when you are charged with the responsibility before the country of carrying legislation, then you must have a party behind you.

Now, that tariff bill not only affected the tariff of the United States, but it also provided an additional means of taxation in order to meet the deficit which was promised, unless some other method of taxation was added to that of the customs and the then existing internal revenue. At first it was proposed to have an inheritance tax, and I recommended that, but the Senate found protests from all the States that they had occupied that field of taxation, and that they desired the United States to keep off that reservation. Accordingly, the question arose, What should we do?

It was proposed in the Senate to pass an income tax law, to pass a law that had been declared by the Supreme Court of the United States to be unconstitutional. That court had held that an income tax was a direct tax, and that a direct tax, under the Constitution must be levied in accordance with the population of states. Nevertheless there was a majority in the Senate of Democrats and Republicans in favor of passing that bill unless some substitute could be devised which would satisfy the Republicans who were in favor of an income tax, and not involve the passage of a bill which had been declared to be unconstitutional. Accordingly it was proposed to have what is now known as the corporation tax, and also to pass an income tax amendment to the Constitution; that is, to propose to the States to amend the Constitution by providing that an income tax might be levied without apportionment as to population between the States. And, accordingly, by almost the unanimous vote of both Houses that amendment has been proposed to the people of the United States, and the corporation tax was passed in the tariff bill.

I propose, first, to allude to the income tax amendment, which may come up at any time in the legislature of any of the States. I sincerely hope that when it does come up it will pass in each State, and the reason why I hope so is that I think that such a power in times of need and disaster is necessary for the central government to maintain itself, and I would not take from the central government a power which in war is necessary to save the government.

We had an experience in the Civil War in respect to that matter. An income tax was levied, and it was supposed, by reason of judicial decision at that time, that the income tax was constitutional, but since that time, as you know, by a late decision—I say late; in 1896 or 1897—it was held to be unconstitutional. I am not in favor of levying an income tax such as that which was provided in the bill, in times of peace. I am not in favor of it because I think it will prove to be too inquisitorial as to individuals, and I think it will be found also that it puts a premium on perjury, so that the gentlemen whom you are especially after, when you levy an income tax, will escape, and only those who are too conscientious will pay more than their share. In times of dire need it is necessary that we should use such a tax, objectionable as it is in certain of its features, and, therefore, I hope it will pass the States.

Now, what is the corporation tax? That is a species of income tax which the Supreme Court has said was constitutional. It proposes to levy one per-cent on the dividends of all corporations as an excise tax, upon the business which they do as corporations. If I understand the decisions of the Supreme Court, that is held not to be a violation of the Constitution, because it is not a direct tax, but it is only a tax on business; it is an excise tax. That brings under Federal control in a sense and under Federal supervision in a sense all corporations. The tax is not levied on incomes of corporations less than $5,000, but all corporations for gain are required to file returns which show their gross receipts, their expenses, their debts, bonded or otherwise, and certain other general facts which will show their condition and enable the tax-gatherer to assess the proper taxation.

If the Commissioner of Internal Revenue shall have reason to believe by evidence that those returns are inaccurate in any case, then he may send an agent who shall examine the corporate officers and the corporate books and such other witnesses as may be necessary to determine what the actual condition of the corporation in question is.

Now, that is a qualified publicity provision with respect to all corporations of the country, and I think it is an excellent incidental benefit of the corporation tax. It is said it is not fair, because on one side of the street is a partnership that is not a corporation, doing exactly the same business that the corporation is doing on the other side of the street. But the corporation on the other side of the street has certain advantages in doing its business which are not enjoyed by the partnership. One advantage, and a very decided one, is that the partners are liable in all their estate for the debts of the partnership, whereas the share-holders in the corporation are liable only to the amount of their stock, or, under some State constitutions, to double that. Again, the corporation lives forever; a partnership dies with the death of one of the partners. Other advantages may occur to you, but these two are sufficient to make a distinction. If the corporation does not choose to continue, and they can divide back again into a partnership, they can do so, and nobody will charge them a tax, but as long as they enjoy the privilege of doing business as a corporation, and carry on their business with that advantage, then the Federal Government has a right to levy, and it seems to me it is a wise tax for the Government to levy.

It is not a heavy tax; one percent—that is one percent on a year's income. If you own ten shares of $100 each, that is $1,000, and you receive six percent; that would be $60, and one percent on that would be sixty cents. It is not a very heavy tax, and I doubt if it will reduce the dividend in the case of any corporation, because a well regulated corporation ordinarily does not declare all of its earnings into the dividends. But whether it does or not, I do not mean to say that it is not a tax, but it is not heavy. It will raise about $26,000,000 or $30,000,000, and that will make up the deficit as it is calculated between the expenditures of the Government and the amount raised from the customs and the internal revenue.

Another provision of the tariff law is the section which declared free trade between the Philippines and the United States, and that, my friends, you are decidedly more interested in from the standpoint of your pocket than I am, because, unless I am no prophet at all, unless I know nothing of the Philippine Islands, and am no judge of the business that is to grow out of our association in free trade with them, you are going to find a trade with the Philippines that will grow each year, that will become more and more valuable to you, that will become more and more valuable to the Philippine Islands; so that when the time comes that we can say to the Filipinos: "Here, we have educated you all up to self-government, and you are at liberty to go and become a separate nation, and cut off our business associations and have a tariff between us," you will find, in my judgment, that neither the Filipinos on the one side, nor we on the other will desire that severance.

The corporation tax, I have said, gives some Federal supervision over corporations. If you were to look into the statistics of the corporations and try to find out how many there are in this country and what business they are doing and what earnings they are having and what their expenses are, I venture to think you would be in a mass of statistics in which you would lose yourselves. The fact is, there are at present no means of telling what our corporations are doing. In some States they are required to make reports, and in others not. All the difficulties that we have had in respect to the standards of business, in respect to monopolies, in respect to those things that Theodore Roosevelt denounced, and intended to bring about legislation which should stop—all those things have arisen out of corporations and the privileges which corporations have been given. Now, I am not here to denounce corporations. We could not get along without corporations—they are a necessary instrument in the business of this country, and in its prosperity; but as we give them privileges, as we give them power, so they must recognize the responsibility with which they exercise that power, and we must have the means of compelling them to recognize that responsibility and to keep within the law.

One of the things that enables us to keep them within the law is to know what they are doing, for one of the things that a corporation does, if you do not supervise and look closely, is to hide everything behind it, and this corporation tax is a step and a long step toward Federal investigation and supervision—I had almost said control—of all corporations. Of course, corporations within the State are State corporations, but they generally do a large interstate business, and after we have established this only modified and qualified supervision of all corporations, we can begin to classify and make more acute and more direct and more thorough our investigation of those particular corporations that we are after. I think, therefore, that this administration has something already to point to in its accomplishment; that it has passed the tariff bill, that it has put free trade between the United States and the Philippines, and that it has taken a long step toward the proper control of the corporations in the passage of the corporation tax law.

Another thing which the tariff bill has done, which has not been commented on particularly, is the provision called the maximum and minimum clause. The European nations have not been slow in levying tariffs themselves. And they have at times discriminated against us in favor of some other country with which they had friendly relations. They have also at times imposed such restrictions, hardly in good faith, upon the importation of our food-stuffs, our lard, our hogs, our beef and other food products, which we send over there, as really to exclude us from their markets; and they have done it in such a way that it was difficult for us to retaliate or to secure an amelioration of the condition of exclusion.

Now, this maximum and minimum provision leaves to the President to say whether any country with which we have business exercises the power of unduly discriminating against American products, and if it does not, then they enjoy the benefit of the minimum or normal rate of tariff in coming into this country with their products. But if it does, then the President shall refuse, if in his judgment their provisions are unduly discriminatory against this country and in favor of some other country. If that is found to be the case, then the President shall refuse to proclaim that the minimum tariff is in effect between us and that country, and thereby the maximum tariff of 25 percent of increase on everything goes into force.

They have maximum and minimum tariffs in other countries. Up to this time we have had none here, and every time we wanted to get even with some country in order to make that country come down and do justice to us, we have had to appeal to Congress to change the rates, and that was a very clumsy and generally an impossible thing to do, because Congress does not want to change one rate without changing a great many others. So this now transfers that power to the Executive, and enables the Executive to act without waiting for Congressional action. What is going to be its effect? Not that we are going into a tariff war—not at all. I sincerely hope I shall not be called upon to exercise this power in a single case with respect to a single country, because the existence of the power is enough to prevent other countries from exercising that discrimination against us when they are advised that we have weapons of our own with which to retaliate.

Another and most important provision of the tariff is that which enables the President to appoint or employ as many experts as he sees fit, consistent with the appropriation of $75,000, made to assist him in the execution of this maximum and minimum tariff clause, and also to assist him and other officers in the execution of the tariff law itself. I construe that to give me power to appoint a board, which I have appointed, which shall go into this tariff business thoroughly, which shall assist me with respect to a knowledge of foreign tariffs, whether they are unduly discriminatory, and if so, how; also to tell me of the operation of this tariff, to tell me the cost of things here, and the cost of things abroad, and to explain to me what these mysterious technical and business expressions in the tariff law mean. You hear a great deal about the tariff, but I would like to have you take up a tariff bill and go through it and then tell me what it means.

Why, it is just like so much Choctaw to a man who is not an expert, and you take an expert on a part of it and he will find that a good deal of the rest that he is not an expert on is Choctaw. So what I wish to use this board for, and what I think under the law I have a right to use it for, is to make a glossary, to make an encyclopedia, to make what is comparable to the United States Pharmacopoeia with respect to drugs, so that when a thing is completed and you take up the tariff law and come to something you do not understand, you can turn to that particular head in the encyclopedia and find out what it means, find out what the exact rate is *ad valorem,* find out where the article is produced, how many factories in this country, how many in other countries are producing it, and in what quantity; find out how it is produced and what labor goes into it, and what the material costs here and abroad. When we have that, we shall have something upon which the Senate and the House and the people can act intelligently in respect to the revision of the tariff.

Now, my friends, that is what has been done. What is there yet to do? In the first place, this administration was elected on a platform that we proposed to carry out the policies of Theodore Roosevelt, and we propose to keep that promise. Let us see what those policies were, speaking generally. I had occasion to say the other night that one little difficulty in carrying out those policies is that there are sometimes indefinite views as to what those policies are. There are some gentlemen, to use an expression that I have heard good Catholics use when they say that a man is even more Catholic than the Pope, who are more Rooseveltian than Mr. Roosevelt; and when they get a fad that Mr. Roosevelt may have heard of or may not have heard of, but which they are very much attached to, they like to gather it in as a part of the Roosevelt policies, and then if you do not subscribe to it, they denounce you as a traitor to the Roosevelt policies.

Well, I was in Mr. Roosevelt's Cabinet four years and had some opportunity to understand what his policies were. The fact is, it fell to my lot to take the platform and discuss them, by his direction and with his sympathy, and therefore I think I know pretty generally what the Roosevelt policies are and what the platform of the Republican party meant when it pledged the party in the administration, if elected, to the carrying out of these policies.

Mr. Roosevelt's chief policy was the determination to make the great corporations of this country obey the law, and those great corporations included two classes; the railroads and the great industrial corporations that did a large industrial business, and that had shown a tendency to try to monopolize that business and control prices and suppress competition. Mr. Roosevelt impressed upon the country, impressed upon Congress, and succeeded in inducing Congress to pass what was known as the Hepburn Rate Bill, and that was for the purpose of enabling the Interstate Commerce Commission to fix rates when complaint was made as to their unreasonableness. Up to that time the only thing that the Commission could do was to say. "We believe this rate is unreasonable, and you must fix another rate"; but that law said: "No, when you find that the rate is unreasonable, then it is your business to go on and fix a reasonable rate."

The law gave greater power to the Commission in other respects in detail, which I shall not dwell upon; but it contained a provision for a court of review. There was considerable discussion as to whether it ought to do so or not. In my judgment it ought to have done so but it did not make any difference whether it did so or not; there would be a court of review of a decision of the Interstate Commerce Commission. A court of review arises from a constitutional right of a railroad company or any other corporation owning property to obtain from its use a fair compensation; and, therefore, if the rates were confiscatory, to complain that it was property taken away from them without due process of law. Hence the situation was this—if you attempted by such a law to prevent recourse to the courts it would invalidate the law; if you gave recourse to the courts, well and good; if you did not say anything about it, then there was recourse to the courts anyhow. So that the question really was a moot one.

Now, the friends of the measure, many of them, dreaded the reference to the court because it was thought that this would delay action and prevent a rapid fixing of rates; and I am inclined to think from the reports of the Interstate Commerce Commission that this fear has proven to be well founded, and that the reference to the court, to the circuit courts and the court of appeals has delayed the remedies sought before the Interstate Commerce Commission, so that we ought to make some other provision in order to expedite those proceedings.

For myself, I think it wise, after a consultation with the Commission, and after conferring with members of the Cabinet, to recommend the establishment of one court of five members to whom all such appeals shall be referred. The fact that they have no other jurisdiction will make them experts; the fact that they sit as five men will enable them to dispose of the business rapidly, and then a case will be ended, except on an appeal to the Supreme Court.

It is possible to go into one of some forty or fifty United States Courts all over the country and file your review or petition for review of the decision of the Interstate Commerce Commission. That produces conflict of decisions between a judge in Oregon and a judge in Massachusetts, and prevents that uniformity which is wanted, necessarily, to establish the proper rights and proper conduct of railroad companies.

Then there are some other features which ought to be amended in the Hepburn Bill, which I shall not stop to call attention to, except to say in the party platform specifically was provided a promise that a law should be passed referring to some tribunal the question of how many bonds and how many shares of stock every interstate railway company may issue. In other words, a measure to prevent the watering of stock in the way in which it has gone on heretofore. That is important in a number of respects. It is important, of course, because when you water stock you only do it to deceive people and get them to pay more than the stock is worth. That is the only object of watering stock. Again, it is wrong because when you come to determine what a railroad company ought to earn, the owners of the railroad company turn at once to their stock and bond account and say: "Here are our shares of stock, and here are our bonds, and we ought to earn 5 percent on our bonds and 6 percent on our stock." If they water the stock and treble it beyond the actual property they have, you see that requires they should pay 18 percent of what was the real value of the railroad, rather than six. In other words, it affects, and affects most injuriously, the rights of the people in determining what a reasonable compensation for a railroad shall be. Another thing is that if you pile up the stocks and bonds of a railroad company in such an amount that they can not even earn, no matter what they charge, their interest charge and the dividend on the stock, you are going to have that company in court in the hands of a receiver; you are going to prevent the expenditure of money needed to make it a good common carrier; you are going to interfere with its usefulness in carrying the interstate trade. And there is where the Federal Government has a right to step in and say, "We propose to supervise your method of doing business, even if you are a State corporation only; you are doing an interstate business, and we have a right to impose such a limitation on your method of doing that business as to secure efficiency and to secure the best kind of a railroad to carry goods and carry passengers."

Then there is the anti-trust law. That law provides that any corporation or any combination or conspiracy in restraint of interstate trade shall be punished. It provides also that a monopoly shall be punished in interstate trade. It is a law most difficult to enforce. It is a law that by its terms is so wide that it includes other restraints of trade than those which are with intent to monopolize or with intent to suppress competition. And if you read some of the decisions of the court by judges who do not appear to be friendly to the law, you will find that the very fact that it seems to cover a great many innocent arrangements which have a tendency to restrain interstate trade serves to make the law ridiculous. Now, what I recommend is that the law be so amended as to narrow it and confine it to combinations and conspiracies to suppress competition and to establish monopolies, and to leave out the denunciation of general restraints of trade. At common law general restraints of trade were not crimes, but men who entered into a contract that had a tendency to restrain trade were left to their own devices to secure its execution. The courts would not enforce it, but this goes farther and denounces as a crime all restraints by contracts and combinations and conspiracies in restraint of trade.

Now, what is the effect of that? One effect has been that the Supreme Court has held that a boycott levied against interstate trade is within that statute, and the labor unions and others have complained that that is an extension of a statute intended to suppress monopolies, trade monopolies and trade suppression and competition, to something which, while the letter of the statute permits it, was not intended by Congress, and was not the evil at which Congress aimed. I am inclined to think that that complaint is not without good foundation, and that we ought not to strain the statute to meet something which in its original conception it was not intended to remedy. I do not think there is any doubt about where I stand in respect to boycotts. If there is, I will just state what I think about them. They are illegal and they ought to be suppressed.

I would never countenance a law which recognizes their legality, and I have not hesitated to say so for a good many years, but I do not think the way to suppress them is to take a Federal statute that was intended for another evil and make it apply to them, although the letter of the statute, and doubtless the judicial construction is right—I am not saying anything against that, I am not criticising the courts, but I am saying it has just happened that the letter of the statute covers their cases. If the statute is changed as I suggest, the letter of the statute will not cover their cases. The labor unions have said they would like to have a definite exception, saying this statute should not apply to labor unions. I would not consent to that at all. Labor unions have got to obey the laws like everybody else. And to introduce a special exception into a statute is to introduce class legislation, and that we do not approve in this country at all. But if by language which narrows this statute and reaches the evil which it was intended to reach, and reaches it better than by language that is broader and gets in a lot of innocent things in addition, we can make it more effective, and in making it more effective we leave out its application to boycotts, I have not the slightest objection. I think it is a good result.

The anti-trust law is a hard law to enforce. It is a hard law to enforce because it is directed against something which the natural tendency in the spirit—the intense spirit of competition—leads business men to. They wanted to avoid competition. They wanted to get ahead of their competitors, and soon they would proceed to unite with their competitors to drive everybody else out of the business, and they would control prices. Twenty or thirty years ago that seemed all right. But when we began to realize what the logical result of that was, and that if it went on we would soon have every business in the hands of a few men, and we would all be subject to the tyranny and the greed of those few men, we saw something had to be done—and this statute was passed.

Now the statute has been most useful and I believe today that due to Theodore Roosevelt's efforts, and due to the crusade which he, like Peter the Hermit of old preached, there has been a new standard introduced into the business of the country; and that men consult statutes now, and consult lawyers to know what the lines of the law are. And it is our business to say to these gentlemen: "Thus far shalt thou go, and no farther"—to point out what that line is. It takes some time for a series of courts to make a decision which shall be plain to the business world. But we are going on with this trust law, and if we amend it as I suggest, we shall draw the lines closer and closer and enable men to know what is legitimate business on the one hand, and what is not on the other.

Now, I have a great many friends in business, and have talked with them on this subject; and I am convinced a good many of them have a good deal to learn.

A gentleman said to me, "We ought to have a trust law that shall permit us reasonably to regulate competition, so that we shall unite to prevent too much competition." Well, he didn't tell me just what kind of a law that was going to be; and he did not tell me, because he could not tell me.

Again, you will hear a gentleman say that we ought not to have a provision for these restraints of trade to suppress competition which shall be unreasonable; and if they only reasonably restrain trade, and reasonably suppress competition, and you get a reasonable monopoly, then it is all right.

Well, I don't know what a reasonable monopoly is. I do know what, at common law, a reasonable restraint of trade is; and I will explain that to you, if you have the patience to listen. I didn't expect to speak this long, but this is a subject most important, and if you will only bear with me I will get through.

The term "restraint of trade," in English law—common law—our law—referred to contracts by which a man agreed that he would not go into business—a certain kind of business—within a certain territory. Now, that contract was enforceable at common law if it was reasonable. If it was unreasonable it was not enforceable. Now, let us see how the courts arrived at the question whether a contract was reasonable or not.

The exception as to reasonableness was introduced for the purpose of enabling a man who had made a good business, and acquired a good will in that business to dispose of that good will for a price, and to give it to someone else so that someone else might enjoy it. As, for instance, there is a merchant doing business in a certain line in the town of Portland, who wants to sell the good will which by twenty years' business he has built up and made valuable, and he goes to John Smith and says, "I want to go out of business; I will sell you all my plant, and I will sell you my good will." "Well," John Smith says, "what is the good will worth if you can sell it to me and then can go into business on the next corner? You will get back all your old customers." "Ah," says the man who is about to sell, "but, I will make a contract with you that I will not go into business in the city of Portland."

Now, that is in restraint of trade. It is in restraint of the man's own trade. But the common law said that was reasonable; because the restraint is limited to that which the man is selling, and which the man is buying. It is what is necessary to protect the good will and make it property on the one hand and enable the man with a business to offer it as something worth having on the other.

Now that is as far as the common law went in saying what was a reasonable restraint of trade. I need not say to you that is a narrow phase which in the great industrial business we are talking about plays no part whatever. But when we talk about reasonable suppression of competition and of a reasonably good trust, assuming that a trust intends to monopolize something, I don't see how you can make any distinction at all, or how a judge can sit on the bench and say, "This monopoly is all right, and that is not." I say all monopoly is wrong, and all combinations to suppress competition—legitimate competition—are wrong. The statute ought to say so, and ought to be enforced in that way. But restraints of trade which are intended to suppress competition are monopolies, and ought not to be regarded at all.

We are going ahead to enforce that statute. As I say, it is a difficult statute to enforce; but I think the country is prepared now to accept that rule of law. I think the business community generally is looking with great care to see whether it is coming within the inhibition of the law; and I hope by urgent prosecution, and by a change in departments, so we can get more rapid action, the law may be more promptly enforced.

There is another Roosevelt policy that we are pledged to, and that is the conservation of resources. I have not time tonight, and I will not detain you with a discussion in detail in respect to that, except to say it covers the treatment of our forests in such a way as to leave something of those forests to posterity; to leave them so that they shall restrain and equalize the water supply. That means also such retention of control over the water powers of this country by the Government, over those water powers which in order to be used men must use the Government land, to retain such control over those that the Government may be able to supervise or regulate the rates charged for the power furnished—the electrical power furnished through those water powers.

Then with reference to the reclamation of arid lands, it means the Government shall go on and by the use of money which the public lands bring to it, increase the productive area of land throughout this arid or semi-arid territory all over this western country.

Again, it means with respect to coal lands, with respect to oil lands, and with respect to land which produces fertilizers, that there should be some provision by which the Government shall prevent the use of those lands by monopolies or syndicates which shall monopolize the use of the coal, the use of the fertilizer, or the use of the oil.

Now, I do not mean to say those problems have all been worked out; but I do say we have gone so far in the matter of the waste of our resources as that men have seen it, and have been able to call a halt and impress the public mind with the necessity for action. And when Congress meets, I propose to bring the matter before them and to ask Congress to amend the statutes so as to put more power in the hands of the Executive in respect to the disposition of this domain, with respect to imposing conditions on the use of the lands which the public gives to its citizens for settlement, in order that there may be a retention of power in respect to these resources, and that they may not be turned over to men who will not observe proper rules, so that on the whole we may not look back upon a field of disaster and waste of which we should not be proud in our history.

Now, my friends, I have talked to you a great deal too long; but these are subjects I am interested in and you came in here and deliberately sat here and didn't move out, and you have had to pay the penalty. I thank you.

33

Remarks to the Pupils of St. Mary's Academy

Portland, Oregon, October 3, 1909

Young Ladies and Gentlemen, Boys and Girls:

You see I make some distinction in the matter of age. His Grace, the Archbishop, called you all his children, as you are, but I have to make a distinction.

I am delighted to see you, and I thank the Archbishop, the clergy and the teachers for giving me an opportunity to come here this afternoon and to look into your faces. I understand that you are curious; that you are interested to see the President of the United States, to see what manner of man he is. I am very much interested to see you and to see in your faces and in your bearing the indications of the coming generation in Oregon.

I was delighted to hear you sing "America." That is our song, although the air first came from Germany, and then was appropriated by England and now is appropriated by us; but it is a beautiful air, and it is the words that make the sentiment, and the sentiment of that song I am sure searches your hearts, as it does those of older people.

Your church teaches that loyalty to God is the same as fidelity to country and reverence for constituted authority, and so do all good churches; and we can be very certain that those who are loyal to their church are certain to be loyal to the country; that those who are good Catholics are good citizens, just as those who are consistent members of every church find in the doing of their duty to the church everything that leads them on to the uplifting of humanity and the observation of all the obligations to government.

And now, my boys and girls, I am going to say goodbye. I wish you all prosperity. I can see in your faces a healthiness, chubbiness and determination, so that when you get into your games you strive to win. I hope you do, but I also hope that when somebody else is a little stronger or a little better or a little fleeter and that somebody else wins, you will have self-restraint to be good losers. For it sometimes takes a good deal more firmness and character and substance that will carry us through life to bear the humiliation of defeat than to achieve success and win; not that you ought not to try to win. You ought to have the feeling when you win a race that the next time somebody will beat you, and if he does, render to him what is due him.

Now my friends, good-bye. I am delighted to have met you. I hope this scene will remain in your memories, as it certainly will in mine. I wish you all prosperity. God bless you all.

34

Address at the Laying of the Cornerstone
of the Universalist Church

Portland, Oregon, October 3, 1909

Mr. Pastor, Mr. Chairman, Ladies and Gentlemen:

I don't know that anybody questions the propriety of my attendance on this occasion, or that it is necessary for me to enter into an explanation. I conceive it to be the duty of the President of the United States to welcome and encourage and support every instrument by which the standard of morals and religion in the community may be elevated and maintained. It was my pleasure and my opportunity to take part in the dedication of an orthodox Congregational Church in Washington in the spring; my pleasure to take part in ceremonies in a Jewish tabernacle in Pittsburgh; to officiate as the layer of the cornerstone of a Roman Catholic university at Helena, and now to take what part I may in the ceremonies of laying the cornerstone of a Universalist Church in this beautiful suburb of Portland. And I do it because I believe that the cornerstone of modern civilization must continue to be religion and morality.

We have in our Constitution separated the civil from the religious. It was at one time my good fortune to visit Rome in order by negotiation to effect a settlement of a number of questions which had arisen between the Roman Catholic Church and the civil government in the Philippines. The government of the Philippines under Spain had illustrated that system known in the Spanish Government as the union of Church and State. Their interests were so inextricably united that it seemed almost impossible to separate them but with the consent and acquiescence of all denominations in this country, I was authorized to go to Rome to meet the head of the great Roman Catholic Church, in order to see if those matters might not be settled amicably. I am glad to say that the result of the visit was a satisfactory settlement, equitable and just to both sides. But I started to mention it in order to relate that I ventured to say to the Pope that the division between Church and State in this country and their separation was not in the slightest degree to be taken as an indication that there was anything in our government or in our people which was opposed to the Church and its highest development, and I ventured to point out that in the United States the Roman Catholic Church had flourished and grown as it had not grown in many European countries, and that it had received at the hands of the government as liberal and as just and as equal treatment as every other church; no better and no worse; but that that was not to be taken as an indication that every officer of the government properly charged with his responsibility would not use all the official influence that he had to encourage the establishment of churches, their maintenance and the broadening of their influence in order that morality and religion might prevail throughout the country.

This is a Universalist Church, known as a liberal church. I think it must have been a Universalist who said that the Universalists believed that they would be saved because God was good; that the Unitarians believed they would be saved because Unitarians were good. But whatever the creed, we have reached a time in this country when the churches are growing together; when they are losing the bitterness of sectarian dispute; when they appreciate that it is necessary, in order that their influence be felt, that they stand shoulder to shoulder in the contest for righteousness. They believe in the Fatherhood of God and the brotherhood of man; and the real broad Christian statesman is glad to accept from every quarter the assistance which will elevate the people and lead them on in that progress that we all believe the American people are making. If they are not attaining higher moral standards, then all this material progress, all this advance in luxury and comfort is worth nothing.

I am an optimist. I believe we are better today than we were fifty years ago, man by man. I believe we are more altruistic. I believe that each man is more interested in his fellow than he was fifty or one hundred years ago. I know you can point to instances of self-depravity, of selfishness and greed, but I believe those instances are made more prominent because we condemn them more, and because by being made prominent the happening of them is made less likely.

I am glad to be here. I hope this church will thrive. I hope it will maintain its high principles of making a good man and a good citizen and mixing them together. I welcome the opportunity to be able as President of the United States to say there is no church in this country, however humble, which preaching true religion, which preaching true morality, will not have my support and my earnest effort to make it more successful when opportunity offers.

35

Subsidy, Merchant Marine, and Conservation of National Resources

Hotel Fairmont, Banquet Tendered by Citizens of
San Francisco, California, October 5, 1909

Mr. Mayor and Men of San Francisco:

This is the fifth time that I have had the honor and the pleasure of visiting your great city. And I am going to come again when I can. I have not had the privilege at any time of staying long. But one of the great advantages of your city is that you do not have to stay long to like it well. There is something so cosmopolitan, something so free and open-hearted in the way in which you take in strangers, something so confident on your part that you have something to give to us which we ought to know and love and feel grateful about as long as San Francisco lives, that I come here always with a feeling that, first, I am coming where I am welcome; second, that I will always carry away in my heart a memory, sweet and always to be called up when I think of my favorite cities.

I shall feel deeply this expression of your good fellowship. You have added to the character of San Francisco in the last three years something that makes you exceptional in the history of the world. I know, because there was a time when I had some responsibility connected with it—I know how that first year after the disaster that visited you seemed an unsurmountable obstacle to your restoring the city to the imperial sway that it had upon this coast. And we in the East were considering whether your power was to pass northward or southward, and were regretting that the Golden Gate and your magnificent harbor were not to be in accord with the city upon its shores. And yet you have overcome all of this.

I do not know how you have done it. Somebody ought to write a history about it and tell how it was that you overcame not alone the disaster, but the difficulties that in your own population you had to meet and that seemed for a time entirely impossible to overcome. I do not wonder that you are proud of it. I do not wonder that your orators can speak of nothing else, for that fills the measure of your memories during the last three years. I had intended to make a staid, sober, dull, business speech to you. It did occur to me as I heard what we had been delighted to hear tonight, that there was an answer to a question which was put to me with respect to the presidential tour. A man said to me, "It's all right in respect to your going and imparting information to the people. But how are they going to impart it to you with reference to the needs of their sections?" It occurred to me as I sat here this evening that if that man had been here tonight he might have heard a hint or two.

Now, there are certain local matters of which I have heard with reference to which I should like to speak, because I am deeply interested in them. You have undertaken to furnish an auxiliary coast artillery force. The United States agrees to equip it and give it instruction, so that if your shores are ever threatened that force will be trained to work the guns for which in the Federal army we have but about a quarter of the men required.

I understand that there is a movement in San Francisco to erect an armory for that coast artillery. I sincerely hope it will succeed. You could not do anything that would aid the Government more than in the preparation and the furnishing of such a force. Infantry are good, and infantry we ought to have. But if you will furnish a trained force to man the guns, you will give us a force that, under ordinary circumstances if we did not have it, would take at least two and perhaps three years to fit men to discharge that duty.

Then I have heard something about the merchant marine. You are the gateway to the Pacific.

The Philippine Islands have at last had justice done to them, and we are going to have free trade between them and this country. And that trade is going to grow. It may be slow at first, but it will grow so substantially and be of such mutual advantage to this country and the Philippines that when the time comes for us to say to them, "Go if you choose; cut off your relations to us; you are fit for self-government," in my judgment neither they nor this country will be willing to say so. I do not mean to say that we should not go on and give them as full a self-government as they desire. But I do mean to say that they will see it to their advantage, as you will, that the bond shall not be broken, and that some sort of relation like that between Australia and England or between Canada and England, shall be retained, and the markets of each country opened to the merchants of the other.

You have Alaska on the north. Its wealth—though it has produced marvellously, measured by the expectations of those who sat up and threw bricks at Seward for spending seven millions to buy it—nevertheless hardly has been scratched. And if I can carry out my purpose, and Congress will follow my recommendation, we will have in that territory a government by a commission which shall have legislative power to attend to the domestic needs of that territory and recommend to Congress the development that ought to be going on there.

Congress—and I do not hesitate to say it—has been derelict. It has not done its duty with respect to Alaska. It ought to do it now. I know there is a disposition to say that we ought to give it popular self-government. But I think that those of you who are familiar with the character of the settlements in that Territory will agree with me that they have not reached the time when that is the safest and best method of government for their real development.

It is easy to catch the applause of the crowd by saying, "We are bound to self-government, and self-government is the best government possible." Well it is—under conditions favorable to it. But there are times and conditions of a temporary character when it is not the best. And we ought to say so.

Then we are building the Panama Canal. We are digging out of it three millions of cubic yards a month. We shall certainly complete it by the first of January, 1915, and I am hoping, oh, so fervently, that it will be a considerable time before that.

China is waking up. It is developing as it never has before. Its future is bright with the prospects of increased activity in its industries and the development of its marvellous resources. Its trade must grow under these conditions, and its international relationship become more and more valuable.

Japan is showing marvellous advance in its commercial strides. And as it does grow in its commercial success it becomes valuable as a neighbor and a trader and a customer.

I am in favor of helping the prosperity of all countries because, when we are all prosperous, the trade of each becomes more valuable to the other.

As has been said tonight, it is true that the future of the world for the next fifty or one hundred years in progress lies in the Pacific Ocean, at your gates. The success of your community as a business community and a trading community is not going to be dependent entirely on whether you have a merchant marine or not. We have gotten along in a wonderful way in increasing our international trade without any merchant marine at all.

But that is no argument and no reason for saying that we might not have made greater strides and might not have directed that trade much more intelligently had we had the ships which helped us to carry that trade to the foreign countries.

The trade of South America is a most valuable one, reaching up nearly to a billion dollars. Of that sum 250 millions is between the United States and South America.

We have word from our consuls that, appreciating the importance of that trade, European countries are stimulating by subsidies, and other means of encouragement that comes to the same thing, the addition to the number of sailings of steamships from European ports to South American ports, and that that addition is showing an effect upon the trade and moving more of it proportionately to Europe.

Now, we must do something. We have a protective system in the United States which encourages industries, and we are able to carry it because these industries are completely within our jurisdiction. But when we enter into competition on the high seas we can only control our own ships. We can not control the ships of other countries. Therefore we must adopt some other method than that which we pursue with respect to the protection of our industries. What method is that? I do not know any that commends itself quite as much to me, because it is on a protective principle, as to furnish to those men who will engage in that trade enough money to make the difference, to equalize the difference that they encounter in their competition with foreign trade by reason of the greater expense of labor, the greater expense of material and the greater cost incident to the stricter regulations that we impose with respect to our sailors, and unless we also add an amount equal to the subsidies which our competing nations give to their own ships.

That is said to be undemocratic doctrine. It is said to be subsidy. It is said to put money in the pockets of private individuals. As Tom Reed said: "That man is opposed to the statute because somebody might make a dollar and a half out of it." It is not true that we put that subsidy into his pocket to enlarge it. We put that subsidy into the pocket of a private individual or a private corporation to enable him or it to render to us a service—that is, to give us a merchant marine, out of which, with the subsidy added, he shall be able to make only a reasonable profit.

Now we make eight or nine million dollars out of our foreign mails. The proposition is to experiment first by using that profit which we thus make to pay mail subsidies and establish lines of those steamships between this coast and the Orient, between this coast and Australia, and between the east coast of this country and South America. Let us try that. Let us see how it works. If it gives us good times, and those lines, by reason of the fact that they carry the United States flag and are put on for the purpose of encouraging American business, do encourage that business—that will be a basis for further trial, further experiment and further building up of a United States merchant marine.

If, on the other hand, that experiment proves to be a failure, the money that we have spent will be well spent in teaching that it was a failure.

Something has been said about the conservation of resources by Governor Gillett—oh, no, there is another thing that I forgot about the Governor. He wants sixteen or eighteen battleships on this side of the water. Well, if you will guarantee that the only attacks which are coming will come on this side, we will let you have the battleships.

But I want to call attention to the fact that if, in two or three or five years, we have a Panama Canal, it in itself will double the efficiency of our navy, and the difference between the east coast and the west coast will be far less in sailing distance than it ever was before. The truth is that my impression about the Panama Canal is that the great revolution it is going to introduce in trade and the trade of the world is in the trade between the east and the west coast of the United States.

I think it is going to affect the transcontinental lines so as to take from them a large part of the heavy bulk merchandise that can not afford to and ought not to pay high rates, and to limit their carriage to that kind of merchandise that needs rapid dispatch and is valuable enough to pay the high rates consistent with that rapid dispatch.

It will also, of course, affect the trade between the eastern coast of the United States and the western coast of South America; for that, with the Panama Canal, will be almost in a straight line. If you will look at your geography, you will see it—your recollection of your geography does not tell you that, but if you will put the ruler there you will find that is just about it. Also, it will develop the trade between the west coast of the United States and European ports.

Everybody in the United States will, I am very sure, feel the benefits of the Panama Canal. How far it will affect the Oriental trade from New York or from Liverpool is a different question. There the competition of the Suez Canal will be so great that the modification will not be, I think, as much as is expected.

But to come to the question of the conservation of resources—the Governor stated it with exactness. We must preserve our forests, but we must preserve them in such a way and with such a knowledge of forestry and the reproduction of the timber as shall permit us to enjoy all the timber that ought to be cut and to leave that which shall insure a constant reforestation of the country.

Now, that is a difficult matter. The Government forests amount to about 195,000,000 acres. I think there are four times that amount in private ownership. Seventy percent of the Government forests are subjected to proper forest regulations, and only about 3 percent of the privately owned forests are so treated. That is a subject probably only within the State jurisdiction. It seems to me that the States ought to be, and doubtless they are, taking immediate steps to bring about the preservation of privately owned forests, because we are all concerned in the maintenance of our trees, in the distribution of the waters, and the equalization of the waters which the forests affect.

And the Federal government, unless in some way or other through the theory that it wishes to maintain navigable streams may exercise that authority, will find it difficult to deal directly with those who own forests and wish to cut them down without regard to the preservation of the trees and the equalization of the falling waters.

Then there are the water-power sites. There are a great many water-power sites that the government does not control, a great many that either are controlled by the States or are owned by the riparian owners. But I think we now know enough of the growing value of that water power to insist that the water-power sites which are still owned by the government shall be treated in such a way that the government may, in its conveyance of these sites, retain sufficient control over the large amount of water power that is still to be used which is on government sites, to prevent a monopoly and the gathering of all that power into a single hand.

And I believe it can be done reasonably by imposing conditions which in the beginning are not burdensome, but which by readjustment, after successful use shall have shown a profit, we can share with the government or with the consuming public, by reduction in rates, the charges that accrue from a continuing use of that water.

In respect to the reclamation of arid land—the irrigation of arid land—no one can visit this western country without realizing that that is perhaps the greatest problem we have. We used to think that our farming and agricultural land was so extensive that we never could exhaust it. The truth is, we are up against it now. And the real reason for the increase in prices in the things that go to make up the food of our inhabitants is the fact that all the good land has been or is rapidly being taken up.

We must, therefore, if we would still retain agricultural control of the world, take some steps to avail ourselves of those great stretches of what seem now to be arid and desert lands, but which, by the application of water, when the water is properly administered, may yield a production marvellous to behold.

So I think this trip has for me been full of information. It has made me much more alive to the immense importance of the conservation of our natural resources, especially of the importance of dealing properly with our arid lands.

The Federal Government has, of course, resources greater than most corporations. How far the Federal Government ought to go in this matter may be a subject for discussion. We certainly ought to encourage, as far as we can, private enterprises in the building of canals, irrigating canals, and in using the water of the streams to bring into agricultural production those desert plains.

But there are a great many enterprises about which it probably may be said that they are too venturesome, too full of risk for private enterprise. These ought to be undertaken by the Government with a hope of furnishing models to private owners thereafter upon which to complete the system and extend it.

I am not a paternalist, and yet I am not a doctrinaire of the laisser-faire school. I think a judicious mixture of paternalism where it trains the children of the Government in the way in which they should go is proper.

If we limit our expenditures on this head, as they are limited in the reclamation act to the proceeds of the sales of public lands and to the proceeds of bonds to be paid out of the sales of public lands—as is now proposed—I don't think we shall have carried the matter to such an excess as will demoralize our people.

I know there was a convention up at Spokane, or somewhere, and a resolution was introduced that we should issue a billion of bonds for reclamation, a billion of bonds for irrigation, a billion of bonds for the improvement of rivers, and then there were two other billions, but I have forgotten just what they were to be applied to. Of course, such propositions send a chill down the back of a member of the appropriation committee, like my friend Senator Perkins; and everybody connected with the expenditure of money in Congress has gooseflesh when you even mention it.

Therefore I warn those who are very earnest in this matter that they must be reasonable and wise as serpents in making their suggestions in respect to the matter so as not to frighten those who feel charged with saving us from financial disaster.

And now, my friends, to return again to the personal element in the reception of today and tonight—I can not speak with the eloquence and fullness of heart that I feel welling up within me. I thank you and the people of San Francisco, for whom, in their stress and trial and admirable recovery I have the highest admiration, and I feel it a great honor to have at their hands such a cordial and sincere welcome as they gave me today, and such a good fellowship welcome as you have given me to-night.

36

He Who Conquers Himself Is Greater
Than He Who Taketh a City

Union Religious Service, City Hall Park,
Fresno, California, October 10, 1909

Mr. Mayor, Clergymen of Fresno, Ladies and Gentlemen, Citizens of Fresno:

It has not been my part in religious exercises, until I began this trip, to
do other than form one of the audience; but I have found it impossible,
under the friendly urgency of ministers of the gospel who occasionally desire
a lay substitute, to keep from taking their places and attempting to preach a
sermon.

I want to say, first, with respect to this audience, that the presence of the
veterans of the Civil War is always a great inspiration to higher thoughts, to
higher moral standards and to everything that goes to make our country
worth living for.

I had discussed the question with some of my companions as to what
subject I might select for this Sunday afternoon as one taking part in religious
exercises, and, with the true California spirit, it was suggested that I ought
to point out to Californians how much they have to thank God for. And
perhaps if I took that subject I could get more earnest sympathy and hearing
than with some other texts more useful. There is a text, however; I do not
know that I can quote it exactly; but to these gentlemen before me who have
taken part in the battles of the war, it will come by reason of its comparison
with great significance, that "He who conquers himself is greater than he

who taketh a city." Now the home application of that text to the individual I need hardly point out. The struggles of a man who is burdened by heredity or otherwise with the taste for strong drink, who having yielded many times has finally struggled and with the aid of God won the victory, those of us who are not so afflicted may yet appreciate and honor. But it is not drink alone. I sometimes think, and perhaps your distinguished Mayor, even more distinguished as a physician, will agree with me, that the appetite for food is one that may well enable a man, if he can control it, to look upon himself as better than the man who taketh a city.

And then there are so many instances in little things. I like to dwell upon the importance of little things in life, for life is not made up of one great series of grand stand plays. It is made up of the little things that go either to make others happy or to make them unhappy. It is the conduct of the husband as he comes home after a tired day in restraining himself when he is met by his eager, curious wife who wants to know how he has been living during that day and what has happened. Perhaps something has happened that does not please him, and he does not like to refer to it, and he cuts her off with a short answer. Oh, I know it and so do you. You have done it. So have I. Now, the overcoming of that disposition, the keeping of her happiness, and not your comfort and disposition constantly in your mind and heart is what makes you greater than if you took a city. And so it is with reference to everyone with whom you come in contact. If you have to say "No" say it in such a way as to indicate to the person to whom you say it that you would like to say "Yes" if you could; and when you do say "Yes" and are able to communicate it to the other person, then you are glad because you know it makes him feel happy. These are the homely illustrations of what I read into that text. But I am expected, I suppose, to look at things from a political and governmental standpoint, and the text appeals to me more strongly in that regard possibly than in any other, because of some very acute experiences that I have had in political matters.

Popular government we all approve of, though sometimes I don't think we know exactly why we do approve it. I think frequently we mistake ends for means. We talk about liberty as something to be secured as an end. We think of popular government as something to be secured as an end. Well, neither is true. Liberty is a means in the pursuit of happiness. Popular government we have because we believe in the long run that it is the best government, that it is the government which makes most people happy, and the reason is this: That in the long run the interests of any particular class, and by that I mean those people who are affected by the same set of circumstances, can by representation in the government be better trusted to look after their own interests than any other class can be trusted to look after those interests, no matter how altruistic that class. So that if every class is represented, assuming that each class has intelligence enough to know its own interest, we can count on that being a better government than a government by one or a few or only a particular class. That is a popular government, but you can not run a popular government merely by calling it so. You must have some means of determining what shall direct the course of government; what shall decide. That is the majority. I do not know any other method in a popular government. We do have checks. We do have indirect means of giving expression to that vote of the majority, but when you get down to the basis, it is the control of the majority. Now you can not have a decent, popular government unless that majority can conquer itself; that is, unless that majority exercises the self-restraint that men with great power ought to exercise if it is to be exercised justly, you can not have popular government. And why? Well, take instances. I am not going into the various parts of the world, but I could call your attention, if it were not that I am in a responsible position now with respect to foreign countries, and must speak with care—I could call your attention to a good many instances where those who are in favor of popular government, and who, if I may use the expression, pull the tail feathers out of the eagle in deifying liberty and apostrophizing everything that we hold dear, think just as soon as they become a majority that that gives them the right to control the minority absolutely, and if the minority show any disposition to question it, they send them to jail. What is the effect of that? They say this is popular rule; this is the rule of the majority. So what does the minority do? Why the minority says "We will take to the woods," and they do take to the woods. And so we have that system that alternates between an election and a revolution and a revolution and an election, and we call that popular government. Now, why is it that it works that way? It is because the majority and the minority do not govern themselves and do not exercise that self-restraint without which popular government is absolutely impossible. And that is the application of the text that comes home to me in thinking and dealing with these countries that are struggling for popular government. A minority that is beaten in the election can not stand the defeat. It has to go to the woods. They are not good losers, and the majority are not good winners. Popular government is a most difficult thing to establish. We have had to hammer it out in a thousand years of Anglo-Saxon suffering and controversy and contest. And now it rests, where? It rests in the common-sense, and the self-restraint of the American people. It rests in the knowledge of the majority that it must keep within the checks of the law and the Constitution if the Government is to be preserved. And it must rest in the view of the minority that it is much more important that the government should be sustained than that the minority should have for the time being control of or a voice in the government. Its rests in the knowledge of the majority that the rights of the minority and the individuals of that minority are exactly as sacred as the rights of the individuals of the majority. Our people exercised government over themselves when they adopted the Constitution of the United States. We do not vote directly under that Constitution. We have a vote which controls the lower House in the selection of the members. We delegate to those members the power to make laws. We do not make them directly. We elect legislatures which elect Senators. Those Senators are reelected every six years. The members of the House are elected every two years, and then we elect a President every four years. Each one of those little joints between popular expression and will and the embodying of that will in the resultant course of the Government, is something which the people voluntarily introduced into our government—for what purpose? To enable them to govern themselves, so that the first wave of popular will should not find immediate expression in legislation, but that the people should take time, should discuss the matter, and should have several delays before they accomplish their entire purpose with respect to the Government.

The people rule, there is no doubt about that, but they rule according to law and under the Constitution, and they voluntarily and willingly placed the restraints of that Constitution upon themselves in order that they might act with deliberation and with the checks that were sure to secure moderate, clear-headed, well-thought out policies, and therefore when the American people voted that Constitution and now are maintaining it and supporting it, as I hope they always will, they are governing themselves, and are more to be credited than he that taketh a city.

And finally even we—or rather even those of the cloth, whose place I humbly take at this hour, have learned to govern themselves in this. There was a time in religious history when the man who was in governmental control and had his own theological theory to work out, worked it out by breaking everybody into believing it or else by cutting off the head or burning the body of the man who didn't agree with him. Well, you can reason out pretty logically sometimes that that was the course to be properly taken. And we tried it on both sides. One church and then another, as it got a chance, took that method of introducing religion into the mind and soul and body of the person thus offered up. After a time there crept into the beliefs and practice of all religion the idea that the way to have religion conquer was to be gentle with views that were contrary to the creed and rely on the arguments and the spirit of the religion to win converts rather than to use the stake and the axe.

They overcame the feeling in themselves that they must make their religion conquer by any means, and they took the method that introduced a broad tolerance of all religious creeds and let each creed and each religion speak for itself gently with a message of good will to all humanity; and that is what we have today. And that is what I am glad to think is illustrated by this meeting today. It means the brotherhood of man as between all Christian religions, the brotherhood of man and the Fatherhood of God. It means tolerance for every belief and every creed that a man honestly and conscientiously entertains. And it means that with that tolerance all the people can be much more surely brought within the circle of those who believe and act upon that belief than by any other method.

37

Panama Canal and Merchant Marine

*Remarks at the Banquet Tendered Him by the Chamber of
Commerce at Los Angeles, California, October 11, 1909*

Mr. Toastmaster, Mr. President, Members of the Los Angeles Chamber of Commerce, Ladies and Gentlemen:

I have attended many banquets. I think that, measuring up for the last ten years, I may be said to be as great an expert on banquets as any that the world affords, and while I have attended larger ones than this I have never attended one more beautifully appointed and never one set with such beautiful gems. It is not for me, a guest, to criticise the arrangement by which the ladies look on and see the animals feed. But it is only a type of their loving patience that they should be willing thus to retire and have the men seem to do the important thing.

It is a great pleasure for me to revisit your beautiful city after now some ten years preceded by a visit ten years before that, so that I claim temporarily to be one of your pioneers.

I came into your city this morning by way of your harbor, and my interest in your city was originally largely developed not from an Eastern standpoint, but from the standpoint of a territory from which I have more right to hail I think than the State of Ohio—I mean the Philippine Islands, and I remember as I went there in 1900 I passed through your city and received the welcome and the wise advice of your distinguished fellow citizen, General

H. G. Otis, who had labored faithfully and well and exposed himself to the dangers of death in order that we might tranquilize a country, which God had placed under our guidance. Then another connection with the Philippines is the fact that after we had made a great General in the Army of the United States—General Chaffee—and fitted him for great tasks, and then retired him because the law required it, you had the good sense to take him and make use of the talents with which he was endowed.

Now, coming in by way of that harbor I learned a lot of things. The fact is, in the trip across the country, I have had to justify my coming at all, and have attempted to explain that in coming I have gathered a great deal of information. But it has been said to me that if I do all the talking, how do I absorb any information. I only want to cite as witnesses those who are present tonight to prove that in the course of my journey there are opportunities for information, and I am delighted to improve them. I thought that story of the hobo and the generous lady was exceedingly apt and that the gentleman who used it followed out to the uttermost the principles of that student of human nature.

But with respect to your harbor, I am bound to say, first, that I have learned today by personal observation a great deal about it and of its value and of its possibility as one of the great harbors of the Pacific Coast that I did not know before. I did know that you were intensely interested in it. No man could live in the neighborhood of your junior Senator and have anything to do with the authority concerning that harbor without having it borne in upon him, as our Methodists say, with an intensity that he doesn't forget. It did not seem to me to be of such immediate importance that the harbor lines away out here on the west coast should be fixed for a particular harbor, but there was nothing for me to do under the circumstances but to end that controversy in view of the attitude that Senator Flint bore toward me, and I made an order that the engineers should fix those harbor lines or else some engineers would suffer. No, I do not ask your gratitude on that account. It was a matter of personal comfort to me, and I fixed them, and they are going to stay there, at least as long as I have control; but, of course, they are going to stay there. They were fixed by an eminent body of army engineers, than whom there are no greater or men of higher character. You were greatly concerned, or some of you were, when the gentleman who preceded the present engineer was assigned to some other duty and the present engineer put in. It is possible I have met Captain Frees. It is a little difficult to keep all the army officers, when there are 3,000 of them, in your mind, but I have met the present engineer—I met him this morning—and if there is any citizen of Los Angeles that is more imbued with the Los Angeles spirit than he is, I have yet to meet him, and I have met a good many. The truth is, with respect to army engineers, they are put where they are to do their duty, and when they are there they do their duty, and the great advantage that we have in building the Panama Canal today is that while we have the most eminent men at the head of that work, if they were to die tomorrow from any cause, yellow fever or pestilence of any kind suggesting immediate death to their successors, we could call upon the members of that corps immediately to furnish men who would step into their places and die if necessary in the discharge of their duty without a question. That is the kind of men we have in the army engineers, and if the time comes under the regulations of that Department for the present lieutenant to move on and acquire the atmosphere of some other enterprising port and harbor and city, he will be followed by a man who will do his duty just as well as the present engineer, and you can count on it.

The last speaker suggested a number of things that you would like to have from the general government. I am not a dispenser of the funds of the general government. I am its distributor, or at least those under me distribute the funds that the Congress of the United States appropriates; but living near the seat of government and having had some experience in the way that the government works and with the matters that influence the committees on rivers and harbors in both Houses, I can give you the benefit of that experience enough to prophesy a few things in regard to that harbor. I do not guarantee it. No wise man ever guaranteed what the verdict of a jury would be or what a Congress would do, but I venture to prophesy with that qualification, first, that you have got a harbor now sufficiently constructed to show that it is worthy of being improved to the uttermost; second, that you have taken the step which most of all will secure from Congress the money needed to make the harbour all that you wish it to be, and that is, you have voted to put your own money into the improvement of that harbor in order that the public may get the benefit of the wharf. The principle that has moved the committees in both Houses is that the Lord helps those who help themselves, and that they are most willing to put the Government's money into those enterprises in which the local communities are so intensely interested that they are willing to make large contributions themselves. Hence, I say without hesitation at all, that with your improvement secured, as you have secured it by a vote of bonds, there isn't any trouble about the improvement of your harbor as you desire. I say as you desire it. Our friend on the left suggested 45 feet depth. Well, that is all right, but what you will do with that extra 10 or 15 feet I do not know until you get boats that have that draft. We had to make the Panama Canal 45 feet because it was a work which was to be constructed for all time. The locks when put in there can not be changed with any reasonable expense, and therefore the law provided that the Canal should be constructed of such dimensions that it would transport or furnish the means of transportation for any vessel now sailing or projected. Well, there were two or three vessels projected of 38 feet maximum loaded draft, 88 feet beam and 800 feet long, and we have put in locks that are 41 feet deep over sill, that are a thousand feet of usable length and are 110 feet wide, but that is for the far future, because it would be most inconvenient and most expensive to change those locks, but it is easy enough to deepen a harbor like this; if you conclude that you have so many ships of 45 feet maximum loaded draft that you need that additional 10 feet I can prophesy that you can get it, but my impression now is if I were you I would not go for 45 feet direct. I would begin with something less.

The Panama Canal is of course the greatest enterprise of a constructive character which has been entered upon for centuries. It will certainly be completed by the 1st of January 1915. We are now engaged in an excavation that equals or nearly equals three millions of cubic yards of material a month, and that would easily finish the Canal some two years before the date that I have mentioned. The uncertainty as to its completion depends upon the construction of the dam and the construction of the locks, and the engineers are not yet in a position to prophesy, as they could with respect to the excavation, when the whole work can be completed. What its effect will be upon the trade of the world is problematical. I do not think that we can always calculate with exactness how trade avenues are to change, but I think there are certain facts with respect to the operation of the Canal upon the commerce of the world that we can make as promises. One is that its most important function will be the trade between the east and west coast of the United States. How far it will affect the transcontinental lines of course it is difficult to say, but that it will make a radical change in the character of the merchandize carried I believe is certain. The next important change that it is going to make is in reference to the trade between this coast and Europe, and the next most important is the trade between the east coast of the United States and the west coast of South America. With respect to all other avenues of trade the Suez Canal is apt to be a competitor and the change that will be effected by a new way of getting through the continent is one that can only be known when the change has been effected and years have been given to allow that change to have all its effect. Certain it is, however, that the city of Los Angeles and the city of San Francisco and the city of Seattle are the cities most to be affected by the completion of the Panama Canal, and no one can criticize, no one has the right to ridicule the effort and the great efforts that your city has made to establish a harbor for your city, so that you shall get the benefit of that great trade which the Panama Canal is certain to bring to the western coast.

I do not know that the increase in the merchant marine is essential to your enjoyment of great benefits from that Canal. I do not think it is. I think if we were to go on as we are now, you still would derive immense benefit by the trade brought in here by foreign vessels and by the trade which could only be brought here by coast vessels—vessels of the United States. Nevertheless, you are on the Pacific; you are on that great ocean surrounded by the Orient on the one side, by the west coast of South America and by the west coast of North America on the other, in which the great commercial progress of the world is to be manifested for the next hundred years. And what that trade shall be is going to be largely influenced by the question of who controls the merchant marine that crosses its waters. Now, we haven't any international merchant marine. I defer to those vessels that are doing the best they can, but I mean, speaking at large, we have none and the question is, how are we going to get it? I do not know that the system of subsidy is to be the correct way of working out that problem, but I do know that it is in accordance with the principle that we have followed in respect to the development of our industries—the protective system. We can not protect it in the sense of controlling foreign bottoms, and therefore, the only equivalent that we can offer is to pay those of our people who will build and operate our ships under our laws enough to equal the difference in condition between their running the ships and foreigners running foreign ships and allowing them a reasonable profit; and I for one am in favor of trying that experiment. It is true that we will pay money into the coffers of private corporations, and it is also true that they will have to render to us a service for the money which we pay into those coffers, because it is undoubtedly true—it is shown in our South American trade—that the control by the flag of the ships that carry the trade greatly influences the trade in favor of the country that owns that flag and owns those ships. We must not be frightened by a word—we must not be frightened by a shibboleth. You say we are going to help along a selfish private corporation by contribution. Well, we are, because the private corporation is the instrument by which we wish to accomplish a great public good. We do not intend to give them any more than a reasonable profit for the good they render us.

There are a good many other subjects that I should like to discuss with you. As I looked at that beautiful map and followed that red eye and green eye across it, and saw where I had inflicted my views on various suffering citizens of the United States at points across its surface, I wondered how long the American people would bear it, and therefore I hesitate to take up the questions that are just as important to you as they are to any of the citizens I have had the honor to address. The truth is, I doubt whether in New York, in Boston, in Chicago, in any city in the country, I should have the honor and opportunity of addressing so cosmopolitan an audience as I now face, an audience made up of the bone and sinew of the community that has builded a beautiful city in a desert; that brings its water 230 miles; that goes 20 miles for a harbor; and that expects to enlarge by the application of water to earth, drawn I do not know from where. You are a marvel. You have got two marvels in California. One in San Francisco that has arisen from its ashes, and the other is Los Angeles that is risen from the desert.

There is one thing that that map has taught me as I looked at it—has only confirmed that which comes to me every time I rise to address an American audience—I don't care whether it is in a small town resurrected from the desert in Colorado, or a large city, or anywhere else—there is in the faces of those people to whom I have talked a sense of contentment, of peace, and of determination to get on and subdue the obstacles that are before them, which they welcome because they are obstacles, in order that they may show their American spirit in overcoming them, and that spirit I find everywhere. Talk about anarchists and socialists and discontent with the situation. It may be that I do not see those people; perhaps I don't. I am not anxious to see them. But I do meet the majority of the American people and they come out to me in order to testify their interest in the government and their pride in their country and their belief that there is nothing that an American can not achieve and can not overcome. I never was so much impressed before with the idea, if I may use a stock-breeder's simile, that we are breeding to a type, that we haven't any Englishmen and we haven't any Irishmen, though there are some that tell stories that are marvellously like it, and we haven't any Germans, we haven't any French, we haven't any Italians or Mexicans, but we only have Americans.

Now, an allusion was made to my predecessor's pronunciation of the name of your desert here. He did not come into this country through a Spanish country, or else he would have known how that name ought to be pronounced. Allusion has been made to the policies of my predecessor. I yield to no one in my admiration for that great man and the map he laid out for those who were to follow him. Sometimes it seems as if it were pretty burdensome for those who do follow them in order to keep up with the procession, but it is a great aid to have his example before me, to have the test of the judgment of the American people which he was able to make, and to know that in following along the general lines which he laid down, the administration which follows him is following the will of the American people.

38

Missions

Glenwood Mission Inn, Riverside, California, October 12, 1909

Mr. Governor and Bishop and Gentlemen of Southern California:

This dinner has assumed a phase that I did not expect. The truth is that the honor of unveiling the tablet to the Rev. Father Serra was one that I had not anticipated, but which I was glad to perform, but had I known what was to come I should have prepared myself with some investigation and some knowledge of the history of the country of that interesting period in California's life when the missions began and continued down to the time that we from the East came into California.

Bishop Conaty has been good enough to refer to some of our experiences in the Philippines, and that enables me to say something appropriate of the settlement by monks of Southern California. I there became aware of the great work which had been done by the missions not only of the Franciscans, but of the Jesuits, the Recolletos, the Dominicans and the Augustinians in the Philippines. I became acquainted with the Spanish character and was made to know its heroic side by a study of what the Spaniards had to do to accomplish what they did accomplish in the Philippine Islands in the 15th and 16th centuries. We are in the habit, we Anglo-Saxons, of looking back to our ancestors with a smug satisfaction and thinking that no one has exactly the right to that pride of ancestry that we have, and I think it reduces our heads somewhat and gives a proper sense of proportion to become aware of the fact that there were others than Englishmen in the 15th and 16th and 17th centuries who were making for progress in the world and were fighting the battles of civilization under the burdens that it now seems impossible for them to bear. When you consider the voyages that were taken by the Spanish and Portuguese sailors, when you consider the hardships that were undergone by the Spanish monks, in advancing the cause of Christian civilization, it is hard to believe the story in the Philippines. They made a people a Christian people, who were the only Christian people, and continue down to today to be the only Christian people, in the Orient. Now I have today enjoyed the privilege of seeing as much of Southern California as one man could see in twelve hours and I think it fitting that the journey should end in a building like this constructed to commemorate the missions that formed so important a part in the history of this region which we have been privileged to visit today. I fully sympathize with the desire to preserve as historical memorials worthy of preservation those missions and the style of architecture that those missions represent. I sympathize with the people of Riverside in desiring their government building to be erected on the mission plan. When we have any past of a picturesque character we ought not to destroy it, and California is one of the few States that reaches back far enough into the past to have an ancient picturesque architecture with which she can well make her present architecture accord.

I have at another time and place delivered myself on the subject of foreign missions, and I am not sure that the time tonight will permit me to go into that subject. My association with the churches in the Philippines and with the Bishops of the various churches and the fortuitous preaching that I have had to do as President of the United States at times makes me feel a little bit like a Bishop. But I know this and I know it from actual experience in the Orient, that the progress of modern Christian civilization is largely dependent on the earnest hard work of the Christian missions of every denomination. The truth is, gentlemen, that where we are advancing the cause of Christian civilization it does not help us to introduce to those whom we would convince of the benefits of Christian civilization, the persons who represent the seamy side of our civilization, and those I am sorry to say, with the exception of the missionaries, are the only persons that advance themselves into heathendom. They go there for the purpose of buying or getting from the heathen what the heathen regards as but little, and what they know to be valuable. In other words, they are there for trading purposes, and when our non-Christian friends say that in those that represent us there is a great deal of guile it does not convince them of the disinterested character of

Christian civilization. It is only through the foreign missionaries who go there pledging their lives to the cause of the advancement of Christianity that we have presented to those whom we would convince of the strength and efficacy of Christian civilization that there is in that Christian civilization a living spirit that they ought to embrace.

Now there is another note in the Bishop's address tonight which I listened to with pleasure, and that is that in Southern California there is a broad tolerance between all denominations which willingly gives credit to the representative of any one who as a man and as a Christian has done all that he could and offered himself up for the advance of the race, and I was glad to note that of those who were interested in preserving the missions in Southern California there were 90 percent who were not members of the Catholic Church. The truth is, gentlemen, we are making progress in Christian tolerance, in the brotherhood of man and the Fatherhood of God, and those who have any responsibility at all in the government of men welcome the progress of all churches as the greatest support of government and of peace on earth and good will to men.

Now I want to respond to what the Governor has said with respect to California. I have valued much and appreciate greatly as an honor his company from one end of California to the other, and during the week that I have spent within the hospitable borders of this State I have felt deeply the welcome of all Californians. I know that welcome is sincere. I don't misconstrue it, but I know that Californians are loyal to the backbone and they are glad to welcome to the borders of their great State the representative of the Nation of which they are proud to be a part. Perhaps you are rather warmer in your welcome, perhaps you are more intense in your hospitality, because you are so far removed from Washington. If I were an everyday story, if you had to see me every week, things might be different. But as it is, I am delighted to take advantage of the fact that you don't know me very well, and therefore that your welcome is entirely unqualified.

But jesting aside, my dear friends, there is no experience in my life more delightful than that which I have had in California. It has been somewhat strenuous, but so life is generally strenuous if it is worth having at all, and I am glad to get out of California with the sweet and pleasant memory of this function held in such a beautiful mansion and suggestive of all the sweet romance of the early history of the State.

39

Statehood

City Hall, Phoenix, Arizona, October 13, 1909

Governor Sloan, Ladies and Gentlemen:

I am glad to meet you. It is a new sensation for me to talk to the people of a territory, and I may say thus far it is a very pleasant sensation.

In the first place, I want to commend myself, and that is by having appointed Judge Sloan your Governor. In the second place I want to congratulate you on having such a territory, such energy and such enterprise as has called forth from the Republican party a pledge that you shall have statehood, and in order to establish my relation with you early, I want to say that so far as I am concerned, I am going to help carry out that promise as far as I can. I say that as a beginning of my speech and not as its ending. Sometimes it is better to postpone the marriage and everything else in a novel to the end, but I always have the habit of looking through to see whether it ends all right before I begin, and I am inclined to think that the ladies before me generally follow that course.

Now, gentlemen, and ladies, for I don't know whether you are going to let the ladies vote or not, and I speak therefore with due consideration, you are anticipating statehood, you are anxious to show what you can do as an independent government, and I am afraid you are anticipating the pleasure of that independence without fully understanding or realizing the responsibilities of it; and therefore if after having made this announcement I point out some of the difficulties that you are to have, you will excuse me. You have got to formulate a constitution after the Congress says you can come in, and I want to say a word about that constitution. In saying it I give you an earnest of the seriousness with which I say that I believe you will be made a State. A constitution is for the purpose of laying down fundamental limitations upon your legislature and your Executive. Now if you think that in the Constitutional Convention you ought to lay down all the limitations that are ordinarily included in a statute, you are going to make a great mistake. The greatest Constitution that was ever made is the Constitution of the United States; and you can go through that in a very short time. You take the last constitution that was made. It is the constitution of Oklahoma, and it is a zoological garden of cranks. I don't mean to say that it has not good ideas in it. It has. But the idea of tying down a legislature which is an experiment, so to speak, with the laws that are to be adapted to a new territory, with a long discourse imposing all sorts of limitations, is a mistake which you ought to profit by.

I want to congratulate you on having room enough in this Territory to grow. It is about four times the size of Ohio, and Ohio is a fairly large State. Of course there is a good deal of soil out here that we would not at first sight value in Ohio, but by your energy and by the application of modern methods of agriculture you seem to be reducing it to a condition where it brings forth wonderful crops and enriches those who devote their attention to its culture. Then the Governor tells me that you have another occupation—you can not call it agriculture or horticulture—I mean the hatching and raising of ostriches. I understand that this is the only State in which ostriches think it worth while to pursue race suicide, and that the result is that there is an industry, to call it by a general term, which is really profitable and which enables you to compete with South Africa. Then the alfalfa fields, the fruit and all the other products which you are able to bring forth make your future one which I need not assure you is most promising. But as I have said in the beginning, your assumption of statehood throws upon you a responsibility that will not enable you thereafter to charge it all to the Federal Government. When you get into difficulty out here and have bad officials you can not say the fault is all at Washington because Washington does not understand your needs. Then the fault will be on your own head. I have no doubt that you will stumble and fall as other peoples and other States have stumbled and fallen, but you are Americans, you are come of a race used to self-government, used to taking hard knocks in the school of experience and profiting by them. And if by a caution I can restrain the desire of those most progressive, or most full of the idea of having limitations on government—can restrain them from making the constitution other than fundamental law with simple rules of limitation, if I can halt and induce the people of this State to take time to deliberate over that instrument which is to follow them so long in the history of their State and in its growth and development, I shall not have let this morning go without its profit.

I thank you for the cordiality of your reception. I like to look into your eyes and see the spirit of enterprise, the spirit of welcome to the man who for the time being represents the Government of the United States of which you are so proud, and your recognition of the sovereignty of your country and a desire on your part to pay respect to him who for the time being represents the dignity of the law.

40

Statehood

Prescott, Arizona, October 13, 1909

Mr. Chairman, Mr. Mayor, Ladies and Gentlemen of Prescott:

My father used to tell me of an old gentleman who lent his coat to another man and said to him as he went away, "Don't swear while you wear that coat." He went away and came back after two or three hours, and the owner of the coat asked him whether he had sworn. He said, "No, I have not sworn, but I never felt so much like lying in my life." [Here the President drank a glass of the famous Hassayampa water, handed him by the Chairman.] After that dose which your Chairman administered to me, I feel like drawing the long bow more than ever on this trip.

I am delighted to meet you. I am willing to admit, as I suppose you will, the truth of the statement of the Chairman, that I have not anywhere had an audience of which this is not a peer. I see you admit it, and you haven't drunk any of that water either. I got some of the water on the way up, but I believe it was from below the crossing. I had it in a canteen, and I expect to try it on some of my party.

My fellow citizens, I am glad to see you because I am glad to know that the population of Arizona, which I believe will soon become a State, is of a character to deserve it. I observe that even out of the mouths of babes and sucklings you hear the desire for statehood. I congratulate you on having such an energetic and pretty city. I have no doubt that here, as elsewhere in Arizona, as elsewhere in the new States which I have had the honor to visit, there is a determination on the part of each citizen in Prescott to make her population double in the next few years, to increase the wealth and prosperity and to make it known as a large place on the map. That spirit I found everywhere throughout the West. I found it subordinate, however, to the interest in the State and still more subordinate to the interest in the development of the country. All these feelings develop into an Americanism that makes a type in which everyone who feels an interest in his country has a right to have great pride. Now I had the honor to address an audience at the capital of your territory this morning, and in the course of those remarks I ventured to prophesy that you would have statehood in the near future. The Republican platform upon which I had the honor to be elected promised statehood to Arizona and to New Mexico separately. I am not, however, the legislature of this government, and all I can do is to prophesy, not to promise. But from what I know, from what I have heard of the discussion, I am quite sure that the movement is proceeding, and that you may count on its success. Now then, if it is to be successful, I want to call your attention to the responsibilities that will be upon you as citizens of a State, as citizens of the country. You will have to select your own State officers, you will have to select your Representatives and Senators, but before all that you will have to make a fundamental law called your constitution, which is to govern your legislature, your lawmakers and your executive thereafter, and that is a responsibility which is very heavy and to which I invite your careful attention. The trouble is that you are so anxious for statehood, so determined to have it, that no matter what your constitution is, if it is presented to you, you will vote for statehood and vote for the constitution. At least that has been the experience in other territories. Therefore it behooves you to see to it that the men who frame your constitution are charged with the responsibility of making a good one. Now we have had constitutions made by territories coming into the Union which were voted and approved, and which did not approve themselves to those men who looked forward and understood what a constitution ought to be. It ought to be simple. It ought to be general. It ought to be comprehensive. It ought not to include every limitation upon the legislature that each member of that constitutional convention thinks would be wise to follow in legislation. You ought to leave something to your legislature. Don't make your constitution read like a statute. Be statesmen and make it read like a fundamental law. Study the Constitution of the United States and see what the greatest instrument of fundamental law was and is, and how simple; how it has been elastic and has yielded to the demands of our increasing country, and yet is today the wonder of the world. Don't allow every fact or every principle, however sound, to be asserted in that constitution. Trust something to your legislature thereafter and don't bind them and yourselves in such a way that you will be struggling for twenty-five years to get away from something that was made in haste and not with the sense of deliberation that you ought to exercise in making a path intended to last for fifty or one hundred years. I am talking sense, I know. You will find in your constitutional convention gentlemen who have radical progressive ideas. Many of the germs of truth ought to be carried out at least in statutes, but don't fasten yourselves down by all the crankisms and by the views of people who want to make laws for a hundred years without knowing exactly what the conditions are under which those laws are to be made. I am not talking just for the sake of talking. I expect that you are going to make a constitution here. I hope you will. I am going to do the best I can to help to give you the power to make it, but don't load down yourselves and your future with restrictions and limitations in your fundamental law like those which are in the Oklahoma Constitution, making it read like a long page of the statutes instead of a fundamental instrument like some of the constitutions of the older States and the Constitution of the United States. Our fathers builded even better than they knew, and we have not gotten in advance of them in the matter of laying down simple principles of constitutional law. We do not know more than our fathers, for in that respect they have proven what they knew by the usefulness of the Constitution of the United States.

Now, my friends, as has been said, I can stay with you but a short time. You give me great courage, and give me great inspiration as I look into your eyes and see that you are deliberate men, that you are intelligent men, and that you propose to exercise your suffrage in such a way as to have a government of law, a government that respects the vested rights of property, that respects the liberty of the individual, and a government that shall reflect credit on your population.

I have passed from Boston to the west coast and down the west coast, and the thought that was uppermost in my mind as I addressed all the audiences which I have seen is that we are here and have for years been breeding to a type of men, not German, not English, not French, not Spanish, not Mexican, not Swiss, or Swedish, but a type adapted to our civilization, a type of Americans by which we can all stand. There may be discontent in this country, but if so I have not found it in any community. In every community, in every hamlet that I have addressed, there is a determination to make things better, both materially, in an educational way and spiritually. All they want is an opportunity and they don't ask odds of anybody. Now, that is the spirit I have found everywhere, and I am proud to be an American, and to know that such a spirit is actuating our people, because its continuance assures the greatness of our country and the making of it such that we can continue to love it with all our hearts.

41

Interviews with President Diaz of Mexico

1. USA
Chamber of Commerce Building, El Paso, Texas, Saturday, October 16, 1909, 11 AM

Those present at the interview were Hon. J. M. Dickinson, Secretary of War; Hon. Frank H. Hitchcock, Postmaster General; the Governor of Texas and other State officials; Captain Archibald W. Butt, U. S. A., the President's Military Aide; Mr. John Hays Hammond; Dr. J. J. Richardson; and Mr. Wendell W. Mischler and Mr. Charles C. Wagner, the President's assistant secretaries.

The President of Mexico was accompanied by General Manuel Gonzales Cosio, Minister of War; Hon. Olegario Molina, Minister Fomento (Industry, Colonization, Mines and Agriculture); Governor Creel of the State of Chihuahua (formerly Ambassador to the United States); Colonel Pablos Escandon, Chief of the Military Staff of President Diaz; and Ignacio de la Barra, Private Secretary to President Diaz.

President Taft: I am very glad to welcome you here, sir; I am very glad indeed.

President Diaz: I am very happy to meet you and to have the honor of being one of the first foreigners to come over to give you a hearty welcome.

President Taft: It gives me not only great pleasure to welcome the President of the great Republic of Mexico, but to welcome the present President of the Republic of Mexico, who has made it so great.

President Diaz: I am very proud to grasp the hand of the great statesman who has made such a record in his life—in the Philippines, in Cuba, and, at present, as the head of the great nation of the United States.

President Taft: I wish to express to you my belief that this meeting is looked upon by both peoples with a great deal of interest not as making stronger but as typifying the strength of the bond between the two countries.

President Diaz: My friendly relations and my personal acquaintance with you will make thousands and thousands of friends of the American and Mexican people, and streams and wonders of beneficial development will have to follow for the good of the countries.

President Taft: You have already met the Secretary of War and the Governor of Texas. I shall be glad to have the privilege of presenting to you the Postmaster General. [The Postmaster General was then presented to President Diaz.]

President Taft; I should be glad to have the privilege of meeting your staff.

[The Minister of War, General Manuel Gonzales Cosio, was thereupon presented to President Taft.]

President Taft: [addressing the Minister of War]: I have been Minister of War, and therefore I have a sympathy with you.

The Minister of War: You have been an excellent Minister of War and I have a good example in you.

President Taft: I should be very glad to have the pleasure of taking you and Governor Creel, who interprets so well and who is my personal friend, into an adjoining room for just a few moments.

[Thereupon President Taft, President Diaz, and Governor Creel retired to an adjoining room for a private interview, which lasted about fifteen minutes.]

Interview with President Diaz of Mexico in the Federal Custom House in Ciudad Juarez, 2. Mexico
Federal Custom House, Ciudad Juarez, Saturday, October 16, 1909, 12:20 PM

Those present at the interview were Governor Creel of the State of Chihuahua (formerly Ambassador to the United States); General Manuel Gonzales

Cosio, Minister of War; Hon. Olegario Molina, Minister Fomento (Industry, Colonization, Mines and Agriculture); Colonel Pablos Escandon, Chief of the Military Staff of President Diaz; and Ignacio de la Barra, Private Secretary to President Diaz.

President Taft was accompanied by Hon. J. M. Dickinson, Secretary of War; Hon. Frank H. Hitchcock, Postmaster General; the Governor of Texas and other State officials; Captain Archibald W. Butt, U. S. A., the President's Military Aide; Mr. John Hays Hammond; Dr. J. J. Richardson; and Mr. Wendell W. Mischler and Mr. Charles C. Wagner, the President's assistant secretaries.

President Diaz: Your excellency, the Mexican people and I feel very proud indeed to have you on Mexican soil. I believe that the personal acquaintance which I have made with you and the friendly feelings which already exist between the United States and Mexico will be a guarantee of the continuance of the friendly, cordial and strong relations between the people of the two countries, and that success and prosperity will follow.

President Taft: This is the first time, so far as I know, that a President of the United States has stepped beyond the border of the United States, either on the north or on the south, and I esteem it a great privilege to be the President at the time when that event has happened. I hope that it is significant of the tightening of the bond between the two countries. Railroads and other means of communication, like the telegraph, have brought us closer to each other, so that the City of Mexico and the City of Washington are far nearer today than they ever were before, and that means a closer union of feeling between the two peoples, a closer feeling between those responsible for the Government of each country, and I esteem it the greatest honor of my life to have the privilege of representing the United States in such a significant ceremony.

President Diaz: I thank you very much.

President Taft: I think your Excellency was good enough on the other side to let me present the gentlemen who accompany me, so that I will not go through that ceremony again.

[President Diaz presented to President Taft his son, Lieutenant-Colonel Porfirio Diaz, Jr., of the Mexican Army; also his nephew, General Felix Diaz, Chief Inspector of the Mexican Police.]

42

Toast of President Diaz at Banquet
Tendered by Him to President Taft

Custom House, Ciudad Juarez, Mexico, October 16, 1909

Mr. President, Gentlemen:

The visit His Excellency, President Taft, today makes to the Mexican territory will mark an epoch in the history of Mexico. We have had in our midst very illustrious American visitors, such as General Ulysses S. Grant and the Honorable Messrs. Seward and Root: but never before have we seen in our land the Chief Magistrate of the great American Union. This striking trait of international courtesy which Mexico acknowledges and appreciates to its full value and significance will henceforward establish a happy precedent for the Latin American Republics to cultivate unbroken and cordial relations among themselves, with us and with every nation of the Continent.

Actuated by these sentiments, which are also those of my compatriots, I raise my glass to the everlasting enjoyment by the country of the immortal Washington of all the happiness and prosperity which justly belong to the intelligent industry and eminent civism that are the characteristics of the manly and cultured American people, and to the enduring glory of its heroic founders. I raise my glass to the personal happiness of its illustrious President who has come to honor us with his presence and friendship whose display will make for the cultivation of the common interests which bind the two neighbor nations whose respective elements of life and progress find in their union reciprocal completion and enhancement.

President Taft's Response to Toast of President Diaz

Responding as befits the cordiality of this auspicious occasion, I rise to express in the name and on behalf of the people of the United States their profound admiration and high esteem for the great, illustrious and patriotic President of the Republic of Mexico. I also take this occasion to pronounce the hearty sentiments of friendship and accord with which my countrymen regard the Mexican people.

Your Excellency, I have left the United States and set foot in your great and prosperous country to emphasize the more these high sentiments and to evidence the feeling of brotherly neighborhood which exists between our two great nations.

The people of the United States respect and honor the Mexicans, for their patriotic devotion, their will, energy, and for their steady advance in industrial development and moral happiness.

The aims and ideals of our two nations are identical, their sympathy mutual and lasting, and the world has become assured of a vast neutral zone of peace, in which the controlling aspiration of either nation is individual human happiness.

I drink to my friend, the President of this great Republic, to his continued long life and happiness, and to the never-ending bond of mutual sympathy between Mexico and the United States.

43

Remarks at the Dedication of the Gift Chapel at Fort Sam Houston, Presented by the Citizens of San Antonio, Texas

October 17, 1909

Mr. Master of Ceremonies, Mr. Ogden, Clergymen of the City of San Antonio, Ladies and Gentlemen:

You will hardly believe me when I tell you that this ceremony and the burden that I am now trying to discharge came to me but today. My itinerary in the last month has been so varied and I have been trying to catch up with it with so much energy that "sufficient unto the day is the evil thereof," and I have had to meet the tasks as they have come; but I should be certainly wanting in power of expression, and in that heartfelt sympathy which makes expression, if I could not say something on this occasion which awakens so many pleasant thoughts in my mind.

The first thought that comes to me is that the exceptional circumstances by which this beautiful building has been contributed by the city of San Antonio, by the people of that city, to the army post here, speaks wonders, both for the people of the city of San Antonio and for the Army of the United States which has been stationed here. It has not always been so at every post, but that you should love the army and that the army should love you under the conditions is a noteworthy fact in which I rejoice. This is a beautiful post. I fear there are some parts of the country which might say that this post has been unduly favored by reason possibly of the assiduity of the Congressman who represented you, and the weakness of the Secretary of War whom he influenced. I am prepared to defend my successor, Mr. Dickinson, who accompanies me and who fortified me in the policy which led to the establishment and the improvement of this great post; and the visit here convinces me that those representatives of the army—officers and enlisted men—who have had the good fortune to be stationed at San Antonio vindicated the reputation of the army and entitled themselves to the consideration, association and friendship of the people of San Antonio. There are places in the country that do not value such association as this which you have in San Antonio, but they make a great error. You have seen the benefit, have encouraged the coming, have made this post a delightful post for everyone in the army connected with it, and by the gift of this building, devoted to religion and morality and the rational amusement of a library, you show what you regard as the highest standard of an army and what it should be.

We do not unite officially under our Constitution Church and State, and sometimes it has been supposed that that indicates a coldness on the part of our government toward religion and morality based on religion. You know and I know that nothing is farther from the truth, but that the government does depend and rest on morality and religion and is anxious in every way possible, except the selection of a particular religion and making it a State religion, to encourage religion and morality in every department, and among all its peoples.

Now, when it comes to the treatment of an army, when we take over a great body from thirty, to sixty, to one hundred thousand men, and house them and feed them and clothe them, give them the places in which to live and surround them with those limitations and restrictions that are necessary for the discipline of the army, as in the navy as well, it becomes the part of the government to furnish to those men the opportunities for the worship of God and for the pursuit of rational amusement in such a way as not to lead them to retrograde steps, and hence it is that we appoint chaplains of different denominations and pay them out of the treasury of the United States; both in the army and the navy, and in the charitable and other institutions of the government. And this is not regarded as uniting Church and State.

I have said that this is a testimony to the generosity and appreciation of the people of San Antonio. It is. It is an expression of generosity that means such and shows that you have a community here that first appreciates a good thing when it sees it and then is willing to go down into its pockets and show that it really feels as it says.

I can not now forbear to speak a word about the Army of the United States of which temporarily I have the honor to be Commander-in-Chief. I am not a member of the army and therefore can speak of it with an entire disinterestedness and impartiality.

The army does not get its share of praise. It sometimes falls to a man in Congress or elsewhere to take what he calls a fall out of the army officer or out of the army establishment and we do not rush forward to defend it as we ought. Army officers by reason of the discipline that must be maintained are obliged to keep quiet and not defend themselves and the establishment as they might. Now, I have no such limitation. I have a right to say what I think about that army of devoted men. I know something about it. I was in the Philippines when they were going through a campaign that in its way was as dangerous to life and limb as any campaign that any army went through. I was there when they had to exercise that self-restraint under provocation that no man can know except the one exposed to the dangers that they there suffered, and I know what efficiency they showed both in the upholding of quasi-civil government and in the pursuit of the men who were seeking to kill them on the one hand and having their children educated in the towns on the other at the same time by the very army which they were attempting in every way to decimate. The army went to Cuba. It stayed there two years. It was extended all over the Island; in every hamlet, in every large town was a detachment of troops. Did you hear of a single trouble occurring in a foreign population guarded by that army? Not one. Of what army in the world can you say that but the army of the United States? In the Philippines it was so that they had to be divided up in 500 different posts. They had to be commanded by captains, and first lieutenants, and second lieutenants, and some posts even by sergeants, and the enlisted men showed there the capacity for leadership. Each man at the head of a post was conceiving a campaign against the enemy in the neighborhood, and they were there. That spirit of self-restraint, intelligent self-reliance, that every American soldier has, is exceptional in the history of the armies of the world. The extension of the members of the army over the entire world now has broadened its knowledge. I don't think we can afford to reduce the army at all. I think we need an army of this character of not more than 100,000 in ninety millions of people. Of course there are some distinguished statesmen who see in that 100,000 a threat to our institutions. Well, I leave it to the people of San Antonio whether the presence in their neighborhood of these men to whom they have given this beautiful evidence of their appreciation—whether they fear that the free institutions of this country are endangered by the existence of an efficient army of 100,000 men.

The occasion tonight is one that fills me with personal pleasure, because it fell to my official lot to have to do with the improvement of this post, and to come here and find not only a beautiful climate in which the army can exercise and drill the year around, but to find a beautiful atmosphere of association with the people of the community that makes everyone who knows anything about it glad to increase the post because the people want it, gratifies me very much.

I don't know that I am making a speech that is exactly adapted to the dedication of a church. I have not been long in the business of preaching, but I am glad here in the name of the people of the United States to receive from the people of San Antonio this beautiful building, this evidence of their love and appreciation of the army and this token that they desire to help the army in its standards of high morality and in religion, and this applies I know both to the officers and enlisted men. It is a most appropriate building for all these purposes, and will remain here as long as the other buildings put up by the government, to show the attachment and loyalty of the people of San Antonio both to the government and to those representatives of the government whose fortune it is to live in this neighborhood.

I now dedicate this edifice to peace, good will and humanity.

44

Conservation of National Resources and Waterways

Corpus Christi, Texas, October 22, 1909

Mr. Mayor, Ladies and Gentlemen:

I am delighted to be here and to meet the citizens of this enterprising city of Corpus Christi, and I am glad to receive their welcome as the temporary head of the Nation. I am glad to see the school children arrayed here, because it speaks well for a community that can have such school children. I think it does them good and gives them a patriotic thrill to come together on an occasion like this to meet the man who for the time being represents the sovereignty of the Nation which they love.

I am glad to be in this southwestern part of Texas. I think it is southwestern. I have been travelling for a good many days and I have not yet gotten to the eastern part of it.

It has been my great fortune to spend three or four days in this neighborhood, and to spend them out in the field, so that I am reasonably confident that you who have had more experience with this productive sun of yours can stand it even better than I.

I am delighted here to have the privilege of meeting and receiving the hospitable greeting of your Governor. The Governor and I have made a little arrangement between ourselves which perhaps, betraying a little confidence, I may tell you all. I am not sure how your local committee will like it, but the Governor has arranged that he is to wear a silk hat in deference to the Presidency, and I am to wear a soft straw hat in deference to the Governorship; so that if you see any apparent lack of congruity in that matter, you will understand that arrangement was made in El Paso.

Seriously speaking, I am exceedingly obliged to your Chief Magistrate for his continued hospitality and his kindness in visiting and welcoming me to the various important parts of the State.

And now, my dear friends, there is another occasion for this meeting to which I must make reference this morning. It is to the object of the Inland Waterways Convention, which manifests its importance by calling so many prominent representatives from all sections of the country to take part in your deliberations.

The subject of the conservation of our national resources received its first impetus from that crusader and reformer, Theodore Roosevelt. He pointed out how wasteful in the past we had been of those blessings which God has showered upon our country and yet which had limitations that if we did not respect would ultimately bring us to a famine in respect to many of them. He pointed out the necessity for the irrigation and reclamation of our arid and semi-arid land. He pointed out the fact that we had conferred upon private individuals and corporations ownerships of great mineral deposits, especially of coal and phosphate; that under our present laws, by mere agricultural settlement, persons and corporations might acquire sites upon which great water power could be obtained from the streams and sold to the public when converted into electrical power. He pointed out the necessity for our saving our forests and reforesting parts where the forests had been destroyed, not only for the purpose of preserving our timber preserves, but also for the purpose of equalizing the rainfall, preventing erosion of the soil by cloudbursts and overfall of rain, as well as by preserving the level in our navigable streams, so that they might be navigated the year round, and thus he led up to the improvement of our waterways all over the country, in order that by the use of these waterways and the cheapness of transportation we might have a substantial means of restraining the excessive railroad rates for the transportation of our produce. Now that program is a long one. It is one in respect to which we have taken some important steps. Of the government forests we have put about 70 percent in forest reservations under control, so that we shall not suffer from the forest fires or the denudation by private greed. We have not taken the steps that ought to be taken, but which doubtless will be, following the model of the general Government by the State governments, which shall preserve the privately owned forests, which are four times the size of those of the Government itself, from fire and from that sort of treatment which shall make the country a waste. We have not yet adopted the laws, but I hope to recommend them to Congress, by which the Government shall retain some control over the use of the coal lands still owned by the Government and still to be put under private use.

We have not yet adopted a law, but I hope to recommend one, by which the water-power sites shall be segregated from other parts of the public domain and parted with only under such conditions as shall enable the Government to secure a proper revenue therefrom, and to regulate the rates of power charged by those who shall take possession of those sites and transform the water power into electricity.

We have not yet adopted a rule, but I hope we may, and I shall recommend it, by which we shall retain some control over the phosphate lands of the Government containing immeasurable wealth in respect to the fertilizers of the soil of the West, leasing them or parting with them on such terms as to prevent the exportation of the phosphate or the charging of too high rates for its use.

The preservation of our waterways is one that has long attracted the attention of the Government; and while we do not permit other people to criticize us, when we get together in a convention and talk to each other confidentially, we must recognize that even we have made mistakes at times.

We have invested about $600,000,000 in our waterways. We have done very good work with reference to sea harbors, and we have done some excellent work, when the work was specified, in helping to make our rivers more navigable; but the trouble with the work has been that it has been done largely by piecemeal. It has not carried out a theory or a great project with reference to the establishment of a great avenue of transportation, and the time has arrived for changing our policy in that regard. Sometimes that body of men who have had charge of our waterways in the execution of the improvements appropriated for, the army engineers, have come under criticism because of the policy pursued by the Government, that is most unjust. That policy has been determined by the river and harbor committees of the Senate and the House—that is, the Commerce Committee of the Senate, and the Rivers and Harbors Committee of the House—and it has usually been determined by the clamor from home for appropriations, and by party considerations, whether there was enough money in the Treasury to justify the appropriations and not subject the party in power to too great criticism for wasteful extravagance.

Now as long as that limitation continues, as long as that state of affairs is allowed to exist, we may be sure of having a piecemeal, and a—what shall I call it ?—a procession by jerks in reference to our improvements. Every man who looks at it from a business standpoint—and a business standpoint is a patriotic standpoint—knows that what ought to be done is for us to agree on the great projects that are necessary to better our conditions; to have those projects surveyed; to have the experts determine whether the proposal is practical; to have it determined by Congress that it will work the improvement hoped for; and then, having made up our minds to do it, to issue the bonds to pay for the construction. I do not think there is any distinction between the improvement of the Ohio River from Pittsburgh to the mouth at Cairo, of the Mississippi River from the headwaters of that stream to New Orleans, from the head of navigation in the Missouri River to its mouth, and the inland waterways of the East, or the inland waterways of the Gulf, or the inland waterways of the West, and the construction of the Panama Canal.

You ought to take each as a measure by itself, determine whether it is worth the expenditure, and then if it is, get your money in the quickest way and build your work in the quickest way, so that you shall get a benefit from it at once. That is economic and it is business-like. Now of course I recognize the danger that there is in the proposition that you issue bonds for such enterprises. In other words, that when you issue bonds you are just like, was it not brother Micawber, who when he had just written a note and turned it over, thanked God that that debt had been paid. There is a disposition, when you pay for an enterprise by bonds, not to realize that some day those bonds have got to be paid, and that that is no payment. Nevertheless, I have confidence in the conservatism of the American people and Congress that they will not adopt every enterprise haphazard and go into the business on the theory that it does not cost anything because we can issue bonds to pay for it, but I believe they will go to work with conservatism, that they will calculate the question whether now is the time to do the work, or whether the country ought to develop more before we make such an expenditure.

Now you will say I am influenced by my beginning. I came from the Ohio Valley, and the Ohio River improvement has reached such a stage that we have gone on and built dams and demonstrated the possibility of making a nine-foot stage of water from Pittsburgh to Cairo and keeping that nine feet every month in the year. That is going to cost sixty-three millions of dollars. It has been surveyed and carefully estimated, and that is the cost we may depend upon within reasonable limits.

Now I say if we are in favor of such an enterprise as that, let us vote the bonds and build it as rapidly as possible. You are not without interest in that Ohio River improvement. The fact is that there are nine feet from Cairo to the Gulf, and if you get your coal down and all those other articles of heavy merchandise that must travel by water, if they are to come to you at all, ultimately you have to count on getting that all the way by water, and that will come through a nine-foot intercoastal canal.

But, my friends, before you can induce Congress to vote the money for that canal, or the bonds, you have to show that you have grown to a point where the trade will justify the expenditure. That is a matter of growth, and whether you have it or not I do not know. I expect, if I took a vote, I would hear a very affirmative expression from the present Convention, but fortunately we do not all pass, that is, we have not a complete vote on everything that affects us in this country.

That the improvement of harbors and waterways is a matter to which we may properly devote our attention is demonstrated by the fact with respect to other harbors that have been made such a success.

Take the harbor of Galveston. That harbor, it was prophesied long ago, could amount to nothing because of the obstacles that were there, and a great deal of money was spent on it, and then the Lord seemed to take a hand and wiped out the entire town. But the energy of those citizens met the obstacles, and the city was rebuilt, and today it is the second port in the United States. But Galveston is a type of what can be done when you have trade that will find its way out, and when you adopt the best means to give expansion to that trade. Now just what ought to be done with reference to the intercoastal canal at this point I do not know. You have had the reports of engineers; you have had your example in a boat which you have here which goes from here to Galveston, as to the reduction of rates. There is not the slightest doubt that the best means of controlling railroad rates is water communication; but that is not the only means, and we ought to see to it that our interstate commerce law is made to accomplish the purpose declared in it by adding to its provisions so as to make it effective.

I am not in favor of drastic legislation against railroads except such as is necessary to keep them within the law and to keep them within reasonable rates. The truth is we want to encourage our railroads. You will rush in a body of 30,000 people in a county, and you will vote bonds for a railroad if it will only come in. Then it will come in, and after a time you won't find a friend of that railroad in that county—except possibly its local attorney. Then you will proceed to legislate and you will do injustice to that railroad, but after a while, after you have done injustice to the point where you don't get the proper accommodations, and where you drive them into a system of economy that does not build up your country, you finally begin to realize that the only good policy as well as the only honest policy is a square deal to the railroads so as to give them the rates they ought to have and not allow popular prejudice to deprive them of reasonable profit for the investment, including the risk that they made when they went into the business.

Now my friends, I did not intend to make as long a speech as this, but I only intended to outline what is before the National Government with reference to the conservation of our resources, the improvement of the waterways, and, in connection with the improvement of the waterways, the strengthening of the hand of the Interstate Commerce Commission so that we may have reasonable rates, so that as this southwestern country here in Texas grows up, as it is bound to grow, changing from a stock country to an agricultural country, to a place where you will produce cotton enough to make you all rich, that you shall have the means of putting that cotton on the market at a reasonable rate, in order that you may get a proper profit out of it.

I do not mean to limit you to cotton. I believe there are lots of other things you can produce, including children, and they all tend to the comfort of your homes, to making you better Texans and to making you better citizens of the greatest Republic on earth.

I want to thank the Confederate and the Grand Army veterans who have honored me by coming here this morning. I hope this test of the Texas sun will not be too much for them. When they were earlier in the field of arms, they were able to withstand the sun a good deal better than some of us that have a little too much avoirdupois, but it is a great scene to see the mixture of those who fought for the blue and those who fought for the gray here in Texas sitting together and worshipping the old flag and feeling a common pride in the deeds of heroism that were done in the Civil War between '61 and '64, and that we remember now and use now only to weld more closely all of those who gather under the starry banner.

45

Conservation of National Resources and Irrigation

Banquet Tendered by the Citizens of Dallas, Texas, October 23, 1909

Mr. Mayor, Bishop Garrett, Senator Culberson, Gentlemen of Dallas and North Texas:

I like an optimist, and I like to sit next to one, and I like an optimist in a prince of the church, too. If they are not optimists, we ought to give up altogether. I congratulate the gentlemen of Dallas and of North Texas on their representative for this evening. I think it was wise, if a statement of needs was to be presented to the general Government, that you should have taken one accustomed to form supplications. If he has left out anything that the general Government ought to attend to, I shall call on my friend, Senator Culberson, with his broad view of the Constitution, to point it out. It has escaped me, at any rate.

With reference to forestry, I am not aware that the United States has any particular ownership in the forests of East Texas, and if they are to be preserved and reforested that must be attended to, I think, by the State of Texas. The Bishop says you would like a little help. Well, there are some propositions with reference to reforesting by the Federal Government on the theory that the Federal Government has the control of navigable streams, and that navigable streams, in order to be navigable, should be navigable the

year round—that forests are useful in the economy of nature for the equalizing of the furnishing of water to those streams, and therefore that it is the
business of the Federal Government to purchase sufficient land that ought
to be forest land to make those streams equal the year round. Now, whether
my friend, Senator Culberson, will follow me in that course of reasoning to
show that that is within the Federal function, I do not know, but I am sure
that my friend, the Bishop, will.

With respect to the boll-weevil and the green fly, they come within the
general welfare clause, and we are doing the best we can. Uncle Jimmie Wilson reports every week at the Cabinet table on the boll-weevil, so that I am
fairly familiar with it. I do not know that it is especially a Texas product, but
we do hear more of it from Texas than any part of the country. The green
fly is a gentleman with whom I am just making an acquaintance. But I shall
consult Secretary Wilson and see that he, too, is covered by the general welfare clause.

With respect to irrigation, we are, if I understand it, engaged in a work
in New Mexico, near enough to the west border of Texas to furnish, when
that project is completed, a very considerable amount of water to that part
of Texas that is exactly like heaven, your Grace, when you get water on it.
The comparison otherwise is different. And I am very hopeful that the project and many others arising, not from the general welfare clause of the Constitution, but due to the enterprise and cupidity of man, may make that vast
country that you have within the borders of this State as full of happy men
and women and as productive as the bringing of water to the soil can make it.

Then, too, the Bishop mentioned ports and waterways. Well, ports do
come within the strict limitation of the Constitution, and we are engaged in
the Government, as far we have money, in improving the ports. My own
impression is, that there is a better and more comprehensive method of at-
tending to this matter than has heretofore been attempted or projected—
that we ought to decide upon particular improvements of extended effect
and determine that these things are to be done, and then do them with as
much dispatch as possible. That involves what I haven't hesitated to say I am
in favor of—when you get a project that ought to be done, I am in favor of
issuing bonds to do it. But that is very far from saying that I am in favor of
every project that is suggested, because it is easy to issue bonds to do it. In
other words, I think that if you adopt that system, you must pursue a method
of rigid examination into the merits of the project to see, not whether in the
distant future it ought to be done, but whether it ought to be done now; and
if it ought to be done now, then to do it in the most economical way, and

the most economical way is to take your money and not wait for it until it accumulates by a surplus from your ordinary revenues, but to issue bonds and do it and share with posterity the burden of that which is of benefit to posterity.

Then the Bishop in that list that he presented alluded to the reclamation of swamp lands. Well, I am not prepared to say that that can not be worked in, having reference to the general welfare clause and the necessity for preserving the navigation of the streams.

Speaking seriously, the conservation of our resources, to which the Bishop has referred, is a subject of immense importance, and it involves not only the construction of waterways and the reforestation of our forests, but also the prevention of reduction in the erosion of our farm lands by the floods, which in theory at least would be largely reduced in volume, and much better able to be controlled, if our forests were extended and certain improvements entered upon in respect to our rivers. All I can say to the Bishop with respect to that is that the matter has been noted and will doubtless be worked out in due time.

The conservation of our resources is going to test the practical operation of our Federal Constitution in cooperation, if I may use that expression, with the State constitutions, and this is going to involve joint operation on the part of the States between themselves, and their cooperation with the Federal Government. I believe it can be worked out. I believe that the Federal Constitution—the greatest instrument that ever was penned by man and adopted as a fundamental law—will prove in the end to be sufficient for our purposes, if we can invoke, as doubtless we can, the cooperation of the States on sensible lines. I think we are going to find that possible in the spirit which, I may say without invidious implication, is present here tonight—the spirit of State pride—which believes that there is nothing that the State cannot accomplish when it attempts to do so, even though it is willing to receive such aid as the general welfare clause of the Constitution will enable the general Government to give it.

The Bishop referred to prejudices that existed against Texas in those early days of the Republic before we knew what Texas was, but we know now, Bishop, and you don't find any such reference or criticism in the conventions of the Episcopal Church and the House of Bishops. You have not only been teaching them, but you in your own person and character have been furnishing an example to them and to all Texas as well.

The truth is, my dear friends, that the United States in one sense has contracted to a degree that our forefathers never in their wildest dreams imagined. You are nearer to Washington today in Dallas than New York was to Washington in the early days of the Republic. Your newspapers and your press, of which the Bishop has spoken so highly, and justly I doubt not—I congratulate you on your exceptional press, which puts you in touch with the center of the nation at Washington so far as the Government is concerned, with the markets of the world in London and New York, and wherever the standard of prices is set. The railroads put you in actual communication in so short a time that we all seem now to be one State rather than forty-six different States.

We have been breeding to a type in America, and what has struck me in going all over the United States is that we are all Americans, that we do not differ in our general mode of thought, we do not even differ in our fashions—the ladies know in Texas and California within the time that it takes the express to take a bonnet from New York to California what the change is, and the change is made, and you generous husbands in Texas know it, just as well as I do.

We are getting closer and closer together, and I thank God that it is so, because with our aims more alike, with our inspirations the same, with our object clearly defined before us of the elevation of the individual in connection with material prosperity, it seems to me that there is nothing that we may not accomplish, because we are engaged in what, for lack of a better term I take from the football language—we are engaged in team work.

Now, you might think that what I have said would demonstrate the lack of necessity for the President to travel around the country; that he ought to gather all the information that there is, because we are all alike and we are all working toward the same end, by sitting in Washington and getting it that way; but I venture to think that there is something in the personal touch between those to whom authority is delegated and those who delegate it that means much for both, certainly for the person who has for the time being to exercise the responsibility of executing what he understands to be the mandate of the people. I believe that I myself can see from the trip which I have thus far taken, the value of coming into contact with the people in all the different parts of the United States. I have not had presented in exactly the same forcible eloquent way the needs of any particular section with as much persuasiveness as the Bishop has put forth that which the State of Texas looks for. I have been able, however, to gather, in every part of the country which I have visited, the general needs of each section, what the people there are thinking about, what they are hoping for, and what they are entitled to. I do not wish to say that those two things differ, but they sometimes differ in the matter of time when they are to receive what they are asking for.

I heard the Bishop speak with great pleasure of that which you are laboring for in Texas—that of unity and an appreciation of the man, no matter what his politics are. I believe that that is true the country over. I think party ties are not quite so binding as they used to be. I think the bitterness of political discussion is by no means what it was in years past. The truth is, if you want to be an optimist, if you want to be happy, you must study the facts with respect to our past political history, and I am sure that we can all trace steps of improvement so marked that we shall find ourselves standing with the good Bishop in believing that the things here are far better than they ever were before, and that the things to come will continue to improve in the same measure.

My friends, I am going to say good night and good-bye. I am going to say to you what comes out of my heart—that I thank you for your very cordial reception. I know it is cordial, I know it is sincere, and you can't help it because I can see it in your faces. Of course, it is rendered to the Chief Magistrate of the nation which you love as true Americans, but nevertheless it is sweet for the time being to be the recipient of that expression of love and patriotism.

46

Conservation and Waterways

The Coliseum, St. Louis, Missouri, October 25, 1909

Governor Hadley, Mr. Chairman, Ladies and Gentlemen:

If you will give me a little quiet and a little time, I will bring that voice back from Texas.

It is a great pleasure to meet the people of St. Louis in this magnificent structure. I feel somewhat at home here, because I attempted to address an audience before it had a roof on it.

I am glad to meet here the distinguished Chief Executive of the State of Missouri, and to congratulate the State on having not only those great qualities and opportunities and resources which he has described, but also on having such a Governor.

We are on the eve of a great journey down the Mississippi River, and cursed be he who calls it a junket! It has reference, as the Governor says, to the problem of transportation by railway and waterway. It is, however, only a part of a still greater movement inaugurated by Theodore Roosevelt, and called by him properly the conservation of our national resources. You in the Mississippi Valley are especially interested in that part of the conservation that looks to the improvement of inland waterways; but you are not lacking in that broad national view that takes in the necessities and the crying necessities of other parts of the Union. The conservation includes, first—and that

305

you are directly interested in—the preservation of our forests because their relation to navigable streams and non-navigable streams has been directly traced by scientific men; the prevention of floods, the prevention of droughts, the prevention of the erosion of the soil and the transportation on your Father of Waters of the farm products of Ohio and Missouri and Iowa to the delta at the mouth of the Mississippi. The part that the United States as a government can claim in this conservation of our resources has not been definitely settled, and it is not likely to be until all the phases of the problem are presented for solution. It is certain that the United States has the right to deal with the land which it owns in such a way as to conduce to the general welfare; and therefore that it owes a duty to the people with reference to the forest lands that it owns to preserve them and develop them as far as possible, to make them useful with reference to our water supply.

But the Government owns only about one-fourth of all the forest lands of the United States. Those other lands are in States, and we must look to the State governments to follow the example of the Federal Government and use all the power possible to preserve those forests from fire and from such denudation as shall destroy their water-equalizing quality throughout the country. The United States has been most bounteous and generous in the sale and disposition of the public lands, and we could point out, if we were hyper-critical, the waste and undue generosity with which we have parted with those lands. But in doing so we are apt to forget the condition of the country that led to that generous policy, and we are apt to ignore the enormous progress that has been made in the country by the carrying out of that generous policy. Therefore, without any tears for what has been done in the past, we can take our stand now on the present conditions and say that a time has come for the inauguration of a new policy with reference to disposing of the lands that remain to the United States.

There would seem to be no reason why we should change the mode of disposing of agricultural land; but there are certain kinds of lands that modern progress shows have an element in them that requires us in their future disposition to be most careful. There are the mineral lands, of which we have disposed of millions of acres as agricultural lands, and yet they have enriched their present owners by the treasures under the soil. There is no reason now why we should not separate the surface of the land and its internal contents, its mineral contents in the disposition, so that a man may settle land as agricultural land and cultivate it as such and not become the owner of the coal or minerals which lie below the surface and of which no one has cognizance at present. That applies to coal land and to oil land and applies to phosphate land, which contains the element by which other soil can be made productive.

Then there has developed in the last decade an enormous power available for all sorts of manufacture and for transportation as well, in electricity. That electricity can be most cheaply produced by water power. A great many sites have been disposed of to private corporations that are now pursuing a course with reference to the development of those powers that ought to be encouraged; and it is quite probable that when they come to sell that power the sovereign power of the State may step in to regulate the rate at which they dispose of that power to other individuals. Meantime there remains in the ownership of the Government enough power sites over which the Government may retain control by the disposition through conditional deeds or leases or some other form of conditional disposition, so that the rates can be directly regulated through the ownership by the Government of those existing power sites. There will then be a number of power sites absolutely owned by private individuals, a number controlled by the States, and still more owned by the Government under the character of title which I have defined, and we may rest assured that under that arrangement monopoly can not possess itself of all the power sites in the country.

And now I come to the subject of waterways. We have done a great deal in this country in the improvement of waterways, and we have spent a great deal of money. I am not criticising the methods then pursued. We were growing. We had a great many things to do, and the first money that was expended ought to have been expended in the development of our harbors on the seacoast. We have spent a good deal of money in the inland waterways. I don't think it has been spent as much to a good purpose as it would have been had we adopted some other theory and some other method, but I am not here to criticise the past, and I think that a great deal could probably be said in defense of the economy that has been pursued in that matter. But I do think we now have reached a time in the history of the development of our waterways when a new method ought to be adopted. Now, I would like to clear away a good many suppositions that I am afraid have lodged in some minds.

This improvement of waterways, the improvement by the irrigation of arid and sub-arid lands, and all this conservation of resources is not for the purpose of distributing "pork" to every part of the country. Every measure that is to be taken up is to be adopted on the ground that it is to be useful to the country at large and not on the ground that it is going to send certain Congressmen back to Congress, or on the ground that it is going to make a certain part of the county prosperous during the expenditure of that money.

If that is the principle—the one which I deprecate—that is to obtain, then I am in favor of going along in the same old way we have gone on before. The method I am in favor of is this: That we should take up every comprehensive project on its merits, and we should determine, by all the means at our command, whether the country in which that project is to be carried out is so far developed as to justify the expenditure of a large sum in carrying out the project, and whether the project will be useful when done. When you have determined that on the general principle of good to the entire country, then I am in favor of doing that work as rapidly as it can be done, and I am in favor of issuing bonds to do it. And if it shall turn out that some part of the country is linked to a particular project by reason of eloquent and large words and a general lively imagination that is not sustained by the facts of cold investigation, then that part of the country must wait until it can grow up to that project and that project come to it.

I am not minimizing the difficulties that are going to arise in selecting what has to be done or in determining the order in which those projects are to be carried out. I know I value more intensely than I ever did in my life the interest and local patriotism that we find all over the United States; but we can not trust that in a plan of improvement which if carried on without sanity and without a knowledge of the good that is to come from it will bankrupt the Government. Now there is a proposition that we issue $500,000,000 of bonds or a billion of bonds for waterways, and then that we just cut that up and apportion a part to the Pacific, a part to the Atlantic, a part to the Mississippi, a part to the Missouri, and a part to the Ohio. I am opposed to it because it not only smells of the "pork barrel," but it will be the "pork barrel." Let every project stand on its own bottom. Let it prove itself by means of its friends and by means of those who know whether it is to be profitable or not, and then enter upon it, but don't let us in the enthusiasm of vague declaration and eloquence embark on a plan that will reflect no credit on our business common sense and will only display the seamy side of that local patriotism which united together makes up our grand Americanism.

And now, my friends, I have subjected you long enough to the croak of a crow, and I am going to ask you to excuse me from speaking further other than to say to you that I have had great pleasure in standing before this magnificent audience of St. Louisans and Missourians, of Congressmen and of Governors, and it makes my heart well up with patriotism to look into your faces and find here in the center of the country the same spirit of determination to overcome all obstacles which are between us and higher living and greater prosperity that I have found from the Atlantic to the Pacific Ocean and from Canada to the Gulf.

47

Remarks at the Waterways Convention

The Atheneaum, New Orleans, Louisiana, October 30, 1909

Governor Sanders, Mr. Chairman, Gentlemen of the Waterways Convention, Ladies of New Orleans:

I mention you last because you are the most important. I am delighted to be present (you see we adopt in our administration the Roosevelt policies to the full) and to head the highly honorable delegation that has come from St. Louis to the Gulf. We have passed through all the dangers of the navigation of the river, and they are not confined to the shoals, sand-banks and the bends, and we are here without the loss of a single man. There are some few of us who have braved the whole way, and I hesitate to speak of those who resorted to the humiliating device of taking land transportation to get here. I hope that will be suppressed in the minutes of this meeting. When "Uncle Joe" addresses your honorable body, don't ask him where he left the river and where he got back to it.

We were honored on our flagship by the presence of the Governor of Louisiana and the Governor of Mississippi. We needed them in our business, for we did not know where we might be thrown ashore on those high banks that frowned down upon us as we rode the river, and you can see from the eloquent tribute and words and kindly, affectionate tone of the Governor how we fooled him.

But, jesting aside, my dear friends, we are delighted to be here, first, because we are reasonable men who know a good thing when we see it, and any man who doesn't welcome an opportunity to come to New Orleans is lacking in all that goes to make up a respectable man; and secondly, we are glad to be here because our coming indicates what we hope may be an epoch in the change of the character of transportation in this country. Do not misunderstand me. I do not think that we are going to fill the bosom of the Mississippi with barges and ocean steamers tomorrow morning. The change which is bound to be effected with respect to that stream will come gradually. It will come with the demand that is certainly growing for an improvement in our transportation and the cheapening of that kind of transportation, to wit, bulky merchandise that ought to be carried more cheaply than it is today.

This trip has been illuminating to many of us, not so much in offering a solution to the problems presented in trying to develop the Mississippi and other rivers for that kind of transportation which will be most beneficial to the country, but it has been illuminating in showing the difficulties that we have to meet and overcome in order that those rivers shall occupy their proper place in transportation.

Now, there are a good many things that come to you when you sit down and think and devote attention to a problem. If your mind is directed toward railroad transportation and the building up of the country by that means, and if public attention is taken off rivers and they are allowed to become nothing but sewers, it is not in human nature that the problems presented by the rivers shall receive the attention which will insure the solution of those problems.

We have seen human ingenuity turned and developed to the highest degree in the growth of our railroad transportation and the economy in the conduct of railroads. But the condition of our rivers, the apparently hopeless task of making them useful, has turned the public attention from them, and there isn't, in reference to river construction or river navigation, that improvement that we ought to have had in the last forty years. I ask you what progress has been made in the last thirty or forty years in reference to river navigation?

Now, we have reached a point where we are bound to use those because the amount that is required to be carried will necessitate it. In Germany and in foreign countries, to which we are pointed to show what can be done with river navigation, the Government exercises control and says that with respect to the rates certain of them shall be such on the river that bulky merchandise must go that way. What do we do? Why, we say to the railroads. "If you will only arrange your rates so as to compete with the river, we will permit you to make them so as to drive the river out of business." Now, that is what has been done, and while the river has served the purpose of regulating rates to a certain extent in reducing them, it nevertheless has not exercised that power and that influence that it might if it were actually used for the purpose.

The Secretary of War yesterday suggested—although he is as far from a government-ownership man as possible—that perhaps it might be well to let the Government experiment a bit in risking some capital to put a few lines on the river to try and see whether something cannot be done with that business. In Kansas City they are investing money today to try it on the Missouri River. And the question whether we can meet the point that you must have some means of gathering the business and getting it on to the boat in order to compete with the railroad, will not give rise to the suggestion that the Government might establish stations along the river for the purpose of housing the merchandise to be sent by the river. All those are suggestions that will have to be worked out before we reach a satisfactory conclusion.

Now, in St. Louis I said I thought that we ought to satisfy ourselves with respect to a great improvement of the river, that it would be useful before we went ahead and invested all the money necessary, and that then we ought to invest that money quickly and issue bonds for the purpose, because that is the most rapid way. Now I think—at least the great weight of opinion is— that we have solved the question of the navigation of the Ohio River for the purpose of improving the trade of that river; and if you are going to make the Mississippi a valuable stream, you must depend on the feeders to that stream, of which the Ohio today is far and away the most important.

Now, you say I come from Ohio, and that that is the reason I think so. Well, perhaps it is, but nevertheless there is a report in which the cost of that improvement has been gone into detail, and the engineers have approved it to the extent of nine feet of water—slack water, throughout the whole year, and it will cost $63,000,000. Now I am in favor of going ahead with that which has been determined to be useful, and issuing bonds and building those improvements, because they have shown by the improvements already erected that the solution there has been reached that it is practical. I am not in favor of delaying the Mississippi River improvement until the Ohio River improvement is completed, but I am in favor of finding out what you ought to do in the Mississippi River succinctly and knowing what it will cost before you go in and spend all your money. The use of a river for navigation is going to determine a good deal of what is needed in it for better navigation. That is the reason why the Kansas City method is a good method and I am hopeful that in some way or other you can increase the amount of business on the Mississippi River.

When I spoke of the Ohio River to a gentleman most interested in the Mississippi, he said, "Oh, well, pshaw; you have got a great coal company up at the top of that river, and it furnishes the business." Well, of course it does, and that is the reason why we are in favor of the improvement. It is demonstrated that the river will carry that coal, and we have the coal to carry. And so it is with respect to the Lakes. They have the iron ore to carry, and its value has been determined time and time again. Now you improve the Ohio River, and we will give you more and more trade for the Mississippi, and in that way you will learn and develop, by investigation and actual experiment, what is needed in the Mississippi.

I have been delighted to read, because I had otherwise a different idea, that the Mississippi has been improved and improved greatly toward the lower end; that the Mississippi River Commission working with Louisiana and Mississippi has developed a system of levees that are wonderful to save a State nearly forty thousand square miles, useful and most productive for agricultural purposes, and that at the same time they have gone on and have discovered means of stopping the sloughing off at the interior of the bends; that by experiment they have found what will stick and what will not stick, and that we are making progress in spite of the fact that the progress is not what it ought to be. The Mississippi River Commission says that in order to carry on even this they ought to have $2,000,000 more a year, and certainly Congress ought to be ashamed not to give it to them.

I am very sure that the Speaker of the House, who although he says he is but one member of the House, nevertheless under the customs which have grown up is more or less a Speaker for the House, is charged with a deep responsibility in regard to this great question; and that he is working as hard as he can to reach a just solution. It is a great deal when your movement has been carried to a point where you command the attention of those in authority to listen to what you have to say in your favor, and that is what you have done. You have brought it to a point where, to use a colloquial expression, we must come down to brass tacks, and where mere general oratory in favor of a waterway does not suffice. It is the question, what can you do, how much will it cost, how long will it take, and what will it result in? Now, when you address yourselves, this body of men, and treat it as a mere question of transportation on a profitable basis, I have not the slightest doubt that you will reach a solution which will appeal to those who have the responsibility of voting the money for the Government, and that you will get what you desire in a measurable time.

I thank you, my friends, from the bottom of my heart for this cordial reception. I thank the Business Men's League of St. Louis for giving me an opportunity to take part in this historical progress down the Father of Waters, and I thank them for delivering us into the hospitable arms and the loving embrace of the Governor of Louisiana and his constituents; and finally I have to advise those who have not experienced the delightful hospitality of New Orleans that they are now sitting in a frame of gems, and that if they will continue here for two or three days in the beauty of the women and their charming qualities, they will almost forget the Mississippi River.

48

Woman's Education

*Address to the Students of the State Institute and College
at Columbus, Mississippi, November 2, 1909*

Young Ladies:

It is a great privilege to address you. Your being here and the character of the institution and of the education that you are receiving and the results to be accomplished by that, are all calculated to inspire in one enthusiasm and sympathy with the work which is going on. I have a lot of maxims and a lot of principles that I would like to advance to young ladies in your situation. I wish that every woman in the world was so situated that she did not think it was necessary for her to marry if she did not want to. Now that is a proposition that I am prepared to defend against all comers. I am the last one to take a position against that old doctrine of the common law that there ought to be nothing to interfere with matrimony. But I would have the matter so arranged that the women when they come to decide and make their choice shall have a full and free choice, and that can only be reached when they are put in a situation where that which they choose is not a life which they select because it is better than some that they expect, but a life that they look forward to with unmixed happiness.

Seriously speaking, I think the most important education that we have is the education which now I am glad to say is being accepted as the proper one, the one which ought to be most widely diffused, that industrial, vocational education which puts young men and young women in a position from which they can by their own efforts work themselves to independence. And I am glad to know that that principle obtains here in its best sense, and I am glad to congratulate these young women on the opportunity which this great institution affords them to carve out their future and their own happiness.

I know it is generally supposed that those who inherit wealth are in the best situation for a future happy life—I mean in this world—but I venture to think that the best legacy that can be left to a young man is a good education and a good character. The necessity that he is under of getting out to hustle is an advantage which he does not appreciate when he is going through the process, but after he has won success and looks back and compares his life with that of the men who, when he entered life had money and means to support themselves, and enjoy themselves, he will be convinced of the great advantage that fate gave him when it did not give him a fortune or a competence. The same thing is true with respect to the young women who are given a fair chance in life to earn and carve out their own futures. The great trouble has been that we have not given the women a fair show. We have not opened all the avenues to livelihood which they are quite as well able to fill, and in certain respects better able to fill, than we are.

I am not a rabid suffragist. The truth is I am not in favor of suffrage for women until I can be convinced that all the women desire it; and when they desire it I am in favor of giving it to them, and when they desire it they will get it too. But I do believe that one of the advantages of giving them that kind of influence will be more certainly to open the avenues of self-support to them than heretofore has been done. The great principle of popular government is that every class in the community, assuming that it has intelligence enough to know its own interest, can be better trusted to look after that interest than any other class, however altruistic that class. While husbands respect the wishes of wives, if they are good husbands, and know what is good for them, I don't know that they always manifest the utmost liberality with reference to the treatment of unmarried women. What we are bound to have in the future through influences working, the effect of which we can see, and the growth into the success of which we can anticipate, is that women are going to be given greater independence in the matter of earning their livelihood, and that then they will reach the point, which I do not think they now have reached, of regarding an education without a competence as a greater benefit than one with the means of support.

I shall be glad that I shall not have any property to leave to my boys, of whom I have two, but only a good character and a pride in themselves and a good education; but for my daughter I am going to scrape together as much as I can give her and as good an education as I can so that she shall take in the lesson which I first sought to announce as the text of my discourse, that she marry only when she chooses to marry and not because of circumstances.

And now, my dear young ladies, I am delighted to have met you. You get a man who lives beyond fifty and he has certain views of life that he reasons about in his own mind and every once in a while he finds an opportunity to give expression to them, and that is what you have offered me this morning, and hence you have had to endure this speech.

49

The Development of the South

Chamber of Commerce Banquet, Birmingham, Alabama,
November 2, 1909

Mr. Chairman, Senator Johnston, Governor Comer, Gentlemen of Birmingham and Citizens of Alabama:

When your distinguished Chairman arose first he advised us that there was to be no reference to politics and that the time of each speaker was limited. He, however, is a toastmaster and, having made the regulation, is entitled to suspend it in his own case, and I make no argument to that at all. It reminds me of an answer made by my friend Judge Howland once, when introduced by a toastmaster whom he called a "roastmaster," with an introduction that took off some of the Judge's peculiarities in advance. He said he had no objection at all because he was reminded of the story of the gentleman who wandered into a saloon in Nevada where a game of poker was going on, and as he sat looking over the game, he saw the dealer transfer four aces from the bottom of the pack into his own hand. He nudged another gentleman who was sitting by him looking over the game. And said, "Did you see that?" "See what," said the man. "See that man take four aces off the bottom of the pack?" His neighbor turned to him and said, "Hell, isn't it his deal?" I am entirely willing to recognize the right of the toastmaster himself to discuss politics and exclude it in the rest of us. I can not, however, refrain from certain observations upon the peculiarities of Alabama politics, and the position of governor in the State. There seems to attach to it a certain necessity for a purgatory after the term, and I am not at all sure that it is not a good arrangement, and that it does not make for excellent senators.

I have listened with a great deal of interest to the statements as to the growth of Birmingham. Those of us who do not live in Birmingham associate it with three or four cities of this country. Perhaps you will decline to accept the association, but as I am a man up a tree, so to speak, I can insist upon the similarity—Birmingham, Atlanta, Pittsburgh, Chicago, Minneapolis, Seattle and Los Angeles are types of a growing prosperity and business development that one who swings around the country as I have done feels the greatest national pride in dwelling upon. They are in the first class. They have a public spirit and a determination to succeed that develop into—I had almost called it a chimney draft and take you off your feet. There seems to be no thing that can limit their growth. You have something substantial and tangible at your doors upon which you can base your future with even more certainty than these other cities that have developed so much.

My friend on the right, who is making Republican voters, has demonstrated that you have a wealth here that is hardly equalled in the world, and I am glad that it is so, glad that you have caught the spirit of your opportunities and are determined to force them to a point where you shall make yourselves certainly the Pittsburgh of the South and one of the great industrial centers of the world. Your Governor has been good enough to suggest that a desire for arbitrary rule is not confined to governors and that it affects the head of the nation as well—the temporary head of the nation—and he has made suggestions as to what I might do with the vacancies that will await me when I get back to Washington. I thought that his suggestion with reference to the associate justiceship was much too indefinite, and that when he made his definite suggestion it received a very much heavier approval. If he will also name his associate justice from the lawyers of Alabama, then he will be really helping me with respect to both offices.

What one sees in Birmingham one also sees in a less degree in every town and State of the United States. It is a spirit of progress and determination to overcome the obstacles that present themselves which I do not think is unjust to call typically American. I haven't found a corner of this country where there is anything but optimism and contentment, anything but a request that they be given an equal chance in the race and a determination to come out first. I can never make a speech on an occasion like this in dealing with our progress as a nation without referring to the fact that has impressed itself on me every time I have stepped onto the platform, in a little town in the

Far West or in a large city like this, and that is the homogeneity of the American people, their having become a type different from that of any other nation, and a type that illustrates all we take pride in, the progressiveness and the courage and the enterprise which have made this country what it is, and which are going to carry it to a development that even we with our optimism can hardly reach in our imagination. And what I long for and hope for and believe is that in that material progress we are not going to lose sight of the fact that unless we accompany it with an elevation of the individual, with an elevation of our business standards, with the making of the character of each citizen better and higher and increasing our moral standards, the material progress will not be worth anything to the nation.

I think that in the last ten years and under the influence of Theodore Roosevelt, we have had called to our attention the dangers into which we might be led by an undue desire to increase our material prosperity at the cost of honesty in business and freedom from monopoly and greed with reference to our corporations and business generally. And now that we are about to resume a prosperity which will grow as I believe in the next four or five years to a point never before seen in this country or in the world, it is wise that we should take into consideration the necessity that we shall not let it come except on condition that it comes with a preservation of equality of opportunity to American citizens and the bettering of our business integrity and the restraint of all those things that tend to monopoly and corruption in politics and in business.

Now, the Chairman said I must keep out of politics, and I will because I believe I am speaking a doctrine to which everybody subscribes, whether he be Republican or Democrat. I am glad to be in Birmingham because it is in the South. It is said to be cosmopolitan, and it has attracted by reason of its great business opportunities many from the North and other places, and yet it is in Alabama and it is in the South and you would not have me say that you are not a Southern community as you are.

I am deeply interested in the development of the South and in her obtaining a share of the national prosperity which came so slowly to her in the last three decades. Birmingham is leading the South in that direction, and she, because of her cosmopolitan character, because she is becoming more and more aware of how close she is to the North and how close she is to the entire country in a business way, is influencing the South as the North is influenced toward her to believe that this country is ceasing to have sections, not ceasing to have traditions, and there is a definition that I want to make as emphatic as possible. I would not have the South give up a single one of her noble traditions. I would not have her abate a single bit of the deep pride she feels in all the great heroes who represented her in that awful struggle between the North and the South. I would have the whole country know, as I believe the South is growing herself to know, that it is possible to preserve all those traditions intact and have a warm and deeply loyal love for the old flag to which she has come back, and to know that the North respects her for those traditions she preserves and does not ask her to discard one, but only wishes to unite with her in the benefits of a common country and of a sympathy and association between the peoples of the two sections that will certainly lead us on to a greater and greater future.

50

Wisdom and Necessity of Following the Law

State Fair Grounds, Macon, Georgia, November 4, 1909

Mr. Chairman, Ladies and Gentlemen, Citizens of Georgia:

I am glad to be back in Georgia. I was a Georgian when I was elected President of the United States. They went through a preliminary canter just a year ago today at the polls, but the real election under the Constitution, as your jurist Senator will tell you, was when I was within the precincts of Georgia, and, therefore, for the time being subject to the Georgian laws, with an allegiance to Georgia, and, I am glad to say, was a Georgian in spirit and in heart. I say so because I came under the delightful influence of Georgian hospitality. I was permitted to work out my own way with a considerateness that I greatly appreciated. I had been engaged in a contest and a controversy that made me wish to lie down for a time, and you permitted me to enjoy that leisure and that rest without disturbing it, but only by your soothing hospitality you enabled me to recover again the strength I needed to meet the responsibilities of the office, for which you had been somewhat innocent in choosing me.

I am greatly indebted to your distinguished Governor, to Senator Bacon, and to your Congressman, Mr. Bartlett, for their representing you in taking me into this beautiful city of Macon, and I may add in giving me a Georgian breakfast. It is an admirable meal—one attractive to me in a way that I hate to admit—but it isn't the best preparation for an oration.

My friends, the note that will rise up in my voice, and which I can not restrain, is one of congratulation to the people of Georgia upon the condition in which they find themselves this year and this decade under the Providence of God. It is, as your Chairman has said, enough to make one stop and think when you realize that out of your cotton crop alone you will receive in gold more than double all the gold that will be mined in the United States during a year.

Now, I sincerely hope that you will spend that to the best advantage. I know from looking about through the town of Macon that you are spending it to make your homes more attractive, and to educate the next generation that is coming on to uphold the high traditions of Georgia, and to maintain its loyalty and support to the National Government.

I have had the privilege of travelling now some 12,000 miles across the United States, down her western border along her southern border, until I reached home in Georgia. And while I would not detract from your natural State pride, and from that feeling, which I know exists, because I have a Georgian, Capt. Archibald W. Butt, as my military aide, that the Georgians are just the best people in the world, nevertheless I want to admit to you that if I were to be put blindfolded, without knowing exactly where I was, before this magnificent audience, it would be a little difficult for me to distinguish between you and some of the audiences that I meet in Ohio. You may not regard that as a compliment, but you must know that I come from Ohio, and the resemblance I like to emphasize, because that is the text of what I would preach both in Georgia and in Ohio.

We have our differences. We differ because the sun differs a little bit in its method of showing its love to you in Georgia and to us in Ohio. We differ because you can raise cotton and we have to get along with corn and wheat. But in the essential, in the aspirations that we have, in our training, in our moral standards, in our political ideals and in our determination to make our condition better with reference to each individual who comes to be part of our people and part of our government, our aims are alike, and we are alike.

Now, you differ from some of us because we have benighted Democrats in Ohio. You differ from us in your view of some political principles. I do not care if you do. If you will only give me such a warmth of reception as you have this morning, I can wipe out the memory of all those principles for the time being and rejoice that you have taken me in as a brother. The truth is, a wholesome difference of opinion with reference to economic and political principles is essential that we reach the truth. If we all agreed—well, there wouldn't be any fun in politics to begin with; if we all agreed, it would indicate an apathy and an indifference to principle that would mean that the country was going downward instead of upward.

The independence of thought that we seek to cherish here must lead to differences of opinion, maintained by argument and voted into the ballot box, and then we all acknowledge acquiescence in the result of that ballot box.

We have been trained a thousand years through our English ancestry in the self-restraint that is absolutely necessary to the success of popular government, and in that quality of being good losers that enabled us to live happily and contentedly under a government selected by a majority of which we are not a part. And the same self-restraint teaches the majority that rules that the limitations of the Constitution, and not only the limitations of law and the Constitution, but limitations of decency, limitations of patriotism, are as strong on the majority as it is possible that law should be. In other words, the power that is enjoyed is the power to be exercised only for the benefit of the people and the country, and not for the purpose of exalting the person who temporarily is vested with power to exercise it.

I always hear, because it is pleasant and because the man who says it believes it, and also because it rounds a full period, about the power of the President of United States, and I doubt not that after I am out of office I shall be able to look back and see where I might have done things in the exercise of power that would have filled me with a consciousness of it, but I am bound to say that under existing circumstances the thing which impresses me most is not the power I have to exercise under the Constitution, but the limitations and restrictions to which I am subject under that instrument. Sometimes a man's head swells a little bit with his momentary authority, and he thinks that there is a good deal of the limitation of the Constitution that might have been safely omitted in his case. Now, here is my friend, Senator Bacon—he and his fellows sit up at the other end of the avenue and they pass on all my appointments. I could get along if they didn't have that power, and for the time being it seems to me that the country would get along a little better if they couldn't put their fingers in, but our forefathers builded well, and they knew what they were doing; and I am not in favor, even if it seems to me that a particular provision ought to be omitted, of changing the Constitution every time you run against the sharp edge of something that indicates that you are only mortal and that the forefathers in making the Constitution distrusted your human nature.

My friends, that leads me up to one little sermon, and that is, the wisdom and necessity of following the law as it is. I know that sometimes in the heat and enthusiasm of reform, there is an impatience with legal limitations and statutes that seem to be directed against that reform, or to prevent its immediate accomplishment, such as to lead us to disregard it or to ignore it. I do not think, and I am sure you will agree with me, that that is the best way of getting rid of a legal limitation that interferes with progress. The best way is to have the people understand that that limitation ought to be removed, and that the statutes of our Government ought to conform so far as may be to our highest ideals and ambitions; but that the first thing that we have got to do after arousing the people to the necessity of change, is to change the law, and not rely upon the Executive himself to ignore the statutes and follow a law unto himself because it is supposed to be the law of higher morality.

Now, that may sound like a lawyer's view. Lawyers are necessary in a community. Some of you who have paid fees—some of you who have lost cases in courts of justice—may have a different view; but as I am a member of that legal profession, or was at one time, and have only lost standing in it by becoming a politician, I still retain the pride of the profession. And I still insist that it is the law and the lawyer that make popular government under a written constitution and written statutes possible, because if you depart in any way from the law as it is, you enter upon a path, which, while entirely certain for one issue in your mind with respect to the higher moral aim of your own soul and that of your fellow-citizens, nevertheless leads into a wilderness, and by which you cannot subsequently guide your steps. Therefore, let us first make the laws to accord to our desires and our ambitions, and then follow them.

I have said that much because I have noticed a tendency among some of our best fellow-citizens to hold the Executive responsible for not doing a great many things in which it is the business of my friends in Congress, with Senator Bacon and Judge Bartlett, to lead the way, and for the Executive only to follow after they have laid down the rules. That does not rid tile Executive of the responsibility of recommending changes in the law. But it does prevent him from going ahead and exercising those changes without the coordinate action of the legislative branch of the Government; and as I intend to recommend a good many measures at the next meeting of Congress, I have taken this method of intimating to you where the responsibility will be if those measures do not pass.

My friends, I am delighted to be here. These surroundings could hardly be surpassed in everything that goes to make up a pleasant meeting. The beautiful ladies and the men with shining eyes and welcoming hospitable hearts, all these surroundings make a man feel as if he could talk from now on until dewy eve. But I am not going to. I only want to say that such a meeting as this confirms me in the view that there is not one single reason why you should not feel as close to the Government at Washington, and as much a part of it, as any other part of the country, and that all that is necessary to have you understand that is to give you the assurance, which I am delighted to give, and which I know you will receive in the same spirit, that we are Americans all together—that you have as much right to be heard by me while I temporarily exercise the powers of the Chief Executive at Washington as any citizens in the land, and that it will gratify me beyond expression if through any act of mine or through the administration as a whole, I can have contributed to bring all the peoples of this country together in one common bond of union, and one sentiment of loyalty to our flag and to our country.

51

Trip of the President and Hospitality of the South

Speech at the Banquet Tendered by the Citizens of Charleston, South Carolina, at the Charleston Hotel, November 5, 1909

Mr. Mayor and Gentlemen of Charleston and of South Carolina:

I thank you for your kindly welcome. It is true that I have been in Charleston just as often as I could come here. And I intend to come as often in the future as possible, as a private citizen or under any conditions. Now, I first came here because I believed Charleston to be the quickest way to go to the Isthmus of Panama. And I haven't changed my opinion about it. Having come here and having become acquainted with the city of Charleston and with its many attractions and with a good many of the interior workings of the city and of South Carolina, they have a fascination for me. I like to come here and renew those pleasurable experiences in the discussions that prevail between the great thunderers in the press. No one who understands the attraction of real hospitality and the friendships that one makes in cities like this, ever comes to Charleston but that he wants to come back again.

Now, I am honored tonight by the presence of the Governor of your State and by that of your two Senators with all of whom, I am glad to say, I am on the most friendly personal terms. And as they cannot make any speeches, because I am to make the only one, that statement has to go down undenied. There are certain advantages in being the only speaker and there are certain disadvantages. When one is making three speeches a day and is searching for subjects upon which to talk, it is of much assistance if other men say something so that one can find suggestion in their ingenuity, and that is missing tonight for me. Last night at Savannah I had it in full and rich measure. Some one has suggested that I would be able to continue my remarks today without having completed all the subjects that were touched upon.

There is one gentleman not here tonight whom I could wish to see, and that is your active, bright, tender-hearted and most able Congressman. I sincerely hope that he is recovering his health completely. He has taken a stay at Fort Bayard, in New Mexico, and that has worked such wonders with other friends of mine similarly afflicted that I am very hopeful he will be restored to you with all his strength and with all his usefulness.

Inasmuch as nobody has been called upon to suggest any subject for discussion, I cannot think of anything to talk about except that which has been present in my thoughts every moment for the last fifty-five days—my present trip. It perhaps needs an explanation. I was invited to go to the Yukon Exposition at Seattle and I agreed to go. That is, I agreed to go if Congress made sufficient provision for my travelling expenses. And Congress did. And so the country had this journey put upon it. But the moment that I accepted that invitation to go to the Exposition, the places which were to be included in the going and coming began to increase in number by reason of the hospitable invitations from a number of places and also by the fact that I seemed to be useful in connection with state fairs and other enterprises that needed encouragement—one of which was the deepening of the Mississippi River—and before I got through, the itinerary had zigzagged across the country so as to aggregate about thirteen thousand miles.

I have had a good many people, especially as I drew near the close of the journey, express sympathy for me as to the endurance test I have gone through. Well, the question is one of temperament, one of taste and possibly one of disposition. If you like people and like to meet them, and if you have an interest in studying the differences and the similarities of the people of the United States, then such a trip as I have undertaken and have gone through with nearly to completion is something which any one having those tastes would enjoy most highly. I can say truly that I have enjoyed every moment of the trip. And I think I can affirm that the people generally in all parts of the country are in favor of having a President travel at least once in four years through the country. They are interested from curiosity perhaps, but also from better reasons, I think, in coming into personal touch with the man who for the time being exercises the executive authority in chief. They not only like to see him, but they like to hear him. I don't know that they pay any particular attention to his views, but they like to get the sound of his voice and hear something from him in order that they may "size up" the man who temporarily is at the head of the nation.

Now, I think that that is a pretty good thing; I think generally that if they see the man and come into a sort of personal touch, they are more sympathetic with him in his difficulties, and I am in favor of sympathy. I am where I need it, and I think we can get along a good deal better where we understand each other and have the means of understanding each other than where the man who is acting on delegated authority is afar from those who have delegated him to act. It certainly has a most beneficial effect upon the man thus charged. It certainly opens his eyes and his mind first to inquiry in reference to the needs of the country in its various sections, and while, on the other hand, it puts the people more or less in sympathy with him as President, it puts him certainly quite in sympathy with sections of whose aspirations and needs and thoughts he may have heard, but he never can have had them impressed on him as they are when he goes into that section, into that State, into that district where the needs arise, and where ambition is stirring the people up to make complaints or claims.

There are times in such a trip when a man feels as if he were on a wild goose chase and not accomplishing much. Those times are usually about five o'clock in the morning, when he is waked up by an earnest crowd, anxious to have him turn out, although he may have gone to bed at one or two o'clock, and make a speech. They can not understand why he should stay in when he is purposely on a trip to show himself.

It has been said that this is a bad precedent, that the present incumbent has been blessed with a digestion and sufficient physical endurance to enable him to make the trip, but that by going about and making a precedent those who follow me and who may not be so blessed may find imposed upon them a burden which it is bad for the public to have their Chief Executive labor under. Well, perhaps that is so. I would not limit the Presidency, certainly, by a civil-service examination as to digestion and physical endurance; but each President, I think, can control that matter largely for himself, and is not governed by the precedents set by other Presidents. The truth is, I don't know any President in my recollection who has been much embarrassed by the precedents set by any other President.

There is one feature of this travelling where you use Sunday, because you have to, and that is that you are called upon to address audiences that are either in churches or in a state of worship, and you have to assume the character of a preacher. I have essayed once or twice in that direction, and I have been very much amused to see the comments of the gentlemen of the clerical profession on my failure in that regard. I notice that I am very subject to criticism by those gentlemen who preside in a sense over the Scriptures—and who resent any attempt to deal liberally with texts from the Scriptures.

One of the difficulties in taking such a trip is that you lose track of the news. You see newspapers only occasionally, and then in such a way that you are not able to keep up with the issues of the day. That has some advantages, but it occasionally presents embarrassment. I am utterly oblivious to the importance and also utterly ignorant of the evidence with reference to the question, Which American discovered the pole? I know that is not the case with anyone who has had the pleasure of being in Charleston for the last sixty days.

Then, too, I have been able to avoid election troubles and even now have not learned all the results, because I have not had an opportunity to see them tabulated or stated. That, too, perhaps, if the elections are not satisfactory, is an advantage. One of the great pleasures of this trip, most gratifying to me, has been what I might almost call the fervor of the receptions that I have had throughout the States of the South. Of course, one in my position, and of limited political experience, might well be misled as to the popular expression and how much of it is substantial and what it means, and yet I have given some attention to the study of human nature and I think I know the Southern people, and I think I correctly construe what it is they have in their minds and hearts when they indicate to me as emphatically and sincerely as they do the pleasure that they have in my presence in their communities. And that is that I am not contemplating a political revolution; that is impossible; but only that I am seeking to smooth out some of the wrinkles that may perhaps have remained from our former differences and am trying to convince the people of the South by such means as the Executive has in his control of my earnest desire to make the South feel that it has influence at Washington, that its foremost men of prominence and influence are entitled to be heard, to be listened to—and that in dealing with the South this Administration looks upon it in no different sense in a general way than upon Ohio or Illinois or the great West.

And now, gentlemen, I have reached the end of my speech. I can only close by saying that, after the very pleasant receptions I have had in the South, it is delightful to come to Charleston and feel that the reception here is not alone the reception of another Southern city, but that it is the reception of a city where I have so many friends already formed that I looked at it rather as coming to a place like home than to a place where I had never visited and which I only regarded as a part of that genial section, with its magnificent traditions, with its enormous possibilities, and with its intense loyalty. I say good-bye now. I hope to come again as soon as I can and I hope that Charleston will retain all her attractiveness; that she will lose none of those residences and those other structures that make her unique throughout the country; that she will continue to have that press which makes each paper so interesting in discussing the other.

52

South Carolina and Her Traditions

Address at the Luncheon Tendered by South Carolinians in the
House of Representatives of the State Capitol,
Columbia, South Carolina, November 6, 1909

Governor Ansel and Gentlemen of South Carolina:

Your committee from Columbia called on me in Augusta before I had assumed the course of office, and were good enough to invite me to come here. I said I would come, and I am here. That is one promise of the Administration that I have redeemed. I don't claim any credit for it, because a man who would not come to Columbia when he could, and enjoy such a festivity and welcome as this, does not understand a good thing when he sees it.

I am greatly honored to be received by you in this the House of Representatives of South Carolina in your magnificent Capitol. I am greatly honored to be received by your representative men of the State, not only by the private citizens but by the Governor, the Senators, the Chief Justice and your Representatives, and I appreciate it to the full. It is the first State in which I have been tendered a welcome within the capitol walls of the State, and I take it as an expression on your part of a desire to show that it is the State and the people of the State that welcome me.

Another and most delightful feature of this reception is the presence of the ladies, the real pride of South Carolina. A gentleman from another part of the State, and I am afraid that in saying this I am betraying something that I ought not to say, but I can not help it, anticipating a meeting with me in another part of the State at some time in the future, said to me, "Come there and we will show you the prettiest women in South Carolina." I resented it, and but for my office and the dignity that necessarily attached to it, I tremble for his fate. We are verging in the right direction. There was a time when we had banquets without the presence of that sex that we all love, and whose influence and control we all secretly recognize. Now we are letting them in to see the animals eat. They show that patience, that sweet sympathy with the selfish side of man, that tolerance of those things about him that even we ourselves do not admire, by allowing this arrangement to continue for a while. But the next time I come to South Carolina I expect to dine with the ladies and the gentlemen.

My friends, I am not inspired to say much today, because I feel so much more than I can say. There is something about South Carolina and her traditions, as I look into the faces of her great men and think what she has done and the part she has played in all the great historical crises of this country, that makes me take this reception from you at your hands with a feeling that I am honored far beyond my deserts. I realize that it is because I represent the whole Nation for the time being, and that you in your loyalty to the flag and country, and with the hospitality for which your State is noted, express to me the feeling that rises in each of your hearts as you think of your country, and as you think of the patriotism of yourselves and the State. I come to Columbia and look out from the steps of the State Capitol and see a city that has arisen since the Civil War—not a city that did not exist before the Civil War, but a city that by its growth and its energy and its taking on life shows that while that Civil War brought to it an evidence of the tremendous strength, the tremendous power of self-sacrifice of its people, it did not destroy their hope for the future, or their willingness again to become a part of the great Union and to make that Union stronger and that country a Nation greater than ever before in its history. And I count it a great privilege to come here, representing the Nation that you love so well, and by this meeting and by your reception, and by what I see, to testify to the fact that while the past is as it is, and while those things come out of it that make us proud on both sides, there is before us in the future a united life in upholding our country, in elevating the standard of citizenship, in making greater the character and the equality of opportunity of the individual that we are glad to seize as a common united people, not separated in any way by our past history, but the more united because while we have those traditions the memory leaves in our mind the awfulness of a separation that now is forever ended.

And now, my friends, I am going to stop. This is the two hundred and fifty-first speech I have made, but in no one of them have I felt so much satisfaction in expressing the truth as I know it.

53

Sanitation and Health of the South

Remarks at the Georgia-Carolina Fair, Augusta, Georgia,
November 8, 1909

Mr. Chairman, Governor Brown, Governor Ansel, Ladies and Gentlemen, Citizens of Georgia and South Carolina:

It is a great pleasure to be here. I have had the pleasure of listening to a governor of a single State in his own State, and I have heard his estimate of his own State approved by his own fellow-citizens; but it is an unusual and exceptional opportunity to have two States represented by two governors, each explaining the excellence and the primacy of his particular State, and when there is thrown into that controversy the question of personal pulchritude, it assumes a character that makes it of exceeding interest.

I want first to express my personal happiness in being again in Augusta, and in seeing and meeting the friends that I made during my stay of about two months last year. There is a lady in Washington whom I am very anxious to see. Nothing could modify my ambitions, nothing restrain the haste with which I would go back to the Capitol City except the pleasure of meeting my old friends in Augusta. I feel always like claiming what Judge Black explained with his constitutional law, that when I was elected President of the United States I was elected from Georgia. And while the part which Georgia took in that ceremony was what we may call negative, it nevertheless was accompanied by the good-will of so many Georgians that I am proud to think of the friends that I have here.

This occasion suggests a number of useful thoughts. It is a meeting of two States to encourage agriculture in both. We have arrived at a time in the development of our country and in the application of our Constitution when the uniform operation of State law upon subjects not covered by the Federal power is becoming more and more important. One of course, can mention the subject of negotiable instruments, of marriage and divorce, and a number of other topics that commend themselves as proper subjects of uniform operation, but it seems to me that the most important scope, the most important collection of subjects is that which relates to the conservation of our national resources. Unless we can have uniform State operation, uniform State legislation with reference to the preservation of our forests, the equalization of water which falls from the clouds, and the preservation of our soil from being washed out to sea, we shall not be able to carry out the program set for us by Theodore Roosevelt, and which to every thoughtful man must commend itself as of the highest importance to the safety and the preservation of our nation.

Another subject which under the influence of your growing manufacturing interests brings itself into one's mind, even though it may suggest a subject of partisan difference, is the question of our mercantile marine. You are making cotton goods in Georgia and South Carolina, and you wish a market in which to dispose of them. Unless our country exercises more control over the mercantile marine of the world than it now does, you are going to find yourselves at great disadvantage in seeking markets of the world in which to dispose of your products. Therefore, I commend to your consideration the question, What means shall we take to establish lines to South America and to the Philippines, to the Orient, to Manchuria, and to all those countries to which you look for the purchases of the products that you here make?

[The President was here interrupted for a few moments by the appearance of a dirigible balloon over the fair grounds.]

I hesitate to occupy your time in discussing an old method of transporting goods when you have before your eyes the newest one invented, and yet I venture to think that it will be some time before that method of transportation will be followed in the matter of cotton bales.

Another subject that is forging ahead and must be considered by the National Government with a great deal more care and with the expenditure of much more money than it has heretofore put into such investigation, is the question of sanitation and the health of the inhabitants of this country. This is peculiarly so in the South, for as you reach nearer to the tropics the danger of the spread of diseases is much greater. We have now various bureaus in Washington that have functions connected with the suppression of diseases and the investigation of their character; but they are scattered, and they need to be united in one bureau, which shall devote its attention, just as the Agricultural Department devotes its attention, to the study of questions of evil under all conditions prevailing in this country, so that by the circulation of the knowledge obtained it may enable the people to live hygienic lives. Now, it is true that the health of the citizens is directly committed to the States, but it is also true that the question of agriculture is committed by the Constitution directly to the States. Nevertheless, the Agricultural Department has found much that with the means at its command it can do to assist the agriculture of the country. Think back two decades, my friends, and see what enormous strides have been made in the proper treatment of the soils, in the development of your crops, in the making available the by-products of those crops, and in an entire change of the character of agriculture from a haphazard, wasteful industry to one in which science and professional knowledge are today of the highest importance. So, too, with respect to sanitation. It is necessary that the towns and States should direct their attention and their money to making better bodies for their citizens as well as better minds, and if the National Government with its resources can follow out lines of investigation that can show proper treatment to be followed, it is well that it should take that step.

I expect to recommend to Congress that there be a union of all the instrumentalities of the Government for the organization of means of health and the study of disease. We have since the Spanish-American War developed a knowledge of diseases, especially of the tropics, that never existed before, and when we have studied the tropical diseases we have gone a long way to help ourselves in all diseases. The truth is that the tropical diseases are only exaggerations generally of the diseases that appear in a less virulent form in the temperate zone, and by reason of the virulence they bear a closer study and give forth a better result in the investigation. Now the consequence is that since the Spanish War we have found out through the study of our army officers and our army surgeons how the yellow fever can be suppressed, how malignant malaria can be suppressed. Without that knowledge, my dear friends, it would have been impossible to build the Panama Canal. We pride ourselves on having done something or being about to do something that France was not able to do with all the millions which De Lesseps was able to command, but we must remember that she did not then have at her command the knowledge which we have had in the suppression of the disease that made life on that Isthmus so dangerous to everyone who attempted to live there. The consequence is that today we have less malaria, or certainly not more on the Isthmus of Panama than you have in your Southern States, and there has not for three years been a case of yellow fever. That can be traced directly to the results of the Spanish War and the labor of American physicians and especially of the surgeons of the United States Army; and if there were no other great result from that war, that single aid to humanity is enough to have justified it.

But I am not going to detain you longer. I am here on my way home after some 13,000 miles of travel studying the American people. I have studied them before. I sought their franchises and that was a considerable study, but it is an aid to go about among them, not asking for their votes but merely seeking from them advice on public policies, their aims, their aspirations and their needs.

I went from Boston clear across the country to the northwest corner in Washington down to the southwest corner at Los Angeles, across the two Territories, through that almost boundless State of Texas, through Arkansas and Missouri, down the Mississippi River, and then through the South to New Orleans, through Mississippi, Alabama, and now to Georgia and South Carolina, and I feel as if I had had an experience that justifies me in saying something about the American people.

Persons have said to me, "If you do all the talking, how can you expect to derive any information from the people whom you address?" Well, that is a relevant question, but I don't do all the talking. I could tell you of some banquets and some meetings where other people did some talking, and a man must be blind and deaf indeed if he can pass through a crowd of intelligent American citizens like this and not draw from them, even through his pores, something of their thoughts, something of their wishes, something of their needs and something of their aims.

The one thought that strikes a judicial mind going about this country is the homogeneity of the American people. We have taken in from abroad millions and millions of foreigners, but we have amalgamated them in such a remarkable way that today as you take the trip that I have taken, there is nothing that strikes you with the same emphasis and with the same certainty as the persistence of the American type. We are not Germans, we are not Britishers, we are not Frenchmen; we are Americans, and we have the same ambitions, the same moral standards and the same love of country. I might also say we have the same love of our respective States and the same faith in the prosperity of our respective counties and towns and cities in which we live. We are looking forward, looking to the future, confident that we can solve the serious problems that stare us in the face, asking no odds of any one, but only an equal opportunity, and with that equal opportunity confident that we can achieve in the future as great victories as our fathers achieved in the past.

Now with respect to the Southland, my reception has been full of sweet gratification to me, because I have felt that the people of the South were glad to see me and wished to show me by their reception that they sympathized with my desire—my earnest desire—to do everything possible in my administration to make completely forgotten all sectional lines and everything that would tend to separate us—not to forget our cherished traditions—not to forget the heroes of our particular sections in that awful struggle that we in the North call the "Civil War" and you call the "War between the States"—not to forget or abate one bit of our pride that has now become a common heritage of all Americans, but to rejoice that, while that great test showed the character of American heroes, the character of American self-sacrifice, it is in the past, and that the future is with nothing but harmony and love between all our people.

54

A Review of Legislation to be Enacted by Congress

The Auditorium, Richmond, Virginia, November 10, 1909

Mr. Mayor, Governor Swanson, Ladies and Gentlemen:

It has been my good fortune to be welcomed to Virginia a number of times by your distinguished Governor, and I can not fail to express to him the gratitude I really feel toward him for making me always at home on Virginia soil. I congratulate you on having such a Governor, and now that he is for the moment to retire to private life, I hope that all success and prosperity may follow him there. I am quite sure that Virginia knows a good thing when it sees it, and that the leisure which he deserves will not be drawn out too long.

I am also indebted to the presence here of the young men of the Virginia Military Institute. I congratulate them on the military appearance that they present as they march along the streets between their admiring fellow citizens of Virginia. I am glad to say that as Secretary of War I came to know that we depend on the Virginia Military Institute as one of two great institutions to furnish to us officers when exigency and the danger to the Government should occur and require us to call for men skilled in arms, and that they have always shown in the attention to duty, in their soldierly bearing, in the high ideals they preserve, the type and character and ideals set for them by

Stonewall Jackson, for whom they entertain, as well they may, the highest respect and the fondest memory.

This, my friends of Virginia, is the last speech I shall make swinging around the circle. I do not know whether you feel glad about it, but I do.

I am glad to be here in Virginia. I feel a certain sort of pride in the fact that I was the only Republican candidate for President who ever ventured in a canvass for the Presidency to address a Virginia audience, and while the result may not have been of such favor as to induce the gentleman who follows me to attempt it again, it proves what I knew was the case, that I could have in Virginia most courteous attention and a most respectful and tolerant hearing.

I left Boston or Beverly on the 14th of September, and I have been travelling and talking and talking and travelling ever since. I have visited and talked to and seen the people of twenty-six States and two Territories. And I think I know something about the United States. One fact that has impressed itself upon me from beginning to end is the spirit of hopefulness, of contentment, of energy, and of enterprise that there is in every corner of this great country, and that spirit is not alone in those States that are full of fertile fields as you see them from the car window, but that spirit prevails in States in which the expanse of the most God-forsaken country man ever looked upon is great and discouraging. But they have been there long enough to know that if they can only catch the water as it falls from the sky and guide it to the soil that looks so forbidding, it will blossom as the rose and bring forth products fourfold what can be cultivated and brought forth in States where they have continuous rain. And so it is that they feel that while the outlook is apparently one of a desert and most discouraging, they have a great advantage over those of us that plod along with the rain from the skies in the somewhat slow and hardly enterprising East. Now when we have those conditions prevailing in the most discouraging part of the country, may we not say that the prospect before us, made necessarily hopeful by the spirit of the inhabitants, is such that we may all be thankful for it?

Another fact that drives itself home in respect to every audience one addresses is the fact that we are all Americans and very much alike. I could if I heard a man pronounce the word "south" or the word "door" or the word "shore" tell fairly well whether he came from the south or north of Mason and Dixon's line. But with that exception, if I could not hear what he said and could only look upon the crowd, as it is, I could not tell whether the audience came from Washington State, from Boston, from California, from the Middle West or from the South. The women's hats are exactly alike, and a mournful husband on my right suggests that they cost as much.

We have taken millions of foreigners into our civilization, but we have amalgamated them, and with the spirit of our free institutions and the energy of our civilization we have made them all Americans. We have bred to a type, and that type is Americanism, a type that commends itself to us as having the highest ideals and the greatest potentiality for elevation of a country and the individual that the world has ever seen.

Now during all this time of sixty days there has been a moment or two of deliberation, and during that time I have been studying what it is the duty of an Executive to recommend to an incoming Congress in respect to future legislation; and when I think of the number of things that Congress ought to do, I am staggered lest it may not find the time to do them.

In the first place there is the conservation of our resources, the reclamation of arid lands. We have reached a time now where a great many people in the West are counting on an immediate supply of water for the land upon which they have settled, which is not forthcoming because the money applied to the reclamation fund does not come in as quickly as expected, or at least quickly enough to meet the exigency of the occasion. I am strongly in favor of anticipating that fund which is a fund raised solely by the sale of public lands, by the issuing of bonds, the payment of which shall be charged to the same source of revenue. That will bring about quickly a change in respect to the arid lands and with respect to the projects already announced by the Reclamation Bureau, so that nobody shall be deceived, and the work which is a work of primary importance shall go on. The truth is, my dear friends, that we are finding that in spite of our enormous domain, in spite of its great productivity, the demand for the products of the soil is greater because of the growing population than the supply under existing circumstances, and we must enlarge our acreage in one way or another, and the plain way seems by reclamation through the application of water to land heretofore a desert and by draining those lands which have heretofore been swamp. Those lands when brought into productivity will yield far more than the lands already under natural tillage. Then we have a great deal of valuable coal land owned by the Government. We have a great many water-power sites, the water power of which will furnish an immense amount of power for use by electrical appliances. Then there are millions of acres of phosphate to be used in the fertilization of the soil. Under existing laws those lands are likely to be parted with merely under a homestead settlement. They are of such peculiar value that it seems wiser that the Government should receive some control over the water-power sites and the coal lands and the phosphates so that they may not come into the hands of one controlling corporation, but may be retained by the Government, with the power to restrict the prices at which the coal, or at least at which the power is sold, to prevent the absorption into one command of all the power on the continent. Just how the problem is to be worked out it is difficult to state, and certainly I would not attempt to state it here, but generous as we have been in the past with respect to mineral lands and the lands which can enjoy water power, we ought now to end that generosity and preserve those things that the Government still owns, in order that hereafter with a much more careful hand we may grant them for useful development.

Then we have the anti-trust law on our hands for enforcement, and the arrangement of the departments of the Government in such a way as to make it more effective if possible.

Then there is the interstate commerce law which certainly needs amendment in order to give the Interstate Commerce tribunal more power to prevent the delays which are now incident to appeals to the courts. In my judgment, the best way is to create a special court and have a court that is charged with the knowledge and practice in regard to railroads, so that the matter can be promptly disposed of.

Then I am strongly in favor of a postal savings bank. I know that in that proposition I come up against a great many conservative bankers, and also of a great many who view with doubt the wisdom of extending paternalism in the Government, but I venture to think that a project ought not to be condemned merely by calling it paternal. We have got beyond the *laisser-faire* doctrine in our Government; and where it happens that the Government is so situated that it can do a thing better than individuals can do it, can do it more economically than individuals can do it, and can supply a want for a means of thrift, I am in favor of its doing it.

The monetary reform is under consideration by a commission. When they will reach a conclusion I do not know. If there ever was a subject-matter that created differences of opinion, it is the question of how to treat our monetary and banking matters. Every man has a different theory, and with every man having a different theory we don't get any farther, but I am hopeful that the Commission may present the conditions that exist here and the conditions as they exist in Europe, and in this way point out to us some steps that may be taken to reform what is certainly today nothing but a patchwork.

Then there is another subject that is very near to my heart. I have been a judge, and legal procedure is a subject I know something about. We must improve our legal procedure so as to make it both in criminal and civil cases more simple, more rapid and less expensive, and I mean to recommend to Congress the appointment of a commission to take that subject up with respect to the Federal procedure; and then if by the Federal procedure we achieve a result that commends itself, it will form a model for the States.

Then there is another subject that especially in the South ought to attract great public attention, and that is the organization of a bureau which shall have control, so far as constitutionally it may be exercised by Federal authority, of the health of the United States. We have offices and bureaus distributed through the Government that are charged more or less with investigation and care and quarantine and that sort of thing, but I believe the time has come—and the medical profession of this country, who ought to know, and who do know, believe that the time has come—for the organization of a health bureau and the concentration in it of all the instruments for the preservation of health and for the investigation of diseases that are now included in the National Government, and such others as may be properly placed there by additional appropriation and direction.

That is a pretty long list of things to do, but if we set our shoulders together we can do a lot in one session or two sessions of Congress. When I was in the South before, and before I became President, but when I had a reasonable expectation of succeeding to that office, I said that I was anxious so far as the Executive could, to show to the Southern people that in the eye of the Executive and the Administration at Washington they were as closely a part of the Union and as much entitled to its consideration in every respect as any other part of the country. That, I said, it was not possible for the Executive to show other than in speech, except by the appointment to Federal office of men whose appointment would commend itself to the communities in which they live, that they might regard those appointees not as agents of an alien government, but as representing their own government. Now in so far as I have been able I have attempted to carry out that policy. A year has not yet elapsed, and you must give me three more years in order to demonstrate my sincerity in that regard. We have reached a point in this country when we can look back, not without love, not without intense pride, but without partisan passion, to the events of the Civil War. We have reached a point, I am glad to say, when the North can admire to the full the heroes of the South, and the South admire to the full the heroes of the North. There is a monument in Quebec that always commended itself to me—a monument to commemorate the battle of the Plains of Abraham; and on one face of that beautiful structure is the name of Montcalm, and on the other side the name of Wolfe. That always seemed to me to be the acme of what we ought to reach in this country, and I am glad to say that in my own alma mater of Yale we have established an association for the purpose of erecting within her academic precincts a memorial not to the Northern Yale men who died, not to the Southern Yale men who died, but to the Yale men who died in the Civil War. And so it is that I venture, without unduly obtruding in something that is none of my business, to hope that the project suggested by my predecessor in office, President Roosevelt, may be alluded to by me with approval and the expression of the hope that it is coming to fruition, to wit, that there should be a great memorial in honor of General Robert E. Lee in the establishment of what he himself would value most highly, a great school of engineering at Washington and Lee University, and I take this opportunity in this presence to express my deep sympathy in that movement and my desire to aid it in every way possible and proper on my part.

My friends, I am going to stop and relieve you. I have had great pleasure in talking to you in this informal way, advising you in some degree of the burdens that I am looking forward to undertaking when I get back to Washington. I do not know whether you have had that experience when you are on the eve of a so-called vacation and your conscience begins to prick you and then your duties grow mountain high so that you can not look over them at all. That is my feeling now. It is a somewhat strenuous life to eat and talk and talk and eat, but there are other things in which you have to exercise great responsibility and give great attention and industry to what you are undertaking for the nation at large, which are even more burdensome, more acute in the consumption of vital energy, than such a tour as I have had the honor of taking.

I look into your faces with the pleasurable thought that you are connected with the last of a very delightful episode in my life. I part with you with the gratitude for your cordial reception, with the belief sincere as possible that you and I agree in respect to sectionalism and its complete obliteration, and with the feeling that you and I rejoice and thank God that we are all Americans under Old Glory.

55

Address at the Washington Convention of the Laymen's Missionary Movement

Continental Memorial Hall, Washington, D. C., November 11, 1909

Mr. President; and Gentleman of the Laymen's Missionary Movement:

I like to think, whether it be true or not, that we have in this generation reached a somewhat different view of the responsibilities of a civilized nation from that which prevailed in the last generation, especially as applied to our country. It was perhaps natural that when we were engaged in digging into the soil and doing the best we could to make enough to live on, we should fall into the habit of thinking that we were a nation by ourselves, with no responsibilities whatever with respect to the rest of the world. So we have had maxims come down to us and a construction put upon Washington's farewell address that would still keep us in a place of isolation, and with pleasant remarks and well and politely expressed hopes for the welfare of other peoples, would cause us to devote ourselves entirely to our own improvement. In the days when that principle was announced and was followed with a good deal of care, there was one doctrine which was utterly at variance with it—the Monroe Doctrine. That did cause some sort of responsibility and did make us assume some sort of protection over and interest in the independent nations and governments of this hemisphere. That is now enlarged into what I think we may call a definite recognition on the part of our public men that we have a very distinct interest in the welfare, and a very

344

distinct duty with reference to the condition, of the countries of this hemisphere, and that we have exhibited it in what was, I think we may almost say, the only altruistic foreign war that history presents—that in which we fought for the liberties of Cuba and the ending of what we regarded at the time as an international scandal. So we have gone on; we have established in a sense a receivership for Santo Domingo and we are helping out that country as well as we may, and we are doing what we can to preserve the peace between the Central American countries; and there lies back in all the history of this continent the possibilities of the heavy obligation resting upon us should unhappiness and chaos arise among any of the people of this hemisphere.

That is one step. The Cuban war illustrated the fact that when you go into a war you never know where you are coming out. We entered lightly— well, not lightly; with a sense of due gravity, but certainly not with a sense of what the possibilities were—at Key West and at Santiago, and we brought up ten thousand miles away at Manila. Then we had to take over that Government; and we still have it. It has cost us a good deal of money. I had a Democratic Senator ask me the other day how much I thought it cost— "right down between us," he said. Well, I explained to him that the War Department accounts showed, so far as the army was concerned, down to 1902, it had cost us about one hundred and seventy millions of dollars, and that the further cost depended upon how you regarded the army. If you thought we could get along with fifteen or twenty thousand men less than we now had, then the whole cost of these men should be imposed on the cost of our Philippine policy, which would be twenty-five or thirty millions of dollars; but that if you thought we ought to have an army as it is now anyway, it has cost by reason of our Philippine policy upward of six million of dollars annually. Perhaps I am a little bit extreme; perhaps my experience in the Philippines has colored my view; but I do not think that the money we have spent even estimating it at the highest sum, has been wasted in any way. I think it has developed our national character; that it has broadened us into a view of our national responsibility that no other experience could. No one can say—I mean conscientiously say, that is "right down between us"—that we have been there for the exploitation of our own business. I do not mean to say that it may not come along, and I think it will and I hope it will; but certainly we have not made any money out of it up to date, and certainly we have not been there and have not done the things we have done with a view to our business profit. We have been there conscientiously—and I think I can speak for part of those who have had to do with its immediate responsibility—for the betterment of the people of the Philippine Islands;

and I am sure we have bettered their condition. We are in the position of many a man who has sought to help another man, and if we go into that sort of thing for undying gratitude we may as well give it up in the beginning. It does not continue and it does not persist, and the only benefit you can get out of it is the consciousness of having tried to do something for another man, and the belief that you have, no matter what he thinks about it.

I was thrown into the Philippines against my will—I won't say that, for I am a person I presume who could say yes or no—but I mean I was led into it by another, by that sweet nature, that most engaging character, that lovely man, William McKinley. I know what actuated him and I know that the spirit that actuated him influenced us all—his successor, Theodore Roosevelt; his Secretary of War, Elihu Root; and all who had the good fortune to serve under those great men. In the control and government of those islands I first came to be aware of the importance of foreign missions; and, if I may say so, I think there is a strong analogy between the spirit that leads a nation into what we have done in Cuba, in Santo Domingo and in the Philippines, and that movement which I am glad to see growing stronger and stronger— the movement in favor of foreign missions. The Philippine Islands themselves are an example of what ancient foreign missions could do. They are the only people, the only race, in the Orient who are Christians, and they were made so three hundred years ago by the earnest efforts of Augustinian and Franciscan friars. They led them on, taught them the agricultural arts, and led them on to a peaceful and religious life. They did not believe in too much education; they did not believe in bringing them into close communion with the European nations. They thought there was a good deal they might learn there that would hurt them. But that which they wrought has been to our great advantage in working out the problem that we are set to there, the problem of teaching them self-government. They are a Christian people, and they look to Europe and America for their ideals, and they recognize those ideals, and that makes it possible to instil in them the principles of civil liberty and the freedom of our institutions. Now there came about in the Islands what is perfectly natural with the prevalence of one denomination, and the division between the Spanish and the native priesthood led to a great deal of demoralization in the church, and led to its taking on a very strong political character. The condition has greatly improved since we went in there, in that regard, because of course we carried with us entire freedom of religion. That has led to the sending in of missionaries of other than the Roman Catholic denomination, and has brought about a spirit of emulation and competition that makes for the good of the entire Islands and for all the churches. But the operation of the foreign missions there, the effect upon the people, the influence upon the people which the church exerts and without which the Government could carry on but few of its reforms, all impress themselves upon a man charged with the responsibility of civil government in those Islands.

In the Orient I could not but take an interest in what occurred on the mainland. Every time you travel around the world, or travel anywhere, you have to refresh your knowledge. The Philippine Islands are about sixty-six hours from Hong Kong, but here we are apt to associate them all together. Distances there do not seem quite so great as they do here, and you do come closer to China when you are in the Philippines than when you are here. We could, those of us who were in the Orient, study somewhat the Chinese question, study somewhat the movements that were going on in that great Empire of four hundred millions of people; and the chief movement that was going on was a movement that found its inspiration, that had its progress, in the foreign missions that have been sent there to introduce Christian civilization among that people. I do not hesitate to say that, because I am convinced of the fact. They are the outposts of the Christian civilization. Each missionary, with his house and his staff, forms a nucleus about which gathers an influence far in excess of the numerical list of the converts. They have a political influence, an influence upon the Government of China itself, upon the Viceroys of China, who exercise so much power there that we do not understand it. The development of China today, and her budding out as she is, and as I hope she will continue to do, is largely the result of, first, the missionary movement, and then the education in America and elsewhere, under the influence of these missionaries, of young Chinamen who are anxious that their country shall take the position that her wealth, and numbers, and resources, and possibilities, and history justify. The same thing is true, though I am not so familiar with it, in regard to Africa. The men who take their lives in their hands and go among the natives are entitled to be called the outposts of civilization. They have been criticised, and I presume that is something that is common to humankind; they have been held up to contempt at times. I have read one book by a very distinguished author who visited China and thought it was wise to poke fun at what he called the assumed self-sacrifice of the missionaries in China. But I am glad to say—I have not seen it myself, but I understand—that the author has withdrawn all these implications and all of this criticism of the men who are fighting for the cause of civilization in that great country. You visit a Chinese mission—I mean a denominational mission in China from this country or Great Britain—and you find a large house, you find a considerable staff, you find as near comfort as they can have in a country that does not know what Occidental comfort is; but you find upon examination that they have to go out among the sick, they have to pursue their course of life far away from friends and homes; they have to undergo that homesickness that no one understands until he has been ten thousand miles away from home and is longing just to breathe in the smoke of his own home, dirty as it is, in order that he may know that he is near where he grew up. The lives they lead, the good they do, and the fact that they represent the highest of our civilization, make it important that they should be sent, with all the instruments of usefulness possible, into those far distant places. I do not want to reflect upon anybody, but I am bound to say that in those distant lands a great many who visit there for gain, and for so-called business, for livelihood that they could not earn at home, are not representatives of our best element at home; and they visit there for other purposes than the spread of Christian civilization. They take in the native when they can, and they do not impress the native, who has only them to judge by, that the civilization that they represent would be any great improvement on that which he has. When you contrast them with the missionaries who go there only for disinterested purposes, risking their lives by going into parts of that country where, should an uprising occur, there is no adequate protection, it makes me indignant to hear contempt expressed for these men who are carrying the banner of Christian civilization and putting themselves in positions where they may be complete sacrifices to the cause. They say they were the cause of the Boxer trouble. Anybody who looks into that knows that they had to bear the danger of it. But the cause of the Boxer trouble came from the fear on the part of China that there was a disposition on the part of a good many Christian powers to divide up, and that the division was going to be parts of China. That was their fear of foreign intervention and they manifested it in a plain way, and the missionaries who were among them for the purpose of spreading Christian civilization had to bear the brunt of it. That is the only excuse for criticism of the missionaries in respect to the Boxer movement.

I sincerely hope that the result of this movement will give to the foreign missions an impetus that, with due respect to our clerical brethren, it can not have unless the whole body of good men in the community press forward. I have spoken of it solely from the laymen's standpoint and not from the purely religious standpoint; but I have spoken the things that I think I know, and I am here not so much to talk as to express by my presence the sympathy I have with the movement that you have so successfully inaugurated.

56

Remarks at the Golden Jubilee
Dedication of St. Aloysius Church

Washington, D. C., November 14, 1909

Father McDonnell, Cardinal Gibbons, Monsignor Falconio, my Fellow Citizens:
 I am glad to be present on this occasion, the golden jubilee of the foundation of this church. In our country, in this Government and under our Constitution there is no union of Church and State, but rather a declared separation of them. This has been sometimes misunderstood by those who did not know our institutions, as an indication that there was something hostile on the part of our Government toward or some lack of sympathy with the Church of God. This is as far as possible from the truth; and I have always sought, in assisting every such church on interesting occasions like this, to testify by my presence and by words of congratulation, that there is nothing which the people and the country of the United States so depend upon for progress and advancement of their ideals as the influence and power of all the churches of the community. They tend to exalt the nation. I am here today therefore to congratulate Father McDonnell and his congregation and the distinguished dignitaries of the Catholic Church on the growth in this community of this Church of St. Aloysius, and on the good that it has done, and to testify as a representative of the Government to the sympathy we have with this instrument and all others that make for righteousness.

57

Waterways

Address at Norfolk, Virginia, on the Occasion of the Convention of the
Atlantic Deeper Waterways Association, November 19, 1909

Mr. Chairman, Governor Swanson, Delegates to the Atlantic Deeper Waterways
Association, Ladies and Gentlemen, Citizens of the Old Dominion:

I am glad again to be on Virginia soil, and I am glad again to be introduced by your distinguished Chief Magistrate, Governor Swanson. He never
introduces me to a Virginia audience that I don't want to come again. He
embodies in what he says that genuine enthusiastic sense of hospitality that
distinguishes Virginia, and therefore I always like to follow him. If I get him
out in Ohio I will give him also a test of Ohio hospitality, but not with the
same eloquence or the same elegance of language. But I am glad to be here
in his company and in the company of the delegates of the Waterways
Association. I have given not enough study, but some, to the proposition,
not so much in this neighborhood as on the Gulf, and I know that along the
Gulf there are places demanding attention where the business that now exists
justifies the claim that money shall be invested in order to make all that network of inner waterways reaching from the Gulf and the Atlantic useful, in
order to reduce rates, or in order to furnish transportation where there really
is no transportation now.

There has been, as your Governor intimates, a general movement over
the country in favor of the expenditure of money to improve our waterways,

inland and coastal; and I am sure that that movement has the support of all the people, has the support of all those responsible to the people for the expenditure of the money raised by taxation or otherwise. All that they require is that there should be shown in an ordinary reasonable way and by evidence that will appeal to sensible men, that the money which we are about to invest will certainly redound to the benefit of the people in the neighborhood where it is spent, not by way of furnishing labor for two or three years, not by way of investing capital for four or five years, but shall redound by way of improving transportation permanently. When you have made your case, then I am sure the Government and Congress will respond to it. That the case can be made I doubt not with respect to definite projects, the operation of which can be shown by reference to the business now done, or the business which certainly will be furnished, but what I wish to deprecate is a general proposition to raise a lot of money and dump some here and some there and some over there and some back here, in order to distribute it equally over the country. I am opposed to that. I am in favor of expending the money for an improvement in Norfolk and not expending it for an improvement somewhere else if the Norfolk project is a good one and that somewhere else is not, and the people who come from somewhere else have got to be judicial and impartial enough to feel that the investment at Norfolk redounds to the whole country, while the investment somewhere else does not redound to anybody but a little local fervor at the time of the expenditure of the money. In other words, we ought to go at this business as if we were business men, spending the money to redound to us in profit and in dividends. When we do that I don't think the people of the United States will grudge a cent of the many millions that it is going to cost to give us the improvements we ought to have, no matter where they are.

Now, my friends, this wind and this great concourse of people whom I am trying to make hear, do not invite a great length of speech, and therefore I am going to pass from the Waterways Association, which calls you here, with the hope that they will proceed in a business-like way to demonstrate what can be done by that which they recommend and commend it to the entire American people; and as one of those exercising temporary authority I want to say that I will take up what is projected and proposed with all the sympathy possible, but nevertheless with what I hope is a judicial spirit to reject what the evidence does not sustain, and to approve what the evidence does sustain.

Now, my friends, there are other thoughts that this meeting suggests. In the first place it must come back to you, as it did to me, and send a thrill down your backs, to see those two columns that stood in front of the reviewing stand, and now stand here, the Blue and the Gray. You say it is getting so common to see them together that it really does not call for comment, and perhaps that is so, but I am just going to make a point of it because I need subjects, and also I want to express to both those columns my appreciation of the honor they have done me in turning out today.

Secondly, you can not stand here and have the breezes come over from Hampton Roads without thinking of that battle of the *Merrimac* and the *Monitor* when it seemed as if the fate of the nation was trembling in the balance, and you can not think of that battle and of the prowess and naval courage and bravery that were shown there on both sides without having your mind come down to those jackies that passed us in presence of the reviewing stand this morning. You can not stand here in Norfolk, which has the most important navy yard and naval base that we have in the United States, without having your mind recur to that arm of the public service which we have done so much to develop, with whose growth I hope we shall do nothing to interfere. I want the Navy to continue to be maintained in a condition worthy of this country. We are not knocking anybody's chip off his shoulder, and we are not having a chip on our shoulder, but we are a great nation of eighty or ninety millions of people, and we must under present conditions in order to maintain the prestige that is proportionate to our stand before the world, have a navy that is worth seeing and able to fight if it has to. Now I am speaking of it here because somehow or other I am convinced in Norfolk that the people of Norfolk are quite judicial in their reference to the growth of the Navy.

There is another thing I want to say that will appeal to you. We have a good many coast defenses—none too many. You are here at the end of Chesapeake Bay, which is the greatest strategic point of naval rendezvous in these United States. We have very heavy and very formidable coast defenses at Fortress Monroe and all about here, but if we wish to protect this coast we ought to protect with as much care as possible the entrance to Chesapeake Bay, and that by erecting an island on the middle ground and putting a fort there that shall be impregnable. That is what I want. That is what I recommended when I was Secretary of War, and that is what I am going to push for the next three years with the hope that I will get it at the end of that time.

And now, my friends, I have talked enough for your comfort and for my throat. I have been talking too much. I talked clear across the continent on the north and down on the west and east on the south, and I have gotten into the habit and I can not help it. My voice has not had any test for more than four or five days, so I am letting it go.

But seriously speaking, my dear friends, I am glad again to be back on the soil of Virginia, and in the Southland, and to find that the warmth of reception that I had all through the South is only repeated in old Norfolk and in the Old Dominion as I visit it again, and that the sentiment in favor of a united country, of cherishing the traditions of both sides as honorable to both, but with a feeling of loyalty to the old flag that was never exceeded in the history before, is still here to make a Northerner and a Southerner rejoice and to make the President of the United States feel that he is entirely at home among you.

58

Industrial Education of the Negro

*Remarks at the Meeting of the Board of Trustees of the Hampton
Institute, Hampton, Virginia, November 20, 1909*

Dr. Frissell, Ladies and Gentlemen, and Members of Hampton Institute:

I have had to do, during the last sixty days, a good deal of speaking
without preparation, and it was my habit to gather the ideas of those who
had preceded me and mix them up and use them to the best advantage. But
the trouble about this afternoon has been that I have been so intensely interested in everything which I have heard that I have not had any time to mix
them up or give them in any different form from that beautiful one in which
they have been presented.

I am very proud that I have had the honor to be elected a member of
the board of trustees of this institution, and I am proud because I have been
thought worthy. I am glad because I know that I can not come into contact
with men like Dr. Frissell, Mr. Ogden, Bishop McVickar, George Foster
Peabody and others who for the joy of service have developed this institution,
without absorbing some of those virtues which have guided their efforts in
building up this wonderful work. Now, in the first place, I could not help
thinking, as I heard Dr. Eliot say what I hoped was true, and what I have
ventured to say before, and what I now know is true because he said it, of
the reform in education here, of another great reform that had come to the
English people in a similar way. The depraved condition of the civil service

354

in the English Government received its remedy and became better, and such a model service as it is now, through the lessons that were learned by the English statesmen from the Indian Civil Service, and so it is here.

We had been struggling along for several hundred years with our system of education. There was presented to General Armstrong, the founder of this institution, the question of what we should do for the Negro and the Indian races in their almost helpless condition as we found them after the war. The necessity for helping their condition led him to undertake this system of education, that of manual dexterity, united with the teaching of life as it was to be. It has now developed not alone for Negroes and Indians, but for the white people throughout this land. I have always thought that, and, when the foremost educator of the land says so, I am going to assert it.

The second thought, and in certain aspects the most important phase of this system which General Armstrong founded and which Dr. Frissell has continued with such success, is the fact that right here in Hampton, in "Little Scotland," we have seen worked out what I regard as the solution of what we call the race question in this country. I do not mean that it is settled and I do not mean that the problem is solved, because problems like that are not solved in a decade. It takes a number of decades. But when you take the speech of former Governor Montague on the one side, and the speech of Major Moton on the other, and put together and give effect to the spirit that actuated both, you have the solution of the race question. Major Moton was sure that he wouldn't make a good Indian or a good white man. Well, I don't know about that; but I am sure that he makes a pretty good Scotchman, if one can judge by the way he leads his chorus in Scotch airs. If ever those beautiful airs were rendered with finer harmony, and better understanding of their meaning, and sweeter tones, than were rendered here this afternoon, I have never heard them—perhaps they are in Scotland.

I am not going to detain you long. I am glad to be here to testify my deep personal interest in this institution, my deep respect for those who have brought it to what it is, my recognition of it as a national institution, the wisdom of the suggestion of Dr. Eliot that there ought to be schools all over this country patterned after it, and while I hold, temporarily, the Presidency of the United States, I am glad to use that office, so far as I can by representation, to testify to the interest of the American people in the problem which is being worked out here.

59

Message to the Two Houses of Congress at the Second Session of the Sixty-First Congress

December 7, 1909

To the Senate and the House of Representatives:

The relations of the United States with all foreign governments have continued upon the normal basis of amity and good understanding, and are very generally satisfactory.

Europe

Pursuant to the provisions of the general treaty of arbitration concluded between the United States and Great Britain, April 4, 1908, a special agreement was entered into between the two countries on January 27, 1909, for the submission of questions relating to the fisheries on the North Atlantic Coast to a tribunal to be formed from members of the Permanent Court of Arbitration at The Hague.

In accordance with the provisions of the special agreement the printed case of each government was, on October 4, last, submitted to the other and to the Arbitral Tribunal at The Hague, and the counter case of the United States is now in course of preparation.

The American rights under the fisheries article of the Treaty of 1818 have been a cause of difference between the United States and Great Britain for nearly seventy years. The interests involved are of great importance to the American fishing industry, and the final settlement of the controversy will remove a source of constant irritation and complaint. This is the first case involving such great international questions which has been submitted to the Permanent Court of Arbitration at The Hague.

The treaty between the United States and Great Britain concerning the Canadian International boundary, concluded April 11, 1908, authorizes the appointment of two commissioners to define and mark accurately the international boundary line between the United States and the Dominion of Canada in the waters of the Passamaquoddy Bay, and provides for the exchange of briefs within the period of six months. The briefs were duly presented within the prescribed period, but as the commissioners failed to agree within six months after the exchange of the printed statements as required by the treaty, it has now become necessary to resort to the arbitration provided for in the article.

The International Fisheries Commission, appointed pursuant to and under the authority of the Convention of April 11, 1908, between the United States and Great Britain, has completed a system of uniform and common international regulations for the protection and preservation of the food fishes in international boundary waters of the United States and Canada.

The regulations will be duly submitted to Congress with a view to the enactment of such legislation as will be necessary under the convention to put them into operation.

The convention providing for the settlement of international differences between the United States and Canada, including the apportionment between the two countries of certain of the boundary waters and the appointment of commissioners to adjust certain other questions, signed on the 11th day of January, 1909, and to the ratification of which the Senate gave its advice and consent on March 3, 1909, has not yet been ratified on the part of Great Britain.

Commissioners have been appointed on the part of the United States to act jointly with commissioners on the part of Canada in examining into the question of obstructions in the St. John River between Maine and New Brunswick, and to make recommendations for the regulation of the uses thereof, and are now engaged in this work.

Negotiations for an international conference to consider and reach an arrangement providing for the preservation and protection of the fur seals in the North Pacific are in progress with the governments of Great Britain, Japan, and Russia. The attitude of the governments interested leads me to hope for a satisfactory settlement of this question as the ultimate outcome of the negotiations.

The Second Peace Conference, recently held at The Hague, adopted a convention for the establishment of an International Prize Court upon the joint proposal of delegations of the United States, France, Germany, and Great Britain. The law to be observed by the tribunal in the decision of prize cases was, however, left in an uncertain and therefore unsatisfactory state. Article 7 of the Convention provided that the court was to be governed by the provisions of treaties existing between the belligerents, but that "in the absence of such provisions, the court shall apply the rules of international law. If no generally recognized rule exists, the court shall give judgment in accordance with the general principles of justice and equity." As, however, many questions in international maritime law are understood differently and therefore interpreted differently in various countries, it was deemed advisable not to intrust legislative powers to the proposed court, but to determine the rules of law properly applicable in a conference of the representative maritime nations. Pursuant to an invitation of Great Britain a conference was held at London from December 2, 1908, to February 26, 1909, in which the following powers participated: the United States, Austria-Hungary, France, Germany, Great Britain, Italy, Japan, the Netherlands, Russia, and Spain. The conference resulted in the Declaration of London, unanimously agreed to and signed by the participating powers, concerning among other matters the highly important subjects of blockade, contraband, the destruction of neutral prizes, and continuous voyages.

The Declaration of London is an eminently satisfactory codification of the international maritime law, and it is hoped that its reasonableness and fairness will secure its general adoption, as well as remove one of the difficulties standing in the way of the establishment of an International Prize Court.

Under the authority given in the sundry civil appropriation act, approved March 4, 1909, the United States was represented at the International Conference on Maritime Law at Brussels. The conference met on the 28th of September last and resulted in the signature *ad referendum* of a convention for the unification of certain regulations with regard to maritime assistance and salvage and a convention for the unification of certain rules with regard to collisions at sea.

Two new projects of conventions which have not heretofore been considered in a diplomatic conference, namely, one concerning the limitation of the responsibility of shipowners, and the other concerning marine mortgages and privileges, have been submitted by the conference to the different governments.

The conference adjourned to meet again on April 11, 1910.

The international conference for the purpose of promoting uniform legislation concerning letters of exchange, which was called by the Government of the Netherlands to meet at The Hague in September, 1909, has been postponed to meet at that capital in June, 1910. The United States will be appropriately represented in this Conference under the provision therefor already made by Congress.

The cordial invitation of Belgium to be represented by a fitting display of American progress in the useful arts and inventions at the World's Fair to be held at Brussels in 1910 remains to be acted upon by the Congress. Mindful of the advantages to accrue to our artisans and producers in competition with their Continental rivals, I renew the recommendation heretofore made that provision be made for acceptance of the invitation and adequate representation in the Exposition.

The question arising out of the Belgian annexation of the Independent State of the Congo, which has so long and earnestly preoccupied the attention of this Government and enlisted the sympathy of our best citizens, is still open, but in a more hopeful stage. This Government was among the foremost in the great work of uplifting the uncivilized regions of Africa and urging the extension of the benefits of civilization, education, and fruitful open commerce to that vast domain, and is a party to treaty engagements of all the interested powers designed to carry out that great duty to humanity. The way to better the original and adventitious conditions, so burdensome to the natives and so destructive to their development, has been pointed out, by observation and experience, not alone of American representatives, but by cumulative evidence from all quarters and by the investigations of Belgian agents. The announced programs of reforms, striking at many of the evils known to exist, are an augury of better things. The attitude of the United States is one of benevolent encouragement, coupled with a hopeful trust that the good work, responsibly undertaken and zealously perfected to the accomplishment of the results so ardently desired, will soon justify the wisdom that inspires them and satisfy the demands of humane sentiment throughout the world.

A convention between the United States and Germany, under which the non-working provisions of the German patent law are made inapplicable to the patents of American citizens, was concluded on February 23, 1909, and is now in force. Negotiations for similar conventions looking to the placing of American inventors on the same footing as nationals have recently been initiated with other European governments whose laws require the local working of foreign patents.

Under an appropriation made at the last session of the Congress, a commission was sent on American cruisers to Monrovia to investigate the interests of the United States and its citizens in Liberia. Upon its arrival at Monrovia, the commission was enthusiastically received, and during its stay in Liberia was everywhere met with the heartiest expressions of good-will for the American Government and people, and the hope was repeatedly expressed on all sides that this Government might see its way clear to do something to relieve the critical position of the Republic arising in a measure from external as well as internal and financial embarrassments.

The Liberian Government afforded every facility to the commission for ascertaining the true state of affairs. The commission also had conferences with representative citizens, interested foreigners and the representatives of foreign governments in Monrovia. Visits were made to various parts of the Republic and to the neighboring British colony of Sierra Leone, where the commission was received by and conferred with the Governor.

It will be remembered that the interest of the United States in the Republic of Liberia springs from the historical fact of the foundation of the Republic by the colonization of American citizens of the African race. In an early treaty with Liberia there is a provision under which the United States may be called upon for advice or assistance. Pursuant to this provision and in the spirit of the moral relationship of the United States to Liberia, that Republic last year asked this Government to lend assistance in the solution of certain of their national problems, and hence the commission was sent.

The report of our commissioners has just been completed and is now under examination by the Department of State. It is hoped that there may result some helpful measures, in which case it may be my duty again to invite your attention to this subject.

The Norwegian Government, by a note addressed on January 26, 1909, to the Department of State, conveyed an invitation to the Government of the United States to take part in a conference which it is understood will be held in February or March, 1910, for the purpose of devising means to remedy existing conditions in the Spitzbergen Islands.

This invitation was conveyed under the reservation that the question of altering the status of the islands as countries belonging to no particular state, and as equally open to the citizens and subjects of all states, should not be raised.

The European powers invited to this Conference by the Government of Norway were Belgium, Denmark, France, Germany, Great Britain, Russia, Sweden, and the Netherlands.

The Department of State, in view of proofs filed with it in 1906, showing the American possession, occupation and working of certain coal-bearing lands in Spitzbergen, accepted the invitation under the reservation above stated, and under the further reservation that all interests in those islands already vested should be protected and that there should be equality of opportunity for the future. It was further pointed out that membership in the conference on the part of the United States was qualified by the consideration that this Government would not become a signatory to any conventional arrangement concluded by the European members of the conference which would imply contributory participation by the United States in any obligation or responsibility for the enforcement of any scheme of administration which might be devised by the conference for the islands.

The Near East

His Majesty, Mehmed V., Sultan of Turkey, recently sent to this country a special embassy to announce his accession. The quick transition of the Government of the Ottoman Empire from one of retrograde tendencies to a constitutional government with a parliament and with progressive modern policies of reform and public improvement is one of the important phenomena of our times. Constitutional government seems also to have made further advance in Persia. These events have turned the eyes of the world upon the Near East. In that quarter the prestige of the United States has spread widely through the peaceful influence of American schools, universities, and missionaries. There is every reason why we should obtain a greater share of the commerce of the Near East since the conditions are more favorable now than ever before.

Latin America

One of the happiest events in recent Pan-American diplomacy was the pacific, independent settlement by the governments of Bolivia and Peru of a boundary difference between them, which for some weeks threatened to cause war and even to entrain embitterments affecting other republics less directly concerned. From various quarters, directly or indirectly concerned, the intermediation of the United States was sought to assist in a solution of the controversy. Desiring at all times to abstain from any undue mingling in the affairs of sister republics and having faith in the ability of the governments of Peru and Bolivia themselves to settle their differences in a manner satisfactory to themselves which, viewed with magnanimity, would assuage all embitterment, this Government steadily abstained from being drawn into the controversy and was much gratified to find its confidence justified by events.

On the 9th of July next there will open at Buenos Ayres the Fourth Pan-American Conference. This conference will have a special meaning to the hearts of all Americans, because around its date are clustered the anniversaries of the independence of so many of the American republics. It is not necessary for me to remind the Congress of the political, social, and commercial importance of these gatherings. You are asked to make liberal appropriation for our participation. If this be granted, it is my purpose to appoint a distinguished and representative delegation, qualified fittingly to represent this country and to deal with the problems of intercontinental interest which will there be discussed.

The Argentine Republic will also hold from May to November, 1910, at Buenos Ayres, a great International Agricultural Exhibition in which the United States has been invited to participate. Considering the rapid growth of the trade in the United States with the Argentine Republic and the cordial relations existing between the two nations, together with the fact that it provides an opportunity to show deference to a sister republic on the occasion of the celebration of its national independence, the proper Departments of this Government are taking steps to apprise the interests concerned of the opportunity afforded by this exhibition, in which appropriate participation by this country is so desirable. The designation of an official representative is also receiving consideration.

Today, more than ever before, American capital is seeking investment in foreign countries, and American products are more and more generally seeking foreign markets. As a consequence, in all countries there are American citizens and American interests to be protected, on occasion, by their Government. These movements of men, of capital, and of commodities bring peoples and governments closer together and so form bonds of peace and mutual dependency, as they must also naturally sometimes make passing points of friction. The resultant situation inevitably imposes upon this Government vastly increased responsibilities. This Administration, through the Department of State and the foreign service is lending all proper support to legitimate and beneficial American enterprises in foreign countries, the degree of such support being measured by the national advantages to be expected. A citizen himself can not by contract or otherwise divest himself of the right, nor can this Government escape the obligation, of his protection in his personal and property rights when these are unjustly infringed in a foreign country. To avoid ceaseless vexations it is proper that in considering whether American enterprise should be encouraged or supported in a particular country, the Government should give full weight not only to the national as opposed to the individual benefits to accrue, but also to the fact whether or not the Government of the country in question in its administration and in its diplomacy faithful to the principles of moderation, equity, and justice upon which alone depend international credit, in diplomacy as well as in finance.

The Pan-American policy of this Government has long been fixed in its principles and remains unchanged. With the changed circumstances of the United States and of the republics to the south of us, most of which have great natural resources, stable government, and progressive ideals, the apprehension which gave rise to the Monroe Doctrine may be said to have nearly disappeared, and neither the doctrine as it exists nor any other doctrine of American policy should be permitted to operate for the perpetuation of irresponsible government, the escape of just obligations, or the insidious allegation of dominating ambitions on the part of the United States.

Beside the fundamental doctrines of our Pan-American policy there have grown up a realization of political interests, community of institutions and ideals, and a flourishing commerce. All these bonds will be greatly strengthened as time goes on and increased facilities, such as the great bank soon to be established in Latin America, supply the means for building up the colossal intercontinental commerce of the future.

My meeting with President Diaz and the greeting exchanged on both American and Mexican soil served, I hope, to signalize the close and cordial relations which so well bind together this republic and the great republic immediately to the south, between which there is so vast a network of material interests.

I am happy to say that all but one of the cases which for so long vexed our relations with Venezuela have been settled within the past few months and that, under the enlightened régime now directing the Government of Venezuela, provision has been made for arbitration of the remaining case before The Hague Tribunal.

On July 30, 1909, the Government of Panama agreed, after considerable negotiation, to indemnify the relatives of the American officers and sailors who were brutally treated, one of them having, indeed, been killed by the Panaman police this year.

The sincere desire of the Government of Panama to do away with a situation where such an accident could occur is manifest in the recent request in compliance with which this Government has lent the services of an officer of the Army to be employed by the Government of Panama as Instructor of Police.

The sanitary improvements and public works undertaken in Cuba prior to the present administration of that Government, in the success of which the United States is interested under the treaty, are reported to be making good progress; and since the Congress provided for the continuance of the reciprocal commercial arrangement between Cuba and the United States assurance has been received that no negotiations injuriously affecting the situation will be undertaken without consultation.

The collection of the customs of the Dominican Republic through the general receiver of customs appointed by the President of the United States in accordance with the convention of February 8, 1907, has proceeded in an uneventful and satisfactory manner. The customs receipts have decreased owing to disturbed political and economic conditions and to a very natural curtailment of imports in view of the anticipated revision of the Dominican tariff schedule. The payments to the fiscal agency fund for the service of the bonded debt of the republic, as provided by the convention, have been regularly and promptly made, and satisfactory progress has been made in carrying out the provisions of the convention looking toward the completion of the adjustment of the debt and the acquirement by the Dominican Government of certain concessions and monopolies which have been a burden to the commerce of the country. In short, the receivership has demonstrated its ability, even under unfavorable economic and political conditions, to do the work for which it was intended.

This Government was obliged to intervene diplomatically to bring about arbitration or settlement of the claim of the Emery Company against Nicaragua, which it had long before been agreed should be arbitrated. A settlement of this troublesome case was reached by the signature of a protocol on September 18, 1909.

Many years ago diplomatic intervention became necessary to the protection of the interests in the American claim of Alsop & Company against the Government of Chile. The Government of Chile had frequently admitted obligation in the case and had promised this Government to settle it. There had been two abortive attempts to do so through arbitral commissions, which failed through lack of jurisdiction. Now, happily, as the result of the recent diplomatic negotiations, the Governments of the United States and of Chile, actuated by the sincere desire to free from any strain those cordial and friendly relations upon which both set such store, have agreed by a protocol to submit the controversy to definitive settlement by His Britannic Majesty Edward VII.

364

Since the Washington Conventions of 1907 were communicated to the Government of the United States as a consulting and advising party, this Government has been almost continuously called upon by one or another, and in turn by all of the five Central American Republics, to exert itself for the maintenance of the conventions. Nearly every complaint has been against the Zelaya Government of Nicaragua, which has kept Central America in constant tension or turmoil. The responses made to the representations of Central American Republics, as viewed from the United States on account of its relation to the Washington Conventions, have been at all times conservative and have avoided so far as possible any semblance of interference, although it is very apparent that the considerations of geographic proximity to the Canal Zone and of the very substantial American interests in Central America give to the United States a special position in the zone of these republics and the Caribbean Sea.

I need not rehearse here the patient efforts of this Government to promote peace and welfare among these republics, efforts which are fully appreciated by the majority of them who are loyal to their true interests. It would be no less unnecessary to rehearse here the sad tale of unspeakable barbarities and oppression alleged to have been committed by the Zelaya Government. Recently two Americans were put to death by order of President Zelaya himself. They were reported to have been regularly commissioned officers in the organized forces of a revolution which had continued many weeks and was in control of about half of the republic, and as such, according to the modern enlightened practice of civilized nations, they were entitled to be dealt with as prisoners of war.

At the date when this message is printed this Government has terminated diplomatic relations with the Zelaya Government, for reasons made public in a communication to the former Nicaraguan chargé d'affaires, and is intending to take such future steps as may be found most consistent with its dignity, its duty to American interests, and its moral obligations to Central America and to civilization. It may later be necessary for me to bring this subject to the attention of the Congress in a special message.

The International Bureau of American Republics has carried on an important and increasing work during the last year. In the exercise of its peculiar functions as an international agency, maintained by all the American Republics for the development of Pan-American commerce and friendship, it has accomplished a great practical good which could be done in the same way by no individual department or bureau of one government, and is therefore deserving of your liberal support. The fact that it is about to enter a new building, erected through the munificence of an American philanthropist and the contributions of all the American nations, where both its efficiency of administration and expense of maintenance will naturally be much augmented, further entitles it to special consideration.

The Far East

In the Far East this Government preserves unchanged its policy of supporting the principle of equality of opportunity and scrupulous respect for the integrity of the Chinese Empire, to which policy are pledged the interested powers of both East and West.

By the Treaty of 1903 China has undertaken the abolition of likin with a moderate and proportionate raising of the customs tariff along with currency reform. These reforms being of manifest advantage to foreign commerce as well as to the interests of China, this Government is endeavoring to facilitate these measures and the needful acquiescence of the treaty powers. When it appeared that Chinese likin revenues were to be hypothecated to foreign bankers in connection with a great railway project, it was obvious that the governments whose nationals held this loan would have a certain direct interest in the question of the carrying out by China of the reforms in question. Because this railroad loan represented a practical and real application of the "open door" policy through cooperation with China by interested powers as well as because of its relations to the reforms referred to above, the Administration deemed American participation to be of great national interest. Happily, when it was as a matter of broad policy urgent that this opportunity should not be lost, the indispensable instrumentality presented itself when a group of American bankers, of international reputation and great resources, agreed at once to share in the loan upon precisely such terms as this Government should approve. The chief of those terms was that American railway material should be upon an exact equality with that of the other nationals joining in the loan in the placing of orders for this whole railroad system. After months of negotiation the equal participation of Americans seems at last assured. It is gratifying that Americans will thus take their share in this extension of these great highways of trade, and to believe that such activities will give a real impetus to our commerce and will prove a practical corollary to our historic policy in the Far East.

The Imperial Chinese Government in pursuance of its decision to devote funds from the portion of the indemnity remitted by the United States to the sending of students to this country has already completed arrangements for carrying out this purpose, and a considerable body of students have arrived to take up their work in our schools and universities. No one can doubt the happy effect that the associations formed by these representative young men will have when they return to take up their work in the progressive development of their country.

The results of the Opium Conference held at Shanghai last spring at the invitation of the United States have been laid before the Government. The report shows that China is making remarkable progress and admirable efforts toward the eradication of the opium evil and that the governments concerned have not allowed their commercial interests to interfere with a helpful cooperation in this reform. Collateral investigations of the opium question in this country lead me to recommend that the manufacture, sale, and use of opium and its derivatives in the United States should be so far as possible more rigorously controlled by legislation.

In one of the Chinese-Japanese Conventions of September 4 of this year there was a provision which caused considerable public apprehension in that upon its face it was believed in some quarters to seek to establish a monopoly of mining privileges along the South Manchurian and Antung-Mukden Railroads, and thus to exclude Americans from a wide field of enterprise, to take part in which they were by treaty with China entitled. After a thorough examination of the Conventions and of the several contextual documents, the Secretary of State reached the conclusion that no such monopoly was intended or accomplished. However, in view of the widespread discussion of this question, to confirm the view it had reached, this Government made inquiry of the Imperial Chinese and Japanese governments and received from each official assurance that the provision had no purpose inconsistent with the policy of equality of opportunity to which the signatories, in common with the United States, are pledged.

Our traditional relations with the Japanese Empire continue cordial as usual. As the representative of Japan, His Imperial Highness Prince Kuni visited the Hudson-Fulton Celebration. The recent visit of a delegation of prominent business men as guests of the chambers of commerce of the Pacific Slope, whose representatives had been so agreeably received in Japan, will doubtless contribute to the growing trade across the Pacific, as well as to that mutual understanding which leads to mutual appreciation. The arrangement of 1908 for a cooperative control of the coming of laborers to the United States has proved to work satisfactorily. The matter of a revision of the existing treaty between the United States and Japan which is terminable in 1912 is already receiving the study of both countries.

The Department of State is considering the revision in whole or in part, of the existing treaty with Siam, which was concluded in 1856 and is now, in respect to many of its provisions, out-of-date.

The Department of State

I earnestly recommend to the favorable action of the Congress the estimates submitted by the Department of State and most especially the legislation suggested in the Secretary of State's letter of this date whereby it will be possible to develop and make permanent the reorganization of the Department upon modern lines in a manner to make it a thoroughly efficient instrument in the furtherance of our foreign trade and of American interests abroad. The plan to have Divisions of Latin-American and Far Eastern Affairs and to institute a certain specialization in business with Europe and the Near East will at once commend itself. These politico-geographical divisions and the detail from the Diplomatic or Consular Service to the Department of a number of men, who bring to the study of complicated problems in different parts of the world practical knowledge recently gained on the spot, clearly is of the greatest advantage to the Secretary of State in foreseeing conditions likely to arise and in conducting the great variety of correspondence and negotiation. It should be remembered that such facilities exist in the foreign offices of all the leading commercial nations and that to deny them to the Secretary of State would be to place this Government at a great disadvantage in the rivalry of commercial competition.

The Consular Service has been greatly improved under the law of April 5, 1906, and the Executive Order of June 27, 1906, and I commend to your consideration the question of embodying in a statute the principles of the present executive order upon which the efficiency of our Consular Service is wholly dependent.

In modern times political and commercial interests are interrelated, and in the negotiation of commercial treaties, conventions, and tariff agreements the keeping open of opportunities and the proper support of American enterprises, our Diplomatic Service is quite as important as the Consular Service to the business interests of the country. Impressed with this idea and convinced that selection after rigorous examination, promotion for merit solely and the experience only to be gained through the continuity of an organized service are indispensable to a high degree of efficiency in the Diplomatic Service, I have signed an executive order as the first step toward this very desirable result. Its effect should be to place all secretaries in the Diplomatic Service in much the same position as consular officers are now placed and to tend to the promotion of the most efficient to the grade of minister, generally leaving for outside appointment such posts of the grade of ambassador or minister as it may be expedient to fill from without the service. It is proposed also to continue the practice instituted last summer of giving to all newly appointed secretaries at least one month's thorough training in the Department of State before they proceed to their posts. This has been done for some time in regard to the Consular Service with excellent results.

Under a provision of the act of August 5, 1909, I have appointed three officials to assist the officers of the Government in collecting information necessary to a wise administration of the tariff act of August 5, 1909. As to questions of customs administration they are cooperating with the officials of the Treasury Department and as to matters of the needs and the exigencies of our manufacturers and exporters, with the Department of Commerce and Labor, in its relation to the domestic aspect of the subject of foreign commerce. In the study of foreign tariff treatment they will assist the Bureau of Trade Relations of the Department of State. It is hoped thus to coordinate and bring to bear upon this most important subject all the agencies of the Government which can contribute anything to its efficient handling.

As a consequence of Section 2 of the rarity act of August 5, 1909, it becomes the duty of the Secretary of State to conduct as diplomatic business all the negotiations necessary to place him in a position to advise me as to whether or not a particular country unduly discriminates against the United States in the sense of the statute referred to. The great scope and complexity of this work, as well as the obligation to lend all proper aid to our expanding commerce, is met by the expansion of the Bureau of Trade Relations as set forth in the estimates for the Department of State.

I have thus in some detail described the important transactions of the State Department since the beginning of this Administration for the reason that there is no provision either by statute or custom for a formal report by the Secretary of State to the President or to Congress and a Presidential message is the only means by which the condition of our foreign relations is brought to the attention of Congress and the public.

Other Departments

In dealing with the affairs of the other Departments, the heads of which all submit annual reports, I shall touch only those matters that seem to me to call for special mention on my part without minimizing in any way the recommendations made by them for legislation affecting their respective Departments, in all of which I wish to express my general concurrence.

Government Expenditures and Revenues

Perhaps the most important question presented to this Administration is that of economy in expenditures and sufficiency of revenue. The deficit of the last fiscal year, and the certain deficit of the current year, prompted Congress to throw a greater responsibility on the Executive and the Secretary of the Treasury than had heretofore been declared by statute. This declaration imposes upon the Secretary of the Treasury the duty of assembling all the estimates of the Executive Departments, bureaus, and offices, of the expenditures necessary in the ensuing fiscal year, and of making an estimate of the revenues of the Government for the same period; and if a probable deficit is thus shown, it is made the duty of the President to recommend the method by which such deficit can be met.

The report of the Secretary shows that the ordinary expenditures for the current fiscal year ending June 30, 1910, will exceed the estimated receipts by $34,075,620. If to this deficit is added the sum to be disbursed for the Panama Canal, amounting to $38,000,000, and $1,000,000 to be paid on the public debt, the deficit of ordinary receipts and expenditures will be increased to a total deficit of $73,075,620. This deficit the Secretary proposes to meet by the proceeds of bonds issued to pay the cost of constructing the Panama Canal. I approve this proposal.

The policy of paying for the construction of the Panama Canal, not out of current revenue, but by bond issues, was adopted in the Spooner Act of 1902, and there seems to be no good reason for departing from the principle by which a part at least of the burden of the cost of the canal shall fall upon our posterity who are to enjoy it; and there is all the more reason for this view because, to date, the actual cost of the canal, which is now half done and which will be completed January 1, 1915, shows that the cost of engineering and construction will be $297,766,000, instead of $139,705,200 as originally estimated. In addition to engineering and construction, the other expenses, including sanitation and government, and the amount paid for the properties, the franchise, and the privilege of building the canal, increase the cost by $75,435,000, to a total of $375,201,000. The increase in the cost of engineering and construction is due to a substantial enlargement of the plan of construction by widening the canal 100 feet in the Culebra cut and by increasing the dimensions of the locks, to the underestimate of the quantity of the work to be done under the original plan, and to an underestimate of the cost of labor and materials both of which have greatly enhanced in price since the original estimate was made.

In order to avoid a deficit for the ensuing fiscal year, I directed the heads of Departments in the preparation of their estimates to make them as low as possible consistent with imperative governmental necessity. The result has been, as I am advised by the Secretary of the Treasury, that the estimates for the expenses of the Government for the next fiscal year ending June 30, 1911, are less than the appropriations for this current fiscal year by $42,818,000. So far as the Secretary of the Treasury is able to form a judgment as to future income, and compare it with the expenditures for the next fiscal year ending June 30, 1911, and excluding payments on account of the Panama Canal, which will doubtless be taken up by bonds, there will be a surplus of $35,931,000.

In the present estimates the needs of the Departments and of the Government have been cut to the quick, so to speak, and any assumption on the part of Congress, so often made in times past, that the estimates have been prepared with the expectation that they may be reduced, will result in seriously hampering proper administration.

The Secretary of the Treasury points out what should be carefully noted in respect to this reduction in governmental expenses for the next fiscal year, that the economies are of two kinds—first, there is a saving in the permanent administration of the Departments, bureaus, and offices of the Government; and, second, there is a present reduction in expenses by a postponement of projects and improvements that ultimately will have to be carried out, but which are now delayed with the hope that additional revenue in the future will permit their execution without producing a deficit.

It has been impossible in the preparation of estimates greatly to reduce the cost of permanent administration. This can not be done without a thorough reorganization of bureaus, offices, and departments. For the purpose of securing information which may enable the executive and legislative branches to unite in a plan for the permanent reduction of the cost of governmental administration, the Treasury Department has instituted an investigation by one of the most skilled expert accountants in the United States. The result of his work in two or three bureaus, which, if extended to the entire Government, must occupy two or more years, has been to show much room for improvement and opportunity for substantial reductions in the cost and increased efficiency of administration. The object of the investigation is to devise means to increase the average efficiency of each employee. There is great room for improvement toward this end, not only by the reorganization of bureaus and departments and in the avoidance of duplication, but also in the treatment of the individual employee.

Under the present system it constantly happens that two employees receive the same salary when the work of one is far more difficult and important and exacting than that of the other. Superior ability is not rewarded or encouraged. As the classification is now entirely by salary, an employee often rises to the highest class while doing the easiest work, for which alone he may be fitted. An investigation ordered by my predecessor resulted in the recommendation that the civil service be reclassified according to the kind of work, so that the work requiring most application and knowledge and ability shall receive most compensation. I believe such a change would be fairer to the whole force and would permanently improve the personnel of the service.

More than this, every reform directed toward the improvement in the average efficiency of government employees must depend on the ability of the Executive to eliminate from the government service those who are inefficient from any cause, and as the degree of efficiency in all the Departments is much lessened by the retention of old employees who have outlived their energy and usefulness, it is indispensable to any proper system of economy that provision be made so that their separation from the service shall be easy and inevitable. It is impossible to make such provision unless there is adopted a plan of civil pensions.

Most of the great industrial organizations, and many of the well-conducted railways of this country, are coming to the conclusion that a system of pensions for old employees, and the substitution therefor of younger and more energetic servants promotes both economy and efficiency of administration.

I am aware that there is a strong feeling in both Houses of Congress, and possibly in the country, against the establishment of civil pensions, and that this has naturally grown out of the heavy burden of military pensions, which it has always been the policy of our Government to assume; but I am strongly convinced that no other practical solution of the difficulties presented by the superannuation of civil servants can be found than that of a system of civil pensions.

The business and expenditures of the Government have expanded enormously since the Spanish War, but as the revenues have increased in nearly the same proportion as the expenditures until recently, the attention of the public, and of those responsible for the Government, has not been fastened upon the question of reducing the cost of administration. We can not, in view of the advancing prices of living, hope to save money by a reduction in the standard of salaries paid. Indeed, if any change is made in that regard, an increase rather than a decrease will be necessary; and the only means of economy will be in reducing the number of employees and in obtaining a greater average of efficiency from those retained in the service.

Close investigation and study needed to make definite recommendations in this regard will consume at least two years. I note with much satisfaction the organization in the Senate of a Committee on Public Expenditures, charged with the duty of conducting such an investigation, and I tender to that Committee all the assistance which the executive branch of the Government can possibly render.

Frauds in the Collection of Customs

I regret to refer to the fact of the discovery of extensive frauds in the collection of the customs revenue at New York City, in which a number of the subordinate employees in the weighing and other departments were directly concerned, and in which the beneficiaries were the American Sugar Refining Company and others. The frauds consisted in the payment of duty on underweights of sugar. The Government has recovered from the American Sugar Refining Company all that it is shown to have been defrauded of. The sum was received in full of the amount due, which might have been recovered by civil suit against the beneficiary of the fraud, but there was an express reservation in the contract of settlement by which the settlement should not interfere with, or prevent the criminal prosecution of everyone who was found to be subject to the same.

Criminal prosecutions are now proceeding against a number of the Government officers. The Treasury Department and the Department of Justice are exerting every effort to discover all the wrongdoers, including the officers and employees of the companies who may have been privy to the fraud. It would seem to me that an investigation of the frauds by Congress at present, pending the probing by the Treasury Department and the Department of Justice, as proposed, might by giving immunity and otherwise prove an embarrassment in securing conviction of the guilty parties.

Maximum and Minimum Clause in Tariff Act

Two features of the new tariff act call for special reference. By virtue of the clause known as the "Maximum and Minimum" clause, it is the duty of the Executive to consider the laws and practices of other countries with reference to the importation into those countries of the products and merchandise of the United States, and if the Executive finds such laws and practices not to be *unduly discriminatory* against the United States, the minimum duties provided in the bill are to go into force. Unless the President makes such a finding, then the maximum duties provided in the bill, that is, an increase of twenty-five per cent, *ad valorem* over the minimum duties, are to be in force. Fear has been expressed that this power conferred and duty imposed on the Executive is likely to lead to a tariff war. I beg to express the hope and belief that no such result need be anticipated.

The discretion granted to the Executive by the term "unduly discriminatory" is wide. In order that the maximum duty shall be charged against the imports from a country not only discriminations in its laws or the practice under them against the trade of the United States, but that the discriminations found shall be undue; that is, without good and fair reason. I conceive that this power was reposed in the President with the hope that the maximum duties might never be applied in any case, but that the power to apply them would enable the President and the State Department through friendly negotiation to secure the elimination from the laws and the practice under them of any foreign country of that which is unduly discriminatory. No one is seeking a tariff war or a condition in which the spirit of retaliation shall be aroused.

Uses of the New Tariff Board

The new tariff law enables me to appoint a tariff board to assist me in connection with the Department of State in the administration of the maximum and minimum clause of the act and also to assist officers of the Government in the administration of the entire law. An examination of the law and an understanding of the nature of the facts which should be considered in discharging the functions imposed upon the Executive show that I have the power to direct the tariff board to make a comprehensive glossary and encyclopedia of the terms used and articles embraced in the tariff law, and to secure information as to the cost of production of such goods in this country and the cost of their production in foreign countries. I have therefore appointed a tariff board consisting of three members and have directed them to perform all the duties above described. This work will perhaps take two or three years, and I ask from Congress a continuing annual appropriation equal to that already made for its prosecution. I believe that the work of this board will be of prime utility and importance whenever Congress shall deem it wise again to readjust the customs duties. If the facts secured by the tariff board are of such a character as to show generally that the rates of duties imposed by the present tariff law are excessive under the principles of protection as described in the platform of the successful party at the late election, I shall not hesitate to invite the attention of Congress to this fact and to the necessity for action predicated thereon. Nothing, however, halts business and interferes with the course of prosperity so much as the threatened revision of the tariff, and until the facts are at hand, after careful and deliberate investigation, upon which such revision can properly be undertaken, it seems to me unwise to attempt it. The amount of misinformation that creeps into arguments *pro* and *con* in respect to tariff rates is such as to require the kind of investigation that I have directed the tariff board to make, an investigation undertaken by it wholly without respect to the effect which the facts may have in calling for a readjustment of the rates of duty.

War Department

In the interest of immediate economy and because of the prospect of a deficit, I have required a reduction in the estimates of the War Department for the coming fiscal year, which brings the total estimates down to an amount forty-five millions less than the corresponding estimates for last year. This could only be accomplished by cutting off new projects and suspending for the period of one year all progress in military matters. For the same reason I have directed that the Army shall not be recruited up to its present authorized strength. These measures can hardly be more than temporary—to last until our revenues are in better condition and until the whole question of the expediency of adopting a definite military policy can be submitted to Congress, for I am sure that the interests of the military establishment are seriously in need of careful consideration by Congress. The laws regulating the organization of our armed forces in the event of war need to be revised in order that the organization can be modified so as to produce a force which would be more consistently apportioned throughout its numerous branches. To explain the circumstances upon which this opinion is based would necessitate a lengthy discussion, and I postpone it until the first convenient opportunity shall arise to send to Congress a special message upon this subject.

The Secretary of War calls attention to a number of needed changes in the Army in all of which I concur, but the point upon which I place most emphasis is the need for an elimination bill providing a method by which the merits of officers shall have some effect upon their advancement and by which the advancement of all may be accelerated by the effective elimination of a definite proportion of the least efficient. There are in every army, and certainly in ours, a number of officers who do not violate their duty in any such way as to give reason for a court-martial or dismissal, but who do not show such aptitude and skill and character for high command as to justify their remaining in the active service to be promoted. Provision should be made by which they may be retired on a certain proportion of their pay, increasing with their length of service at the time of retirement. There is now a personnel law for the Navy which itself needs amendment and to which I shall make further reference. Such a law is needed quite as much for the Army.

The coast defenses of the United States proper are generally all that could be desired, and in some respects they are rather more elaborate than under present conditions are needed to stop an enemy's fleet from entering the harbors defended. There is, however, one place where additional defense is badly needed, and that is at the mouth of Chesapeake Bay, where it is proposed to make an artificial island for a fort which shall prevent an enemy's fleet from entering this most important strategical base of operations on the whole Atlantic and Gulf coasts. I hope that appropriate legislation will be adopted to secure the construction of this defense.

The Military and Naval Joint Board have unanimously agreed that it would be unwise to make the large expenditures which at one time were contemplated in the establishment of a naval base and station in the Philippine Islands, and have expressed their judgment, in which I fully concur, in favor of making an extensive naval base at Pearl Harbor, near Honolulu, and not in the Philippines. This does not dispense with the necessity for the comparatively small appropriations required to finish the proper coast defenses in the Philippines now under construction on the island of Corregidor and elsewhere or to complete a suitable repair station and coaling supply station at Olongapo, where is the floating dock "Dewey." I hope that this recommendation of the joint board will end the discussion as to the comparative merits of Manila Bay and Olongapo as naval stations, and will lead to prompt measures for the proper equipment and defense of Pearl Harbor.

The Navy

The return of the battle-ship fleet from its voyage around the world, in more efficient condition than when it started, was a noteworthy event of interest alike to our citizens and the naval authorities of the world. Besides the beneficial and far-reaching effect on our personal and diplomatic relations in the countries which the fleet visited, the marked success of the ships in steaming around the world in all weathers on schedule time has increased respect for our Navy and has added to our national prestige.

Our enlisted personnel recruited from all sections of the country is young and energetic and representative of the national spirit. It is, moreover, owing to its intelligence, capable of quick training into the modern man-of-warsmen. Our officers are earnest and zealous in their profession, but it is a regrettable fact that the higher officers are old for the responsibilities of the modern navy, and the admirals do not arrive at flag rank young enough to obtain adequate training in their duties as flag officers. This need for reform

in the Navy has been ably and earnestly presented to Congress by my predecessor, and I also urgently recommend the subject for consideration.

Early in the coming session a comprehensive plan for the reorganization
of the officers of all corps of the Navy will be presented to Congress, and I
hope it will meet with action suited to its urgency.

Owing to the necessity for economy in expenditures, I have directed the
curtailment of recommendations for naval appropriations so that they are
thirty-eight millions less than the corresponding estimates of last year, and
the request for new naval construction is limited to two first-class battleships
and one repair vessel.

The use of a navy is for military purposes, and there has been found need
in the Department of a military branch dealing directly with the military use
of the fleet. The Secretary of the Navy has also felt the lack of responsible
advisers to aid him in reaching conclusions and deciding important matters
between coordinate branches of the Department. To secure these results he
has inaugurated a tentative plan involving certain changes in the organization of the Navy Department, including the navy yards, all of which have
been found by the Attorney-General to be in accordance with law. I have
approved the execution of the plan proposed because of the greater efficiency
and economy it promises.

The generosity of Congress has provided in the present Naval Observatory, the most magnificent and expensive astronomical establishment in the
world. It is being used for certain naval purposes which might easily and
adequately be subserved by a small division connected with the Navy Department at only a fraction of the cost of the present Naval Observatory.
The Official Board of Visitors established by Congress and appointed in 1901
expressed its conclusion that the official head of the observatory should be
an eminent astronomer appointed by the President by and with the advice
and consent of the Senate, holding his place by a tenure at least as permanent
as that of the Superintendent of the Coast Survey or the head of the Geological Survey, and not merely by a detail of two or three years' duration. I fully
concur in this judgment, and urge a provision by law for the appointment
of such a director.

It may not be necessary to take the observatory out of the Navy Department and put it into another department in which opportunity for scientific
research afforded by the observatory would seem to be more appropriate,
though I believe such a transfer in the long run is the best policy. I am sure,
however, I express the desire of the astronomers and those learned in the
kindred sciences when I urge upon Congress that the Naval Observatory be
now dedicated to science under control of a man of science who can, if need

be, render all the service to the Navy Department which this observatory now renders, and still furnish to the world the discoveries in astronomy that a great astronomer using such a plant would be likely to make.

Department of Justice

Expedition in Legal Procedure

The deplorable delays in the administration of civil and criminal law have received the attention of committees of the American Bar Association and of many state bar associations, as well as the considered thought of judges and jurists. In my judgment, a change in judicial procedure, with a view to reducing its expense to private litigants in civil cases and facilitating the dispatch of business and final decision in both civil and criminal cases, constitutes the greatest need in our American institutions. I do not doubt for one moment that much of the lawless violence and cruelty exhibited in lynchings is directly due to the uncertainties and injustice growing out of the delays in trials, judgments, and the executions thereof by our courts. Of course these remarks apply quite as well to the administration of justice in State courts as to that in Federal courts, and without making invidious distinction it is perhaps not too much to say that, speaking generally, the defects are less in the Federal courts than the State courts. But they are very great in the Federal courts. The expedition with which business is disposed of both on the civil and the criminal side of English courts under modern rules of procedure makes the delays in our courts seem archaic and barbarous. The procedure in the Federal courts should furnish an example for the State courts. I presume it is impossible, without an amendment to the Constitution, to unite under one form of action the proceedings at common law and proceedings in equity in the Federal courts, but it is certainly not impossible by a statute to simplify and make short and direct the procedure both at law and in equity in those courts. It is not impossible to cut down still more than it is cut down, the jurisdiction of the Supreme Court so as to confine it almost wholly to statutory and constitutional questions. Under the present statutes the equity and admiralty procedure in the Federal courts is under the control of the Supreme Court, but in the pressure of business to which that court is subjected it is impossible to hope that a radical and proper reform of the Federal equity procedure can be brought about. I therefore recommend legislation providing for the appointment by the President of a commission with authority to examine the law and equity procedure of the Federal courts of first instance, the law of appeals from those courts to the courts of appeals and to the Supreme Court, and the costs imposed in such procedure upon the private litigants and upon the public treasury and make recommendation with a view to simplifying and expediting the procedure as far as possible and making it as inexpensive as may be to the litigant of little means.

Injunctions Without Notice

The platform of the successful party in the last election contained the following:

"The Republican party will uphold at all times the authority and integrity of the courts, State and Federal, and will ever insist that their powers to enforce their process and to protect life, liberty, and property shall be preserved inviolate. We believe, however, that the rules of procedure in the Federal courts with respect to the issuance of the writ of injunction should be more accurately defined by statute, and that no injunction or temporary restraining order should be issued without notice, except where irreparable injury would result from delay, in which case a speedy hearing thereafter should be granted."

I recommend that in compliance with the promise thus made, appropriate legislation be adopted. The ends of justice will best be met and the chief cause of complaint against ill-considered injunctions without notice will be removed by the enactment of a statute forbidding hereafter the issuing of any injunction or restraining order, whether temporary or permanent, by any Federal court, without previous notice and a reasonable opportunity to be heard on behalf of the parties to be enjoined; unless it shall appear to the satisfaction of the court that the delay necessary to give such notice and hearing would result in irreparable injury to the complainant and unless also the court shall from the evidence make a written finding, which shall be spread upon the court minutes, that immediate and irreparable injury is likely to ensue to the complainant, and shall define the injury, state why it is irreparable, and shall also indorse on the order issued the date and the hour of the issuance of the order. Moreover, every such injunction or restraining order issued without previous notice and opportunity by the defendant to be heard should by force of the statute expire and be of no effect after seven days from the issuance thereof or within any time less than that period which the court may fix, unless within such seven days or such less period, the injunction or order is extended or renewed after previous notice and opportunity to be heard.

My judgment is that the passage of such an act which really embodies the best practice in equity and is very like the rule now in force in some courts will prevent the issuing of ill-advised orders of injunction without notice and will render such orders when issued much less objectionable by the short time which they may remain effective.

Anti-Trust and Interstate Commerce Laws

The jurisdiction of the general Government over interstate commerce has led to the passage of the so-called "Sherman Anti-trust Law" and the "Interstate Commerce Law" and its amendments. The developments in the operation of those laws, as shown by indictments, trials, judicial decisions, and other sources of information, call for a discussion and some suggestions as to amendments. These I prefer to embody in a special message instead of including them in the present communication, and I shall avail myself of the first convenient opportunity to bring these subjects to the attention of Congress.

Jail of the District of Columbia

My predecessor transmitted to the Congress a special message on January 11, 1909, accompanying the report of Commissioners theretofore appointed to investigate the jail, workhouse, etc., in the District of Columbia, in which he directed attention to the report as setting forth vividly,

"the really outrageous conditions in the workhouse and jail."

The Congress has taken action in pursuance of the recommendations of that report and of the President, to the extent of appropriating funds and enacting the necessary legislation for the establishment of a workhouse and reformatory. No action, however, has been taken by the Congress with respect to the jail, the conditions of which still are antiquated and insanitary. I earnestly recommend the passage of a sufficient appropriation to enable a thorough remodeling of that institution to be made without delay. It is a reproach to the National Government that almost under the shadow of the Capitol dome prisoners should be confined in a building destitute of the ordinary decent appliances requisite to cleanliness and sanitary conditions.

Post-Office Department

Second-Class Mail Matter

The deficit every year in the Post-Office Department is largely caused by the low rate of postage of one cent a pound charged on second-class mail matter, which includes not only newspapers, but magazines and miscellaneous periodicals. The actual loss growing out of the transmission of this second-class mail matter at one cent a pound amounts to about $63,000,000 a year. The average cost of the transportation of this matter is more than 9 cents a pound.

It appears that the average distance over which newspapers are delivered to their customers is 291 miles, while the average haul of magazines is 1,049, and of miscellaneous periodicals 1,128 miles. Thus, the average haul of the magazine is three and one-half times and that of the miscellaneous periodical nearly four times the haul of the daily newspaper, yet all of them pay the same postage rate of one cent a pound. The statistics of 1907 show that second-class mail matter constituted 63.91 percent of the weight of all the mail, and yielded only 5.19 percent of the revenue.

The figures given are startling, and show the payment by the Government of an enormous subsidy to the newspapers, magazines, and periodicals, and Congress may well consider whether radical steps should not be taken to reduce the deficit in the Post-Office Department caused by this discrepancy between the actual cost of transportation and the compensation exacted therefor.

A great saving might be made, amounting to much more than half of the loss, by imposing upon magazines and periodicals a higher rate of postage. They are much heavier than newspapers, and contain a much higher proportion of advertising to reading matter, and the average distance of their transportation is three and a half times as great.

The total deficit for the last fiscal year in the Post-Office Department amounted to $17,500,000. The branches of its business which it did at a loss were the second-class mail service, in which the loss, as already said, was $63,000,000, and the free rural delivery, in which the loss was $28,000,000. These losses were in part offset by the profits of the letter postage and other sources of income. It would seem wise to reduce the loss upon second-class mail matter at least to the extent of preventing a deficit in the total operations of the Post-Office.

I commend the whole subject to Congress, not unmindful of the spread of intelligence which a low charge for carrying newspapers and periodicals assists. I very much doubt, however, the wisdom of a policy which constitutes so large a subsidy and requires additional taxation to meet it.

Postal Savings Banks

The second subject worthy of mention in the Post-Office Department is the real necessity and entire practicability of establishing postal savings banks. The successful party at the last election declared in favor of postal savings banks, and although the proposition finds opponents in many parts of the country, I am convinced that the people desire such banks, and am sure that when the banks are furnished they will be productive of the utmost good. The postal savings banks are not constituted for the purpose of creating competition with other banks. The rate of interest upon deposits to which they would be limited would be so small as to prevent their drawing deposits away from other banks.

I believe them to be necessary in order to offer a proper inducement to thrift and saving to a great many people of small means who do not now have banking facilities, and to whom such a system would offer an opportunity for the accumulation of capital. They will furnish a satisfactory substitute, based on sound principle and actual successful trial in nearly all the countries of the world, for the system of government guaranty of deposits now being adopted in several Western States, which with deference to those who advocate it seems to me to have in it the seeds of demoralization to conservative banking and certain financial disaster.

The question of how the money deposited in postal savings banks shall be invested is not free from difficulty, but I believe that a satisfactory provision for this purpose was inserted as an amendment to the bill considered by the Senate at its last session. It has been proposed to delay the consideration of legislation establishing a postal savings bank until after the report of the Monetary Commission. This report is likely to be delayed, and properly so, because of the necessity for careful deliberation and close investigation. I do not see why the one should be tied up with the other. It is understood that the Monetary Commission have looked into the systems of banking which now prevail abroad, and have found that by a control there exercised in respect to reserves and the rates of exchange by some central authority panics are avoided. It is not apparent that a system of postal savings banks would in any way interfere with a change to such a system here. Certainly in most of the countries in Europe where control is thus exercised by a central authority, postal savings banks exist and are not thought to be inconsistent with a proper financial and banking system.

Ship Subsidy

Following the course of my distinguished predecessor, I earnestly recommend to Congress the consideration and passage of a ship subsidy bill, looking to the establishment of lines between our Atlantic seaboard and the eastern coast of South America, as well as lines from the west coast of the United States to South America, China, Japan, and the Philippines. The profits on foreign mails are perhaps a sufficient measure of the expenditures which might first be tentatively applied to this method of inducing American capital to undertake the establishment of American lines of steamships in those directions in which we now feel it most important that we should have means of transportation controlled in the interest of the expansion of our trade. A bill of this character has once passed the House and more than once passed the Senate, and I hope that at this session a bill framed on the same lines and with the same purposes may become a law.

Interior Department

New Mexico and Arizona

The successful party in the last election in its national platform declared in favor of the admission as separate States of New Mexico and Arizona, and I recommend that legislation appropriate to this end be adopted. I urge, however, that care be exercised in the preparation of the legislation affecting each territory to secure deliberation in the selection of persons as members of the convention to draft a constitution for the incoming state, and I earnestly advise that such constitution after adoption by the convention shall be submitted to the people of the territory for their approval at an election in which the sole issue shall be the merits of the proposed constitution, and if the constitution is defeated by popular vote means shall be provided in the enabling act for a new convention and the drafting of a new constitution. I think it vital that the issue as to the merits of the constitution should not be mixed up with the selection of state officers, and that no election of state officers should be had until after the constitution has been fully approved and finally settled upon.

Alaska

With respect to the Territory of Alaska, I recommend legislation which shall provide for the appointment by the President of a governor and also of an executive council, the members of which shall during their term of office reside in the territory, and which shall have legislative powers sufficient to enable it to give to the territory local laws adapted to its present growth. I strongly deprecate legislation looking to the election of a territorial legislature in that vast district. The lack of permanence of residence of a large part of the present population and the small number of the people who either permanently or temporarily reside in the district as compared with its vast expanse and the variety of the interests that have to be subserved, make it altogether unfitting in my judgment to provide for a popular election of a legislative body. The present system is not adequate and does not furnish the character of local control that ought to be there. The only compromise, it seems to me, which may give needed local legislation and secure a conservative government is the one I propose.

Conservation of National Resources

In several Departments there is presented the necessity for legislation looking to the further conservation of our national resources, and the subject is one of such importance as to require a more detailed and extended discussion than can be entered upon in this communication. For that reason I shall take an early opportunity to send a special message to Congress on the subject of the improvement of our waterways, upon the reclamation and irrigation of arid, semi-arid, and swamp lands; upon the preservation of our forests and the reforesting of suitable areas; upon the reclassification of the public domain with a view to separating from agricultural settlement mineral, coal, and phosphate lands and sites belonging to the Government bordering on streams suitable for the utilization of water power.

Department of Agriculture

I commend to your careful consideration the report of the Secretary of Agriculture as showing the immense sphere of usefulness which that Department now fills and the wonderful addition to the wealth of the nation made by the farmers of this country in the crops of the current year.

Department of Commerce and Labor

The Light-House Board

The Light-House Board now discharges its duties under the Department of Commerce and Labor. For upward of forty years this board has been constituted of military and naval officers and two or three men of science, with such an absence of a duly constituted executive head that it is marvelous what work has been accomplished. In the period of construction the energy and enthusiasm of all the members prevented the inherent defects of the system from interfering greatly with the beneficial work of the Board, but now that the work is chiefly confined to maintenance and repair, for which purpose the country is divided into sixteen districts, to which are assigned an engineer officer of the Army and an inspector of the Navy, each with a light-house tender and the needed plant for his work, it has become apparent by the frequent friction that arises, due to the absence of any central independent authority, that there must be a complete reorganization of the Board. I concede the advantage of keeping in the system the rigidity of discipline that the presence of naval and military officers in charge insures, but unless the presence of such officers in the Board can be made consistent with a responsible executive head that shall have proper authority, I recommend the transfer of control over light-houses to a suitable civilian bureau. This is in accordance with the judgment of competent persons who are familiar with the workings of the present system. I am confident that a reorganization can be effected which shall avoid the recurrence of friction between members, instances of which have been officially brought to my attention, and that by such reorganization greater efficiency and a substantial reduction in the expense of operation can be brought about.

Consolidation of Bureaus

I request Congressional authority to enable the Secretary of Commerce and Labor to unite the Bureaus of Manufactures and Statistics. This was recommended by a competent committee appointed in the previous administration for the purpose of suggesting changes in the interest of economy and efficiency, and is requested by the Secretary.

The White Slave Trade

I greatly regret to have to say that the investigations made in the Bureau of Immigration and other sources of information lead to the view that there is urgent necessity for additional legislation and greater executive activity to suppress the recruiting of the ranks of prostitutes from the streams of immigration into this country—an evil which, for want of a better name, has been called "The White Slave Trade." I believe it to be constitutional to forbid, under penalty, the transportation of persons for purposes of prostitution across national and state lines; and by appropriating a fund of $50,000 to be used by the Secretary of Commerce and Labor for the employment of special inspectors it will be possible to bring those responsible for this trade to indictment and conviction under a Federal law.

Bureau of Health

For a very considerable period a movement has been gathering strength, especially among the members of the medical profession, in favor of a concentration of the instruments of the National Government which have to do with the promotion of public health. In the nature of things, the Medical Department of the Army and the Medical Department of the Navy must be kept separate. But there seems to be no reason why all the other bureaus and offices in the general Government which have to do with the public health or subjects akin thereto should not be united in a bureau to be called the "Bureau of Public Health." This would necessitate the transfer of the Marine-Hospital Service to such a bureau. I am aware that there is a wide field in respect to the public health committed to the States in which the Federal Government can not exercise jurisdiction, but we have seen in the Agricultural Department the expansion into widest usefulness of a department giving attention to agriculture when that subject is plainly one over which the States properly exercise direct jurisdiction. The opportunities offered for useful research and the spread of useful information in regard to the cultivation of the soil and the breeding of stock and the solution of many of the intricate problems in progressive agriculture have demonstrated the wisdom of establishing that department. Similar reasons, of equal force, can be given for the establishment of a bureau of health that shall not only exercise the police jurisdiction of the Federal Government respecting quarantine, but which shall also afford an opportunity for investigation and research by competent experts into questions of health affecting the whole country, or important sections thereof, questions which, in the absence of Federal governmental work, are not likely to be promptly solved.

Civil Service Commission

The work of the United States Civil Service Commission has been performed to the general satisfaction of the executive officers with whom the Commission has been brought into official communication. The volume of that work and variety and extent have under new laws, such as the Census Act, and new executive orders, greatly increased. The activities of the Commission required by the statutes have reached to every portion of the public domain.

The accommodations of the Commission are most inadequate for its needs. I call your attention to its request for increase in those accommodations as will appear from the annual report for this year.

Political Contributions

I urgently recommend to Congress that a law be passed requiring that candidates in elections of Members of the House of Representatives, and committees in charge of their candidacy and campaign, file in a proper office of the United States Government a statement of the contributions received and of the expenditures incurred in the campaign for such elections, and that similar legislation be enacted in respect to all other elections which are constitutionally within the control of Congress.

Freedman's Savings and Trust Company

Recommendations have been made by my predecessors that Congress appropriate a sufficient sum to pay the balance—about 38 percent—of the amounts due depositors in the Freedman's Savings and Trust Company. I renew this recommendation, and advise also that a proper limitation be prescribed fixing a period within which the claims may be presented, that assigned claims be not recognized, and that a limit be imposed on the amount of fees collectible for services in presenting such claims.

Semicentennial of Negro Freedom

The year 1913 will mark the fiftieth anniversary of the issuance of the Emancipation Proclamation granting freedom to the Negroes. It seems fitting that this event should be properly celebrated. Already a movement has been started by prominent Negroes, encouraged by prominent white people and the press. The South especially is manifesting its interest in this movement.

It is suggested that a proper form of celebration would be an exposition to show the progress the Negroes have made, not only during their period of freedom, but also from the time of their coming to this country.

I heartily indorse this proposal, and request that the Executive be authorized to appoint a preliminary commission of not more than seven persons to consider carefully whether or not it is wise to hold such an exposition, and if so, to outline a plan for the enterprise. I further recommend that such preliminary commission serve without salary, except as to their actual expenses, and that an appropriation be made to meet such expenses.

Conclusion

I have thus, in a message compressed as much as the subjects will permit, referred to many of the legislative needs of the country, with the exceptions already noted. Speaking generally, the country is in a high state of prosperity. There is every reason to believe that we are on the eve of a substantial business expansion, and we have just garnered a harvest unexampled in the market value of our agricultural products. The high prices which such products bring mean great prosperity for the farming community, but on the other hand they mean a very considerably increased burden upon those classes in the community whose yearly compensation does not expand with the improvement in business and the general prosperity. Various reasons are given for the high prices. The proportionate increase in the output of gold, which today is the chief medium of exchange and is in some respects a measure of value, furnishes a substantial explanation of at least part of the increase in prices. The increase in population and the more expensive mode of living of the people, which have not been accompanied by a proportionate increase in acreage production, may furnish a further reason. It is well to note that the increase in the cost of living is not confined to this country, but prevails the world over, and that those who would charge increases in prices to the existing protective tariff must meet the fact that the rise in prices has taken place almost wholly in those products of the factory and farm in respect to which there has been either no increase in the tariff or in many instances a very considerable reduction.

60

Address at the Sixth Annual Convention of the National Rivers and Harbors Congress

New Willard Hotel, Washington, D. C., December 8, 1909

Mr. President, Members of the National Rivers and Harbors Congress, Ladies and Gentlemen:

I don't know that I have any right to be here to talk about waterways, unless it makes a man an expert on the subject to have gone down the Mississippi River. The dangers to which one was exposed on that journey, by reason of the shoals and the other obstacles and temptations of the journey, certainly offered an opportunity for careful study and deliberation. Now I think I am a sufficiently established resident of Washington to make what I have to say an address of welcome. I am delighted that you selected Washington as your place of meeting. You have done it wisely, first, because when you want a thing done it is just as well to get close to the men who are to do it; and secondly, Washington is always a good place to come to, and you can induce the ladies of the family to come with you, which is always an assurance of both work and pleasure.

I congratulate this Congress on having brought the subject of waterways to such a point that the Representatives in Congress, from one end of the country to the other, recognize it as a subject that calls for action. They have not come to a definite conclusion as to the policy that ought to be adopted, but they have come to the conclusion that some policy must be adopted with reference to the development of these instrumentalities which nature has furnished for the transportation of goods and for the controlling of railroad rates.

You in your declaration say that you are in favor of a policy and not in favor of any particular project. I think that a wise platform to take; and yet when it comes to the practical enforcement and accomplishment of something, you have got to go into projects. You may insist that a policy ought to be adopted, and you have insisted, and I do not doubt that you have— indeed I know you have—made that distinguished member of Congress, the head of the Rivers and Harbors Committee, sit up nights to devise a policy which shall be presented to the country and satisfy the demand that has arisen in such a—I had almost said—unanimous way the country through. But you are coming now near to the detail of projects.

One has to travel over the country to find out what the country is thinking about. You go into the Northwest and you find the development of the Columbia River as one of the great projects of many who live in that neighborhood. You go into far-distant Texas, and you find that they have an inland waterways project there reaching into Louisiana, into the bayous of Texas, and down along the Gulf, that has demonstrated its usefulness as to part, and that only needs further addition and improvement to carry out a great system of waterways there that shall reach farms and plantations that are even beyond railroads now. And so, as you come up the eastern shore of this country, you find the inland—I don't think they call it inland waterways exactly, but it is the inside waterway—the Atlantic Deeper Waterways Association. Now, it is well that there is in almost every part of the country a project of that sort to awaken the interests of those who live in that part of the country, for while we are all patriots, and while we are all in favor of all the country, we are just a little more intensely in favor of that which is nearest than we are in favor of that which is very far away. The danger to this movement, the test of the value of the movement, is going to be seen when you get off that very safe platform, that you are in favor of a policy and not in favor of a project, and get down to the business of pushing projects.

One of the things that I think we ought to do is not to decry the past. It is to take from the past that which is valuable and build on it. The trip down the Mississippi River was an eye-opener to many of us. The work which has gone on at the end of the river and near its mouth, up along the banks in Mississippi and Louisiana, and up into Arkansas, is a work that commends itself to everyone who sees it. It is work in the direction both of the preservation of farms and the establishment of a great waterway there. The work which has been done by the National Government through its army engineers in strengthening the banks of that river is a work of experimentation, but work which has now demonstrated the possibility of treating that river in such a way as to hold the banks and keep the river within it, and insuring a reasonable depth where steamers may go.

Then we have had an investigation by the army engineers into the practicability of deepening to six feet the Missouri River, from Sioux City to St. Louis; of deepening the Mississippi River from St. Paul to St. Louis; of deepening and keeping at an eight-foot depth the river from St. Louis to Cairo; and also of a project for the maintenance of a nine-foot depth the year round in the Ohio River. I recognize the gentlemen who applaud, as coming from the Columbia River district and illustrating that disinterested enthusiasm that is certain to carry all the projects through.

Now I don't think I betray a secret when I say that the gentleman who has most to do with the initiation of projects in Congress is fully charged with the necessity for doing something in the next Congress to foreshadow, or rather to begin, a policy with respect to those rivers. You have the Missouri, the upper Mississippi, the Mississippi between St. Louis and Cairo, and the Ohio between Pittsburgh and Cairo, all of them satisfying the requirements that you have to put in your platform with respect to the improvement of the waterways. That is an improvement in the heart of the country, an improvement that reaches to more States than any other improvement that can be mentioned in this entire country. It affects not only the States along whose borders the improvements will be made, but it affects all the states along the borders of the Mississippi beyond Cairo, for the project will also include and must include the investment of a sufficient amount of money to keep the nine-foot stage always between Cairo and New Orleans.

I am aware that there are a great many gentlemen in this country who are in favor of something more than nine feet between Cairo and the Gulf, but you must get nine feet before you get fourteen. When you once get that system that I have outlined into operation so as to show the benefits that can be derived from it, what will go on thereafter no man can foresee. The truth is that the engineers will tell you that after you have harnessed the Mississippi River by protecting its banks, no man can tell what the depth of that river will be made by the river itself confined within reasonable banks. In other words, what I am urging, what I am laboring for, is something practical in the way of a moderate project in order that you may go on and gradually develop a larger project than that which was in your minds at its initiation— that you do something practical by taking the materials that you have, and as you go on and as the business increases, demonstrate to those in the country who are not so near to that improvement its advantage to the entire country in the reduction of railroad rates and in the actual transportation of that kind of business that the river will attract.

Now speaking to this assembly—I think it was this assembly (we have got so many congresses in favor of so many good things that sometimes there is a little difficulty in distinguishing, and when you all meet together in Washington at the same time there is danger of mistaken identity as to associations)—but at any rate a year ago President Roosevelt and I were together on a platform before the Conservation of Resources Convention, I think it was, in which we both advocated the issuing of bonds in order that a project improving waterways when begun should be completed in a reasonable time. Now I am still a consistent advocate of that theory. I believe that the Government is entitled to as rapid a method of developing an enterprise and putting it through as private corporations, and as they always issue bonds, or generally do (some of them are fortunate enough not to have to), in order to expedite the completion of these projects, it would seem wise for the Nation to do so where it will accomplish the same result.

But I want to suggest a word of caution. You are going to encounter in Congress great opposition to the policy of issuing bonds right out of hand. You are much more likely to get from Congress a declaration of policy in the shape of a declaration that a certain improvement ought to be carried out and spread upon the minutes of Congress in the form of a resolution or a declaration in a statute. Now, what I advise you to do is to get that declaration. Then when the time comes that political exigency shall prevent the appropriation of sufficient amounts from the current revenues to put the proper part of the project through the coming year or the coming two years as economy requires, the question of issuing bonds will arise. I would get the declaration first, and not have the bonds first, for the reason that you will encounter the objection of Congress that the issuing of bonds and the receipt of the money will develop a desire to be extravagant. That may not meet your views, but I have thought it over, and I know something about Congress. I know where you are going to encounter opposition, and I believe the best way is the natural way with those gentlemen. You lead them on to declare in favor of the Missouri improvement, in favor of the St. Louis to St. Paul improvement, in favor of the Cairo to St. Louis improvement, in favor of the Ohio improvement, all of which have been approved by the army engineers, and get them recorded in the statutes of this country as declaring that those things are to be carried out and let them make their first appropriation from the revenues of the country, and then you have them where they must issue bonds, unless the revenues afford a sufficient amount each year to carry that project on economically and with due rapidity.

I tell you, gentlemen, you are getting, as the boys and girls used to say in "finding the button"—you are getting warm. You are at a point where you can accomplish something if you don't stop it by doing it the wrong way. I don't feel justified in giving advice to a body like this on a subject which they have studied so much, or, I should not feel it except that I have had pretty close association as Secretary of War and otherwise with the army engineers, who have given their lives to the study of these improvements.

I know those army engineers very well. Doubtless you do, as you have met them in the districts to which they were assigned. I venture to say that in your whole experience you have never met men of a higher standard of character, of a higher devotion to public duty, and of greater skill in their profession than those same army engineers. They are selected from the first ten or the first five of the graduates of West Point, and they have a little ring in the Army, which I might betray to you by reason of some inside information. If a class comes out that has not developed very good material in the way of engineers and mathematicians, somehow or other the Chief of Engineers advises the Secretary of War that for that year they do not need any particular addition to the corps; and so it is that they have acquired a greater proportion of the mathematical and engineering ability of those who graduated from West Point than they really were entitled to. They have gone on, and, with but one exception, their record is clear, in the honesty, and I had almost said the severity, with which they have expended the Government's funds, and have seen to their being put into material at a cost which was an honest cost. But it has been said that they were crotchety; that at times they did not apparently catch the sound of progress; that they were slow sometimes in the building up of improvements. I am not prepared to say that those criticisms with reference to individuals were not well founded. You can not take a great corps like that, numbering as it does a great many officers within it, and not find men who fail to keep up with the procession, but I am very sure from talking with General Marshall and with a number of the other men at the head of the corps that they are fully charged with the increased interest in this country among the people and among the business men in the development of the inland waterways, and that you could not have a safer body of men to advise than the army engineers.

I count it one of the great good fortunes of this country that when the country had to build the Panama Canal, after using the great ability of civil engineers, we finally settled down upon the army engineers to carry that project through.

So it is with respect to the waterways. They have recommended to the chairman of the waterways committee in the House a system of improvements that I believe will meet the judgment of this convention, if it be moderated to the possibilities of what can be accomplished. I think you can secure upon the statute books of this country a declaration in favor of continuing contracts to build the four or five projects which the engineers have recommended, in such a way, even if you do not get the bonds voted at first, that if the time arises when the revenues will not permit their use, I mean the current revenues, to continue that work with reasonable rapidity, you can move upon the Government for the issuing of bonds. I would make the fight for bonds when the conditions strengthen the argument in their favor. It is a strong argument that you will have to meet; that if you are going to issue a large amount of bonds just for the purpose of putting them into the waterways as their necessity may develop, then there is a temptation to extravagance. Perhaps it is my judicial experience, but I always feel as if you ought to shape your policy in order to win, not according to the enthusiastic suggestions of your imagination, but in order to overcome the obstacles that you are likely to encounter in winning the end which you seek.

And, now, ladies and gentlemen, I am very much obliged to you for giving me such attention. I realize that what I have said comes from the lips of a mere tyro, but it comes from one who has some temporary responsibility in respect to the matter, and from one who is thoroughly in sympathy with the general object which you seek here, to wit, the development of all the waterways of this country by a general policy in such a way as to reduce and control railroad rates and in such a way as to stimulate upon the bosom of the waters the transportation of such merchandise as is peculiarly fitted to that character of carriage.

61

Remarks to the Ohio Valley
Improvement Association

The White House, December 9, 1909

Mr. Chairman and Gentlemen:

This is the first time in my life I can remember that I am sorry I am from Ohio. It is because, coming from Ohio, I can not make my recommendation in respect to the necessity for the improvement of the Ohio as strong as I might if I had not come from Ohio, for my motives will be questioned. You gentlemen who figure in private life do not have to encounter that. Those of us who do are rapidly getting used to it.

With respect to the Ohio improvement, it is the first one out of all the conventions, out of all the oratory and out of all the indefinite nebulous appeals for waterways that has a definite scope, a plain reason for being, a clear estimate of cost and a plain possibility of execution. You have six locks now completed, and where those six locks operate, the success of the system of slack water has been demonstrated. You have seven locks under construction, and there are fifty-four locks in all necessary to establish slack water at nine feet the year round from Pittsburgh to Cairo, and that improvement in the long run is to cost—I should not say in the long run, for no one knows how much it would cost in the long run—but under the present estimates of engineers, if done with business-like rapidity, it would cost $63,000,000.

There is an additional advantage in this proposal.

I have not looked into waterways very much, but I have gathered the impression from such reading and discussion as I have been able to do and to hear, that it does not always follow because you have waterways with sufficient depth for steamers, for barges and for other transportation, that you are going to attract business on that waterway. The question is, whether you have the kind of business that the waterway will attract. In Europe I am told that there are rivers on which the traffic is all up-stream, or largely so, because the merchandise and material to be carried are at the mouth of the stream; and the place where they are to be landed is along near its sources, and that those steamers after carrying up the stream the material to be used come down partly empty, which is an indication that in order to justify improvements of this sort, those who contend for them must point out the utility by showing the proper business to be done.

Now, in respect to the Ohio improvement you have the present business. You can point to your coal mines and to your heavy products of manufacture in Pittsburgh and throughout that neighborhood which can be carried cheaply down the Ohio River clear to the mouth and to the Gulf; and having the business and having the estimate and having the water and having the plans, there is not any reason why improvement should not be made.

I observe that there are a number of gentlemen who think that I cast a wet blanket over the convention yesterday by what I said there. I did not intend to do so. I only intended to help it along by pointing out the practical method of accomplishing what you are here for.

You have had enough experience with Congress to know that it is *sui generis* to have to deal with it as a body different from any other body, as it is different from any other body, being representative of three hundred and ninety-one districts of the United States, with differing interests and differing views. When you approach Congress with a proposal for the issuing of bonds, you are going to arouse great opposition and that opposition will arise and demand why, and they will demand an answer not in general expressions, not in resounding oratory, but they will want facts and estimates and a statement of something definitely useful into which they are going to put their money which they may even have to borrow in order to carry through the enterprise. You in the Ohio Valley have an enterprise in respect to which you can give the sufficient answers. All I can hope is that you shall find enough disinterested people in the country to support the Ohio improvement with some others that I mentioned yesterday that might be just as well carried along together, right in the heart of the country. The improvement of the Ohio River is not alone to improve the Ohio River and help the States along its border, but it is also to help the Mississippi River and the States that border on the Mississippi River down to the Gulf and the whole country.

I am only a coordinate branch of this Government and the least important of those branches, but such influence as I can bring to bear you can count on my bringing to bear in favor of the Ohio River, and it is not because I was born and brought up in Ohio and looked across the Ohio River until I left Ohio, but it is because I have looked into the question of the improvement, and if I came from the Columbia River I should still be in favor of the improvement of the Ohio.

62

Remarks to the Committee of the
Lakes-to-the-Gulf Deep Waterways Association

The White House, December 9, 1909

Governor Deneen, other Governors, and Gentlemen of the Deep Waterways Association:

I am glad to renew our old and our delightful association. The presence of gubernatorial timber on that trip sweetens every recollection of the trip. It will be, I doubt not, an epoch in the history of this country in fixing, more than any other one event, the attention of the country upon the necessity for action in respect to our inland waterways, the most important of which everyone admits, of course, is the Mississippi River.

How these details are to be worked out is a question that must be solved in the near future. I am sure that this coming Congress will take steps; I say I am sure—I mean I have received assurances from those gentlemen connected with the committees that have to do with legislation of that sort—that this whole matter will receive earnest consideration, and that steps will be made of an important character toward the development of a system of improvement in the heart of the country. That this may not meet the views of the most aspiring of those who are interested will probably be the case. With deference to Senator Warner and other members of that body called Congress, it never does quite meet the aspirations of everybody, but that "something is doing," if I may use a colloquial expression; that the interest of those who heretofore have turned a cold shoulder to the entire subject has been aroused, no one at all familiar with the atmosphere of Washington can deny. And I hope that we are all engaged in a work in which we stand shoulder to shoulder without respect to a particular locality, and that if you gentlemen who are interested in a particular improvement find that your view may not be entirely met and that your particular project may not be the first one taken up in a substantial way, it will not prevent your welcoming a step by the Congress of the United States which when taken means the embracing of every improvement that ought to commend itself to those who are familiar with Congress.

And, now, Governor Deneen, I am glad to renew the association and acquaintance which, though it was not begun on the broad bosom of the Mississippi, certainly received an impetus so that we shall never forget the company that we met there under auspices which our hosts, the Business Men's Association of St. Louis, made so delightful.

63

Address at a Mass Meeting in Celebration of the
Diamond Jubilee of Methodist Episcopal
Missions in Africa

Carnegie Hall, New York, December 13, 1909

Ladies and Gentlemen:

I am very glad to be here to bear witness to my very great interest in that which this meeting celebrates—the attack of the Methodist Church upon Africa. I like to think of Methodism among the denominations as an affirmative, aggressive, pushing, practical church militant, and it needed to be that to tackle Africa. Since I have had the honor to occupy public office, it has fallen to me to address meetings of many different churches, and I always seize the opportunity—when invited to any other church than my own, and I hope I don't leave out my own—to be present, because I like to feel and imbibe in my nature the sense of tolerance and increase in the feeling of the Fatherhood of God and the brotherhood of man among all the denominations of the churches; and my own reception by churches, not my own, makes me feel certain of the growing and wide catholicity of the Christian Church. Doubtless it is because I was not aroused to the importance of the missionary spirit and the great things that were being done years ago, that it seems to me that it is only within recent times that this missionary feeling has taken such a hold upon the people.

I have observed that each man dates the spread of public opinion on a particular subject from the time that he began to think of it; but the history of our country does offer a date and an epoch when it seems to me that people of the United States acquired a wider and a world feeling, and an interest and a responsibility for all the people of the world, as distinguished from those who enjoy our opportunities of living under the Stars and Stripes.

It is not perhaps appropriate to date a religious movement from a war, but it does seem to me as if our people acquired a world feeling from the time we undertook the responsibility of freeing Cuba and saying what should be done by our neighbors with reference to internal government when that internal government seemed to us to pass the bounds of what we thought to be civilized. We began our war expecting to finish it shortly, and we landed in the Philippines and we are still there. But our horizon has widened much beyond those gems of the Pacific Ocean by reason of the responsibilities which we have been obliged to assume with reference to the entire world. We are a great power in the world, and we may be, and hope we are, a great power for usefulness, a great power for the spread of Christian civilization, and we must be so if we would justify our success and vindicate our right to enjoy the opportunities that God has given us in this fair, broad land of building of wealth and comfort and luxury and education and making ourselves, what we like to think we are, the foremost people of the world.

There are those who would read the last words of Washington in his farewell message as an indication that we ought to keep within the seas and not look beyond; but he was addressing thirteen states that had much to do before they could make themselves a great nation and that might well avoid entangling alliances, or any foreign interference, or any foreign trouble, while they were making themselves a nation.

But now we are a nation with tremendous power and tremendous wealth, and unless we use that for the benefit of our international neighbors (and they are all neighbors of ours, for the world is very small)—unless we use that power and that wealth, we are failing to discharge the duties that we ought to feel as members of the international community. This world is very small. It is only 10,000 miles to the Philippine Islands, and I am carried back, as I look into the face of my brother, Homer Stuntz, to many a platform that he and I sat upon in the Philippine Islands and talked about the possibilities of what we might do in developing those islands and bringing those people to a realization of what good government was. I thought your church ought to have established a bishopric out in the Philippines, and we had a candidate out there. I haven't lost hope that you may know a good thing when you see it. But it is true that when you live in the Philippines, 10,000 miles away from here, and meet people coming and going, see people on the streets of Washington that you met in Mindanao, or in Luzon, or in Panay, or in

Samar, and shake hands with them as if it were only yesterday when you last saw them, the world does not seem very big around. And so I can understand, though I don't quite have the feeling, that Africa is not so dark, is not so far away from anything that you would wish to be in when your interest is excited, when your knowledge is full of the needs of the 160,000,000 of people who are in that continent, and of the possibilities of developing them into a Christian people who shall learn after a time all the arts of peace, and learn to govern themselves.

I confess, if I were a missionary, I would prefer to try my hand in a country like China that has a history of two or three or four or five thousand years, than to go into Africa that hasn't any history at all except that which we trace to the apes. But you can not read the account of the missions that your church is carrying on in that continent without knowing that there is the seed which is to lead those people on to be useful citizens and useful members of the community and of the world. Now, as I understand it, the Methodist Church has taken the continent in front and rear at Madeira, at Algiers, in Arcola, in Portuguese East Africa, and in Rhodesia, and that there are missions and a stream of them in which the practical, sensible methods of modern missionaries have been adopted, and accompanying instruction in the Christian religion and the leading on to Christian civilization, of lessons in agriculture, in the simple mechanical arts, in primary education, and in leading them on to feel that debt of gratitude which reaches a native's heart as nothing else can, the ministrations of the physician when the dear ones of those native savages seem about to be taken away.

The mission is a nucleus and epitome of the civilization that is expected to widen out in that neighborhood. I have heard missions criticized. I have heard men say that they would not contribute to foreign missions at all; that we had wicked people enough at home and we might just as well leave the foreign natives and savages to pursue their own happy lives in the forests and look after our own who need a great deal of ministration. I have come to regard that as narrow-minded as a man who does not like music, who does not understand the things that God has provided for the elevation of the human race. The missionaries in China and the missionaries in Africa are the forerunners of our civilization, and without them we should have no hope of conquering the love and the admiration and the respect of the millions of people whom we hope to bring under the influence of Christian civilization.

Those who go for mercantile purposes into those distant lands, I am sorry to say, are quicker to catch the savage tendencies than the savages are to catch from them the basis of our Christian civilization, and if they had to depend for their belief in the good that is to come to them from embracing Christianity and accepting a civilization that we offer them, to that which they learn from the adventurers who go far into the interior to buy things from them at a price much too low and much below what ought to be paid, we should never succeed at all. I speak that with all the sense of moderation that I know I ought to have in dealing with countries so far from here and in saying things that can not be contradicted. If there is anything that promotes lying and the abuse of imagination, it is the impunity that a man enjoys in telling a story about something that happened 25,000 miles away, in a country that you can not reach and from which you don't hear more than once a year.

Now, as to these statements that missionaries have an easy time, which have been made by a good many travelers, I remember that a leading correspondent of one of the newspapers wrote a book in which he sought to illustrate and prove it. I am glad to say he has taken it back now, but he described the great houses that the missionaries lived in, the number of servants that they had, and the comfortable life generally that they led, which he said was much more comfortable than that which they would have had at home; but he did not go into the lives that they really lead; he did not see the work that they had to perform; he did not encounter, he did not know that terrible drain upon the vitality of being so many years away from home and from the people you love, from the communities you love, and the surroundings you love, and if he had been talking about African missions he would not have been able to describe their large houses or their comfortable quarters. A man who goes into Africa as a missionary goes into a place where he must be content to put up with all sorts of sacrifices and a very possible death from the malignant fevers that he is constantly exposed to, unless he goes clear into the interior onto the tablelands. I admire the missionaries who go to India and China and the Philippines, because I know they are doing good work, and I know that they have many sacrifices to make; but the men whom I wish most to commend are those who in the face of all the obstacles that certainly tend to discourage the bravest, enter the dark continent of Africa in an attempt to win those people to Christianity and civilization.

Of course, there has been great improvement in Africa; that is, they have surveyed it enough and investigated it enough to divide it up between the European nations. Well, I hope that is an improvement. I have no doubt it is. I have no doubt that their governments there have defects as other governments have, and have the natural defects that governments so far removed from civilization must have. But it is a sign of progress that the boundaries have been fixed throughout Africa, and that European nations are becoming responsible for the governments in that country. The United States has not any territorial interest there. We did make an experiment, or encouraged an experiment some seventy odd years ago in Liberia, and we do have that interest that we ought to have in trying to preserve the integrity of that little Negro republic that was begun so many years ago. But you know, and the nations of the world know, that we are not in Africa to spread our territory. We have enough. Some people think we have a good deal more than enough, but certainly there is no one quite so imperialistic as to desire to share a part of the dark continent; but because we are not going in there to assume the powers of government does not furnish the slightest reason why we should not in every way possible encourage such movements as this under the auspices of other governments, to aid those governments, and to aid the people under those governments in the progress toward Christian civilization. We have the money here and we have the men and women who are willing to make the sacrifice; and those of us who sit back and come every two or three years to hear the stories of what has been done there by representatives of this country, may well afford to be generous in helping out that movement.

It is curious to see how the Almighty works His ways. Our interest in Africa for many years was the interest to suppress the slave trade. We were all responsible—New England got out of it a little earlier than the rest—for a time in the encouragement of that trade. And now we have living with us ten millions of people who are descended from the slaves that were taken by force—the Negroes that were taken by force from that dark continent, taken with all the cruelties incident to the middle passage; and yet no one would say that the descendants of those people thus brought here are not to be congratulated on the fact that their ancestors were brought here, so that they have been able to enjoy the proximity to civilization and are a hundred years in advance of their relatives in Africa; and yet they came here by the greed and the sin of those for whom we, by reason of ancestry, must be responsible. I think that is a very curious working out of the ways of God that no one could have anticipated. It is natural that the Negroes of America, who have had the advantage of an association in a Christian country, with modern civilization, so that they are civilized and educated, should yet retain an intense interest in the development of the continent from which their ancestors came; and I am glad to note the fact that there is an interest among the race, both as to Liberia and the maintenance of that republic, and this missionary movement through the dark continent, to bring all the black races into Christian civilization.

Now, my friends, I ought not to have spoken at all tonight on this subject, because I haven't any information about Africa which you do not have;

but I have acquired the habit of speaking at foreign mission meetings, and the managers of the meetings think that there is something missing in the support of the Government unless I appear to testify in my insufficient and inadequate way to the interest that the country all has in the success of this movement. Now, my dear friend, Bishop Hartzell I hope has realized what he came here to bring about, and I hope he will take back in his pocket that $300,000 that is necessary to aid him in the great work he is there carrying on. I wish he had $3,000,000 instead of $300,000, but it is a good deal easier to wish it than to get it; and if we have secured $300,000, we ought to be as smiling and as happy as possible in the thought of the good which that will do.

64

Remarks at the New Bowery Mission

New York City, December 13, 1909

My Friends:

I am just about as much surprised at being here as you are at seeing me. I had a note from your benefactor. Dr. Klopsch, asking me to come down to a mission which he had established in the Bowery, after the meeting at Carnegie Hall. Now, I have known Dr. Klopsch—well, not very long—but I have known him in a way that perhaps you know him. I know him by what he has done.

It has been my fortune in life to play a good deal of the part of a figurehead. Some men do the work and others are figureheads; and nature developed me in such a way that I play a pretty good part as a figurehead. So they put me at the head of the Red Cross, and as the head of the Red Cross I came to know the enormous energy and the tremendous power for good which Dr. Klopsch could exercise through the Christian Herald in raising hundreds of thousands of dollars to relieve human suffering wherever it might be in the world. And so when he wrote and asked me to come here, I was not exactly advised as to where I was coming, except that it was on the Bowery, and I have always had a good deal of curiosity (for I have not lived in New York) to know the Bowery, and I felt certain that where Dr. Klopsch and the Bowery met there would probably be the best part of the Bowery, and so I came here.

Now, your superintendent has been good enough to say some complimentary things about my coming from Carnegie Hall down to the Bowery to meet you. I am not conscious of deserving any credit for that at all. As I look into your faces I see that you are earnest American citizens. To use a colloquial expression, some of you are "down on your luck" perhaps, but nevertheless responding in every fiber of your body to the same sentiments of loyalty and patriotism and love of country and decency and aspirations for better things that I hope every other man in this country has. I am glad to be here, if, by being here and saying so, I can convince you that the so-called chasm between you and people who seem for the time to be more fortunate is not a chasm, and that there is extending over whatever is between you and them a deep feeling of sympathy and a deep earnest desire that you shall have that equality of opportunity, that means of getting onto your feet, of earning your livelihood, of supporting your families, that we hope every man under the Stars and Stripes may fully enjoy. I am glad to come here and to testify by my presence as to my sympathy with the great work of Dr. Klopsch in this mission by which he shall from time to time and constantly, help you and other men over hard places, help you over the times when things seem desperate, when it seems as if the Lord and everybody else had turned against you—help you over those times to believe that there are people in the world who sympathize with you and wish for better things, and enable you to achieve those better things that the equality of opportunity may, I hope, in this country enable you to achieve.

I know it is difficult for you to believe that I, who for the time being am receiving a large salary from the United States and living in comfort, could understand or take into my heart, the feeling that you may have of desperation and of a sense of injustice that you have not had the chance that other men have had; and yet I assure you that, in spite of that seeming difference, your fellow-citizens and mine are not the greedy, oppressive persons that sometimes people would make you believe, but that, more today than ever in the history of the world, their hearts are open and their desires to help the needy and lift the suffering out of their suffering are greater today than ever before and are growing every month. Dr. Klopsch is one of those through whom I hope that thought is being conveyed to you, so that you may not burn with a sense of injustice, but that you may hope on and struggle on with the belief that the future is brighter for you.

65

Interstate Commerce and Anti-Trust
Laws and Federal Incorporation

January 7, 1910

To the Senate and House of Representatives:

I withheld from my annual message a discussion of needed legislation under the authority which Congress has to regulate commerce between the States and with foreign countries, and said that I would bring this subject-matter to your attention later in the session. Accordingly, I beg to submit to you certain recommendations as to the amendments to the interstate commerce law and certain considerations arising out of the operations of the anti-trust law suggesting the wisdom of Federal incorporation of industrial companies.

Interstate Commerce Law

In the annual report of the Interstate Commerce Commission for the year 1908, attention is called to the fact that between July 1, 1908, and the close of that year sixteen suits had been begun to set aside orders of the commission (besides one commenced before that date), and that few orders of much consequence had been permitted to go without protest; that the questions presented by these various suits were fundamental, as the constitutionality of the act itself was in issue, and the right of Congress to delegate to any tribunal authority to establish an interstate rate was denied; but that perhaps the most serious practical question raised concerned the extent of the right of the courts to review the orders of the commission; and it was pointed out that if the contention of the carriers in this latter respect alone was sustained, but little progress had been made in the Hepburn Act toward the effective regulation of interstate transportation charges. In twelve of the cases referred to, it was stated, preliminary injunctions were prayed for, being granted in six and refused in six.

"It has from the first been well understood," says the commission, "that the success of the present act as a regulating measure depended largely upon the facility with which temporary injunctions could be obtained. If a railroad company, by mere allegation in its bill of complaint, supported by *ex parte* affidavits, can overturn the result of days of patient investigation, no very satisfactory result can be expected. The railroad loses nothing by these proceedings, since if they fail it can only be required to establish the rate and to pay to shippers the difference between the higher rate collected and the rate which is finally held to be reasonable. In point of fact it usually profits, because it can seldom be required to return more than a fraction of the excess charges collected."

In its report for the year 1909 the commission shows that of the seventeen cases referred to in its 1908 report, only one had been decided in the Supreme Court of the United States, although five other cases had been argued and submitted to that tribunal in October, 1909.

Of course, every carrier affected by an order of the commission has a constitutional right to appeal to a Federal court to protect it from the enforcement of an order which it may show to be *prima facie* confiscatory or unjustly discriminatory in its effect; and as this application may be made to a court in any district of the United States, not only does delay result in the enforcement of the order, but great uncertainty is caused by contrariety of decision. The questions presented by these applications are too often technical in their character and require a knowledge of the business and the mastery of a great volume of conflicting evidence which is tedious to examine and troublesome to comprehend. It would not be proper to attempt to deprive any corporation of the right to the review by a court of any order or decree which, if undisturbed, would rob it of a reasonable return upon its investment or would subject it to burdens which would unjustly discriminate against it and in favor of other carriers similarly situated. What is, however, of supreme importance is that the decision of such questions shall be as speedy as the nature of the circumstances will admit, and that a uniformity of decision be secured so as to bring about an effective, systematic, and scientific enforcement of the commerce law, rather than conflicting decisions and uncertainty of final result.

For this purpose I recommend the establishment of a court of the United States composed of five judges designated for such purpose from among the circuit judges of the United States to be known as the "United States Court of Commerce." which court shall be clothed with exclusive original jurisdiction over the following classes of cases:

(1) All cases for the enforcement, otherwise than by adjudication and collection of a forfeiture or penalty, or by infliction of criminal punishment, of any order of the Interstate Commerce Commission other than for the payment of money.

(2) All cases brought to enjoin, set aside, annul, or suspend any order of requirement of the Interstate Commerce Commission.

(3) All such cases as under section 3 of the act of February 19, 1903, known as the "Elkins Act," are authorized to be maintained in a circuit court of the United States.

(4) All such mandamus proceedings as under the provisions of section 20 or section 23 of the Interstate Commerce Law are authorized to be maintained in a circuit court of the United States.

Reasons precisely analogous to those which induced the Congress to create the Court of Custom Appeals by the provisions in the tariff act of August 5, 1909, may be urged in support of the creation of the Commerce Court.

In order to provide a sufficient number of judges to enable this court to be constituted, it will be necessary to authorize the appointment of five additional circuit judges, who, for the purposes of appointment, might be distributed to those circuits where there is at the present time the largest volume of business, such as the second, third, fourth, seventh, and eighth circuits. The act should empower the Chief Justice at any time when the business of the Court of Commerce does not require the services of all the judges, to reassign the judges designated to that court to the circuits to which they respectively belong; and it should also provide for payment to such judges while sitting by assignment in the Court of Commerce of such additional amount as is necessary to bring their annual compensation up to $10,000.

The regular sessions of such a court should be held at the capital, but it should be empowered to hold sessions in different parts of the United States if found desirable; and its orders and judgments should be made final, subject only to review by the Supreme Court of the United States, with the provision that the operation of the decree appealed from shall not be stayed unless the Supreme Court shall so order. The Commerce Court should be empowered in its discretion to restrain or suspend the operation of an order of the Interstate Commerce Commission under review pending the final hearing and determination of the proceeding, but no such restraining order should be made except upon notice and after hearing, unless in cases where irreparable damage would otherwise ensue to the petitioner. A judge of that court might be empowered to allow a stay of the commission's order for a period of not more than sixty days, but pending application to the court for its order or injunction, then only where his order shall contain a specific finding based upon evidence submitted to the judge making the order and identified by reference thereto, that such irreparable damage would result to the petitioner, specifying the nature of the damage.

Under the existing law, the Interstate Commerce Commission itself initiates and defends litigation in the courts for the enforcement, or in the defense, of its orders and decrees, and for this purpose it employs attorneys who, while subject to the control of the Attorney-General, act upon the initiative and under the instructions of the commission. This blending of administrative, legislative, and judicial functions tends, in my opinion, to impair the efficiency of the commission by clothing it with partisan characteristics and robbing it of the impartial judicial attitude it should occupy in passing upon questions submitted to it. In my opinion all litigation affecting the Government should be under the direct control of the Department of Justice; and I therefore recommend that all proceedings affecting orders and decrees of the Interstate Commerce Commission be brought by or against the United States *eo nomine*, and be placed in charge of an assistant attorney-general acting under the direction of the Attorney-General.

The subject of agreements between carriers with respect to rates has been often discussed in Congress. Pooling arrangements and agreements were condemned by the general sentiment of the people, and, under the Sherman Antitrust Law, any agreement between carriers operating in restraint of interstate or international trade or commerce would be unlawful. The Republican platform of 1908 expressed the belief that the Interstate Commerce Law should be further amended so as to give the railroads the right to make and publish traffic agreements subject to the approval of the commission, but maintaining always the principle of competition between naturally competing lines and avoiding the common control of such lines by any means whatsoever. In view of the complete control over rate-making and other practices of interstate carriers established by the acts of Congress and as recommended in this communication, I see no reason why agreements between carriers subject to the act, specifying the classifications of freight and the rates, fares, and charges for transportation of passengers and freight which they may agree to establish, should not be permitted, provided copies of such agreements be promptly filed with the commission, but subject to all the provisions of the Interstate Commerce Act, and subject to the right of any parties to such agreement to cancel it as to all or any of the agreed rates, fares, charges, or classifications by thirty days' notice in writing to the other parties and to the commission.

Much complaint is made by shippers over the state of the law under which they are held bound to know the legal rate applicable to any proposed shipment, without, as a matter of fact, having any certain means of actually ascertaining such rate. It has been suggested that to meet this grievance carriers should be required, upon application by the shipper, to quote the legal rate in writing, and that the shipper should be protected in acting upon the rate thus quoted; but the objection to this suggestion is that it would afford a much too easy method of giving to favored shippers unreasonable preferences and rebates. I think that the law should provide that a carrier, upon written request by an intending shipper, should quote in writing the rate or charge applicable to the proposed shipment under any schedules or tariffs to which such carrier is a party, and that if the party making such request shall suffer damage in consequence of either refusal or omission to quote the proper rate or, in consequence of a misstatement of the rate, the carrier shall be liable to a penalty in some reasonable amount, say two hundred and fifty dollars, to accrue to the United States and to be recovered in a civil action brought by the appropriate district attorney. Such a penalty would compel the agent of the carrier to exercise due diligence in quoting the applicable legal rate, and would thus afford the shipper a real measure of protection, while not opening the way to collusion and the giving of rebates or other unfair discrimination.

Under the existing law the commission can only act with respect to an alleged excessive rate or unduly discriminatory practice by a carrier on a complaint made by some individual affected thereby. I see no reason why the commission should not be authorized to act on its own initiative as well as upon the complaint of an individual in investigating the fairness of any existing rate or practice; and I recommend the amendment of the law to so provide; and also that the commission shall be fully empowered, beyond any question, to pass upon the classifications of commodities for the purposes of fixing rates, in like manner as it may now do with respect to the maximum rate applicable to any transportation.

Under the existing law the commission may not investigate an increase in rates until after it shall have become effective; and although one or more carriers may file with the commission a proposed increase in rates or change in classifications, or other alterations of the existing rates or classifications, to become effective at the expiration of thirty days from such filing, no proceeding can be taken to investigate the reasonableness of such proposed change until after it becomes operative. On the other hand, if the commission shall make an order finding that an existing rate is excessive and directing it to be reduced, the carrier affected may by proceedings in the courts stay the operation of such order of reduction for months and even years. It has, therefore, been suggested that the commission should be empowered, whenever a proposed increase in rates is filed, at once to enter upon an investigation of the reasonableness of the increase and to make an order postponing the effective date of such increase until after such investigation shall be completed. To this, much objection has been made on the part of carriers. They contend that this would be, in effect, to take from the owners of the railroads the management of their properties and to clothe the Interstate Commerce Commission with the original rate-making power—a policy which was much discussed at the time of the passage of the Hepburn Act in 1905–6, and which was then and has always been distinctly rejected; and in reply to the suggestion that they are able by resorting to the courts to stay the taking effect of the order of the commission until its reasonableness shall have been investigated by the courts, whereas the people are deprived of any such remedy with respect to action by the carriers, they point to the provision of the Interstate Commerce Act providing for restitution to the shippers by carriers of excessive rates charged in cases where the orders of the commission reducing such rates are affirmed. It may be doubted how effective this remedy really is. Experience has shown that many, perhaps most, shippers do not resort to proceedings to recover the excessive rates which they may have been required to pay, for the simple reason that they have added the rates paid to the cost of the goods and thus enhanced the price thereof to their customers, and that the public has in effect paid the bill. On the other hand, the enormous volume of transportation charges, the great number of separate tariffs filed annually with the Interstate Commerce Commission, amounting to almost 200,000, and the impossibility of any commission supervising the making of tariffs in advance of their becoming effective on every transportation line within the United States to the extent that would be necessary if their active concurrence were required in the making of every tariff, has satisfied me that this power, if granted, should be conferred in a very limited and restricted form. I therefore recommend that the Interstate Commerce Commission be empowered, whenever any proposed increase of rates is filed, at once, either on complaint or of its own motion, to enter upon an investigation into the reasonableness of such change, and that it be further empowered, in its discretion, to postpone the effective date of such proposed increase for a period not exceeding sixty days beyond the date when such rate would take effect. If within this time it shall determine that such increase is unreasonable, it may then, by its order, either forbid the increase at all or fix the maximum beyond which it shall not be made. If, on the other hand, at the expiration of this time, the commission shall not have completed its investigation, then the rate shall take effect precisely as it would under the existing law, and the commission may continue its investigation with such results as might be realized under the law as it now stands.

The claim is very earnestly advanced by some large associations of shippers that shippers of freight should be empowered to direct the route over which their shipments should pass to destination, and in this connection it has been urged that the provisions of section 15 of the Interstate Commerce Act, which now empowers the commission, after hearing on complaint, to establish through routes and maximum joint rates to be charged, etc., when no reasonable or satisfactory through route shall have been already established, be amended so as to empower the commission to take such action, even when one existing reasonable and satisfactory route already exists, if it be possible to establish additional routes. This seems to me to be a reasonable provision. I know of no reason why a shipper should not have the right to elect between two or more established through routes to which the initial carrier may be a party, and to require his shipment to be transported to destination over such of such routes as he may designate for that purpose, subject, however, in the exercise of this right to such reasonable regulations as the Interstate Commerce Commission may prescribe.

The Republican platform of 1908 declared in favor of amending the Interstate Commerce Law, but so as always to maintain the principle of competition between naturally competing lines, and avoiding the common control of such lines by any means whatsoever. One of the most potent means of exercising such control has been through the holding of stock of one railroad company by another company owning a competing line. This condition has grown up under express legislative power conferred by the laws of many States, and to attempt now to suddenly reverse that policy so far as it affects the ownership of stocks heretofore so acquired, would be to inflict a grievous injury, not only upon the corporations affected but upon a large body of the investment-holding public. I, however, recommend that the law shall be amended so as to provide that from and after the date of its passage no railroad company subject to the Interstate Commerce Act shall, directly or indirectly, acquire any interests of any kind in capital stock, or purchase or lease any railroad of any other corporation which competes with it respecting business to which the Interstate Commerce Act applies. But especially for the protection of the minority stockholders in securing to them the best market for their stock I recommend that such prohibition be coupled with a proviso that it shall not operate to prevent any corporation which, at the date of the passage of such act, shall own not less than one-half of the entire issued and outstanding capital stock of any other railroad company, from acquiring all of the remainder of such stock; nor to prohibit any railroad company which at the date of the enactment of the law is operating a railroad of any other corporation under lease, executed for a term of not less than twenty-five years, from acquiring the reversionary ownership of the demised railroad; but that such provisions shall not operate to authorize or validate the acquisition, through stock ownership or otherwise, of a competing line or interest therein in violation of the anti-trust or any other law.

The Republican platform of 1908 further declares in favor of such national legislation and supervision as will prevent the future overissue of stocks and bonds by interstate carriers, and in order to carry out its provisions I recommend the enactment of a law providing that no railroad corporation subject to the Interstate Commerce Act shall hereafter for any purpose connected with or relating to any part of its business governed by said act, issue any capital stock without previous or simultaneous payment to it of not less than the par value of such stock, or any bonds or other obligations (except notes maturing not more than one year from the date of their issue), without the previous or simultaneous payment to such corporation of not less than the par value of such bonds, or other obligations, or, if issued at less than their par value, then not without such payment of the reasonable market value of such bonds or obligations as ascertained by the Interstate Commerce Commission, and that no property, services, or other thing than money shall be taken in payment to such a carrier corporation, of the par or other required price of such stock, bond, or other obligation, except at the fair value of such property, services, or other thing as ascertained by the commission; and that such act shall also contain provisions to prevent the abuse by the improvident or improper issue of notes maturing at a period not exceeding twelve months from date, in such a manner as to commit the commission to the approval of a larger amount of stock or bonds in order to retire such notes than should legitimately have been required.

Such act should also provide for the approval by the Interstate Commerce Commission of the amount of stock and bonds to be issued by any railroad company subject to this act upon any reorganization, pursuant to judicial sale or other legal proceedings, in order to prevent the issue of stock and bonds to an amount in excess of the fair value of the property which is the subject of such reorganization.

I believe these suggested modifications in and amendments to the Interstate Commerce Act would make it a complete and effective measure for securing reasonableness of rates and fairness of practices in the operation of interstate railroad lines, without undue preference to any individual or class over any others; and would prevent the recurrence of many of the practices which have given rise in the past to so much public inconvenience and loss.

By my direction the Attorney-General has drafted a bill to carry out these recommendations, which will be furnished upon request to the appropriate committee whenever it may be desired.

In addition to the foregoing amendments of the Interstate Commerce Law, the Interstate Commerce Commission should be given the power, after a hearing, to determine upon the uniform construction of those appliances—such as sill steps, ladders, roof handholds, running boards, and hand brakes on freight cars engaged in interstate commerce—used by the trainmen in operation of trains, the defects and lack of uniformity in which are apt to produce accidents and injuries to railway trainmen. The wonderful reforms effected in the number of switchmen and trainmen injured by coupling accidents, due to the enforced introduction of safety couplers, is a demonstration of what can be done if railroads are compelled to adopt proper safety appliances.

The question has arisen in the operation of the Interstate Commerce Employer's Liability Act as to whether suit can be brought against the employer company in any place other than that of its home office. The right to bring the suit under this act should be as easy of enforcement as the right of a private person not in the company's employ to sue on an ordinary claim, and process in such suit should be sufficiently served if upon the station agent of the company upon whom service is authorized to be made to bind the company in ordinary actions arising under State laws. Bills for both the foregoing purposes have been considered by the House of Representatives, and have been passed, and are now before the Interstate Commerce Committee of the Senate. I earnestly urge that they be enacted into law.

Anti-trust Law and Federal Incorporation

There has been a marked tendency in business in this country for forty years last past toward combination of capital and plant in manufacture, sale and transportation. The moving causes have been several: First, it has rendered possible great economy; second, by a union of former competitors it has reduced the probability of excessive competition; and, third, if the combination has been extensive enough, and certain methods in the treatment of competitors and customers have been adopted, the combiners have secured a monopoly and complete control of prices or rates.

A combination successful in achieving complete control over a particular line of manufacture has frequently been called a "trust." I presume that the derivation of the word is to be explained by the fact that a usual method of carrying out the plan of the combination has been to put the capital and plants of various individuals, firms, or corporations engaged in the same business under the control of trustees.

The increase of the capital of a business for the purpose of reducing the cost of production and effecting economy in the management has become as essential in modern progress as the change from the hand tool to the machine. When, therefore, we come to construe the object of Congress in adopting the so-called "Sherman Anti-trust Act" in 1890, whereby in the first section every contract, combination in the form of a trust or otherwise, or conspiracy in restraint of interstate or foreign trade or commerce, is condemned as unlawful and made subject to indictment and restraint by injunction; and whereby in the second section every monopoly or attempt to monopolize, and every combination or conspiracy with other persons to monopolize any part of interstate trade or commerce, is denounced as illegal and made subject to similar punishment or restraint, we must infer that the evil aimed at was not the mere bigness of the enterprise, but it was the aggregation of capital and plants with the express or implied intent to restrain interstate or foreign commerce, or to monopolize it in whole or in part.

Monopoly destroys competition utterly, and the restraint of the full and free operation of competition has a tendency to restrain commerce and trade. A combination of persons, formerly engaged in trade as partnerships or corporations or otherwise, of course eliminates the competition that existed between them; but the incidental ending of that competition is not to be regarded as necessarily a direct restraint of trade, unless of such an all-embracing character that the intention and effect to restrain trade are apparent from the circumstances or are expressly declared to be the object of the combination. A mere incidental restraint of trade and competition is not within the inhibition of the act, but it is where the combination or conspiracy or contract is inevitably and directly a substantial restraint of competition, and so a restraint of trade, that the statute is violated.

The second section of the act is a supplement to the first. A direct restraint of trade, such as is condemned in the first section, if successful and used to suppress competition, is one of the commonest methods of securing a trade monopoly, condemned in the second section.

It is possible for the owners of a business of manufacturing and selling useful articles of merchandise so to conduct their business as not to violate the inhibitions of the Anti-trust Law and yet to secure to themselves the benefit of the economies of management and of production due to the concentration under one control of large capital and many plants. If they use no other inducement than the constant low price of their product and its good quality to attract custom, and their business is a profitable one, they violate no law. If their actual competitors are small in comparison with the total capital invested, the prospect of new investments of capital by others in such a profitable business is sufficiently near and potential to restrain them in the prices at which they sell their product. But if they attempt by a use of their preponderating capital and by a sale of their goods temporarily at unduly low prices, to drive out of business their competitors, or if they attempt, by exclusive contracts with their patrons and threats of non-dealing except upon such contracts, or by other methods of a similar character, to use the largeness of their resources and the extent of their output compared with the total output as a means of compelling custom and frightening off competition, then they disclose a purpose to restrain trade and to establish a monopoly and violate the act.

The object of the Anti-trust Law was to suppress the abuses of business of the kind described. It was not to interfere with a great volume of capital which, concentrated under one organization, reduced the cost of production and made its profits thereby, and took no advantage of its size by methods akin to duress to stifle competition with it.

I wish to make this distinction as emphatic as possible, because I conceive that nothing could happen more destructive to the prosperity of this country than the loss of that great economy in production which has been and will be effected in all manufacturing lines by the employment of large capital under one management. I do not mean to say that there is not a limit beyond which the economy of management by the enlargement of plant ceases; and where this happens and combination continues beyond this point, the very fact shows intent to monopolize and not to economize.

The original purpose of many combinations of capital in this country was not confined to the legitimate and proper object of reducing the cost of production. On the contrary, the history of most trades will show at times a feverish desire to unite by purchase, combination, or otherwise all plants in the country engaged in the manufacture of a particular line of goods. The idea was rife that thereby a monopoly could be effected and a control of prices brought about which would inure to the profit of those engaged in the combination. The path of commerce is strewn with failures of such combinations. Their projectors found that the union of all the plants did not prevent competition, especially where proper economy had not been pursued in purchase and in the conduct of the business after the aggregation was complete. There were enough, however, of such successful combinations to arouse the fears of good, patriotic men as to the result of a continuance of this movement toward the concentration in the hands of a few of the absolute control of the prices of all manufactured products.

The anti-trust statute was passed in 1890 and prosecutions were soon begun under it. In the case of the *United States v. Knight,* known as the "Sugar Trust" case, because of the narrow scope of the pleadings, the combination sought to be enjoined was held not to be included within the prohibition of the act, because the averments did not go beyond the mere acquisition of manufacturing plants for the refining of sugar, and did not include that of a direct and intended restraint upon trade and commerce in the sale and delivery of sugar across State boundaries and in foreign trade. The result of the Sugar Trust case was not happy, in that it gave other companies and combinations seeking a similar method of making profit by establishing an absolute control and monopoly in a particular line of manufacture a sense of immunity against prosecutions in the Federal jurisdiction; and where that jurisdiction is barred in respect to a business which is necessarily commensurate with the boundaries of the country, no State prosecution is able to supply the needed machinery for adequate restraint or punishment.

Following the Sugar Trust decision, however, there have come along in the slow but certain course of judicial disposition, cases involving a construction of the anti-trust statute and its application until now they seem to embrace every phase of that law which can be practically presented to the American public and to the Government for action. They show that the Anti-trust Act has a wide scope and applies to many combinations in actual operation, rendering them unlawful and subject to indictment and restraint.

The Supreme Court in several of its decisions has declined to read into the statute the word "unreasonable" before "restraint of trade," on the ground that the statute applies to all restraints and does not intend to leave to the court the discretion to determine what is reasonable restraint of trade. The expression "restraint of trade" comes from the common law, and at common law there were certain covenants incidental to the carrying out of a main or principal contract which were said to be covenants in partial restraint of trade, and were held to be enforceable because "reasonably" adapted to the performance of the main or principal contract. And under the general language used by the Supreme Court in several cases, it would seem that even such incidental covenants in restraint of interstate trade were within the inhibition of the statute and must be condemned. In order to avoid such a result, I have thought and said that it might be well to amend the statute so as to exclude such covenants from its condemnation. A close examination of the later decisions of the court, however, shows quite clearly in cases presenting the exact question, that such incidental restraints of trade are held not to be within the law and are excluded by the general statement that, to be within the statute, the effect of the restraint upon the trade must be direct and not merely incidental or indirect. The necessity, therefore, for an amendment of the statute so as to exclude these incidental and beneficial covenants in restraint of trade held at common law to be reasonable does not exist.

In some of the opinions of the Federal circuit judges there have been intimations, having the effect, if sound, to weaken the force of the statute by including within it absurdly unimportant combinations and arrangements, and suggesting therefore the wisdom of changing its language by limiting its application to serious combinations with intent to restrain competition or control prices. A reading of the opinions of the Supreme Court, however, makes the change unnecessary, for they exclude from the operation of the act contracts affecting interstate trade in but a small and incidental way, and apply the statute only to the real evil aimed at by Congress.

The statute has been on the statute book now for two decades, and the Supreme Court in more than a dozen opinions has construed it in application to various phases of business combinations and in reference to various subjects-matter. It has applied it to the union under one control of two competing interstate railroads, to joint traffic arrangements between several interstate railroads, to private manufacturers engaged in a plain attempt to control prices and suppress competition in a part of the country, including a dozen states, and to many other combinations affecting interstate trade. The value of a statute which is rendered more and more certain in its meaning by a series of decisions of the Supreme Court furnishes a strong reason for leaving the act as it is, to accomplish its useful purpose, even though if it were being newly enacted useful suggestions as to change of phrase might be made.

It is the duty and the purpose of the Executive to direct an investigation by the Department of Justice, through the grand jury or otherwise, into the history, organization, and purposes of all the industrial companies with respect to which there is any reasonable ground for suspicion that they have been organized for a purpose, and are conducting business on a plan which is in violation of the Anti-trust Law. The work is a heavy one, but it is not beyond the power of the Department of Justice, if sufficient funds are furnished, to carry on the investigations and to pay the counsel engaged in the work. But such an investigation and possible prosecution of corporations whose prosperity or destruction affects the comfort not only of stockholders but of millions of wage-earners, employees, and associated tradesmen, must necessarily tend to disturb the confidence of the business community, to dry up the now flowing sources of capital from its places of hoarding, and produce a halt in our present prosperity that will cause suffering and strained circumstances among the innocent many for the faults of the guilty few. The question which I wish in this message to bring clearly to the consideration and discussion of Congress is whether in order to avoid such a possible business danger something can not be done by which these business combinations may be offered a means, without great financial disturbance, of changing the character, organization, and extent of their business into one within the lines of the law under the Federal control and supervision, securing compliance with the anti-trust statute.

Generally, in the industrial combinations called "trusts," the principal business is the sale of goods in many States and in foreign markets; in other words, the interstate and foreign business far exceeds the business done in any one State. This fact will justify the Federal Government in granting a Federal charter to such a combination to make and sell in interstate and foreign commerce the products of useful manufacture under such limitations as will secure a compliance with the anti-trust law. It is possible so to frame a statute that while it offers protection to a Federal company against harmful, vexatious, and unnecessary invasion by the States, it shall subject it to reasonable taxation and control by the States, with respect to its purely local business.

Many people conducting great businesses have cherished a hope and a belief that in some way or other a line may be drawn between "good trusts" and "bad trusts," and that it is possible by amendment to the Anti-trust Law to make a distinction under which good combinations may be permitted to organize, suppress competition, control prices, and do it all legally if only they do not abuse the power by taking too great profit out of the business. They point with force to certain notorious trusts as having grown into power through criminal methods by the use of illegal rebates and plain cheating, and by various acts utterly violative of business honesty or morality, and urge the establishment of some legal line of separation by which "criminal trusts" of this kind can be punished, and they, on the other hand, be permitted under the law to carry on their business. Now the public, and especially the business public, ought to rid themselves of the idea that such a distinction is practicable or can be introduced into the statute. Certainly under the present Anti-trust Law no such distinction exists. It has been proposed, however, that the word "reasonable" should be made a part of the statute, and then that it should be left to the court to say what is a reasonable restraint of trade, what is a reasonable suppression of competition, what is a reasonable monopoly. I venture to think that this is to put into the hands of the court a power impossible to exercise on any consistent principle which will insure the uniformity of decision essential to just judgment. It is to thrust upon the courts a burden that they have no precedents to enable them to carry, and to give them a power approaching the arbitrary, the abuse of which might involve our whole judicial system in disaster.

In considering violations of the Anti-trust Law we ought, of course, not to forget that that law makes unlawful, methods of carrying on business which before its passage were regarded as evidence of business sagacity and success, and that they were denounced in this act not because of their intrinsic immorality, but because of the dangerous results toward which they tended, the concentration of industrial power in the hands of the few, leading to oppression and injustice. In dealing, therefore, with many of the men who have used the methods condemned by the statute for the purpose of maintaining a profitable business, we may well facilitate a change by them in the method of doing business, and enable them to bring it back into the zone of lawfulness without losing to the country the economy of management by which in our domestic trade the cost of production has been materially lessened and in competition with foreign manufacturers our foreign trade has been greatly increased.

Through all our consideration of this grave question, however, we must insist that the suppression of competition, the controlling of prices, and the monopoly or attempt to monopolize in interstate commerce and business, are not only unlawful, but contrary to the public good, and that they must be restrained and punished until ended.

I therefore recommend the enactment by Congress of a general law providing for the formation of corporations to engage in trade and commerce among the States and with foreign nations, protecting from them undue interference by the States and regulating their activities, so as to prevent the recurrence, under national auspices, of those abuses which have arisen under State control. Such a law should provide for the issue of stock of such corporations to an amount equal only to the cash paid in on the stock; and if the stock be issued for property, then at a fair valuation, ascertained under approval and supervision of Federal authority, after a full and complete disclosure of all the facts pertaining to the value of such property and the interest therein of the persons to whom it is proposed to issue stock in payment of such property. It should subject the real and personal property only of such corporations to the same taxation as is imposed by the States within which they may be situated upon other similar property located therein, and it should require such corporations to file full and complete reports of their operations with the Department of Commerce and Labor at regular intervals. Corporations organized under this act should be prohibited from acquiring and holding stock in other corporations (except for special reasons upon approval by the proper Federal authority), thus avoiding the creation, under National auspices, of the holding company with subordinate corporations in different States, which has been such an effective agency in the creation of the great trusts and monopolies.

If the prohibition of the Anti-trust Act against combinations in restraint of trade is to be effectively enforced, it is essential that the National Government shall provide for the creation of national corporations to carry on a legitimate business throughout the United States. The conflicting laws of the different States of the Union with respect to foreign corporations make it difficult, if not impossible, for one corporation to comply with their requirements so as to carry on business in a number of different States.

To the suggestion that this proposal of Federal incorporation for industrial combinations is intended to furnish them a refuge in which to continue industrial abuses under Federal protection, it should be said that the measure contemplated does not repeal the Sherman Anti-trust Law and is not to be framed so as to permit the doing of the wrongs which it is the purpose of that law to prevent, but only to foster a continuance and advance of the highest industrial efficiency without permitting industrial abuses.

Such a national incorporation law will be opposed, first by those who believe that trusts should be completely broken up and their property destroyed. It will be opposed, second by those who doubt the constitutionality of such Federal incorporation, and even if it is valid, object to it as too great Federal centralization. It will be opposed, third, by those who will insist that a mere voluntary incorporation like this will not attract to its acceptance the worst of the offenders against the anti-trust statute, and who will therefore propose instead of it a system of compulsory licenses for all Federal corporations engaged in interstate business.

Let us consider these objections in their order. The Government is now trying to dissolve some of these combinations, and it is not the intention of the Government to desist in the least degree in its effort to end those combinations which are today monopolizing the commerce of this country. Where it appears that the acquisition and concentration of property go to the extent of creating a monopoly or of substantially and directly restraining interstate commerce it is not the intention of the Government to permit this monopoly to exist under Federal incorporation or to transfer to the protecting wing of the Federal Government a State corporation now violating the Sherman Act. But it is not and should not be, the policy of the Government to prevent reasonable concentration of capital which is necessary to the economic development of manufacture, trade, and commerce. This country has shown a power of economical production that has astonished the world, and has enabled us to compete with foreign manufactures in many markets. It should be the care of the Government to permit such concentration of capital while keeping open the avenues of individual enterprise, and the opportunity for a man or corporation with reasonable capital to engage in business. If we would maintain our present business supremacy, we should give to industrial concerns an opportunity to reorganize and to concentrate their legitimate capital in a Federal corporation, and to carry on their large business within the lines of the law.

Second. There are those who doubt the constitutionality of such Federal incorporation. The regulation of interstate and foreign commerce is certainly conferred in the fullest measure upon Congress, and if for the purpose of securing in the most thorough manner that kind of regulation, Congress shall insist that it may provide and authorize certain agencies to carry on that commerce, it would seem to be within its power. This has been distinctly affirmed with respect to railroad companies doing an interstate business, and interstate bridges. The power of incorporation has been exercised by Congress and upheld by the Supreme Court in this regard. Why, then, with respect to any other form of interstate commerce like the sale of goods across State boundaries and into foreign commerce, may the same power not be asserted? Indeed, it is the very fact that they carry on interstate commerce that makes these great industrial concerns subject to Federal prosecution and control. How far as incidental to the carrying on of that commerce it may be within the power of the Federal Government to authorize the manufacture of goods, is perhaps more open to discussion, though a recent decision of the Supreme Court would seem to answer that question in the affirmative.

Even those who are willing to concede that the Supreme Court may sustain such Federal incorporation are inclined to oppose it on the ground of its tendency to the enlargement of the Federal power at the expense of the power of the States. It is a sufficient answer to this argument to say that no other method can be suggested which offers Federal protection on the one hand and close Federal supervision on the other of these great organizations that are in fact federal because they are as wide as the country and are entirely unlimited in their business by State lines. Nor is the centralization of Federal power under this act likely to be excessive. Only the largest corporations would avail themselves of such a law, because the burden of complete Federal supervision and control that must certainly be imposed to accomplish the purpose of the incorporation would not be accepted by an ordinary business concern.

The third objection, that the worst offenders will not accept Federal incorporation, is easily answered. The decrees of injunction recently adopted in prosecutions under the Anti-trust Law are so thorough and sweeping that the corporations affected by them have but three courses before them:

First, they must resolve themselves into their component parts in the different States, with a consequent loss to themselves of capital and effective organizations and to the country of concentrated energy and enterprise; or

Second, in defiance of law and under some secret trust, they must attempt to continue their business in violation of the Federal statute, and thus incur the penalties of contempt and bring on an inevitable criminal prosecution of the individuals named in the decree and their associates; or

Third, they must reorganize and accept in good faith the Federal charter I suggest.

A Federal compulsory license law, urged as a substitute for a Federal incorporation law, is unnecessary except to reach that kind of corporation which, by virtue of the considerations already advanced, will take advantage voluntarily of an incorporation law, while the other State corporations doing an interstate business do not need the supervision or the regulation of a Federal license and would only be unnecessarily burdened thereby.

The Attorney-General, at my suggestion, has drafted a Federal incorporation bill, embodying the views I have attempted to set forth, and it will be at the disposition of the appropriate committees of Congress.

66

Conservation of National Resources

January 14, 1910

To the Senate and House of Representatives:

In my annual message I reserved the subject of the conservation of our national resources for discussion in a special message as follows:

"In several departments there is presented the necessity for legislation looking to the further conservation of our national resources, and the subject is one of such importance as to require a more detailed and extended discussion than can be entered upon in this communication. For that reason I shall take an early opportunity to send a special message to Congress on the subject of the improvement of our waterways; upon the reclamation and irrigation of arid, semi-arid, and swamp lands; upon the preservation of our forests and the reforesting of suitable areas; upon the reclassification of the public domain with a view to separating from agricultural settlement mineral, coal, and phosphate lands and sites belonging to the Government bordering on streams suitable for the utilization of water power."

In 1860 we had a public domain of 1,055,911,288 acres. We have now 731,354,081 acres, confined largely to the mountain ranges and the arid and semi-arid plains. We have, in addition, 368,035,975 acres of land in Alaska.

The public lands were, during the earliest administrations, treated as a national asset for the liquidation of the public debt and as a source of reward for our soldiers and sailors. Later on they were donated in large amounts in aid of the construction of wagon roads and railways, in order to open up regions in the West then almost inaccessible. All the principal land statutes were enacted more than a quarter of a century ago. The homestead act, the preemption and timber-culture act, the coal land and the mining acts were among these. The rapid disposition of the public lands under the early statutes, and the lax methods of distribution prevailing, due, I think, to the belief that these lands should rapidly pass into private ownership, gave rise to the impression that the public domain was legitimate prey for the unscrupulous, and that it was not contrary to good morals to circumvent the land laws. This prodigal manner of disposition resulted in the passing of large areas of valuable land and many of our national resources into the hands of persons who felt little or no responsibility for promoting the national welfare through their development. The truth is that title to millions of acres of public lands was fraudulently obtained, and that the right to recover a large part of such lands for the Government long since ceased by reason of statutes of limitation.

There has developed in recent years a deep concern in the public mind respecting the preservation and proper use of our national resources. This has been particularly directed toward the conservation of the resources of the public domain. The problem is how to save and how to utilize, how to conserve and still develop; for no sane person can contend that it is for the common good that Nature's blessings are only for unborn generations.

Among the most noteworthy reforms initiated by my distinguished predecessor were the vigorous prosecution of land frauds and the bringing to public attention of the necessity for preserving the remaining public domain from further spoliation, for the maintenance and extension of our forest resources, and for the enactment of laws amending the obsolete statutes so as to retain governmental control over that part of the public domain in which there are valuable deposits of coal, of oil, and of phosphate, and, in addition thereto, to preserve control, under conditions favorable to the public, of the lands along the streams in which the fall of water can be made to generate power to be transmitted in the form of electricity many miles to the point of its use, known as "water-power" sites.

The investigations into violations of the public land laws and the prosecution of land frauds have been vigorously continued under my administration, as has been the withdrawal of coal lands for classification and valuation and the temporary withholding of power sites.

Since March 4, 1909, temporary withdrawals of power sites have been made on 102 streams, and these withdrawals therefore cover 229 percent more streams than were covered by the withdrawals made prior to that date.

The present statutes, except so far as they dispose of the precious metals and the purely agricultural lands, are not adapted to carry out the modern view of the best disposition of public lands to private ownership, under conditions offering on the one hand sufficient inducement to private capital to take them over for proper development, with restrictive conditions on the other which shall secure to the public that character of control which will prevent a monopoly or misuse of the lands or their products. The power of the Secretary of the Interior to withdraw from the operation of existing statutes tracts of land the disposition of which under such statutes would be detrimental to the public interest, is not clear or satisfactory. This power has been exercised in the interest of the public, with the hope that Congress might affirm the action of the Executive by laws adapted to the new conditions. Unfortunately, Congress has not thus far fully acted on the recommendations of the Executive, and the question as to what the Executive is to do is, under the circumstances, full of difficulty. It seems to me that it is the duty of Congress now, by a statute, to validate the withdrawals which have been made by the Secretary of the Interior and the President, and to authorize the Secretary of the Interior temporarily to withdraw lands pending submission to Congress of recommendations as to legislation to meet conditions or emergencies as they arise.

One of the most pressing needs in the matter of public land reform is that lands should be classified according to their principal value or use. This ought to be done by that Department whose force is best adapted to that work. It should be done by the Interior Department through the Geological Survey. Much of the confusion, fraud, and contention which has existed in the past has arisen from the lack of an official and determinative classification of the public lands and their contents.

It is now proposed to dispose of agricultural lands as such, and at the same time to reserve for other disposition the treasure of coal, oil, asphaltum, natural gas, and phosphate contained therein. This may be best accomplished by separating the right to mine from the title to the surface, giving the necessary use of so much of the latter as may be required for the extraction of the deposits. The surface might be disposed of as agricultural land under the general agricultural statutes, while the coal or other mineral could be disposed of by lease on a royalty basis, with provisions requiring a certain amount of development each year; and in order to prevent the use and cession of such lands with others of similar character so as to constitute a monopoly forbidden by law, the lease should contain suitable provision subjecting to forfeiture the interest of persons participating in such monopoly. Such law should apply to Alaska as well as to the United States.

It is exceedingly difficult to frame a statute to retain government control over a property to be developed by private capital in such manner as to secure the governmental purpose and at the same time not to frighten away the investment of the necessary capital. Hence, it may be necessary by laws that are really only experimental to determine from their practical operation what is the best method of securing the result aimed at.

The extent of the value of phosphate is hardly realized, and with the need that there will be for it as the years roll on and the necessity for fertilizing the land shall become more acute, this will be a product which will probably attract the greed of monopolists.

With respect to the public land which lies along the streams offering opportunity to convert water power into transmissible electricity, another important phase of the public-land question is presented. There are valuable water-power sites through all the public-land States. The opinion is held that the transfer of sovereignty from the Federal Government to the territorial governments as they become States, included the water power in the rivers except so far as that owned by riparian proprietors. I do not think it necessary to go into discussion of this somewhat mooted question of law. It seems to me sufficient to say that the man who owns and controls the land along the stream from which the power is to be converted and transmitted, owns land which is indispensable to the conversion and use of that power. I can not conceive how the power in streams flowing through public lands can be made available at all except by using the land itself as the site for the construction of the plant by which the power is generated and converted and securing a right of way thereover for transmission lines. Under these conditions, if the Government owns the adjacent land—indeed, if the Government is the riparian owner—it may control the use of the water power by imposing proper conditions on the disposition of the land necessary in the creation and utilization of the water power.

The development in electrical appliances for the conversion of the water power into electricity to be transmitted long distances has progressed so far that it is no longer problematical, but it is a certain inference that in the future the power of the water falling in the streams to a large extent will take the place of natural fuels. In the disposition of the domain already granted, many water-power sites have come under absolute ownership, and may drift into one ownership, so that all the water power under private ownership shall be a monopoly. If, however, the water-power sites now owned by the Government—and there are enough of them—shall be disposed of to private persons for the investment of their capital in such a way as to prevent their union for purposes of monopoly with other water-power sites, and under conditions that shall limit the right of use to not exceeding fifty years, with proper means for determining a reasonable graduated rental, and with some equitable provision for fixing terms of renewal, it would seem entirely possible to prevent the absorption of these most useful lands by a power monopoly. As long as the Government retains control and can prevent their improper union with other plants, competition must be maintained and prices kept reasonable.

In considering the conservation of the natural resources of the country, the feature that transcends all others, including woods, waters, minerals, is the soil of the country. It is incumbent upon the Government to foster by all available means the resources of the country that produces the food of the people. To this end the conservation of the soils of the country should be cared for with all means at the Government's disposal. Their productive powers should have the attention of our scientists that we may conserve the new soils, improve the old soils, drain wet soils, ditch swamp soils, levee river overflow soils, grow trees on thin soils, pasture hillside soils, rotate crops on all soils, discover methods for cropping dry-land soils, find grasses and legumes for all soils, feed grains and mill feeds on the farms where they originate, that the soils from which they come may be enriched.

A work of the utmost importance to inform and instruct the public in this chief branch of the conservation of our resources is being carried on successfully in the Department of Agriculture; but it ought not to escape public attention that State action in addition to that of the Department of Agriculture (as for instance in the drainage of swamp lands) is essential to the best treatment of the soils in the manner above indicated.

The act by which, in semi-arid parts of the public domain, the area of the homestead has been enlarged from 160 to 320 acres has resulted most beneficially in the extension of "dry farming," and in the demonstration which has been made of the possibility, through a variation in the character and mode of culture, of raising substantial crops without the presence of such a supply of water as heretofore has been thought to be necessary for agriculture.

But there are millions of acres of completely arid land in the public domain which, by the establishment of reservoirs for the storing of water and the irrigation of the lands, may be made much more fruitful and productive than the best lands in a climate where the moisture comes from the clouds. Congress recognized the importance of this method of artificial distribution of water on the arid lands by the passage of the Reclamation Act. The proceeds of the public lands create the fund to build the works needed to store and furnish the necessary water, and it was left to the Secretary of the Interior to determine what projects should be selected among those suggested, and to direct the Reclamation Service, with the funds at hand and through the engineers in its employ, to construct the works.

No one can visit the Far West and the country of arid and semi-arid lands without being convinced that this is one of the most important methods of the conservation of our natural resources that the Government has entered upon. It would appear that over thirty projects have been undertaken, and that a few of these are likely to be unsuccessful because of lack of water, or for other reasons, but generally the work which has been done has been well done, and many important engineering problems have been met and solved.

One of the difficulties which have arisen is that too many projects in view of the available funds have been set on foot. The funds available under the reclamation statute are inadequate to complete these projects within a reasonable time. And yet the projects have been begun; settlers have been invited to take up and, in many instances, have taken up, the public land within the projects, relying upon their prompt completion. The failure to complete the projects for their benefit is, in effect, a breach of faith and leaves them in a most distressed condition. I urge that the nation ought to afford the means to lift them out of the very desperate condition in which they now are. This condition does not indicate any excessive waste or any corruption on the part of the Reclamation Service. It only indicates an overzealous desire to extend the benefit of reclamation to as many acres and as many States as possible. I recommend, therefore, that authority be given to issue not exceeding $30,000,000 of bonds from time to time, as the Secretary of the Interior shall find it necessary, the proceeds to be applied to the completion of the projects already begun and their proper extension, and the bonds running ten years or more to be taken up by the proceeds of returns to the reclamation fund, which returns, as the years go on, will increase rapidly in amount.

There is no doubt at all that if these bonds were to be allowed to run ten years, the proceeds from the public lands, together with the rentals for water furnished through the completed enterprises, would quickly create a sinking fund large enough to retire the bonds within the time specified. I hope that, while the statute shall provide that these bonds are to be paid out of the reclamation fund, it will be drawn in such a way as to secure interest at the lowest rate, and that the credit of the United States will be pledged for their redemption.

I urge consideration of the recommendations of the Secretary of the Interior in his annual report for amendments of the Reclamation Act, proposing other relief for settlers on these projects.

Respecting the comparatively small timbered areas on the public domain not included in national forests because of their isolation or their special value for agriculture or mineral purposes, it is apparent from the evils resulting by virtue of the imperfections of existing laws for the disposition of timber lands, that the acts of June 3, 1878, should be repealed and a law enacted for the disposition of the timber at public sale, the lands after the removal of the timber to be subject to appropriation under the agricultural or mineral land laws.

What I have said is really an epitome of the recommendations of the Secretary of the Interior in respect to the future conservation of the public domain in his present annual report. He has given close attention to the problem of disposition of these lands under such conditions as to invite the private capital necessary to their development on the one hand, and the maintenance of the restrictions necessary to prevent monopoly and abuse from absolute ownership on the other. These recommendations are incorporated in bills he has prepared, and they are at the disposition of the Congress. I earnestly recommend that all the suggestions which he has made with respect to these lands shall be embodied in statutes, and, especially, that the withdrawals already made shall be validated so far as necessary, and that the authority of the Secretary of the Interior to withdraw lands for the purpose of submitting recommendations as to future disposition of them where new legislation is needed shall be made complete and unquestioned.

The forest reserves of the United States, some 190,000,000 acres in extent, are under the control of the Department of Agriculture, with authority adequate to preserve them and to extend their growth so far as that may be practicable. The importance of the maintenance of our forests can not be exaggerated. The possibility of a scientific treatment of forests so that they shall be made to yield a large return in timber without really reducing the supply has been demonstrated in other countries, and we should work toward the standard set by them as far as their methods are applicable to our conditions.

Upward of 400,000,000 acres of forest land in this country are in private ownership, but only 3 percent of it is being treated scientifically and with a view to the maintenance of the forests. The part played by the forests in the equalization of the supply of water on watersheds is a matter of discussion and dispute, but the general benefit to be derived by the public from the extension of forest lands on watersheds and the promotion of the growth of trees in places that are now denuded and that once had great flourishing forests, goes without saying. The control to be exercised over private owners in their treatment of the forests which they own is a matter for State and not national regulation, because there is nothing in the Constitution that authorizes the Federal Government to exercise any control over forests within a State, unless the forests are owned in a proprietary way by the Federal Government.

It has been proposed, and a bill for the purpose passed the lower house in the last Congress, that the National Government appropriate a certain amount each year out of the receipts from the forestry business of the Government to institute reforestation at the sources of certain navigable streams, to be selected by the Geological Survey, with a view to determining the practicability of thus improving and protecting the streams for Federal purposes. I think a moderate expenditure for each year for this purpose, for a period of five or ten years, would be of the utmost benefit in the development of our forestry system.

I come now to the improvement of the inland waterways. He would be blind, indeed, who did not realize that the people of the entire West, and especially those of the Mississippi Valley, have been aroused to the need there is for the improvement of our inland waterways. The Mississippi River, with the Missouri on the one hand and the Ohio on the other, would seem to offer a great natural means of interstate transportation and traffic. How far, if properly improved, they would relieve the railroads or supplement them in respect to the bulkier and cheaper commodities is a matter of conjecture. No enterprise ought to be undertaken the cost of which is not definitely ascertained and the benefit and advantages of which are not known and assured by competent engineers and other authority. When, however, a project of a definite character for the improvement of a waterway has been developed so that the plans have been drawn, the cost definitely estimated, and the traffic which will be accommodated is reasonably probable, I think it is the duty of Congress to undertake the project and make provision therefor in the proper appropriation bill.

One of the projects which answer the description I have given is that of introducing dams into the Ohio River from Pittsburgh to Cairo, so as to maintain at all seasons of the year, by slack water, a depth of nine feet. Upward of seven of these dams have already been constructed and six are under construction, while the total required is fifty-four. The remaining cost is known to be $63,000,000.

It seems to me that in the development of our inland waterways it would be wise to begin with this particular project and carry it through as rapidly as may be. I assume from reliable information that it can be constructed economically in twelve years.

What has been said of the Ohio River is true in a less complete way of the improvement of the upper Mississippi from St. Paul to St. Louis, to a constant depth of six feet, and of the Missouri, from Kansas City to St. Louis, to a constant depth of six feet and from St. Louis to Cairo to a depth of eight feet. These projects have been pronounced practical by competent boards of army engineers, their cost has been estimated, and there is business which will follow the improvement.

I recommend, therefore, that the present Congress, in the river and harbor bill, make provision for continuing contracts to complete these improvements.

As these improvements are being made, and the traffic encouraged by them shows itself of sufficient importance, the improvement of the Mississippi beyond Cairo down to the Gulf, which is now going on with the maintenance of a depth of nine feet everywhere, may be changed to another and greater depth if the necessity for it shall appear to arise out of the traffic which can be delivered on the river at Cairo.

I am informed that the investigation by the Waterways Commission in Europe shows that the existence of a waterway by no means assures traffic unless there is traffic adapted to water carriage at cheap rates at one end or the other of the stream. It also appears in Europe that the depth of the non-tidal streams is rarely more than six feet, and never more than ten. But it is certain that enormous quantities of merchandise are transported over the rivers and canals in Germany and France and England, and it is also certain that the existence of such methods of traffic materially affects the rates which the railroads charge, and it is the best regulator of those rates that we have, not even excepting the governmental regulation through the Interstate Commerce Commission. For this reason, I hope that this Congress will take such steps that it may be called the inaugurator of the new system of inland waterways.

For reasons which it is not necessary here to state, Congress has seen fit to order an investigation into the Interior Department and the Forest Service of the Agricultural Department. The results of that investigation are not needed to determine the value of, and the necessity for, the new legislation which I have recommended in respect to the public lands and in respect to reclamation. I earnestly urge that the measures recommended be taken up and disposed of promptly, without awaiting the investigation which has been determined upon.

67

Uniformity of State Legislation

Address Before the National Civic Federation, Belasco Theatre,
Washington, D.C., January 17, 1910

Mr. President, Ladies and Gentlemen:

In the first place, I am glad to welcome the Civic Federation to Washington. I think the sun shines a little brighter in Washington than it does anywhere else along on the same latitude, and it is a very pleasant place either to live in or to be in; and therefore, I congratulate the Civic Federation on having had the good sense to come here.

You are not the only citizens of the United States who look in this direction. I am glad that you came here at the same time that the Governors did, so that your deliberations and theirs in the same direction, and the right direction, as they doubtless will be, will have the weight of two great forces, not only upon the National Legislature, but upon the State legislatures, for from Washington everything radiates to the ends of the country.

In the discussion of uniformity of legislation, when you take a man who has gotten out of the practice of the law, so that he does not remember with great exactitude those principles that are applied in actual cases, he can not help falling back on a discussion of the Constitution. The constitutional lawyer is a gentleman who has gotten out of the practice and who has gone into politics.

Now, my friend, Senator Root, whom I am delighted to class with me in the same category, some years ago was greatly misunderstood with reference to his view of the Constitution and the trend under the Constitution toward centralization of government. If I understood him, his view was that, unless the States did their duty in the exercise of the functions which it was necessary they should exercise in the interest of good government, there would be a tendency toward the enlargement of the Government at Washington; and he uttered a warning to the States that if they would retain the power given to them under the Constitution in all its integrity, they must see to it that they exercised that power in the interest of the people and in the interest of the country generally. The misunderstanding led to ascribing to him views in favor of centralization that would certainly have been most radical, but I am sure he does not have them. We have a nation and we have a centralized government, and the reason why we have it is because John Marshall was put at the head of the Supreme Court early and exercised that power which a good judge always exercises with his colleagues. He did not minimize the power of the Supreme Court to construe that Constitution authoritatively. And so construing it, he made this a nation with all the powers incident to a nation. And then when he left the Bench, after that long period of useful service, he was succeeded by Chief Justice Taney and his associates, and at that time the trend toward national power and authority of the party, from which Chief Justice Taney was selected, led him right along the same path that Marshall had marked out, until we came to the war. And then with the war amendments, the same tendency to make this government a Nation as distinguished from a Federation, continued to the present day.

Now, it is said that we have centralized too much. There are jurisdictions which might be asserted under the Constitution that Congress has not asserted, notably in the jurisdiction of the Federal courts. So, too, in bankruptcy; so, too, in elections. With respect to the jurisdiction of the Federal courts, there is a large measure which Congress does not assert which it might take away from that which the State courts now exercise. And so, with respect to bankruptcy, it might be made much more exclusive of State jurisdiction in that regard, and with respect to elections, they have gone back entirely to the States.

There are other matters under the Constitution which I shall not stop to mention, which show that all the power conferred upon the National Government has not yet been exercised; but the reason why it seems as if we were becoming a more centralized government is not because of a change in the construction of the Constitution, but a change in the importance of the power which was always given to the National Government under that Constitution, to wit: the interstate commerce clause. When the Constitution was framed, the state traffic as distinguished from the interstate traffic was as 75 to 25, and now, instead, the interstate traffic is to the state traffic as 75 to 25—a complete reversal of the amount of interstate business done as compared with the state business. And that is the reason why the National government's power seems to have grown so largely because its power covers more volume than it ever did before. With respect to that, I am inclined to think that it will be found wise after a time to recognize these great organizations, concentrations of wealth, and plant and capital that do a country-wide business, going into every State, whose business is almost wholly interstate, to recognize them as instrumentalities of interstate commerce and to incorporate them in order that we may get them more directly under the control of the National Government.

I admit there is ground for dispute, and I have only recommended this as something that I look forward to in the future as a means of saving to the public what is valuable; as there is a great deal that is valuable in those trusts, and eliminating permanently that which is vicious and contrary to public policy. But you are not Congress, and I did not come here to convince you on that subject. I only mention it in passing.

There has been, during the last ten or fifteen years, an earnest desire on the part of some people to minimize State power altogether. They say—I heard the distinguished Governor of Massachusetts say, the United States can better regulate child labor than can the States—so what's the use of talking! Why not put that power into the United States Government? And so, with reference to every power, the suggestion is that the Central Government has more capital; being more centralized, its execution of the laws is more certain and less affected by local conditions, and therefore it is wise in the interest of effective government to put what we can in the Central Government. Therefore we invoke the old "general welfare clause." We have got the money in the Treasury, and we can spend the money there for anything we choose, because there is no court to prevent it. We cannot issue an injunction against the Secretary of the Treasury dishonoring an appropriation of Congress. And when it comes to the expenditure of money, the history of the United States is full of appropriations and expenditures that can not be explained on any ground except that of old "General Welfare." And the way they propose to expend it when there is a particular subject that needs attention is to organize a bureau, and let that bureau occupy an advisory relation and experimental relation to the States in the exercise of that jurisdiction which is undoubtedly theirs. They have got to a point where, just before I sent in my message, in the list of bureaus that was asked for was a bureau on earthquakes. I assume that the argument was that as earthquakes did not know any State bounds neither did the exercise of jurisdiction with respect to them know any State bounds.

Now, the lesson that this teaches is that we have a Constitution by which the Government of the United States can not accomplish all reform, and that there is a burden and there is a heavy responsibility, eloquently described by Mr. Root, upon the States with reference to meeting the demands of those who call themselves progressive, and who are in favor of the reforms to uplift the people and to make the comfort of the individual greater.

In no department of government, in no reform, is this uniformity of legislation going to be more important than in the conservation of our resources. The Federal Government has no power to compel owners of forests to attend to those forests with a view to the welfare of the community, of the neighbors who live there, or of those who are affected by the denudation of the land of the trees. That must be done through the State government if it is done at all. And so with respect to many of the streams. Indeed, if one follows out legal reasoning, it will seem, I think, that there is more to be done by the States in the conservation of resources even than by the Federal Government, large an influence as that Federal Government may have by reason of its ownership of the public domain.

Now there are many other subjects that ought to occupy the States with reference to uniform legislation. If I had been a member of the Constitutional Convention, I would have voted to have included marriage and divorce in the Federal jurisdiction, but it will never get there now.

The theory upon which they put in bankruptcy was that where a man was declared a bankrupt it fixed his status, and that status ought not to vary in one State from the status in another. But when a man is married, he has established a status and certainly that status ought not to vary between the States, but as it is not possible to secure an amendment to the United States Constitution placing that subject within Federal cognizance, it certainly calls for uniform legislation on the part of the States. I state that because I think everybody will agree with me. Then I am not going on to say what kind of legislation there ought to be, because I am told that in that discussion as yet even the Civic Federation has not reached a result.

Then there is another subject upon which there may well be uniformity of legislation after we, in the Federal Government, have adopted a proper system, and that is with respect to judicial procedure. If there is anything in our whole Government, state and national, that justifies an attack upon our present system of living, it is the delays in our judicial procedure, and the advantage that wealth gives in the struggle in the courts against those who have not the means to meet the expense that is now imposed on them.

If we can do something in the National Government to introduce the simplicity of the English procedure in equity and in law, perhaps uniting them, that will be a model for State legislatures in adopting a uniform system.

I might go on with respect to other subjects; I have said a good deal more than I intended to, and I have only—so to speak—"shot on the wing"; but if you had to write a message a week perhaps you would only write when you have to.

68

Uniformity of State Legislation

Address at the Conference of Governors, East Room,
White House, January 18, 1910

My dear Fellow Executives and Fellow Sufferers:

I am delighted to greet you in the White House. I should have been glad to have had you here during all your sessions so that you might have made the White House your headquarters, but in discussing this matter with the committee it occurred to them, and it occurred to me, that it would possibly be better for you to hold your sessions in a neutral place, so to speak, where you would feel more independent, and where doubtless things could be said and things could be done which perhaps might be a little embarrassing in doing when you were under the Executive shadow.

When you were here before, Mr. Roosevelt, I think, extended to you the hospitality of the White House, and the meetings were held here, but those meetings were so fully his, in the sense of being called by him, that it seemed entirely appropriate; whereas now, I hope this is a movement among the Governors to have some sort of a permanent arrangement that shall bring them here without suggestion from any one but the Governors themselves.

For my own comfort, it would have been better if the Civic Federation and the Governors had united in the initial meeting, for I made a speech yesterday and said all I could think of saying on the general subject that called you here.

mine"; but that was because I occupied a different relation to him from that which the army occupied toward him.

Then there comes what the army did there. My friend, the Senator, thinks it was nothing to be proud of. That is because my friend the Senator does not know what the army did, and what the navy did in a less way. It was upon the army that there fell the burden of eliminating an insurrection that extended the islands' full length, and they had to be divided up into five hundred different posts and they had to put small detachments of the army under command of lieutenants and second lieutenants, and even sergeants, and trust to the ability of the non-commissioned officer and the young commissioned officers to carry on independent campaigns in the neighborhood of the post to which they were assigned in stamping out this insurrection. No army, and I assert it without any fear of contradiction, could have offered that knowledge, that independence of judgment, that self-reliance on the part of those young officers that enabled it as a whole ultimately and quietly and softly—and—I had almost said—peaceably to bring about a condition of pacification in the islands and to stamp out an insurrection so difficult to overcome. And in those campaigns there was an opportunity for individual bravery and courage that is not exceeded by any opportunity in the Civil War or any other war that this country was engaged in.

And this Signal Corps which was referred to tonight in a jocular way, may point to a record of loss in death and wounds in those islands that I think has been equaled by no other signal corps, and perhaps by no other corps in any other army.

Now the Senator says that he has been allowed to think but the officers of the army have not been. Well, I confess that under the circumstances, with the result of the fight I think the army is ahead of the Senator. What we went to the Philippines to do was to defeat the fleet of an enemy in a war that was begun as no other war in the history of the world—no other foreign war—from pure altruism; and we got into the islands and we had them on our hands before we knew what the consequences were to be. And when they came into our hands there seemed to us—at least to those of us who were responsible—and my friend the Senator has had the advantage for the last fifteen years—I hope he may continue to have it for fifteen years—of not being at all responsible for the Government—the obligation of doing the right thing. The question was, "What are we going to do?" Are we going to let those islands go into chaos, are we going to turn them back to Spain with the charges against the domination of Spain that were made? Or are we to take them ourselves and develop them as best we may under our institutions?

Now my friend the Senator is troubled about taxation without representation, and about the Declaration of Independence. I am not going into those arguments and I am not going to point out to my friend the Senator some of the most glaring instances that I could point out in his view of the Constitution in South Carolina and his view of the Philippines. What I do say is, and say it with a knowledge of McKinley, and I know the Senator and I share in the respect for President McKinley's memory that President McKinley went into those islands with great reluctance and assumed the burdens which were most heavy to him of introducing a government there which should be the best for the islands. Now, of course it is a matter of dispute how good a government we have there. Having taken part in its formation, perhaps it is improper—or at least I speak as a prejudiced witness—but I believe that the ten years of government in the Philippines has made that people a far happier people than they would have been under any other conditions that might have been presented by our taking a different course. They enjoy today a free trade tariff on the one hand and the right to sell in a protected market on the other. That was long coming, but we have ultimately secured it. We have saved the rice of our friend the Senator from South Carolina. We were asked to stave off a little bit of the injury to the tobacco and the sugar of other parts of the country. They are now beginning, as I believe, an industrial progress there that means an elevation of those people intellectually and spiritually in such a way that we can continue to extend to them, from time to time, additional self-government. We now have put them under one chamber which is elected popularly, sharing the government with a commission upon which there are a number of Filipinos.

Now the cost has been considerable. Five hundred million dollars has been mentioned. My impression is that the cost is not so much, and that will have to include what is the cost of a war, and a war always costs most heavily. But the actual cost depends upon how you count the army, whether you would count it that we would have an army of the present size if we did not have the Philippines, or would not. Personally, I should have an army of this size, whether we have the Philippines or not, and therefore I don't think the cost goes beyond six or seven million dollars a year. Counting it the other way it is very considerably more.

Now a third question which arises is the effect of the Spanish War and our going to the Philippines upon the country at large, upon our standing before the nations of the world, and upon our opportunities for usefulness as a prosperous, powerful country. And I think in that record perhaps the Spanish War and what followed are more important than in any other aspect. I know it is easy to make fun of a proposition that we as a nation have an obligation because of our power and wealth to assist other nations that may be thrown upon us in such a way as to call for our aid and support; but I do believe in the brotherhood of nations, and I do believe that nations are like members of a community and a neighborhood where the wealthy and the powerful and the more fortunate owe it to the weaker and the less fortunate to assist them when circumstances point in that direction.

As a matter of fact the result of the Philippine War, our ownership of the Philippines, our ownership of Puerto Rico, our friendship for and close relation to Cuba, our assertion of an interest in South America and an interest in the Isthmus bringing us into close relations with Central America, and our assertion of a right to the "open door" in China, have put us in a position forefront among the nations of the world; and I believe we have no right to neglect the opportunity to take such a position or the opportunity to use that position for the progress of civilization in the world. Now the result of that war, short as it was, involving as little blood as it did, was remarkable. The expansion of the United States as a great world power dates from that time. We are not going about seeking to aggrandize ourselves, seeking for territory in China or anywhere else.

We are building the Panama Canal now for the benefit of the world, and at the same time to aid us in our commerce and to strengthen and double the force of our Navy. The broadening of our people with regard to those problems, the liberalizing of the army, or making the army a body—and especially the officers—a body of well-read gentlemen, men of affairs—all date from that time.

Now I deprecate the tone of my friend Senator Tillman's statement that we are ashamed of all this. Well, I am not ashamed of it, because if it had not come that way I should not have been in the White House, I know, and if he expects me to shed tears over that he is mistaken. I think I know our army and navy well enough to know that while they sing these songs that at times hold up to ridicule our "little brown brothers" in the Philippines, they look back to that service with pride, and with the belief that they accomplished what no other army could have accomplished in the same time and under the same circumstances, with as little blood and as little oppression. It may be as I say that I am a prejudiced witness. I am. Nevertheless a witness may be prejudiced but he may have such an advantage in opportunities for observation which are denied to those who are only free from prejudice, as to make his evidence better than the judge who sits on the case. I am sorry I did not have the opportunity of welcoming to the Philippine Islands my Brother Tillman. There were some of his Democratic brethren whom I entertained there with great pleasure and into their sphere of vision I think we introduced some things that changed their aspect, changed their views I should say, of the situation there. They deplored what we had to do, but they thought we were doing it well. The truth is, while my friend the Senator comes from South Carolina and the South, I think I know something of the attitude of his brethren in the South with reference to the Philippine Islands and this general policy of expansion, and I think we could have a vote on that alone without introducing the race question and all that sort of thing— the wisdom of our taking the Philippines as we have taken them, and developing them as we are developing them, teaching them English and extending to them, as they show themselves fit, self-government. Then the time may come, and I hope it may come soon, when they shall be ready to take over a government like that of Australia or Canada, and I say so not because we might not be willing to part with them, but because they will find that under the present arrangement, under the tariff as arranged there and the tariff as arranged here, it is greatly to their advantage to retain some sort of bond, no matter how light, which will justify their continuing to enjoy the benefit of our markets with a free trade tariff toward the Orient.

And now, my friends, I have talked a good deal longer than I intended to; but my friend the Senator whispered to me that he would not have said a word if he had not desired to start me up, so I had to gratify his desire and show him that he was successful. I thank you my friends for giving me this opportunity to bring back the reminiscences of the Philippines. There were times in the Philippines when the nervous strain upon those who were responsible was tremendous and the more tremendous because we were so far removed, it seemed, from Washington and the people of United States. There were times, and there were many, when the beauties of life in that country, when the associations that we made there, when the feeling that we did have a people who were grateful at times and who listened to us as children depending on us and having confidence in us—gave us pleasure in doing the good which we thought we were doing a pleasure that knows no measure, for there is nothing in life equal to the consciousness of having attempted to do good for a people and having in a measure succeeded.

There is one other thought that I wanted to give you, and that was in relation to the carabao. He too received, I must say, unmerited condemnation from my friend the Senator, not for lack of sympathy with the dumb beast, but again for lack of opportunity for observation. There is no animal that is the friend of the Filipino like the carabao. He moves slowly, he moves deliberately, but he moves always in the right direction, and he gets there after a time without respect to obstacles. It is unwise in dealing with the Filipino or in dealing with anything in the tropics to suppose that you are going to make headway suddenly. The carabao represents the right policy in working out the problems in the East, and I congratulate you on having selected that animal as an indication that you know how to accomplish things in the Philippines. Ill as I was in 1902, for three or four months, and confined to my bed in the First Reserve Hospital in the Philippines, Mrs. Moses sent me a full set of Kipling's volumes, and in the head note to one of the chapters entitled "Nauhlahka" I found a verse that gave me a great deal of consolation, and I can remember it. I want to recite it as a justification for your selection of this animal as typical of your policy and our policy and our hopes and yours in the Philippines:

> Now it is not good for the Christian's health to hustle the Aryan brown;
> For the Christian riles and the Aryan smiles and he weareth the Christian down;
> And the end of the fight is a tombstone white, with the name of the late deceased;
> And the epitaph drear, "A fool lies here who tried to hustle the East."

70

The Republican Party's Promises

Address at the Lincoln Birthday Banquet of the Republican Club of the City of New York, February 12, 1910

Mr. President, Gentlemen of the Republican Club, and Fellow-Guests:

The birthday of the man whose memory we celebrate tonight is an appropriate occasion for renewing our expressions of respect and affection for the Republican party, and our pledges to keep the part which it plays in the history of this country as high and as useful as it was during the administration of Abraham Lincoln. The trials which he had to undergo as President, the political storms which the party had to weather during the Civil War, the divisions in the party itself between the radical anti-slavery element and those who were most conservative in observing the constitutional limitations, are most interesting reading, and serve to dwarf and minimize the trials through which the Republican party is now passing, and restore a sense of proportion to those who allow themselves to be daunted and discouraged, in the face of a loss of popular confidence thought to be indicated by the tone of the press.

In what respect has the Republican party failed in its conduct of the Government and the enactment of laws, to perform its duty? It was returned to power a year ago last November by a very large majority, after a campaign in which it made certain promises in its platform, and those promises it has either substantially complied with or it is about to perform within the present session of Congress.

Let us take up these promises in order:

In the Republican platform of last year, upon which the campaign was made, appears the following plank in regard to the tariff:

"The Republican party declares unequivocally for the revision of the tariff by a special session of Congress immediately following the inauguration of the next President, and commends the steps already taken to this end in the work assigned to the appropriate committees of Congress which are now investigating the operation and effect of existing schedules. In all tariff legislation the true principle of protection is best maintained by the imposition of such duties as will equal the difference between the cost of production at home and abroad, together with a reasonable profit to American industries. We favor the establishment of maximum and minimum rates to be administered by the President under limitations fixed in the law, the maximum to be available to meet discriminations by foreign countries against American goods entering their markets, and the minimum to represent the normal measure of protection at home, the aim and purpose of the Republican policy being not only to preserve, without excessive duties, that security against foreign competition to which American manufacturers, farmers, and producers are entitled, but also to maintain the high standard of living of the wage earners of this country, who are the most direct beneficiaries of the protective system. Between the United States and the Philippines, we believe in a free interchange of products with such limitations as to sugar and tobacco as will afford adequate protection to domestic interests."

We did revise the tariff. It is impossible to revise the tariff without awakening the active participation in the formation of the schedules of those producers whose business will be affected by a change. This is the inherent difficulty in the adoption or revision of a tariff by our representative system.

Nothing was expressly said in the platform that this revision was to be a downward revision. The implication that it was to be generally downward, however, was fairly given by the fact that those who uphold a protective tariff system defend it by the claim that after an industry has been established by shutting out foreign competition, the domestic competition will lead to the reduction in price so as to make the original high tariff unnecessary.

In the new tariff there were 654 decreases, 220 increases and 1,150 items of the dutiable list unchanged, but this did not represent the fair proportion in most of the reductions and the increases, because the duties were decreased on those articles which had a consumption value of nearly $5,000,000,000, while they were increased on those articles which had a consumption value of less than $1,000,000,000. Of the increases, the consumption value of those affected which are of luxuries, to wit, silks, wines, liquors, fumeries, pomades, and like articles, amounted to nearly $600,000,000; while the increases on articles not of luxury affected but about $300,000,000, as against decreases on about $5,000,000,000 of consumption. I repeat, therefore, that this was a downward revision. It was not downward in reference to silks or liquors or high-priced cottons in the nature of luxuries. It was downward in respect to nearly all other articles except woolens, which were not affected at all. Certainly it was not promised that the rates on luxuries should be reduced. The revenues were falling off, there was a deficit promised, and it was essential that the revenues should be increased. It was no violation of the promise to increase the revenues by increasing the tax on luxuries, provided there was downward revision on all other articles. The one substantial defect in compliance with the promise of the platform was the failure to reduce woolens. Does that defect so color the action of the Republican party as to make it a breach of faith leading to its condemnation? I do not think so. Parties are like men. Revisions are like the work of men—they are not perfect. The change which this tariff effected was a marked change downward in the rate of the duties, and it was a recognition by the party that the time had come when instead of increasing duties they must be decreased, when the party recognized in its platform, and in much of what it did, that the proper measure of protection was the difference in cost in the production of articles here and abroad, including a fair profit to the manufacturer. There was a dispute as to what that difference is, and whether it was recognized in the change of all the duties downward. Particularly was this the case on the materials that enter into the manufacture of paper and paper itself. The reduction on print paper was from $6 to $3.75, or about 37 percent.

There was a real difference of opinion on the question of fact whether the new duty correctly measured the difference in the cost of production of print paper abroad and print paper here. It affected the counting-rooms of the newspapers of the country and invited the attention of the newspaper proprietors who had associated themselves together like other interests for the purpose of securing a reduction of the tariff. The failure to make a larger reduction showed itself clearly in the editorial columns of a great number of the newspapers, whatever their party predilection. The amount of misrepresentation to which the tariff bill in its effect as a downward revision bill was subjected has never been exceeded in this country, and it will doubtless take the actual operation of the tariff bill for several years to show to the country exactly what the legislation and its effect are. It is perhaps too early to institute the fairest comparisons between the Payne-Aldrich Bill and the bill which preceded it, but the Payne-Aldrich Bill has been in operation now for six months, and figures are at hand from which we may make a reasonable inference, first as to whether it is a revision downward, and, second, as to its capacity for producing revenue; for it must be borne in mind that the passage of the law was demanded not only for the purpose of changing rates in their effect upon the industries of the country, but also for the purpose of increasing the revenues; and the success of the measure is to be judged by its results in both these respects.

The Bureau of Statistics is authority for the statement that during the first six months of the operation of the Payne law, which has just ended, the average rate of duty paid on all imports was 21.09 percent ad valorem. The average rate of duty paid on all imports for the same six months for the four preceding years under the Dingley law was 24.03. This would show that the reduction in the Payne law is 2.94 percent of the value of the goods, or that the reduction below the previous tariff rates is 12 percent showing a downward revision to this extent. But this is not all. Under the Payne law 51.6 percent of the gross imports for the last six months have been entered free, while under the four years preceding for the same six months the free list amounted to 45.46 percent of the total importations; so there was not only a reduction of duty on gross imports of about 12 percent but also an enlargement of about the same percentage of the free list.

For the production of revenue, the Payne law is even more an improvement on the Dingley Bill. During the six months that the Payne tariff was in force, from August 5 to the night of February 5, the customs receipts amounted to $166,002,856.54. Under the Gorman-Wilson tariff the semiannual average was $83,147,625.90. Under the Dingley tariff the semi-annual average was $130,265,841.84. Under the Wilson tariff the monthly average was $13,857,937.65. Under the Dingley tariff the monthly average was $21,710,973.64; while under the Payne tariff the monthly average has been $27,667,142.75, or 100 percent greater than the monthly average under the Wilson tariff, and 26 percent greater than the monthly average under the Dingley tariff.

Of course as the country increases in population, the customs receipts increase, but even considering the population, the increase in the tariff receipts has been marked. Under the Wilson tariff the average annual customs receipts per capita were $2.38; under the Dingley tariff $3.23; while under the Payne tariff they are $3.71.

For the six months that the Payne tariff has been in force the total receipts both from customs and internal revenue have been $323,899,231.91, while the disbursements have been $332,783,283.08, showing an excess of disbursements over receipts of about $8,884,051.17, with no collection as yet from the corporation tax. For the corresponding period last year the expenditures exceeded the receipts by over $40,000,000. This showing indicates that under the present customs law the deficit will be promptly wiped out, and that to meet our normal expenditures we shall have ample revenue.

I therefore venture to repeat the remark I have had occasion to make before, that the present customs law is the best customs law that has ever been passed, and it is most significant in this: that it indicates on the part of the Republican party the adoption of a policy to change from an increase in duties to a reduction of them, and to effect an increase of revenues at the same time.

The act has furnished to the Executive the power to apply the maximum and minimum clause in order to prevent undue discrimination on the part of foreign countries, and this is securing additional concessions in respect to impositions on our foreign trade.

The act has done justice to the Philippine Islands by giving them free trade with the United States.

More than all this, the new tariff act has provided for the appointment of a tariff board to secure impartial evidence upon which, when a revision of the tariff seems wise, we shall have at hand the data from which can be determined with some degree of accuracy the difference between the cost of producing articles abroad and the cost of producing them in this country.

The great difficulty in the hearing and discussion of the present tariff bill was the absence of satisfactory and credible evidence on either side of the issues as to low or high tariffs. The importer on the one hand and the manufacturer on the other were present to give their fallible judgments affected by their own pecuniary interests as to the facts under investigation. Men who were struggling to find the truth were greatly perplexed by the conflicting testimony.

The tariff bill authorizes the President to expend $75,000 in employing persons to assist him in the administration of the maximum and minimum clause and to assist him and other officers of the Government in the administration of the tariff law. I have construed this to mean that I may use the board appointed under this power not only to look into the foreign tariffs, but also to examine the question with respect to each item in our tariff bill, what the cost of production of the merchandise taxed is, and what its cost is abroad. This is not an easy task for impartial experts, and it requires a large force. I expect to apply to Congress this year for the sum of $250,000 to organize a force through which this investigation may go on, the results to be recorded for the use of the Executive and Congress when they desire to avail themselves of the record. In this way any subsequent revision may be carried on with the aid of data secured officially and without regard to its argumentative effect upon the question of raising or lowering duties. Taken as a whole, therefore, I do not hesitate to repeat that the Republican party has substantially complied with its promise in respect to the tariff, and that it has set itself strongly in the right direction toward lower tariffs and furnished the means by which such lower tariffs can be properly and safely fixed.

An investigation by the tariff board of the sort proposed will certainly take a full two years or longer. Meantime the operation of the present tariff promises to be consistent with the prosperity of the country and with the furnishing of sufficient funds with which to meet the very heavy but necessary expenditures of carrying on our great Government.

The Republican national platform contained the following:

"We favor the establishment of a postal savings bank system for the convenience of the people and the encouragement of thrift."

A bill has been introduced to establish a postal savings bank. The great difficulty in the bill seems to have been to secure a proper provision for the management and investment of the money deposited. The great advantage of a postal savings bank is the encouragement to thrift of those whose fears of the solvency of any depository except a government depository tempts them away from saving. A government promise to repay seems to be specially effective in leading people to save and deposit their savings. The machinery of the Post-Office, with its 60,000 post-offices and 40,000 money-order offices, offers an economical and far-reaching machine for the reception in places remote from banks, and among people who fear banks, of that which but for the opportunity, they would not save, but spend. The low interest offered to it, that of 2 percent, prevents such postal savings banks from interfering with regular savings banks whose rate of interest always is in excess of 2 percent.

In the present stage of the Senate bill there have been inserted amendments drawn apparently for the purpose of having money deposited as savings in government post-offices distributed through the locality where deposited in the banks, state and national, and so deposited as to make it impossible for the trustees of the fund appointed under the law to withdraw the money for investment in any other form. I regard such an amendment as likely to defeat the law. First, because it takes away a feature which ought to be present in the law to assure its constitutionality. If the law provided that the trustees to be appointed under the law with the funds thus deposited could meet the financial exigencies of the Government by purchase or redemption of the government 2 percent and other bonds the measure would certainly be within the Federal power, because the postal banks would then clearly be an instrument of the National Government in borrowing money. We have now about $700,000,000 of 2 percent bonds with respect to which we owe a duty to the owners to see that those bonds may be taken care of without reduction below the par value thereof, because they were forced upon national banks at this low rate in order that the banks might have a basis of circulation.

This implied obligation of the Government, the postal savings bank funds would easily enable it to meet. Secondly, if the funds are to be arbitrarily deposited in all banks, state and national, without national supervision over the state banks, and a panic were to come, it is difficult to see how the Government could meet its obligations to its postal savings bank depositors, because with every bank suspending payment, the funds of the postal savings banks would be beyond the control of the Government, and we should have a financial disaster greater than any panic we have heretofore met. A provision that when the money is not needed to invest in government bonds or to redeem the same it may be deposited in national banks, in the neighborhood of the place of deposit, will avoid the great danger of a panic and will strengthen a banking system which is an arm of the Federal Government. I sincerely hope that before the measure is hammered into its final shape it may take on these characteristics which shall give it a constitutional validity and sound financial strength and usefulness. Those who insist upon the elimination of these two necessary characteristic features of the bill will put the party in the position where it can not hope to escape the charge that it is not in good faith seeking the passage of a postal savings bank act, and is not seeking, therefore, to comply with the promise of the Republican platform in that regard.

On the subject of railroads the Republican platform said:

"We approve the enactment of the Railroad Rate Law and the vigorous enforcement by the present administration of the statutes against rebates and discriminations as a result of which the advantages formerly possessed by the large shipper over the small shipper have substantially disappeared; and in this connection we commend the appropriation by the present Congress to enable the Interstate Commerce Commission to thoroughly investigate and give publicity to the accounts of interstate railways. We believe, however, that the Interstate Commerce Law should be further amended so as to give railroads the right to make and publish traffic agreements subject to the approval of the commission, but maintaining always the principle of competition between naturally competing lines and avoiding the common control of such lines by any means whatsoever. We favor such national legislation and supervision as will prevent the future overissue of stocks and bonds by interstate carriers."

A bill to carry out these declarations has been introduced in both the House and the Senate, and is now being considered before the appropriate committees of those two bodies, and there is every hope that the bills thus introduced in substantially the same shape as introduced will pass and be enacted into law. Indeed this railroad measure goes further than the promise of the platform, for while it subjects the issue of stock and bonds to the restrictive supervision of the commission and prevents future watering of securities and forbids the acquisition by a railroad company of stock in a competing line, it also puts very much more power into the hands of the commission for the regulation of rates, and it facilitates in every way the ease of supervision by the commission of the railroads to secure compliance by the railroads with the rights of the public and of the shipper. The bill was prepared by the Attorney-General, after a full conference with the Interstate Commerce Commission, with the representatives of the shippers and with the representatives of the railroads, and while it was not the result of an agreement between all the parties in interest, it was drafted with a view to meeting all the fair objections and suggestions made by every one of them.

The platform further provided:

"The Republican party will uphold at all times the authority and integrity of the courts, State and Federal, and will ever insist that their powers to enforce their process and to protect life, liberty, and property shall be preserved inviolate. We believe, however, that the rules of procedure in the Federal courts with respect to the issuance of the writ of injunction should be more accurately defined by statute and that no injunction or temporary restraining order should be issued without notice, except where irreparable injury would result from delay, in which case a speedy hearing thereafter should be granted."

A bill to carry out exactly this promise has been introduced into both the Senate and House and will doubtless come up for consideration and passage. The bill does not go as far as Mr. Gompers and the Federation of Labor demand, but it goes as far as the Republican convention was willing to let it go, and it is so drawn as to make an abuse of the issuance of injunction without notice very improbable. It requires that no injunction shall be issued without full notice and hearing, unless to prevent irreparable injury, and that in such case the court shall make a finding from the evidence adduced, pointing out what the injury anticipated is and why irreparable, and why there is not time to give notice; and after the injunction shall be issued without notice, it is provided that such injunction shall lose its force at the expiration of five days, unless a hearing is had.

The platform also promised statehood to Arizona and New Mexico, and the bill providing such statehood has passed the House and has been favorably considered by the committee of the Senate, so that there seems to be no reasonable doubt that this promise will be fully kept.

The Republicans in their platform spoke further, as follows:

"We indorse the movement inaugurated by the Administration for the conservation of natural resources; we approve all measures to prevent the waste of timber; we commend the work now going on for the reclamation of arid lands, and reaffirm the Republican policy of the free distribution of the available areas of the public domain to the landless settler. No obligation of the future is more insistent and none will result in greater blessings to posterity. In line with this splendid undertaking is the further duty, equally imperative, to enter upon a systematic improvement upon a large and comprehensive plan, just to all portions of the country, of the waterways, harbors, and Great Lakes, whose natural adaptability to the increasing traffic of the land is one of the greatest gifts of a benign Providence."

In accordance with this plank, measures for the conservation of the public domain, for the reclassification of lands according to their greatest utility, and the vesting of power in the Executive to dispose of coal, phosphate, oil, and mineral lands, and of water-power sites in such a way as to prevent their monopoly, and union of ownership in one syndicate, or combination, have been already introduced, and will doubtless in a form approved by Congress be made into law. The subject has attracted the widest interest, and its importance is becoming more and more impressed upon the American people.

The river and harbor bill, which has just been reported by the River and Harbor Committee of the House, has been framed with a view to complying with the plank of the platform I have just above quoted. It has taken the plan for the improvement of the Ohio from Pittsburgh to Cairo as a project to be carried out in a certain number of years; and it has treated similar projects for the improvement of the Missouri from Kansas City to St. Louis, for the improvement of the Mississippi from St. Paul to St. Louis, and of the same river from St. Louis to Cairo; and by continuing contracts and regular appropriations, these projects will go on until they are completed. This is a change from the previous plans, and is the result of an extended popular agitation in favor of such a system.

Following the panic of 1907, the governmental revenues fell off and the expenditures continued as before, leaving a deficit for the years 1907, 1908, and 1909. There was, however, no deficit in the whole administration of Mr. Roosevelt when the expenses are compared with the revenues. Indeed it will be found that under the operation of the Dingley Bill, which covers most of his administration and the first six months of the present administration, the surplus on the whole was about $250,000,000. At the beginning of this Administration, however, it was perfectly evident that with expenses increasing and revenues decreasing, there would be a continuous deficit, and this the Republican party, with its majority in Congress and the responsibility placed upon it, has proposed to meet by reducing expenditures and increasing revenues.

I have already shown what the increase in revenues has been. The present administration in its estimates for the year ending June 30, 1911, cut them some forty odd million dollars below the actual appropriations of the year before, and now it is proposed to appoint a joint commission, consisting of Senators, Representatives, and members appointed by the Executive, who shall examine the organization of the various departments and bureaus, and by the elimination of duplication, the consolidation of bureaus, and the increase in efficiency of the individual civil servant shall decrease the regular permanent cost of governmental operation.

With respect to trusts the Republican party spoke as follows in its platform:

"The Republican party passed the Sherman Anti-trust Law over Democratic opposition and enforced it after Democratic dereliction. It has been a wholesome instrument for good in the hands of a wise and fearless administration. But experience has shown that its effectiveness can be strengthened and its real objects better attained by such amendments as will give to the Federal Government greater supervision and control over and secure greater publicity in the management of that class of corporations engaged in interstate commerce having power and opportunity to effect monopolies."

Since this plank was adopted prosecutions of the Tobacco trust and the Standard Oil trust, begun in the last administration, have gone on and have resulted in decrees in the Court of Appeals of the Second and Eighth circuits, which are now pending on appeal in the Supreme Court. The decrees in each case tear apart the congeries of subordinate corporations which, united by holding companies, make up the trust in each case and enjoin individuals from a further maintenance of the illegal combination of such corporations to carry on the business for which it was organized.

It has been said that the Republican party made a promise so to amend the law as to ameliorate and soften the application of the trust law in its interdiction upon business as conducted by the greatest corporations, but I find nothing in the platform to justify such a construction. The principle of the anti-trust law is that those engaged in modern business, especially of manufacture and transportation, shall pursue the policy with respect to their competitors of "Live and let live," and that they shall not use the bigness of their concerns to frighten exclusive patronage from customers and eliminate smaller concerns from competition and thus control output and fix prices.

The Attorney-General has prepared a bill which, he thinks, and I think, will offer to those who wish to pursue a lawful method of business, the means of easily doing so. A lawful interstate business under the protection of a Federal charter which, while it will subject the business of the concern to the closest scrutiny of government officers, will save the business from harassment by State authorities and will give it that protection which a peaceful pursuit of its business as a Federal corporation will necessarily secure it. This measure has not met the approval of those who fear too great concentration of power in the Federal Government, of those who deny the right of the Federal Government in such cases to grant incorporation. I believe the act to be constitutional, and I believe that if enforced it would furnish a solution of our present difficulties; but as it was not specifically declared for in the Republican platform, I do not feel justified in asking the adoption of such an act as a party matter. I have brought it forward, however, as a suggestion for meeting the difficulties which are likely to be presented in the prosecution of suspected illegal trusts as a means by which they can put their houses in order and take their places among those engaged in legitimate business.

If the other measures to which I have referred are enacted into law, and the pledges of the Republican party performed, there would seem to be no good reason why the party should not receive renewed approval by the electors of the country in the coming congressional campaign. But there are signs which many construe as an indication that the Republican majority in the present Congress will change to a Democratic majority in the next. This is based chiefly on the dissensions in the Republican party, and upon the very severe attacks, made by a great many of the newspapers having Republican tendencies, upon the party and its leaders in Congress and in the nation. I am glad to say that so far as the legislation which I have indicated above is concerned, there seems to be a clear party majority in both Houses in favor of its passage and the consequent redemption of the party pledges. There is, however, a very decided difference as to the proper rules to prevail in the House and as to the personnel of the leadership.

It would seem as if these questions were questions that might well be solved within the party lines, but they have been so acute as to produce what has been called an insurrection and to awaken the country over a controversy between the insurgents and the regulars, so-called. I am hopeful that as we approach the lines of battle for the next year, the settlement of these internal questions can be effected without such a breach of the party as to prevent our presenting an unbroken front to the enemy.

We among the Republicans may be discouraged when we consider our own dissensions, but when we look to the possibility of any united action on the part of the Democrats for any policy or any line of policies we must take courage. It was General Grant who said that when he first went into battle he had a great deal of fear, but he overcame that feeling by maintaining in his mind the constant thought how much more afraid his opponent was. And so we who find ourselves at times given over to the thought that Republican control is at an end should not forget to consider not only our own factional strife but also that of our ancient enemy. If the Democratic party were a solid, cohesive opposition, guided by one principle and following the same economic views as a whole, the situation would be far more discouraging than it is. The Republican party has been the party responsible for the Government for the last seventeen years. It has discharged those responsibilities with wonderful success. The problems growing out of the Spanish war and those which have come from the rapid accumulation of wealth, and the greed for power of its accumulators, it has fallen to the party to meet, and while they have not yet all had a perfect solution, the record is one of which we have no reason to be ashamed.

Mr. Roosevelt aroused the country and the people to the danger we were in of having all our politics and all our places of governmental authority controlled in corporate interests and to serve the greed of selfish but powerful men. During his two terms of office, by what almost may be compared to a religious crusade, he aroused the people to the point of protecting themselves and the public interest against the aggressions of corporate greed, and left public opinion in an apt condition to bring about the reforms needed to clinch his policies and to make them permanent in the form of enacted law.

But as an inevitable aftermath of such agitation, we find a condition of hysteria on the part of certain individuals, and on the part of others a condition of hypocrisy manifesting itself in the blind denunciation of all wealth and in the impeachment of the motives of men of the highest character, and by demagogic appeals to the imagination of a people greatly aroused upon the subject of purity and honesty in the administration of government. The tendency is to resent attachment to party or party organization, and to an assertion of individual opinion and purpose at the expense of party discipline. The movement is toward factionalism and small groups, rather than toward large party organization, and the leaders of the party organization are subjected to the severest attacks and to the questioning of their motives without any adequate evidence to justify it.

I am far from saying that the Republican party is perfect. No party which has exercised such power as it has exercised for the last seventeen years could be expected to maintain either in its rank and file or in its management men of the purest and highest motives only. And I am the last one to advocate any halt in the prosecution and condemnation of Republicans, however prominent and powerful, whose conduct requires criminal or other prosecution and condemnation. It should be well understood that with the Republican party in its present condition, with its various divisions subjected to the cross fire of its own newspapers and its own factions, any halt or failure on the part of those in authority to punish and condemn corruption or corrupt methods will be properly visited upon the party itself, however many good men it contains.

We shall be called upon to respond to the charge in the next campaign that the tariff, for which we are responsible, has raised prices. If the people listen to reasonable argument, it will be easy to demonstrate that high prices proceed from an entirely different cause, and that the present tariff, being largely a revision downward, except with respect to silks and liquors, which are luxuries, can not be charged with having increased any prices. But this will not prevent our Democratic friends from arguing on the principle of *post hoc propter hoc,* that because high prices followed the tariff, therefore they are the result of it. And we must not be blind to the weight of such an argument in an electoral campaign. The reason for the rise in the cost of necessities can easily be traced to the increase in our measure of values, the precious metal, gold, and possibly in some cases to the combinations in restraint of trade. The question of the tariff must be argued out. The prejudice created by the early attacks upon the bill and the gross misrepresentations of its character must be met by a careful presentation of the facts as to the contents of the bill and also as to its actual operation and statistics shown thereby. I believe we have a strong case if we can only get it into the minds of the people. Should disaster follow us and the Republican majority in the House become a minority in the next House, it may be possible that in the Democratic exercise of its power, the people of this country will see which is the party of accomplishment, which is the party of arduous deeds done, and which is the party of words and irresponsible opposition.

I only want one more word. From time to time attacks are made upon the Administration, on the ground that its policy tends to create a panic in Wall Street and to disturb business. All I have to say upon that subject is this: That certainly no one responsible for a government like ours would foolishly run amuck in business and destroy values and confidence just for the pleasure of doing so. No one has a motive as strong as the Administration in power to cultivate and strengthen business confidence and business prosperity. But it does rest with the National Government to enforce the law, and if the enforcement of the law is not consistent with the present method of carrying on business, then it does not speak well for the present methods of conducting business, and they must be changed to conform to the law. There was no promise on the part of the Republican party to change the anti-trust law except to strengthen it, or to authorize monopoly and a suppression of competition and the control of prices, and those who look forward to such a change can not now visit the responsibility for their mistake on innocent persons. Of course the Government at Washington can be counted on to enforce the law in the way best calculated to prevent a destruction of public confidence in business, but that it must enforce the law goes without saying.

I am glad to be present at this meeting of the Republican Club of New York and here meet your distinguished Governor, whose name is such a power before the people of this State and of the country, that to lose him as a candidate for Governor by his voluntary withdrawal is to lose the strongest asset that the Republican party has in the State to enable it to win at the next election.

I am glad to be here at the meeting of the Republican Club on Lincoln's birthday, because my knowledge and information with respect to the club is that it stands for stalwart Republicanism, believes in party organization and party discipline, but insists on the highest ideals and methods in formulating the policies of the party and carrying them out.

71

Government Expenses and Economies

Address at the Banquet of the Board of Trade,
Newark, New Jersey, February 23, 1910

Gentlemen of the Board of Trade of the City of Newark:

It is an opportunity to be able to speak to the business men of New Jersey, of whom this is a most representative gathering. The proximity of New Jersey to New York, and the fact that from the West one can hardly get to New York without passing through New Jersey, make one forget at times the importance of Newark and of all the rest of the hive of industry that spreads west from the Hudson River far into and across this prosperous State. It comes to a stranger with considerable surprise to find a city of 350,000, nine miles west of Jersey City, so extended in its manufacturing industries, so solid in its invested capital.

When I accepted the invitation to come here, I learned that I was to have the pleasure of being a fellow–guest with my friend, Senator Lodge, and that he was to take up the question of high prices, a question which has occupied the attention of all the people and has invited the investigation into its causes of the Congress of the United States and some of the State legislatures.

For my part of the evening, I should like to direct your attention to a more prosy subject, to the question of government expenses and government revenues, and the possible economies, and what expenditures are essential at whatever burden of taxation.

In the first place, it should be said that we have been so far from exhausting the resources of national taxation, and Federal revenues have been collected so easily and in such an amount, that we have failed in the past to adopt a budget system which is practiced in every other civilized country. By a budget system I mean a reference of proposed expenditures and receipts to some one authority or tribunal, which after determining what the revenues are to be, must also determine what the expenditures can be, and make a budget without a deficit.

In our legislative body, which provides the revenue and authorizes the expenditures, time was when the Committee on Ways and Means, on the one hand, determined the revenues of the Government, or provided the laws for raising them, and, on the other hand, determined the appropriations and measured the expenditures. But for many years in our Congress these functions have been divided. The revenues are provided by the Ways and Means Committee of the House and the Finance Committee of the Senate, and submitted to their respective Houses, while the appropriations are made by the appropriation committees of the House and the Senate, and in too many instances without apparent reference to the revenues which are to be available to meet the appropriations.

It has so happened that in many years of the past, the revenues have increased more rapidly than the expenditures and there has been a surplus. During the life of the Dingley Bill, which carried us from 1896 to 1908, the appropriations exceeded the expenditures by about $250,000,000; but the surplus took place in the earlier years, so that in 1908 we had a deficit, and in 1909 we had a deficit. The pinching effect of the falling off of the revenues and the continuance of the expenditures at the same rate attracted the attention of Congress, so that now a preliminary duty is thrown upon the Secretary of the Treasury to make a budget; that is, by law he is required to receive all the estimates of all the Departments, himself to make an estimate of the probable revenues, and if his calculations show a deficit, to recommend legislation for additional taxation or the raising of money by bonds sufficient to meet it.

The calculation of the Secretary of the Treasury for the present year showed that the deficit was likely to be $34,000,000 in respect to ordinary receipts and expenditures. I am glad to say that the operation of the new tariff bill has been so much more productive of income that this deficit for the current year is likely to be considerably reduced. In addition, however, to the ordinary deficit, we have to add the Panama Canal expenditures for immediate provision $38,000,000; or what was estimated to be a total deficit of $72,000,000 is now reduced considerably by the better rates under the present tariff bill.

By meeting the expenditures on the Panama Canal with the proceeds of bond issues, we have enough cash in the Treasury to meet the deficit in our ordinary expenses for the current year, and if we meet the expenditures on the Panama Canal for the following year, we shall have a surplus of $35,000,000; or if the revenue–producing capacity of the new tariff keeps up to its present indications, this surplus may be increased to $50,000,000. On the other hand, if the Congress proposes to add to the expenditures of the Government over those estimated for, for new enterprises in the Rivers and Harbors Bill, and for the construction of Federal buildings under a building act, it will be very easy to consume or exceed the entire surplus.

Everyone must admit the wisdom of providing for the payment of the canal expenditure by bonds. The original act made provision for the issuing of bonds, and while the amount therein estimated was far short of the actual cost, the policy of the Government in supplying funds for the enterprise by bonds was sufficiently declared. This is a work of a permanent character for the millions who come after us, and it seems only fair that that which we provide in such a generous measure for posterity should be paid for, in part at least, by posterity.

Not only is the application of such a principle just and right in the case of an enterprise like the Panama Canal, but it seems to me wise and appropriate to adopt it with reference to other projects which commend themselves to Congress, and the economical completion of which requires the issuing of bonds. I refer to those definite projects that have been agreed upon in respect to the improvement of our inland waterways. I would not begin the expenditure of any money on any project the wisdom of which had not been fully vindicated by experts and the cost of which had not been fully ascertained by the most experienced engineers; but having determined to put through the improvement, it ought not to be done by fits and starts, but it ought to be done as one job, and provision for its completion ought to be made by the issuing of bonds, unless the current revenues afford a sufficient amount to complete it within a reasonable time.

This statement has peculiar application to the River and Harbor Bill, which now has passed the House. There the Ohio River improvement, to cost $63,000,000, is entered upon, and an appropriation made for its continuing. The same thing is true of the improvement of the Mississippi from St. Paul to St. Louis, and the same river from St. Louis to Cairo; and of the

Missouri River from Kansas City to St. Louis. These projects seem to be warranted by the traffic in sight.

While I am dealing with the Panama Canal, however, I ought to refer to the discrepancy between the estimated cost of the enterprise and the actual cost as we are now able to fix it with very considerable accuracy within four or five years of its completion. The estimated cost of the engineering and construction of the canal was $139,700,000. Its actual cost for engineering and construction will be $297,000,000, an increase of about $157,300,000. This increase is to be explained first by the very great appreciation in the cost of labor and material between the time when the estimate was made in 1900 and the time when the work was done between 1904 and 1909. Second, by the fact that the canal has been enlarged substantially beyond the original dimensions estimated for. You know that the great work of excavation in the canal is called the Culebra Cut. This is where the backbone of the continent, reduced to its lowest height, is cut through in order to permit the flowing of the canal; and through five miles of that cut, which altogether is about nine miles long, for purposes of economy the original plan and estimate made the bottom of the canal in the rock 200 feet wide. This would not enable two of the largest steamers to pass each other in the canal with any degree of safety, and would require that one of them should tie up to the bank while the other went by. In order to avoid this delay in that part of the canal it has been thought wise to increase the bottom width from 200 to 300 feet in a place and in material that of course make the change most expensive. So, too, in order that the canal may be adapted to the largest size of steamers possible, the dimensions of the six locks have been increased from 900 feet, usable length, by 90 feet width, to 1,000 feet, usable length, and 110 feet width. This was done at the insistence of the Navy Department, on the ground that they could look forward in the future and see vessels of a beam exceeding 100 feet.

It has also been found necessary to change the character of the canal on the Pacific side from a lake with a dam and locks on the shore of the Bay of Panama to a sea level canal running four miles inland, so as to remove the locks four miles inland and beyond the possible reach of the guns of an enemy in Panama Bay. These two changes also have added very considerably to the cost.

Again it has been found wise to enlarge the canal into a lake or basin at the foot of the Gatun locks, and with other variations in the plans which experience in the construction has demonstrated the necessity for, the more than doubling of the cost of construction and engineering has been made necessary. In addition to this, the cost of sanitation and government, without which the canal could not have been built, will be about $73,000,000, and will carry the entire cost of the canal to $373,000,000.

To return to the state of finances, I repeat that the surplus for the year ending June 30, 1911, for which we are now making provision in this Congress by appropriation, will be about $35,000,000, if the estimates made by the Departments as transmitted by the Secretary of the Treasury to Congress are not exceeded, and if the revenue from the tariff bill equals that which the Secretary of the Treasury has estimated it as likely to be. This surplus is also upon the supposition that the $38,000,000 necessary annually in the construction of the Panama Canal will be met by bonds.

In view of the threatened shortage for the year ending June 30, 1911, I directed the heads of Departments in making their estimates to cut them to the quick and to avail themselves of every possible economy and reduction. The result was that the total of the estimates forwarded by the Secretary of the Treasury was $42,818,000 less than the total of the appropriations for the previous year, ending June 30, 1910.

A river and harbor bill has now been introduced and has passed the House, which appropriates nearly $40,000,000. This is a very considerable increase over the amount estimated for by the Secretary of the Treasury. If, in addition to this, a building bill passes Congress, appropriating $15,000,000 or $20,000,000 for the coming fiscal year, there may still be a deficit unless the receipts from the tariff bill and the corporation tax exceed what was originally estimated from them. I am bound to say that the results of the tariff bill thus far indicate a considerable increase over the estimate of the Secretary.

Now, I would like for a moment to go into the question of what it was that we cut down in our estimates for the coming year in the departments.

The reduction in the estimate of the War Department below the appropriations of last year amounted to $10,000,000. The reduction in the estimate of the Navy Department for the expenses of the year ending June 30, 1911, also amounted to $10,000,000. The reduction in the Interior Department of estimated expenses for 1911 below the appropriations for 1910 amounted to $8,000,000. The reduction in the Treasury and in the Post-Office Department made up the balance of the $42,000,000.

Speaking with reference to the Army and the Navy, it should be said that the reductions were not in what may be called the permanent expenses of the Departments, but were rather in cutting down proposed improvements, which if the plans of the Departments are properly carried out must be some time met. In other words, it is a postponement only of expenditures that are necessary until the income shall be sufficient to meet them.

Let us take the War Department. There was a very considerable cut in the expenditures needed to complete with modern appliances the coast defences on the Pacific and Atlantic seaboard. There is needed at the mouth of Chesapeake Bay, between Cape Henry and Cape Charles, an artificial island upon the so–called middle ground, which shall command the entrance to Chesapeake Bay. Chesapeake Bay is the most important body of water from a strategic naval standpoint on the whole Atlantic coast, and must be defended.

So, too, we have now determined that the great naval base of the Pacific for us is to be Pearl Harbor, near Honolulu. For years there was discussion as to whether we ought to make the naval base at Subig Bay or at Cavite, in Manila Bay, in the Philippines. By unanimous consent of naval and military authorities, it is now concluded that we do not need a naval base in the Philippines at all; that we ought to make Corregidor Island, at the mouth of Manila Bay, impregnable, establish a naval supply station in Subig Bay, but rely upon the Sandwich Islands as our base. This will all involve a heavy expenditure at Honolulu, but for the present the amount proposed is comparatively small.

In the naval expenditures we have retained a provision for two battleships of the large 25,000 ton capacity, and we have done this on the ground that until the Panama Canal is completed we ought to go on and add to our naval strength. The Panama Canal will certainly be completed in 1915, and if we have two battleships a year until that time, the opening of the canal will so double the efficacy of our Navy for the protection of our Pacific and Atlantic coasts that we can then abate and reduce our expenditures in new construction.

The reductions in the Treasury Department were I think more of them in the administration than in the expenditures for improvements, and this was also the case in the Post–Office Department.

The reduction in the Interior Department was $5,000,000 of it due to a reduction of the amount of pensions to be paid out, and we may reasonably expect that as the years now go on this amount will gradually be reduced.

On the other hand, there are certain of our Departments, to wit, the Agricultural Department, with its Forestry Bureau, the War Department in so far as it is a constructive department for the improvement of rivers, the Department of Commerce and Labor, including as it ought, it seems to me, a Bureau of Health, which, as the opportunities for bettering the condition of the people by governmental investigation increase, grow in importance and in cost and we ought not to expect a reduction either in the expenses growing out of a conservation of our resources.

For some time it has been said that we have "billion dollar" Congresses. The statement in itself is an unjust one, because it is generally construed to mean that the total expense of the Departments to be paid out of taxation amounts to a billion dollars a year. This is quite an error, for the reason that in making up the billion dollars the expenses for the Post–Office Department are always included, whereas the expenses of the Post–Office Department are not paid for out of the proceeds of taxes. They are paid for out of the receipts of that Department from the sale of stamps, with the exception of $17,500,000, which was the excess of the cost of the Post–Office Department last year over its receipts. This, therefore, reduces the cost of the Government by taxation each year to something like $750,000,000.

It is now proposed to appoint a Congressional commission to look into the question of a general reorganization of the Departments of the Government, with a view to reducing the expense of administering the Government. I think I have already made clear the distinction between those expenditures of the Government that go into permanent improvements and that may be reduced one year and must be increased another, and the actual routine cost of administration. A reduction in the cost of proposed improvements is not an elimination of them, but merely a postponement of them; whereas a reduction in the cost of administration would be a permanent economy that, of course, on that account, becomes most important.

It has been stated on the floor of the Senate that it will be possible by this commission to reduce the cost of administering the government $100,000,000 a year, and that if a free hand were given to a businessman the reduction in the expense of administration might be doubled or trebled. I am unable to confirm these statements as to exact amount, but I am very sure that a conservative, prudent, and fearless commission could make a most material reduction in the cost of administering the government. They will find opposition in Congress to every change recommended, because there is no branch or bureau so humble that it can not secure its adherents and defenders within the legislative halls. But, if by the totals that it shows this commission shall justify its existence, it is probable that it can secure a majority sufficient to carry through its proposed reforms. This Government has been constructed not all at one time, but bureau has been added to bureau, and department to department, and it has been impossible to avoid duplication and expensive methods. In creating a new bureau, there was no time to go back and reform the Government with reference to the adjustment of that bureau to its proper place or to consider the work of the entire Government with reference to it. This proposed commission, as I understand it, is to take up the bureaus of all the Departments, to see whether they may not often be consolidated, and also to lay down such rules governing the civil service as will secure the utmost efficiency from each civil servant or each unit of labor. It is undoubtedly true to–day that we have a great many more persons employed in the government than we would need, if every person in the government rendered to the government a service of a high degree of efficiency. This commission will have to take up the question, which has troubled great industrial corporations and great railroads, as to the method of disposing of superannuated servants. Our military pensions have reached so large an annual sum, to wit $150,000,000, that we have avoided the suggestion of civil pensions, but I am convinced that some method must be adopted by which superannuated civil servants may be retired on an income sufficient to support them, and that such a provision will ultimately bring about great economy in the administration.

It has been reported by the Postmaster–General that we are carrying in the Post–Office Department the weekly periodicals and magazines at a loss to that department of upward of $60,000,000, and that the business of the Government in the Post–Office Department is now run at a general loss of $17,500,000. The committees of Congress are investigating the correctness of this view. The owners of magazines dispute the correctness of the figures. There ought to be some way certainly of determining this fact, and if it is a fact it calls for a reform, and an increase in the postage of a sufficient amount at least to take away the deficit in the Post–Office Department. Should the two postal committees not be able to reach a conclusion satisfactory to them upon this question, the whole matter may well be left to the commission to consider. It will be essential for this commission to employ expert men who have had to do with the organization of great businesses and who are familiar with the most modern methods of economy. The truth is that the success of modern business has been the adoption of successful economies, and the time has come for us to make an effort at least to introduce something of these economies into an administration of the greatest business that we have in this country, the business of our Federal Government.

I am quite aware that things done by the Government are done under conditions so different from those of a business concern that there are certain expenditures necessary, in view of the fact that the government business is done for the benefit of all the people, and that therefore all the people are entitled to know how it is done, and a number of them are entitled to be selected in a fair way to share in its doing. But in spite of the added expenditure of administration incident to the requirements of popular government, everyone familiar with government methods now in vogue must recognize the possibility of reforms leading to great economy, if the Congress shall have the courage to adopt plans which may be recommended by this commission after a full examination by business experts.

I have already occupied your time too much, and I perhaps have not made this statement very informing or interesting, but I cannot close without congratulating you and myself on the prospect that the present tariff bill offers such an increased income as to make deficits under any condition unnecessary. Of course if there were to be a halt in our prosperity and a panic, the reduction in imports might be so substantial as to lead to deficits again. Let us hope, however, that the prosperity of our country is founded on such a substantial basis that no flurry in the stock market and no other temporary cause may prevent the continuance of good business on a substantial basis.